BOOKS SHOULD BE RETURNED ON OR BEFORE THE LAST DATE SHOWN
BELOW. BOOKS NOT ALREADY REQUESTED BY OTHER READERS MAY
BE RENEWED BY PERSONAL APPLICATION, BY WRITING, OR BY
TELEPHONE. TO RENEW, <u>GIVE THE DATE DUE AND THE NUMBER ON
THE BARCODE LABEL</u>.

FINES CHARGED FOR OVERDUE BOOKS WILL INCLUDE POSTAGE
INCURRED IN RECOVERY. DAMAGE TO, OR LOSS OF, BOOKS WILL BE
CHARGED TO THE BORROWER.

LAST LENDING COPY

Leabharlanna Poiblí Bárdas Átha Cliath
Dublin Corporation Public Libraries
Dolphins Barn Branch Tel. 4540681

MELTING
SNOW

MELTING SNOW

An Irishman in Moscow

Conor O'Clery

Appletree Press
Belfast

For my wife Zhanna

First published and printed by
The Appletree Press Ltd
7 James Street South
Belfast BT2 8DL
1991

British Library Cataloguing in Publication Data
O'Clery, Conor, *1940–*
Melting Snow: an Irishman in Moscow.
I. Title
947.0854

ISBN 0 86281 291 7

Grateful acknowledgement is made to Jonathan Cape, The
Random Century Group Ltd, for permission to use material
from *Against the Grain* by Boris Yeltsin (London: 1990).

9 8 7 6 5 4 3 2 1

Contents

NORWEGIAN SEA

NORWAY

SWEDEN

FINLAND

Murmansk

NOVAYA
ZEMLYA

WHITE SEA

Tallinn

Kaliningrad

LATVIA

ESTONIA

Riga

LITHUANIA

Vilnius

Leningrad

POLAND

BYELORUSSIA

Pechora

Torzhok

Gorky

Minsk

HUNGARY

L'vov

Chernobyl

MOSCOW

Pripyat

Kiev

Tula

Ryazan

Kama

ROMANIA

Don

BULGARIA

UKRAINE

Volga

Odessa

SEA OF
AZOV

Tobol

CRIMEA

Yalta

Volgograd

BLACK SEA

Ural

On

TURKEY

GEORGIA

Tbilisi

CASPIAN SEA

KAZAKHSTAN

Yerevan

ARMENIA

UZBEK-
BAIJAN

ARAL
SEA

Alma Ata

TURKMENIA

UZBEKISTAN

Tashkent

KIRGHIZIA

Samarkand

IRAN

TAJIKISTAN

AFGHANISTAN

Kabul

ARCTIC OCEAN

NEW SIBERIAN ISLANDS

EAST SIBERIAN SEA

BERING SEA

KARA SEA

LAPTEV SEA

KAMCHATKA

SIBERIA

Lena

SEA OF OKHOTSK

• Yakutsk

Yenisey

Angara

Krasnoyarsk •

Bratsk

Lake Baykal

Novosibirsk •

Irkutsk •

NORTH
KOREA

SEA OF JAPAN

SOUTH
KOREA

MONGOLIA

CHINA

THE SOVIET UNION

| 0 | 200 | 400 | 600 | 800 miles |

| 0 | 250 | 500 | 750 | 1000 | 1200km |

Preface

B Y OPENING a bureau in Moscow in March 1987, *The Irish Times* became the first Irish newspaper, indeed the first Irish company, to ever establish an office behind the Iron Curtain. At the time perestroika was just beginning to break down the rigid ideology which held Russia in its totalitarian grip, sometimes in conditions of terror, for seven decades. It was becoming evident that a political springtime had arrived in the Soviet Union, and we too sensed the first tremors of the convulsions which were about to shake Soviet society and rip down the Iron Curtain as a mood of anti-communism swept through Russia and Eastern Europe.

It was my job to establish *The Irish Times* bureau and meet the growing appetite for information about the Soviet Union as it attempted to change from a communist to a democratic society. This book is an account of my experiences, not just as a reporter and observer of the great and historic events which have affected all our lives, but as a traveller throughout the country, as a resident of its capital city, Moscow, and as a Kremlin-watcher, parliamentary correspondent, newspaper reader, cinemagoer, shopper, queuer, tenant, crime victim, churchgoer, explorer and student and devotee of Russia, its language and people. This book is an account of what I saw and experienced as an Irishman in Moscow at a time when history was on the move, in that period which began with great optimism and ended with Russia facing hunger and chaos.

It was also a period when Western correspondents were able for the first time to talk freely with Russians as they lost the centuries-old fear of giving information to foreigners. We became the travelling people of the Soviet Union. We could, and did, wander throughout the country almost as we pleased, sometimes to places closed for decades to outsiders. The traditional courtesy shown to foreigners, the ending of official supervision of interviews, and the belief that information published outside the Soviet Union would bring greater understanding and sympathy, combined to open doors everywhere. In the nationalist republics we were overwhelmed with hospitality and treated as the harbingers of freedom.

I am grateful for the company and comradeship of several colleagues with whom I commuted around the USSR, including Rupert Cornwell and Helen Womack of the London *Independent*, Stephen Handelman of the Toronto *Star*, Jonathan Steele of the *Guardian*, Quentin Peel of the *Financial Times*, Kyosti Karvonen of the *Helsingin Sanomat*, Mike McIvor of the Canadian Broadcasting Corporation, Robert Haupt of the *Sydney Morning Herald*, Alison Mitchell of *Newsday*, and John Lombard of the Australian Broadcasting Corporation – a fellow Irishman with the claim to fame of once being the first Protestant reporter to be hired by the *Irish Independent* back in the 1960s. I am particularly grateful to Xan and Jane Smiley of *The Daily Telegraph* and Helen Womack of *Reuters* for advice and hospitality in the early days, and to Patrick and Jan Cockburn of the *Financial Times*, Celestine Bohlen of the *Washington Post* and Chuck and Fiona Mitchell and Jack and Catherine Redden of United Press International for help with accommodation and communications in the first few months before the foreign ministry assigned me an office, apartment, telex machine and telephone. I should record my gratitude to the Irish embassy and to Soviet Foreign Ministry officials who helped in one way and another to get over the rough patches, especially Yuri Sapounov and *Irish Times* interpreters, first Angela Gallagher and then Alexei Zinin, who assisted me with their translations and suggestions while I was beginning a long struggle to become competent in Russian.

I have the great good fortune to work for *The Irish Times*, whose former editor, Douglas Gageby, to whom I owe my journalistic career, first sent me to Russia as a visiting reporter in 1980, and whose successor, Conor Brady, asked me to go back as permanent correspondent in 1987. He and *The Irish Times* foreign editor Paul Gillespie gave me complete freedom to report not just on what was happening in the Soviet Union, but on what it was like to live there at a time of change. This book is a result of the licence they gave me to travel freely and to write not only about news events, but about the people who live, work, dream and suffer, in the Soviet Union. I am grateful also to all those who offered advice and suggestions, but I alone bear responsibility for any errors which occur.

Nothing, however, would have been written without the help, guidance and inspiration of my wife Zhanna, who shared so many of the experiences recounted in these pages, who read and helped shape the text, and to whom the book is dedicated.

Introduction

MY FIRST encounter with a Russian was when I was arrested at the point of an AK-47 automatic assault rifle by a soldier of the Red Army on a snow-swept road, high in the Afghanistan mountains. It was January 1980. I had arrived in Afghanistan from Pakistan a few days earlier, crossing over at the Khyber Pass and driving to the capital, Kabul, through spectacularly beautiful yellow and purple hills capped with snow. Only when I passed through the icicle-hung Kabul Gorge and emerged on to the 7,000-foot high central plateau did I catch my first sight of the Russian soldiers who had occupied the country on 31 December. From Kabul I drove further north with a few colleagues in an old Russian-made Volga towards the Soviet border, passing through the Salang Pass in the Hindu Kush mountains. Russian soldiers seemed glad to see us, as if the presence of fellow Europeans from the Western press might bring a respite from the Afghan rebel attacks on the highway, which had become their life-line from the Soviet Union. They even posed, smiling shyly, for snapshots at checkpoints on the twisting, climbing road where golden eagles occasionally swooped down from miniature alpine-like peaks, though they warned us not to photograph any of their light parachute regiment tanks or radio emplacements. At the highest point, as snow blew like dry sand over the black road, one of our number decided to take a sneak photograph from the back window of the car. A soldier who had been smiling and waving spotted the little Olympus, raised his AK-47, and angrily ordered all of us out of the vehicle – *The Irish Times*, the BBC, the *Daily Express* and the guilty one, the *Daily Telegraph*.

We were convoyed a few miles to a command post, a wooden-floored former Afghan army guard-house tucked into the mountain-side with nine bunks along the concrete walls of the operations room, two of them occupied by off-duty soldiers reading novels printed on cheap paper. In the centre stood a large, very hot wood-burning stove. The lieutenant in charge spoke a few words of English and questioned us about our movements. 'Why are you here, it's so cold?' he asked. 'Why are you here?' one of us said, but he didn't reply. He took our press cards and relayed our names over a field radio to his headquarters. When we tried to talk to each other he ordered us to remain quiet. Outside it was getting dark and a freezing wind blew the snow into the room everytime a soldier came in or out. After an hour an orderly brought us *borshch*, made from beetroot, rice with mutton and sweet, clear tea. Even high in the Hindu Kush mountains, Russian hospitality demanded that guests be fed. We gave our cigarettes in turn. It was all done in silence. We supped our tea as the lieutenant waited for instructions on what to do with us.

It was a ridiculous thought, but it occurred to me as we sat in the guard-room, eyeing our captors, that I was seeing Russian soldiers in colour for the first time. The lieutenant I noticed had brown hair, blue eyes, a pink neck, red wind-burned cheeks and turquoise shoulder flashes on a green shirt. The image of the Soviet army had been typographed in my mind when I was younger by black-and-white pictures in the newsreels of the 1950s and 1960s. I grew up in the Northern Ireland seaside resort of Newcastle and my window on the world that lay behind the Iron Curtain was Pathé news in the Palace Cinema where I saw Russian troops marching into Budapest or Prague, and grey Soviet leaders standing grim-faced on the Lenin mausoleum in Moscow. The voice of the announcer on Radio Moscow, which I could occasionally get on the short-wave band of my father's wireless set, was also a colourless monotone. The gift postcards which Radio Moscow sent me when I wrote off for a programme guide were all of Moscow University, a fairy castle of socialist realism, also in black and white. Despite, or perhaps because of these negative impressions (in the photographic sense), I had a great curiosity to find out more about this strange world. My mother and father were not so happy, however, about letters arriving from communist Russia for their fourteen-year-old son. In Ireland in those days, communists were people who shut down churches in Russia, killed missionaries in China or were spies. Anti-communist propaganda was so intense that Dr MacQuaid, the Archbishop of Dublin, had tried to stop an Ireland-Yugoslavia soccer match because it meant contact with communist players. My parents' more immediate concern in those Cold War days centred on a counter clerk at the post-office who had a reputation for malicious gossip. A letter from Moscow put us in danger of being portrayed as the reds among the resort's rather genteel population. When programme guides and postcards began arriving every month, my mother firmly insisted that I write to Radio Moscow and ask them to terminate the correspondence. I did so and the letters stopped.

I was interrupted in my reveries by the jangling of the field telephone. The lieutenant barked several *da*'s into the receiver, then turned to us and demanded that we open our cameras so that he could confiscate our film. He apologetically extracted the blank spools we had managed to insert while being taken to the command post – the used ones we had slipped down our socks – and then told us we were free to go. He gave us an escort part of the way down the mountain towards Kabul, past soldiers in white snow-suits manning machine-gun posts in the darkness, and shook hands before we parted.

The encounter was the start of my long association with Russia and the Russians. Because of the intensification of the Cold War caused by the occupation of Afghanistan, my editor, Douglas Gageby, asked me when I returned from Afghanistan shortly afterwards to go to the Soviet Union and spend some time travelling around in order to get an impression of the mood of the country. He gave me a few weeks to lean some Russian and I made strenuous efforts at mastering the rudiments of the language under the tuition of Martin Bates, the Irish army's expert at reading Russian military manuals and who also taught at University College Dublin. It was an impossible task, but much, I was to discover, could be achieved in those days by a naive enthusiasm, a mastery of the alphabet and the ability to remember a few phrases.

It had been a hard winter and snow covered the fields and parks when I arrived in Moscow on a chill April morning. The Moscow River was still frozen and fishermen in black overcoats and hats sat over ice holes. The streets were full of the smell of petrol fumes and of Russian cigarettes. People crowded into unmarked shops in new concrete structures or shabby nineteenth-century buildings. The university with its mock-Gothic spires, one of seven wedding-cake edifices erected by Stalin in the Soviet capital, was as eerily majestic, and just as black and white, at least from a distance, as I remembered it from the postcards. I was struck by the complete absence of advertising, except for Communist Party slogans, and the immense faces of Soviet leader Leonid Brezhnev and the state founder, V I Lenin, gazing sternly into the far distance from gable walls. This was the time which later became known as the era of stagnation. Shortly after I arrived, less than four months after he had sent the tanks into Afghanistan, Brezhnev awarded himself his fifth Lenin prize, an occasion celebrated by identical headlines in all the Soviet newspapers praising his 'constant struggle for peace'. The same journals carried no news of human rights abuses in the USSR, where more than 1,000 dissidents were in prison camps or psychiatric hospitals. Nobel prize-winning scientist Dr Andrei Sakharov was forced to live in internal exile in a shabby apartment in Gorky for speaking out on Afghanistan, and the great Russian writer Alexander Solzhenitsyn was banished to the United States for exposing Stalin's camps. People were afraid to communicate with foreigners beyond polite conversation. At the same time the Soviet bureaucracy employed an army of interpreters and guides to shepherd tourists around. Visiting correspondents were assigned assistants from the Soviet Union of Journalists or the news agency *Novosti*, who were assumed by foreign correspondents in Moscow to be working for the KGB.

The day I arrived at Moscow's Sheremetyevo Airport, I found Nikolai waiting for me. Nikolai, a thirty-nine-year-old former *Tass* correspondent who had worked in the Arab emirates, looked remarkably like the actor Cyril Cusack. He had a knee-length leather coat which strained at the buttons. He had been put at my service, he told me, by the Union of Journalists. He would arrange interviews, travel with me round the Soviet Union, eat with me, sleep at the same place, even give me money if I ran short. I decided to confront Nikolai with my suspicions. 'You are a KGB agent, aren't you?' I said as we were driven along Kalinin Prospect in a black Volga. He looked at me sharply, then grinned and winked. He put an arm around my shoulder and squeezed my knee with his other hand. 'Ho, ho', he cried. 'And what are you? MI6?' So that's how they're trained to react, I thought.

Nikolai was, nevertheless, indispensible in penetrating the bureaucracy of the Soviet Union, where appointments had to be made days in advance, where telephone books were unattainable and where government ministries did not have switchboards. If one did not have an official's direct line, there was no way of getting in contact. At short notice Nikolai, who had access to all the right numbers, arranged a series of interviews and assignments. His regulation blond haircut and black coat became a familiar sight in the lobby of the Intourist Hotel every morning. 'Better to have one good friend than one hundred roubles', he would grunt to me, playfully punching my shoulder as we set off along Gorky Street. Nikolai was not my only escort. My Intourist Hotel voucher entitled me to a guide/interpreter for three hours a day, and the elfin-like face of Tania from Intourist also appeared regularly each morning behind Nikolai in the lobby of the hotel. Off we would go, with a dour-faced driver, to arrive at an official's office for an interview in the manner of a *delegatsia* rather than a lone reporter.

It was, of course, possible to take a day to oneself and wander unaccompanied through the streets. I visited the Jewish *refusnik* professor, Alexander Lerner, a scientist who had been refused permission to emigrate, without any sign of being followed either to or from his apartment – though he assured me that our conversation was taped by the KGB. The permanent correspondents I met in Moscow at that time were also convinced that their offices and apartments were bugged. A state ambulance was suspected of taking away secret recording tapes each week from the big foreigners' compound in Kutuzovsky Prospect. Their despatches were not censored but they sometimes imposed censorship on themselves. One American advised me, 'Back home they just don't want to be bothered with feature articles on the Russian way of life. They want only space launchings, dissidents and what the Soviet press is saying about foreign policy. Human-interest stories are out. I guess they wouldn't go down well in the United States at present.' He thought for a moment and then added, 'What the hell. They never have anything good to say about America.' Another resident correspondent spoke despairingly of his frustrations. 'I love Russia, but the trouble is the system wears you down after about six months. You can't get any scoops. You have to walk in the park to have any sort of confidential discussion. You mix with diplomats in your ghetto and develop anti-Soviet attitudes simply because you are looking out at them all the time.' Some observers spent hours scouring the columns of the daily newspapers for hints of real news, such as a disaster or a change of policy or personnel. The Irish ambassador at the time, Ned Brennan, had the reputation of being the best informed of the EEC envoys, mainly because he had fluent Russian and devoted hours to reading not just the national but the provincial newspapers, which he prevailed upon people travelling beyond Moscow to bring back to the embassy.

Despite the ease with which Nikolai arranged interviews, I came up against the official reluctance to give any real information to foreigners. This was said to be a trait deeply ingrained in the Russian psyche. In 1839 the French Marquis de Custine wrote, 'In Russia, secrecy presides over everything administrative, political and social.' This fallacy was to be laid to rest under glasnost, but by 1980 nothing had changed and the authorities had plenty to hide. The administration-by-command system had brought the economy to a crisis, destroyed people's trust in the law, perverted human rights and brought about wholesale pollution of the environment. Any statistics published were largely invented to fit the image of a system that was working.

The official Soviet media, I discovered, was part of the conspiracy to withhold information from foreigners and Russian citizens alike. I was brought to the headquarters of the Soviet news agency, *Tass*, one day, so that I could discuss Soviet news-reporting with Vladimir Goncherov, the foreign editor. It wasn't an intimate conversation. I was flanked by Nikolai and Tania, and Goncherov was accompanied by a row of *Tass* executives, including Yuri Ustimenko, the first *Tass* correspondent in Dublin who had also written a book about Ireland in the 1970s. The role of the Soviet press was not primarily to disseminate news, explained Goncherov. The first principle was that information must serve the needs of the Soviet state. 'Any publication of news which goes against the moral principles of our society is prohibited', he said sternly, wagging a finger. I asked him what instructions he gave his correspondents covering the war in Afghanistan and if they reported casualties. They were told, he replied, to report the result of reforms carried out by the revolutionary government. The Soviet media did not concern itself with casualties, which were inflicted by 'bandits' and therefore not relevant. Leaning across the polished wooden table he asked suddenly, 'Have you ever heard of our writer Sholokhov, author of *Quiet Flows the Don*? He put it well. He said, "We write from our hearts and our hearts belong to the party."'

In those prereform days interviews with all public figures were closely monitored. A correspondent could not question a Russian Orthodox priest or bishop, for example, without a government official from the Council for Religious Affairs sitting in on the discussion. The council officially liaised between church and state, but in reality was supervised by the KGB (confirmed by a former director in 1989), which controlled church activities, restricting their publications and public activities. Its chairman then was Leonid Shcherbakov, an unsmiling bureaucrat in a pin-striped suit who made no secret of his distrust of the people whose well-being he was supposed to look after. 'You know,' he told me in his office, beneath a large portrait of Lenin, 'we still meet more people opposed to Soviet power among believers than unbelievers.' In those days the church was demoralised, with many of its beautiful onion-domed buildings wrecked inside and used as storehouses or tractor-sheds, having been confiscated first under Stalin and then in a second wave and with greater zeal by Khrushchev. Priests were forbidden to teach religion, do charitable work or say anything about the state of society from their pulpits. Those who did, like Father Dmitri Dudko, were put in jail because, said Shcherbakov, they tried to make their sermons political. 'Priests cannot use their churches as political clubs; they are Soviet citizens subject to soviet laws', he said, waving his cigarette in the air.

There were signs, however, of a reviving interest in religion in those days of social and spiritual stagnation. The Easter service at the Novodevichy Monastery in Moscow that year – it had escaped the closures – was so packed I could hardly get in. Large crowds gathered near the sixteenth-century Trapeznaya church long before the service began. Most were sturdy *babushkas*, the old women who fill Russian churches generation after generation, but many of those who flowed in past the birch trees, or picked their way across the snow-covered graveyard where Gogol and Chekhov – and Khrushchev – lay buried, were in their twenties or thirties. Groups of teenagers, some tipsy, others embracing, hung around police-barriers watching with curiosity as churchgoers bought red wax tapers at wooden stalls. At midnight, robed Orthodox priests with magnificent beards and cylindrical hats led the choir in procession around the outside of the church. As they re-entered, the crowd was so tightly packed that those of us caught up in the sweating mass of people were pushed and shouldered helplessly through the porch. Inside, the aroma of incense and candle smoke mingled with the smell of scorched hair and fur as tiny flames brushed against people and clothing. Six decades of atheism had clearly not extinguished the spiritual fervour of the Russian people. Religious observance might have been even greater, one sensed, if the fear of being seen in church was removed. One of Tania's colleagues, a middle-aged interpreter, said frankly she wanted very much to attend the Easter ceremony, but 'It wouldn't be worth it. I would be called in at Intourist and asked to account for myself. I might even lose my job.'

Another place where career-minded people did not care to be seen in the Brezhnev days was the Moscow Hippodrome, where I made my way one afternoon to watch the Russian Oaks, discovering that there was yet another side to Moscow life which communism had not completely discouraged despite a complete absence of information in the Russian newspapers. Even in the columns of *Sovietsky Sport* there was no mention of this high point of the Russian racing season. Nor could one glean from the next day's newspapers that the Oaks I had watched was won by Saba, ridden by Yakovlev, jockey of the second class. Such news clearly 'offended against the moral principles' of Soviet society, as Goncharov would put it. Racing, the sport of kings, was not a fashionable socialist pastime, though it was very much the sport of the Moscow proletariat, attracting what people in the West would consider a doggie rather than a racing crowd, with fag ends in their mouths and beaten dockets underfoot.

In later years when things went wrong with Mikhail Gorbachev's reforms and shortages became acute, some Russians would express nostalgia for those days of stagnation, but the forays I was able to make without Nikolai and Tania to shops in the city centre and the suburbs, enabled me to learn that *deficit* items that April in 1980 included not just green vegetables and every kind of fruit except apples, but toothpaste, electric light bulbs and thread. When I began travelling round the Soviet Union, accompanied by Nikolai, I found that despite his best efforts to show the good side of everything, the situation was much worse than in the capital. A quick walk around the streets of Bratsk in Siberia one morning while Nikolai was still shaving in the hotel revealed food shops with no fresh food and meat shops with only lumps of gristle on display.

When Nikolai and I set off on our journey, it became more difficult to make contact with ordinary Russians. At airports, always crowded with people on the move, we were kept apart from the masses along with other foreigners who happened to be travelling on the plane. At every airport from Moscow to Omsk, Bratsk, Irkutsk, Alma Ata, Tashkent, Samarkand and back to Moscow, an otherwise empty bus would take us from the plane to a special section of the terminal building with a private coffee bar and hard-currency souvenir shop. Tourists of the revolution were not required to endure, or witness, the frustration of Soviet citizens waiting days for a place on a flight in miserable air terminals with filthy toilets. Protests were useless. 'We look after our friends', Nikolai would say, squeezing my arm and pushing me through the waiting proletariat. And the further away from Moscow, the more the escort business got out of hand. In Irkutsk, a visit to the local vegetable market entailed squeezing into a groaning Chaika with Nikolai, a local Intourist guide, an elderly provincial journalist, a driver and the driver's plump and cheerful blonde wife who came along because it was a Sunday and it was also their wedding anniversary and she wasn't going to sit at home.

In the evenings it was practically impossible not to socialise with Nikolai. We were staying in Intourist hotels with only each other for company. In Samarkand, however, I managed to break away and make some discoveries which gave me a glimpse of the under side of life in the Soviet Union. I had asked to visit this ancient city in Uzbekistan to talk to Moslem leaders about the role of Islam inside the Soviet Union, especially relevant then in view of events in Afghanistan where the ethnic cousins of the Tajikhs and Uzbeks who lived on the Soviet side of the Afghanistan border were fighting Soviet troops in what they regarded as a holy war. The day had been taken up instead with a guided tour of the magnificent but tourist-only mosques and mausoleums. 'In Samarkand, better one look than a hundred descriptions', said the local Intourist guide. The mosque of Bibi Khanym with its flower patterns and glazed tiles was truly a magnificent sight, but despite promises we did not meet the Moslem leaders. They had left town, I was told, and in any event, only 4 per cent of the Uzbeks were practising Moslems. Why should I concern myself with them? Back at the Hotel Samarkand after this tour, feeling frustrated and angry, I met a Finnish journalist in the hard-currency bar, relaxing with his Soviet minder from the *Novosti* news agency. I asked him if he felt like going for a walk, unaccompanied, through the old part of the town before darkness fell. Nikolai overheard us and cried, 'Let's have a drink.' He grabbed both of us by the arm and called for a bottle of Bulgarian champagne and four glasses which appeared within seconds on the counter, but we wriggled free from his leather-sleeved embrace and not-so-playful punches and managed to set off alone along the dusty streets of the old town, where elderly men in black, four-cornered caps sat in chairs along the footpath, children played volleyball in the alleys and youths with wispy moustaches drank large bottles of watery beer in open bars. Were they *Musslimani*, we asked them. Of course, everyone was a Moslem in Samarkand, they said. (The answer was revealing, but deceptive. I learned many years later that an Uzbek will claim to be a *Musselman* in the same way a Belfastman will say he is a Protestant. Religious beliefs might not come into it.) They didn't make a secret of their feelings about life under Soviet power. One olive-skinned young man with jet-black hair said with sudden vehemence, 'I fuck communists', and spat out a sunflower seed.

Uzbekistan was run then by a mafia which controlled the cotton crops and whose practice of paying bribes had corrupted many high officials in Moscow, another scandal which was later to break under glasnost. Everything was done to prevent foreign journalists from poking their noses into Uzbek affairs. My attempt to visit a collective farm in the Asian republic showed the lengths to which the authorities would go while keeping up a show of hospitality. On this occasion I had four escorts, a fat, retired journalist from Samarkand, a male Intourist guide, an Uzbek driver and Nikolai. We arrived first at the headquarters of the 4,500-acre cotton and tobacco farm, situated at the side of the road with a picture of the first cosmonaut, Yuri Gagarin, on the outside wall and nearby a statue of Lenin. The director, a squat Uzbek in a blue suit and brown homberg who could have played Dr No in the James Bond film, was waiting to greet us, along with three similarly attired party officials.

Before seeing the farm we must eat, he insisted. We retreated from the midday sun through a door marked 'Club' where a table was laden with nuts, apples, oranges, cucumbers, olives, bread and extremely large tomatoes. A large glass of Samarkand vodka was poured for each person. After every toast – and there were many – the glass was refilled. Hot dishes were brought in. The speeches and the lunch went on for two hours. This was followed by an excursion to a scenic point in the hills some miles away and then back to the club where the man in the homberg was waiting to host another meal, this time of Uzbekistan pilaf, and offer yet more toasts to Soviet-Irish relations. Everybody was by then quite drunk, and when the grizzled head of the local journalist fell on to the table, we called it a day. In the back of the car I complained bitterly to Nikolai about not even seeing the cotton fields or being allowed to walk on the farm. 'You can look at the fields from the car window', he replied before he nodded off. We caught the plane back to Moscow that evening. When we woke as we approached the capital, Nikolai reproached me angrily about my behaviour in the hotel lobby where, apparently, I had referred to him rather loudly as 'my KGB man'. 'It's your own fault', I replied.

I returned to Moscow later that year for the Olympics. The city was cleaned up and partly depopulated to accommodate the foreign guests. The extent of the exercise only became known in later years. There were no criminals or prostitutes on the streets in July or August, nor any children. However, the authorities couldn't completely sanitise the Soviet capital and I caught another memorable glimpse of the alternative Moscow during the games. On 28 July, an interpreter at the Olympics press centre whispered to me that I should go to Taganskaya Square where a crowd had gathered to mark the death of a forty-two-year-old actor, poet and folk singer, Vladimir Vysotsky. Few people in the West had heard of Vysotsky, but he was a much-loved figure in the Soviet Union, an actor whose Hamlet in the Taganki Theatre was regarded as a classic. Vysotsky's irreverent, satirical ballads sung in a gravelly voice expressed sympathy for the people's everyday misery and humiliations. The state recording company Melodiya would not produce any of his songs, but most people in Russia, even Brezhnev, had pirated copies of his tapes. I found a huge crowd gathered in the square calling for his picture to be displayed in a window of the theatre. It appeared briefly and was taken away as mounted police shouted to people to go home. Some raised clenched fists and there was a crescendo of whistling. It was an astonishing manifestation of defiance in the Soviet Union of 1980. Vysotsky's funeral service was conducted by a remarkable priest, Father Alexander Men, who was unofficial chaplain to Moscow intellectuals and to dissidents within the church. Vysotsky's grave in Vakhtangova cemetery immediately became a place of pilgrimage for people visiting Moscow. Many would go to place flowers there before queuing for Lenin's tomb across town.

Perhaps the lowest point in the Cold War period of the 1980s came when Yuri Andropov, who followed Brezhnev as Communist Party first secretary, was succeeded in 1984 by old-style communist Konstantin Chernenko. I returned once more to Russia for Andropov's funeral, this time in the most unorthodox manner. The USSR's borders had been closed to foreign journalists for the period of mourning. When the Soviet embassy, as expected, refused to give me a journalist's visa, I turned for help to Sean Donlon, head of the Irish Department of Foreign Affairs in Dublin. He listed me as a member of the small official party accompanying the Irish head of state, President Hillery, to the funeral and notified the Soviet embassy, which promptly reversed its decision and issued a visa; I arranged to leave as soon as possible. The next day, before I had arrived in Moscow, the Soviet ambassador received an urgent inquiry from Moscow about my status. He dropped in on Sean Donlon – they were near neighbours in central Dublin – to discuss the matter. It was clear that to identify me as a journalist would result in the immediate cancellation by Moscow of the visa. A glass or two of wine was drunk and by the time the reply was eventually despatched by the sympathetic ambassador, I was walking through immigration in Moscow and disappearing into the city on a suburban bus. I stayed in a spare room in the apartment of the Irish embassy's second secretary, Joe Hayes, with the status of non-person but with an as yet uncancelled visa on my passport. Not only did I get to the funeral, but the Irish ambassador, Padraig Murphy, took me to the lying-in-state in the embassy car, with militiamen saluting us every few yards. We stood solemnly for a few seconds in front of the bier of the deceased party boss while an orchestra played somber music. During the funeral service, which only ambassadors and invited foreign guests could attend, I went for a walk in Gorky Park and discovered that the official mourning had not affected several young people who continued to skate merrily around the ice on the flooded paths even as the city's sirens and factory hooters commanded people to stand to attention as the body was lowered into the grave.

When the Communist Party selected seventy-two-year-old Konstantin Chernenko to succeed Andropov it seemed the Soviet Union was to continue to stagnate. However, the next year, 1985, he died and Mikhail Gorbachev became Soviet leader. Very soon Gorbachev was to raise hopes both within the USSR and the West that Russia was about to awaken from its slumbers and open up to the outside world. The reform programme he announced, called perestroika, or rebuilding, and the new foreign policy which accompanied it, held out promise for great changes inside the Soviet Union and throughout the world. A new generation of foreign correspondents began arriving in Moscow. I was among them, this time to establish an *Irish Times* bureau, the first ever Irish newspaper bureau behind the Iron Curtain, still firmly drawn across Europe. Until then I had had only superficial impressions of Russia, many of them negative. I knew little about the people. Most Russians I met had been officials – or soldiers. But like many visitors to Russia I sensed that part of me belonged there; I was happy to go and live through and witness, in full technicolour, what was happening.

1

The Russia House

T HE THAW began early in the spring of 1987 and melting snow
was running across the roads from huge drifts, filthy with
the pollution and cigarette butts of the winter months. On
23 March 1987 I arrived to set up the *Irish Times* bureau, my
suitcase weighed down with the *Cambridge Encyclopedia of Russia*,
the Moscow correspondent's bible. I checked into the Rossiya Hotel,
a twenty-storey structure of glass and concrete beside the Kremlin,
with narrow corridors almost a kilometre in length, built around a
square courtyard.

This time there was no Nikolai or Tania to take me in hand. There
was, however, an Olga, who made her appearance the next day. She
was about twenty-three with a round face and red lips and wearing a
camel-hair coat and knitted cap. She approached me in Red Square,
as if by chance, to ask directions. When she established that I spoke
English she said she was a student of languages and remarked how
wonderful it would be if she could speak to me for a few minutes to
practise her English. Olga talked non-stop for fifteen minutes, during
which time she made several critical remarks about the failings of
the Soviet system. I couldn't believe my good fortune at meeting an
outspoken Muscovite on my first day. Contacts with ordinary Russians
were still difficult for correspondents, even after two years of glasnost.
I suggested we continue the conversation over coffee, whereupon she
hailed a taxi, gave the driver some instructions, and a few minutes
later we were sitting at a café table in the Ukraine Hotel which
happened to be, as she pointed out after a while, just across the
road from a *Beriozhka*, a foreign-currency shop selling sportswear.
Soviet citizens were not permitted to possess hard currency and such
shops were closed to them, she told me sadly. She was also an athlete
and could never get proper track suits. Would I mind buying her a
sports outfit in the shop if she give me the equivalent of the price?
It didn't seem too much to ask in return for her insights into Soviet
life. I bought the track suit for her. Only later did I discover that it
was worth twenty times the rouble value on the black market. My
first inkling that our transaction may not have been quite legal came

25

when she insisted on going into a dark corner of a nearby chemist shop to give me the roubles. She then confessed she hadn't quite enough money and suggested meeting again the next day. I decided I had been conned and that I should write the whole thing off to naivety and inexperience. The next day, however, she turned up with the roubles she owed me and with a new proposition: she was very unhappy, she said; what would make her happy was a video recorder from the *Beriozhka*, to help with her language studies. In return she would arrange for me to get Bolshoi tickets from her sister who worked in the theatre and, more intriguing, would introduce me to her sister's husband 'who was a Communist Party organiser who would be able to help you in your work'. This was an almost irresistable inducement to a newcomer but alarm bells began to ring. Naive as I had been, the suggestion smacked not of racketeering but of something else – the KGB. I took the roubles she owed me, declined the offer and, as we say, made an excuse and left. Subsequent events convinced me I was right and that I had escaped some sort of snare. I hadn't given her my telephone number in the Rossiya – every one of its 3,172 rooms has its own outside line – but she managed to get it, an almost impossible achievement for a mere student, and kept ringing for several days. The hotel, by chance, moved me to a different room, and the calls came there too. I kept hanging up and after I moved out of the hotel nineteen days later I heard no more from her. An alarming incident a year later reinforced my suspicions. A Russian friend was approached by the KGB and asked to arrange to introduce someone to me – a party organiser who could 'help me in my work'. The request was rejected, despite veiled threats about the consequences, and I was told nothing more came of it.

I soon escaped from the Rossiya corridors to an apartment block for foreigners known as Sad Sam, a shortened version of its address on the inner ring road Sadovaya Samotechnaya. It was a solid block with high-ceilinged drawing-rooms, built by German prisoners of war as one of the first foreign ghettoes established in Moscow in the late 1940s, before which foreign correspondents had to work from rooms in the Metropole Hotel. Among other transient residents, Sad Sam housed the Irish-born *Financial Times* correspondent, Patrick Cockburn, who suggested I move into his apartment while he and his wife Jan were on leave. The foreign community in Moscow, a city within a city confined to a dozen 'diplomatic compounds', had its own hierarchal structures, with ambassadors at the top and nannies, often better informed through their Russian boyfriends about what was really going on in Moscow, at the bottom. Its floating population was listed in a British publication called *Information Moscow*, a who's who which provided addresses and telephone numbers, with convenient symbols to denote whether a person was married or single. Foreigners were not listed in the Moscow telephone directory, which was a classified Soviet document made available by the authorities only to women who gave out telephone numbers at street kiosks. A variety of other measures further isolated foreigners from their adopted city and its citizens. Russian apartment blocks had no front doors, and security huts with little eye-level windows were strategically placed at the corners of their buildings so that militiamen could observe everyone entering or leaving the yard at the back. We were also distinguishable by the colour of our car number plates – yellow for journalists – and a registration coding system so that a policeman knew immediately the status and country of origin of the owner. I was assigned the registration K-037, K for *korrespondent* and 037 for Ireland. Irish diplomats had D-037. Americans were 004, the British 001. The French drove around with the James Bond number 007.

Life in the compounds was removed from the real Moscow. To drive into the yard past the militia hut was to leave Russia and its people behind. The militiamen harassed the occasional Russian visitors and were so unpopular that residents delighted in telling newcomers the story of the great wind which hit Moscow one day, blowing over a guard-box with its occupant inside and prompting one tenant to shout from a window, 'Do it again, God.' For some foreigners, especially those who had come unwillingly to Moscow as a spouse, life was an endless round of dinner parties, often with the same people retelling the same stories of Soviet stupidity. The only Russians they encountered were maids and drivers. They were never required to stand in queues in Moscow shops as there were three *Beriozkas* in the city where Western drinks and groceries, even bread, could be bought for hard currency and, in one store, for diplomatic coupons. Fresh vegetables, meat and milk could be ordered directly from Stockman's department store in Helsinki, from where they were despatched by train in refrigerated boxes. Special 'diplomatic' beaches were provided for swimming and picnicking. The foreign community even had its own games, including broomball, in which two sides wearing soft shoes chased a ball around an ice-rink with brooms made from twigs. Going out for a drink in the evening was practically impossible. The beerhalls, packed and sweaty with standing room only and long queues outside, closed at 7.00 p.m. Hard-currency bars in the foreigners-only hotels were frequented by tourists and, quite often, prostitutes. Some big diplomatic missions like the American embassy provided entertainment for their own communities, and on Friday nights there was a bar at the Australian embassy which sold that day's British newspapers for a dollar each – a considerable luxury when foreign newspapers took two weeks to arrive by post. But people mostly preferred to entertain at home, and in those relatively quiet days before the Soviet Union plunged into crisis, correspondents like myself were able to find time for Tuesday night poker games. Some of the embassies sponsored special schools for children, who could not be expected to cope with the demands of Russian in state educational establishments, but inevitably found themselves all day in an environment where they had little contact with the people or the language of the country they inhabited. Little wonder that their vision of the society around them came to reflect the often superior attitude of their parents to the Russians.

While it was deliberate Soviet policy to isolate foreigners and to keep them under surveillance, there were other good reasons for the compound system, one of them being the need to provide security for residents who possessed much-desired and unavailable items, such as computers, stereos and hard currency which might tempt Moscow's criminals to pay a visit. The isolation also gave rise to a comradeship among foreigners, a feeling 'we're all in this together'. People helped each other, especially journalists. I was offered temporary accommodation not just by Patrick Cockburn but by Jack Redden and Chuck Mitchell of UPI and Celestine Bohlen of the *Washington Post* before moving into my own apartment, and was able to return the compliment in later years to new arrivals. Such was the neighbourly atmosphere inside Sad Sam and the sense of security provided by the militiamen on duty at the archway leading into its tiny courtyard, that residents could and often did leave their apartment doors unlocked. Patrick didn't even have a snib on his hall door. This block was also noted for the Sad Sam summer party, an all-night mid-June revelry where the narrow courtyard was bedecked with Japanese and American bunting and a Union Jack and a French flag were draped over the back wall. A Russian jazz band played until dawn as ambassadors and nannies rubbed shoulders with foreign ministry officials and correspondents at trestle tables piled high with pork sausages from London, sushi from Tokyo and other national delicacies flown in from various world capitals. If the tanks had rolled into the Kremlin on the night of a Sad Sam summer party, no one would have noticed.

Some new arrivals had been known to wait for a year to be assigned an apartment, but after a month, along with several other new correspondents who formed the Class of '87, I was summoned to the foreign ministry's housing department and assigned what was to become my home for the indefinite future. I was given a document and told to take it to 1 Marksistskaya Street where the *dezhurnaya*, or caretaker, was waiting to admit me to the building. I hailed a taxi and arrived to find the address was a seventeen-storey concrete apartment block in the final stages of completion, towering above a supermarket on the edge of Taganskaya Square. I had been alloted two modest flats on the top floor, the smaller with only a single large room to serve as an office. In my apartment I found three women painters covered from head to toe with emulsion, having a smoke with a couple of electricians. They made fun of my halting Russian. Their ashtray, one said with great seriousness, was *originalne*, unique. An old sardine tin was held up for my inspection and they fell about laughing. The *dezhurnaya* presented me with two rental agreements and a large bunch of keys and told me that everything would be ready in two weeks.

The apartment block was less than one kilometre up-river from the Kremlin. It would have no militia hut, I was delighted to discover, and in another break with Cold War practice would be shared with Muscovites, though our wing at the western end was to be exclusively for foreigners. We were the first beneficiaries of a small breakthrough in 'new thinking'. The new arrivals included Rupert Cornwell of the London *Independent*, a quintessential Englishman and a brilliant linguist who lent a flavour of intrigue to the building by virtue of the fact that he was a brother of the spy novelist John le Carré; Ian Glover James of Independent Television News (ITN), who was later to be expelled in a futile tit-for-tat exchange between Moscow and London; and the correspondents of *Haagsche Courant* of the Netherlands, *Proti* of Greece and *Newsday* of New York. We found ourselves thrust into the heart of one of the busiest and most interesting centres of the capital, where the prerevolutionary city merged with modern Moscow. There were three metro stations in the square and people from the country were always crowding into the supermarket below us or pushing and shoving to get into the beerhall on the opposite side. To get a feel for the mood of the city or to find out the latest shortages or, more important, to ascertain what was available in the shops, I simply had to walk out my front door. We were one of the city's firework centres – the tiny park which formed a traffic island in the middle of the square was used as a firing point when fireworks were set off from army lorries around Moscow on festival days. Nearby was the Jewish Theatre, and the Moscow Synagogue was only a ten-minute walk away. The narrow roadway outside it where people congregated on Saturdays was known as the Jewish club and was then the only place in the city where political debate took place in the open. Derzhinsky Square with the notorious Lubyanka Prison, and behind it Moscow's only Roman Catholic church, was just a little further on. Across the square was the Taganky Theatre, where I had seen the crowds of mourners after Vysotsky's death in 1980 and which was just beginning to enjoy a revival of its rich theatrical traditions in the new spirit of cultural freedom. Next door to it was the Vysotsky Bar, a tiny restaurant with a picture of the singer in the foyer, patronised by theatre people. At night a violinist, jazz trumpeter, magician, accordionist and a *balalaika* player strolled among the tables arranged around a fountain, and a scantily clad contortionist went through her paces, smiling at customers from between her legs. On the picture frieze above, two roosters strutted above the hunting murals and sometimes fluttered down on to the tables.

A short walk from the bustling square another quieter world existed, with roads as deserted as a village street on a hot afternoon. It contained little parks and children's playgrounds, almost all adorned with a bust of Lenin. At the end of one quiet street I found the best bread shop in Moscow where the currant loafs, the French-type batons and the round white *bulkas*, the traditional Moscow bread, were often piping hot. This old part of Moscow had hundreds of decaying wood and plaster buildings and nineteenth-century merchants' houses in green and yellow pastels. Here and there could be found a beautiful, neglected church, like the eighteenth-century temple of St Martin the Confessor, built in imitation of St Paul's in London, standing unused in the permanent shade of poplar trees, and a derelict but beautiful monastery on the river embankment which had been one of the ring of fortified monastic settlements guarding Moscow against Tatar invasions. In a narrow street off the square stood a tiny working church with an icon of the Virgin Mother facing the pavement which old women would stop to kiss. Another tiny seventeenth-century church with five cupolas nestled in a corner of the yard beneath my balcony, but it was used as an office by the local Soviet.

The apartment was eventually declared finished, but I soon discovered that it needed perestroika even before I could move in. Every wall was crooked. Door handles came off in my hand, the television cable socket was cemented over, doors and windows were out of alignment and didn't shut properly, the balcony floor sloped away from the walls and the purple mozaic tiles on the outside walls were uneven, broken and plastered with cement. Shortly after I arrived, a window toppled into the living-room in a crash of wood and splintering glass. Light fittings fell from the ceiling. Pipes rumbled like ship engines and scalding hot water came from every tap, as well as the lavatory cistern, giving a new meaning to the phrase 'hot flush'. I made emergency plans with Rupert, whose ninth-floor apartment had only cold water, whereby I could brush my teeth in the cold water of his flat and he could take a bath in mine. One, and sometimes both, lifts were frequently out of action. The situation often bordered on farce. I was given a telephone with a number which the engineer said had been that of the plumber servicing the building. Ten minutes after he left, my pipes began to growl and shudder and I was faced with the prospect of dialling my own number to get it stopped. The wallpaper was stained and had to be removed. The plasterers had to come back and do the walls again. There was talk of a rent strike, and furious representations were made to our landlord, the housing department, known by its initials as UPDK, which usually resulted in visits by tut-tutting delegations and promises of instant action. The head of one of these groups of officials, a pleasant middle-aged woman, explained to me that the building was a disaster even by Moscow standards. It had been constructed by a work collective prepared to cut corners – literally – to get it erected quickly, and UPDK had been forced to hire one wing to cope with the pressure on accommodation brought about by the wave of foreign journalists, diplomats and business people arriving because of the reforms. The worst time was to come in the winter when we began to suffer blackouts because of circuit overloading. When the power cuts occurred, the *Reuters* and *Tass* wire machines in my office would stop their chatter in mid-sentence, the telex, my only reliable link with Dublin, would go dead, and the screen on my Amstrad word processor would give a green flash and wipe away a half-completed despatch. The power cable had not been designed to cope with the equipment installed in our offices or with the blow heaters of the African diplomats who had also been assigned apartments in the building and who wanted to boost the temperature above that provided by the communal central heating. While the candle was to become the symbol of freedom in the revolutions that shook Eastern Europe, for us it became a metaphor for Soviet power, or the lack of it, before the cable was eventually replaced and the blackouts stopped.

Furnishing the apartment presented problems peculiar to Moscow. Furniture was a *deficit* item in the Soviet capital. To buy a bed, a wardrobe, a kitchen table or even a bookshelf, ordinary Muscovites had to obtain from their work collectives or trade unions certificates to testify that they were genuine workers and not black-marketeers.

Only with these testimonials could furniture be ordered. A wait of up to a year could then follow for the simplest kitchen unit. The only option for the foreigner was to take the night train to Helsinki and spend a day in Stockman's multi-floored department store, ordering everything from divans and cups to typewriters and paper-clips. These were shipped to the Soviet capital where customs allowed new residents to import personal items duty-free for the first year. What I didn't realise at the time was that the furniture displayed in the Helsinki department store was disassembled before despatch and arrived in boxes in small pieces, with packets of screws and hinges and instructions in Finnish on how to put it together again. I had to wrestle for many hours to erect a wardrobe with sliding, latticed doors and to put together chrome and leather office chairs and various cupboards. I also purchased a duty-free Russian car, a Lada, in Helsinki. At that time it was almost impossible to get a foreign car properly serviced in Moscow, and the high-grade petrol needed for Volvos or Toyotas was available only with special coupons. In Finland, too, Soviet cars were better finished and, unlike in Moscow, available on demand.

The drive back to Moscow via Leningrad in the Lada was a shock course, both educationally and physically, into the ramshackle state of the Soviet infrastructure. The highway linking Leningrad and Moscow, the two main cities of the Russian empire, was pitted with potholes and for much of the way reduced to two-lane traffic. It passed through dozens of villages of carved wooden *izbas*, peasant houses with piles of firewood stacked outside, where old women trudged along paths carrying water from the wells and geese and hens pecked at the verges. In one village where I stopped to buy bread, a young woman with a large handbag led a cow nonchalantly across the road. There were few private cars in the Russian countryside, but dozens of motorcycles with sidecars. When it was raining, mud splattered the windscreen; in sunshine, clouds of dust rose behind. I counted twenty-three broken-down lorries being attended to along the roadside. I quickly learned to steer away from the crumbling verges and to avoid the potholes. Conditions were made worse on the day I travelled by driving rain and the fact that few lorries had mud-flaps. Petrol stations were equipped with antiquated pumps with clock faces of the kind found at village garages in the west of Ireland in the postwar years and they offered no services. You had to guess how much petrol the car would take, then slide the money through a slot to a woman sitting in a wooden hut and serve yourself. There were few cafés along the way, though the ones I found had a rural charm, like the Lubava, a little restaurant built entirely from tree trunks and half-hidden in a clump of lilac trees beside an ornamental pond. Inside, two girls served lorry drivers at long, varnished log tables. For a rouble, I got chicken-and-potato broth delivered in a huge earthenware bowl with a lacquered wooden spoon. There was no piped music in the Lubava, nor any Formica or plastic, reinforcing the impression of being back in time. One had always to keep an eye out for the traffic police who mounted frequent radar speed traps (though oncoming cars warned of their presence with a friendly flash of headlights) and who supervised movement in both directions at glass watch-towers positioned every thirty kilometres, where they waved down vehicles at random to check documents.

In Moscow the grey-uniformed police, the militia, seemed to be everywhere, swinging their white sticks at street corners, standing astride the centre lanes or cruising around in little orange-and-green Zhiguli cars, constantly on the lookout for minor traffic infringements. Police pulled in drivers for crossing a white line, for turning a corner too sharply or simply for having a dirty car. The traffic police invariably greeted their victims with a courteous salute, then delivered a sharp lecture and more likely than not imposed an on-the-spot fine – or accepted a donation to the annual police ball. About the worst thing a driver could do was to collide with a police car, a feat which I managed in my first few nervous days behind the wheel of the Lada. It wasn't so much a crash as a bang, which happened at 7.25 p.m. on a Tuesday evening as I was backing towards a petrol pump, the only way to approach it due to the layout of the filling station. When the driver of a little police car tried to jump the queue by accelerating backwards past me into the space, the inevitable happened. We both got out and silently surveyed the damage. I had a scraped bumper, but the nearside back-wing of his Zhiguli was bashed in. He glared at me angrily but, incredibly, did nothing and merely drove off in a fury after filling his tank. It was probably no coincidence that I was stopped for a traffic misdemeanour by two police Zhigulis a few hours later when conveying the Irish Labour Party leader, Dick Spring, who was in Moscow for a Socialist International conference, back to his hotel after dinner. After a long argument, unintelligible to both sides, I had to pay the militiamen a large fine. To make matters worse for my distinguished passenger, when I located the hotel on the wrong side of a busy highway I found myself driving several miles to find a *raz*, a spot where U-turns were allowed, and got hopelessly lost, at one point stalling on tram-lines as a tram clanked towards us. We were

rescued by a middle-aged pedestrian called Grigor who hopped into
the car and guided us back to the hotel. Things were often to happen
that way in the early days in Moscow. When frustrated and annoyed,
trying to cope with the system, along would come a person like Grigor
to restore one's faith in the concern of the ordinary Muscovite for a
foreigner in difficulty.

I eventually learned all the tricks used by Muscovites to whizz
around town avoiding militiamen and trams. It wasn't because I
couldn't cope with the driving, however, that I hired a driver. Every
correspondent employed or shared a driver, without whom life would
be unbearable in Moscow. His job was not so much to drive as to
pay bills, buy travel tickets, collect and deliver letters, convey requests
for interviews, make bookings, withdraw money from the bank and
maintain the car. In Moscow every official request had to be made in
writing on headed notepaper, with an office stamp over the signature,
and delivered by hand. A simple transaction like taking cash from the
bank was the work of a whole morning and collecting a parcel from
customs could take up a day. *The Irish Times* was assigned – we had
little choice in such matters – Valery Chervyakov, an experienced
Muscovite who had worked several years for the American embassy
until all Soviet employees were withdrawn in 1986 in a superpower
row over spying. He knew the city and its shortcuts and such essential
information as where to get a replacement pair of wipers if I was
careless enough to leave them on the car at night and found them gone
in the morning. Wipers were deficient too, and were kept inside cars to
avoid being stolen. It was not uncommon to see dozens of Ladas and
Volgas pulling on to the side of the road and drivers quickly affixing
their wipers when a sudden shower came on. I was also allocated
an interpreter secretary, Alexei Zinin, a sensitive Muscovite with
Ukrainian blood who rarely expressed political opinions but who
once abruptly interrupted my musings about Soviet history by saying,
before it became fashionable to express such views, 'You must always
remember, Conor, that Stalin was a monster.' Without him I could not
have coped with Russian officialdom, which demanded a deference to
bureaucrats more appropriate to the world of Gogol's 'Government
Inspector' than to the age of perestroika.

One of the first letters which Zinin wrote on my behalf, and which
Valery, of course, had to deliver, brought home to me the self-esteem
and time-wasting encouraged by those who serve the public in Russia.
It was addressed to the head of the railway ticket office. 'Respected
honourable administrator', it began, 'The Moscow bureau of *The Irish
Times* pays its respects and asks you not to refuse the favour of the

following. The matter is that Conor O'Clery, chief of the Moscow bureau of *The Irish Times*, is leaving for Minsk on the evening train on the 14th inst. Your respected cashier did not, however, give us the number of the train when purchasing the ticket. At the same time the Ministry of Foreign Affairs of the USSR cannot authorise the trip unless the number of the train is given to them. We imploringly ask you to clarify the number of the train and inform us in the nearest future. Thank you for your co-operation. With much respect, etc.'

I didn't know quite how Kafkaesque Soviet bureaucracy was until I went to sell *The Irish Times's* Lada some years later to a Russian friend, Vladimir. At first I was told that the car could not be sold to a Soviet citizen as customs had registered it as a temporarily imported vehicle. However, an official in UPDK explained that there was a way around this. The car could be given outright to the Soviet citizen and Vladimir could pay me for the 'present' if he wished. I should go to customs and get their permission to 'give it away'. There was a small problem, however, to be ironed out first. The car was registered with *The Irish Times*. By law it must first be transferred to my name before it could be 'given' to anyone. I wrote to customs asking for permission to transfer the car to my name. After a few days the officials agreed and gave me documents to take to the traffic police to change the name of the registered owner. This involved getting new number plates from a different department at a cost of 160 roubles. I then wrote to customs again asking for permission to 'give' the car to Vladimir. After a three-day delay an official advised me that the easiest way to effect the transfer was to drive to Helsinki, bringing Vladimir with me, and get a new set of entry documents in his name. This was a catch-22 situation. Getting a visa to visit Finland would take months for Vladimir while the round-trip with the car would take at least four days. I said this was out of the question. It would be cheaper in the long run, the official replied, because – I believe he enjoyed telling me this – they would have to impose a tax on me for 'giving away' the car, amounting to 100 per cent of its value. I appealed to his better nature. Surely so many obstructions should not be put in the way of giving a Soviet citizen a three-year-old Lada? 'I'll think about it', he said.

This bureaucrat did have a better nature. A week later he called to say that permission would, after all, be granted to 'give away' the Lada, with a service charge of eighty roubles. If I called at customs with the car documents and Vladimir's internal passport, they would issue the necessary consent form. The next step was to take this written permission to a state lawyer to obtain a legal certificate stating the car was being given as a present to a Soviet citizen. Without this the police would not issue Vladimir documents entitling him to drive the car. Such certificates are produced by a notary's office, a bureau of state solicitors who issue the mountains of legal documents which control the lives of Soviet citizens. If the helpful official in customs is the hero of this story, the notary's office is the villain. We went early to the city-centre bureau and found its waiting-room full of people queuing to get in. We were number 40 on the list. By lunchtime they had only got to number 19. We were then told we should go to the local notary's office in Tagansky region. After queuing again, a thin, unsmiling woman examined our papers and told us triumphantly that no legal document could be issued without a valuation for the car, certified by the traffic police. The next day we took the car to a co-operative (private) valuer who, for forty roubles, issued a certificate stating the car was worth 7,000 roubles. We went to the traffic police once more (another long queue), had the Lada certified and then returned. The thin lady inspected the documents and – another triumph – discovered that the police had not written my name in Russian letters. We went to another office to get the certificate retyped at a cost of three roubles. Only then did she give us a legal certificate saying the car was Vladimir's. The notary's bill came to 7 per cent of the value of the car; 490 roubles. We took the legal document to the police to get the car registered in Vladimir's name. This time the officer refused to do so without a letter from UPDK authorising the transfer from my name to his. Back we went to UPDK, which also decided to charge 7 per cent of the value of the car, and another 490 roubles exchanged hands. The total cost of 'giving away' the car so far amounted to 1,183 roubles.

Having paid up and obtained the letter we went back to the police. The officer on duty looked through the documents and shoved them back: the lawyer had given us a copy of the legal certificate and kept the original, which he needed. We returned to the thin woman's office. Without a word of apology she provided the correct paper. Back at the traffic police there was one last obstacle. The number plate had to be changed again. After parting with another fifty roubles, temporary registration plates were provided to allow Vladimir to drive to his home outside Moscow. When he arrived, he would have to pay for yet another registration number, the fourth in as many weeks. This process took two weeks out of our lives and the bureaucracy still hadn't finished with us. Vladimir was carrying several thousand roubles in fifty and one-hundred rouble notes, his life savings, to meet all the necessary expenses. Just as the whole process was being concluded the government decided on shock monetary reform. The Kremlin declared all such notes worthless, except for the first 1,000 roubles. Vladimir saw most of his savings wiped out overnight. For the benefit of *The Irish Times* accountants I should record that he eventually managed to get most of it back and was able to compensate the bureau for the 'gift'.

The journey to Minsk which Alexei arranged was one of dozens of expeditions to different parts of the Soviet Union I was to undertake as first ripples and then tidal waves of change swept through the fifteen republics. We were permitted to travel to most cities without special permission, though the foreign ministry required forty-eight hours notice by telex of time, details of travel, hotel and purpose of journey. The information was, everyone knew, passed on to the KGB. If the destination was one of the closed zones, which included much of the greater Moscow region and such cities as Archangelsk, Astrakhan, Chelyabinsk, Gorky, Kaunas, Krasnoyarsk, Magnitogorsk, Omsk, Perm, Sverdlovsk and Vladivostok, or if the area was temporarily out of bounds because of unrest, then we were telephoned and informed that our trip was 'not registered'; that is, we could not go. Anyone who violated the rules was liable to a fine and, in an extreme case, expulsion.

In 1987, despite two years of perestroika and glasnost, the political and cultural transformation of society had hardly begun. The talking had started – it was to become a torrent of political self-analysis – but for ordinary people, and for journalists, almost nothing had changed. Alexei Zinin spent most of the day ploughing through the newspapers and journals, finding occasional advances in glasnost which sometimes made interesting stories, but there was as yet no serious political news or analysis. *Pravda* looked as dull and uninformative as it had in 1980. The foreign ministry, under its Georgian minister Eduard Shevardnadze, was, however, beginning to lead the way in opening up Soviet society: the foreign ministry press centre, equipped with simultaneous translation from Russian into English, German, French and Spanish, was being used to host increasingly open press conferences, to give advance screenings of daring new films and to reintroduce figures like Andrei Sakharov to public life. We were briefed regularly by the foreign ministry spokesman Gennady Gerasimov, who had the authority of a senior ambassador and a knack of supplying quotable quotes. I went to see him on getting my accreditation, an occasion which I felt should be marked by the presentation of a bottle of Bushmills Black Label Irish whiskey. 'Aha, a small corruption', he said. 'All right, I'll take it.' I promised him I would not ask a question at a press conference until I could do it in Russian, a pledge I kept some days later by mumbling a few words learned off by heart into the microphone. It was still possible in those days to get by without Russian and most senior correspondents could speak no more than a few words, relying completely on their interpreters and the synchronised translation service in the foreign ministry. But sensing that those days were going fast, the Class of '87 devoted many hours a week to learning the language, a commitment which was to pay off when democratic politics came to the Soviet Union in the following years and correspondents could not function properly if unable to talk to political activists, watch television programmes, follow a parliamentary debate, interview deputies in the lobbies of the Kremlin or simply talk to people in the street.

In those early days of awakening interest in Russia, however, the function of a correspondent like myself was not just to report and analyse changes but to describe what it was like to live in a vast country where living conditions, as Mikhail Gorbachev was now telling his own people with increasing frankness, were so desperate. There was an immense appetite in Ireland for an insight into this society, which had got stuck in a time warp somewhere in the 1950s and whose people shared many characteristics with the Irish, not least their humour, their love of poetry and their drinking habits. There was sympathy for and a curiosity about the Russians and the task Gorbachev had undertaken and a sense of great historic change in the making, though no one guessed how dramatic it would be. As I struggled to set up shop in Marksistskaya Street, I began to get letters from readers wishing me well in Moscow. Irish tourists rang me from their hotels and brought gifts to cushion me against the hardships they imagined that I had to endure, as a result of which there was always a bottle of Irish whiskey in my apartment. Colm Connolly of RTE came with a camera crew to interview me about living and working in Russia and asked, as a final, throw-away question, what I missed most. 'Marmalade', I replied. Within a month I had received eighteen jars of marmalade from Ireland, and even a tin of Mamade which filled a further half-dozen jampots.

2

'... but home is better ...'

I was struck when I arrived in Moscow in spring 1987 how, even a year after the Chernobyl nuclear accident, the Soviet capital was still rife with rumours about radioactive contamination of food. There were frequent official assurances that all produce had been checked for radiation, but there was deep and, as it turned out, justifiable, distrust of government claims. Shoppers in queues would ask where potatoes or cabbage came from and would refuse to take them if they had been grown in the Ukraine, though it was rarely possible to establish satisfactorily where any produce originated. As time went by, they would discover that food from Byelorussia was potentially even more dangerous, and they had to wait until three years after the accident before it emerged that huge tracts of Russian land had also been contaminated.

The lack of precise information and the instinctive feeling that the government was covering up the true extent of the effects of the disaster contrasted with the situation in Sweden. I had gone to Scandinavia the previous September to find out how serious had been the contamination from heavy rains which fell in central Sweden some hours after the explosion and fire at Chernobyl. What I found there left me with no illusions about the plight of the residents of great sections of the western Soviet Union.

The official Swedish government report on the impact of Chernobyl stated: 'The radiation level started to rise on 27 April as the first cloud of contaminated air from the Chernobyl accident reached Sweden. The air activity reached a maximum around 29 April. The outdoor radiation level was continuously followed by gamma-monitoring stations. The highest increase, a factor of ten, was registered at Umea in northern Sweden.' Umea was a university town on the Swedish coast at the same latitude as Reykjavik. The beautiful, forested countryside between the town and the Norwegian border was rich in wildlife. Elk, hare and woodcock were plentiful. The landscape's countless rivers and lakes were alive with trout, char, salmon and carp and the forest floor was ankle-deep in plants bearing black, red and blueberries, wild raspberry bushes and clumps of *hjortron*, the yellow cloudberries used for distinctive-tasting jam and liquor. Mushrooms sprouted around pale patches of reindeer lichen.

Almost everything had been rendered inedible because of the invisible blight which had descended from the skies with the rain. The woodcock were highly radioactive. So too were the fish, whose feeding cycle guaranteed that they would absorb more radioactive particles and become more contaminated as years went by. The forest floor was sprouting radioactive mushrooms. Some of the berries were not fit to pick. The lichen on which the reindeer fed had absorbed cancer-inducing caesium with a half-life of thirty years like a sponge. The Swedish government had decreed that any food with more than 300 *bequerels* of contamination per kilo could not be sold for consumption. The *bequerel* was a unit for measuring radioactive caesium particles, though experts disagreed on what the proper safety limit was. In Norway it was set at 600 *bequerels* and in Finland, 1,000. The more *bequerels*, the greater was the chance of getting cancer in later years. The Swedish government report went on: 'After six weeks the ground activity was dominated by caesium 137 and caesium 134 ... the following peaks have been reported: for hare, around 5,000 *bequerels*; venison, 8,000 *bequerels*; woodcock, 16,000 *bequerels*; and moose, 1,000 *bequerels*. For vegetable foodstuffs values above the permissible level have been obtained ... primarily for early species such as chives, parsley and nettles. For later species, such as rhubarb, lettuce, berries and potatoes, no alarming values have so far been reported. Reindeer killed in the highly contaminated regions show caesium concentrations at or above the permissible level and in a large fraction of cases more than 10,000 *bequerels*. The levels cannot be counted on to decrease to below 300 *bequerels* over the coming years in the highest contaminated areas without special counter measures.' Roland Olofsson, the co-owner of a reindeer meat plant in Vilhelmina, not far from Umea, showed me the bulletins he had received of readings in his district. In one lake a perch registered 137 *bequerels*, in another 5,523. On Lillorsjon Lake a small salmon was discovered with 13,770 *bequerels*. A mushroom picked nearby had 4,984. People were advised that if eaten a little at a time and infrequently, elk with up to 1,500 *bequerels* were safe enough. Most people had stopped eating elk, even though the majority shot in the forest had levels of less than 300. A few grazing in 'hot spots' had been found with more than 1,500 *bequerels*.

This avalanch of information allowed the Swedes to decide what not to do and what not to eat. I discovered in Moscow that no one in the Soviet Union knew about *bequerel* levels or even what the government safety limit was. People were given no information about how decisions were made to declare food fit for human consumption. The Soviet authorities relied instead on an invisible border, the circumference of a twenty-mile exclusion zone which had been declared around the nuclear reactor. Anything which grew within this circle was considered unfit for consumption. Everything outside was harvested as normal. It took little account of wind or rainfall on the night of the fire.

Driving to Chernobyl from Kiev, eighty miles to the south, on a hot June morning in 1987, we passed at first through dozens of typical Ukrainian villages, housing double lines of wooden *izbas* with intricate carvings around the windows, where life was going on as normal. Twenty miles from Chernobyl the landscape suddenly gave way to deserted roadside villages whose people had been evacuated. The lanes between the cottages, blocked off with wooden barriers, were choked with grass and dandelions. Gardens, vegetable plots and orchards were overgrown and running wild. In open country the grain crop, which had not been harvested since the accident, had reseeded, producing vast, unkept expanses of waist-high spring wheat mixed with weeds. From my experience in Sweden, I guessed that some patches in the forbidden territory could be relatively clean, with low *bequerel* levels. What none of us knew as we drove into the exclusion zone was that more vast tracts of land in the Ukraine, Byelorussia and Russia were so badly contaminated that tens of thousands of people had to be evacuated from towns and villages when the full truth came out in 1989 and 1990.

The exclusion area resembled a war zone. No civilians were allowed to enter without an army escort. Lorries and buses travelled along the roads carrying workers and soldiers wearing white face masks. Some soldiers resting by the roadside could be seen with the masks hanging loosely around their necks. How healthy would they be in five or ten years? Ten thousand soldiers were involved in removing the contaminated top soil and dumping it in huge concrete-encased pits set in clay beds. Most were volunteer reservists, I was told. Even then, more than a year after the fire spewed radioactive particles for miles around, water trucks patrolled the roads day and night to keep down radioactive dust. A hose pipe continuously flooded the steps of the entrance to the two-storey Communist Party headquarters in the sleepy town of Chernobyl, about six miles from the plant. It too had been mostly evacuated and the party building had been converted into a centre for instructing visitors on how to behave in the closed zone. 'It is forbidden to open the windows or use air-conditioning in buses or cars', a stocky man with silver teeth told our small party. 'You may not enter the forest. You may not walk on the grass. You must not drink spring water. You must stay together. You are recommended to wear sunglasses and you should not smoke. If you smoke you are more likely to inhale aerosols from the air or from your fingers.' He finished speaking and lit up a Kosmos cigarette. His forefinger and thumb were stained with nicotine. Which would get him first, we wondered, the nicotine or the radioactivity? He then took us to Pripyat.

The journey to Pripyat, three miles from the stricken power plant, was an excursion into unreality. We found a modern Soviet town as empty of life as an abandoned film set. The only things working were the traffic lights which signalled at empty streets. On the balcony of a second-floor apartment some washing was hanging on a string line: a vest, two shirts, a sheet and a couple of socks. Through a gap in the lace curtains could be seen a row of potted plants. The clothes had been drying there for 412 days. The geraniums, if that is what they had been, were brown, withered stalks. Forty-nine thousand people, many of them workers at the power plant, had lived there until Sunday afternoon, 28 April 1986, the day Pripyat died. They left in a fleet of 1,200 buses. The first bus departed at 2.00 p.m. By 4.00 p.m. practically everyone had gone. For two days radioactive dust from the burning reactor at Chernobyl had rained down on Pripyat's new ten-storey apartment blocks and wide streets, contaminating trees, grass, soil, cars, bicycles, prams, swings, slides, washing, tables, chairs, beds, kettles, books, picture frames and everything else in contact with the air. Nothing could be taken away. Some residents hid from the buses, unable to comprehend the catastrophe. Two old women, aged seventy-two and eighty-five, were found six weeks after the evacuation in their apartment, living on tinned food and ignoring the amplified announcements from police cars which occasionally crawled through the streets. All the things which defined the daily lives of the people were still in place: the apartments with their books, clothes, icons and personal treasures; the shops; the big gasometer; the Prometheus Cinema; the Forest Glade Hotel where young couples had their wedding receptions; the city council offices; the huge portrait of Lenin in the main square. The streets were absolutely silent in the afternoon heat. Nothing stirred except the sand, spiralling across the asphalt in the hot breeze and drifting against the kerbstones as if this settlement in the heart of the Ukraine was a seaside resort. Since the evacuation, all the contaminated top-soil in the parks, flowerbeds and lawns around the apartment blocks had been trucked away and protective yellow sand had been spread in its place. Here and there lanky strands of new grass sprouted through pavement cracks. Weeds had pushed through the sandy expanse that used to be the turf of the city football and athletics stadium. Down a sidestreet, in a grove of coniferous trees behind a five-foot concrete wall, were parked 300 Lada, Moskvich and Volga cars and dozens of Minsk and Yava motorcycles. Some of the motorbikes with sidecars had been parked in neat rows in a shallow pond. All these gleaming vehicles were too contaminated to be used. The pine trees which shaded them were drooping and withered, killed by the radioactive emissions. A colleague wondered aloud if the cars and bikes and the thousands of invaluable spare parts they contained would be destroyed or end up on the black market, so acute were the shortages of private motor vehicles in the Soviet Union. The radioactive assault on Pripyat was erratic. Some flats were more contaminated than others. A few owners had been allowed to return briefly to take away some personal belongings which had remained unaffected deep in a drawer or a cupboard. An official said there was no prospect of former residents coming back to live in Pripyat in their generation, though by then one third of the apartments had been officially 'decontaminated' using a new chemical spray.

In the middle of this desert stood the city greenhouses. The windows had been open when radioactive dust fell over the town. Inside, scientists worked in white coats. The contaminated gravel and soil beds had become a laboratory for experiments to find plants which absorbed the radionuclides from the soil and then purified them. Under the command of Professor Nikolai Arkhipov, a gang of agricultural workers wearing white masks over their faces were bused in every day to cultivate cucumbers, strawberries, lettuce, tomatoes, roses and 200 other varieties of plants. One of their aims was to find out which plants would produce clean products from contaminated soil. There had been surprising results. Heavy fertilising with calcium had helped eliminate strontium 90 from some species. With some misgivings I munched a freshly picked cucumber at the insistence of the cheerful Dr Arkhipov as the sand blew lightly on the greenhouse glass from the wasteland outside.

There was a notice in large letters outside the gates of the Chernobyl power-station proclaiming: 'We say no to nuclear madness'. Beside it was a poster of a nuclear missile being crushed by a huge fist. With bizarre irony this slogan, erected by the Chernobyl work collective, referred to Soviet disarmament policy rather than to the results of the environmental catastrophe their own Number 4 reactor had caused when it exploded and went on fire at 1.23 a.m. on 26 April 1986. The Chernobyl station, with its hundreds of electricity pylons, was isolated in the centre of a man-made desert stretching as far as the eye could see over the flat Ukrainian landscape. For miles around, tracts of highly contaminated forest and topsoil had been bulldozed away and replaced with sand. On the horizon, where clearing work continued, clumps of brown, withered pine trees stood on strips of new grass. At the entrance to the plant where two reactors were still working, pop music was playing over loudspeakers, ABBA adding to the sense of unreality with 'Money, Money, Money'. The Number 4 reactor was encased in concrete and clad in black metal so that it resembled the upturned hulk of an ocean-going liner. We were allowed to observe it across waste ground from a roadway 500 yards distant. A foreign ministry official with me, a young married man in his twenties who had expressed great misgivings about having to go anywhere near Chernobyl, switched on his Geiger counter. The needle showed 1.2 millirems of radioactivity, the average for the area around the power-station and about ten times higher than normal. He walked away a few paces, stopped, and called me over. 'See what it is now', he said grimly. The needle had shot up to 12.8 millirems. 'It's a hot spot, let's get back in the car.' In Kiev we had been given a report by the Ukrainian Supreme Soviet on the Chernobyl accident, especially prepared for the foreign press, which said nothing about hot spots. It declared that emissions from the reactor had more or less ended a year earlier. We found out later that this was a lie. 'To stop the release of radioactive substances to the atmosphere, over 5,000 tons of sand, clay, dolomite, lead and boron were dropped on the damaged reactor from helicopters from 27 April to 10 May', it said. 'This made it possible to reduce the radiation levels drastically. The total emission of fission products amounted to some fifty megacurie, which is about 3.5 per cent of the overall amount of radionuclides that had been in the reactor. In May the emissions had practically ceased.'

As we gazed at the black metal tomb, I recalled the words of Bessmertny, one of the characters in *Sarcophagus*, a play about Chernobyl written by Vladimir Gubaryev, the science editor of *Pravda* who had given me a copy of the text. In it Bessmertny said to the power-station director, 'Tens of thousands of years ahead, none of us will be here, not even our great-great-great grandchildren. All our cities will have gone. Even the pyramids of Egypt will be just a handful of dust, yet the sarcophagus around this reactor of yours will still be standing . . . that's some monument to leave our descendants, isn't it?' In real life the director of Chernobyl was fifty-two-year-old Mikhail Umanets. In his office behind windows lined with heavy antidust curtains, he too assured us that there were 'practically no new emissions' from the sarcophagus and declared, 'we don't have to worry about working here'.

We drove on to Green Cape, a settlement for the 6,000 workers who serviced the Chernobyl power-station, erected just outside the contaminated zone. In that postnuclear commuter town of barrack-type wooden buildings fenced off from the outside world, children and grandparents were banned. So too was money. It was a cashless society with clothes, food and entertainment provided free of charge so that contaminated objects would not be filtered back to Kiev where most of the workers had their families. They could not go outside for their entertainment. A notice invited inhabitants to a disco or to play 'hunt the dragon' that evening. The workers were the former inhabitants of Pripyat. Most had been given apartments in Kiev after the accident and came back to spend two weeks every month living in Green Cape. We saw a shift of workers returning from the nuclear station in their brown uniforms and white face masks. Before entering they had to pass through a radiation check at a turnstile where security guards ran a Geiger counter over their bodies. About one in fifty failed the test and was taken away for clothes-disposal and a thorough scrubbing, which I was told was a very unpleasant experience. As we left we recalled the hot spot we had stood on near the sarcophagus and tested our shoes with the counter. Both pairs showed 4.0 millirems, forty times higher than normal. We decided to burn them when we got back to Moscow.

After three hours of driving through the flat Ukrainian landscape, putting the radiation zone far behind us, we arrived at the village of Hebrat. Hebrat had 560 houses, all sturdy chalets of brick and wood with glass-covered verandas. Each occupied a third of an acre and had tiny wooden railings fronting the paved streets. It could have been a suburb in rural America. A year before, Hebrat also didn't exist. All its 1,622 inhabitants had lived in the village of Zavesia, half-a-day's drive to the west. Most of them worked on what had been the Bolshevik collective farm and in their spare time looked after privately owned cows, pigs and vegetable plots. Zavesia was less than ten miles from the Chernobyl power-plant. On 4 May 1986, eight days after the disaster, confused and frightened and wearing only the clothes on their back, since burned, the inhabitants were driven for several hours away from the danger zone and billeted with peasant families in a cluster of hamlets. Within days construction workers arrived from all over the Soviet Union. Before the eyes of the villagers, Hebrat rose from a disused pasture meadow. On 1 September they were able to move in. They found the houses sturdily built and adequately furnished and their shop assistant from Zavesia, plump, good-natured Olga Yanchenko, behind the counter of a new general store. There were little recesses in the street occupied by benches where the old people could sit and gossip in the summer evenings, just like in Zavesia. The collective farm had also been transferred to Hebrat, taking up 9,000 acres of old grazing land. The soil wasn't as good but it was responding to heavy fertilisation. Little monuments dotted the streets, including an ornamental anchor donated by construction workers from Sevastopol. All the villagers, who were among the 43,000 country people moved out of the contamination zone, had received or were due to receive what they said was generous financial compensation. It was a showpiece of Soviet caring and relief work.

Nevertheless, they only wanted to go home. 'Everybody here wants to go back; people are used to their own place, especially country people', said the chairman of the village soviet, Vasily Timochenko, a squat, round-faced village boss in a brown suit with thick hair sleeked back. 'It's not easy for them, even though we have kept neighbours and friends in the same street.' Down a side road, Ivan Smirnov, a retired miner, invited me into his new house. A carpet hung on the wall and a television set played in the corner. It was better than he had ever had, but 'the old house was good enough for me', he said. In another part of the village, Mikhail Fedoretz, leaning on his bicycle, told me how this had been the second evacuation of Zavesia in half a century. In 1944, the Nazis had forced all the residents to move to a nearby town as the Soviet army approached. The Germans had killed forty people from the village. In nearby Raza, they had exterminated 620 villagers, and in the next hamlet, Borodyanka, had dumped seventy-two bodies in a well. No one from the village had died this time, but for all its horrors and brutalities, it was evident that the war was something the old people understood better than they did the invisible radiation. What drove them from their homes was something intangible. No one had shown any signs of serious illness in their monthly check-ups. A woman in a headscarf hurrying by saw my notebook. 'Tell them it's good here but we want to go home and that that electricity station should be closed down', she shouted. Outside the post-office, fifty-seven-year-old Anna Romanchenko smiled and said, 'Houses are fine but home is better.' She had tended cattle all her life, only to see 650 cows and 600 pigs owned by the villagers taken away for slaughter in the days after the accident. A thirteen-year-old schoolboy, Sergei, who had stopped cycling to watch a stork gliding by, said, 'I want to go home, so do all my friends.' It is unlikely that Sergei will be allowed to go back to take up residence in Zavesia, should he live to be an old man. Of the sixty-nine settlements evacuated after the disaster, twenty-seven would never be resettled. Zavesia is one of them. Some villagers had been allowed to return briefly. Ivan Smirnov was able to retrieve a family portrait from the sideboard of his old home. 'There were lots of fish in the river', he said sadly, 'and no one to catch them.'

They did not know it, but they were among the lucky ones. Across the border in Byelorussia, 30,000 people were evacuated from similar villages caught inside the twenty-mile contaminated zone. Not until 1990 did the full truth come out, that persistently high levels of caesium 137 had been recorded in seventeen other districts of Byelorussia up to 160 miles north of Chernobyl. The Byelorussian foreign minister, Pyotr Kravchanka, told the United Nations in October that year that one fifth of the Byelorussian population, or 2,200,000 people, including 800,000 children, had become innocent victims of the radioactive contamination. One third of its territory, about 70,000 square miles, was a radiation desert. Between 120,000 and 150,000 residents of high-risk zones were still waiting for their relocation into settlements under construction in clean areas. In his UN speech Kravchanka quoted from the book of revelations which speaks of a great star named wormwood falling from the sky, and 'a third of the waters turned bitter and many people died from waters that had become bitter'. Chernobyl means wormwood in slavic languages. Chernobyl was an apocalypse, he said, which had left hanging over the children the possibility of long-term genetic defects which could give rise in the future to a 'sect of outcasts' in marital and other spheres of human relations.

The movement of nuclear refugees wasn't all one way. By 1990 some 2,000 old people had gone back to their villages in the Ukraine and in Byelorussia despite an official ban, saying they would rather die in five years from cancer than in ten years away from home. The government casualty figures showed that three and a half years after the accident, only eighty-six people had died of radiation sickness which, along with the immediate victims of April 1986, brought the death toll up to 117. A Chernobyl veterans group set up in Estonia in 1989 voiced public scepticism. It cited men working near the reactor who complained of a sweet acid taste in their mouth long afterwards, and who had suffered hair and teeth loss, claiming some had died without being included in the official statistics.

Nobody disputes that if it hadn't been for the bravery of the Chernobyl firemen, the disaster could have been much worse. A museum was opened in Kiev to the memory of the six men who lost their lives putting out the flames. Their portraits were displayed along a long, narrow room with dramatic photographs of the fire and its aftermath, including a five-foot picture of the stricken reactor, illuminated from below by an artificial coal fire from an electric heater. There were framed press-cuttings, including one from a British tabloid with a headline, 'The Bravest Man in the World'. It referred to Colonel Leonid Telyatnikov who led the fire fighters. His photograph, with head completely bald because of radiation sickness, appeared in a clipping from *Izvestia* with the words, 'Thank you, hero of Chernobyl'. There were tributes to the hero of Chernobyl and his team from all over the world, ranging from a message sent by Rangers fans at Ibrox to lines of praise written by Russian poet Andrei Voznesensky:

> When the robot failed to switch off the tragedy
> A man stepped into the radiant block
> We both stayed alive, you and I,
> Because that was a real man.

Colonel Telyatnikov had recovered and greeted us at the museum in an olive green uniform. He described the night of the fire. 'You had the impression you could see the radiation', he said. 'A lot of the substances there were glowing, luminescent, a bit like sparklers. There were flashes of light springing from place to place as if they were being thrown. And there was a kind of gas on the roof, a kind of fog.' He passed out after half an hour's exposure to the radiation and came to in hospital in Pripyat, from where he was evacuated to Moscow for special treatment. His hair fell out, his energy drained away. 'I wanted nothing; neither to see nor to hear nor eat nor drink', he said. He only learned of the deaths of his companions three months later when his recovery began. This hero of the Soviet Union and devoted party member became the living symbol of what the museum described as 'the victory of Soviet man over the calamity'. He was also a testimony to the possibility of recovery, even if only temporary, from radiation sickness. His ginger hair had regrown, his fingernails had come back to life and he was shaving again. His face looked waxen but his health was improving all the time, he said. He was back at work as an instructor. He was thirty-four when the disaster occurred. 'I expect to grow old', he said, smiling bravely.

3

'I didn't send you there . . .'

I N THE MORNING sunlight the two magnesium flares looked like tiny pieces of red hot coal trailing white smoke as they passed beneath the Afghan Air Ilyushin descending towards Kabul at the end of a four-hour flight from Moscow. They were fired from a Soviet helicopter gunship to intercept heat-seeking missiles from the rebel-held mountains around the Afghan capital. We had begun our descent from 20,000 feet above the city, which sprawled across a wide brown plateau surrounded by snow-covered peaks. Three times the sun flashed blindingly through the window beside me as we plunged around and down in narrowing circles to the airport. The helicopter gunships had appeared at around 4,000 feet, firing flares every five seconds beside and beneath us until we had landed. The manoeuvres undertaken by civilian airlines over Kabul, and the flares which filled the blue skies above the city all day with sparks and white ribbons of smoke, underlined for the new arrival in January 1988 the fact that the Soviet intervention in Afghanistan which began eight years earlier had failed to achieve its purpose. Rebel activity had become so intense that the capital was under a state of siege. Up to 200 planes had already been brought down in the war, several of them civilian aircraft, by American-made stinger missiles, and the number was growing rapidly.

It was becoming evident by then that the Soviet leadership was preparing the ground for a withdrawal of what it always called its 'limited contingent' of 115,000 troops from Afghanistan. The Soviet presence on the territory of its southern neighbour, which had caused the 1980 Olympic boycott and plunged the Cold War into deep freeze, hampered the search by Mikhail Gorbachev and his advisers for major foreign-policy successes to aid their reforms. Opposition, too, was simmering at home as casualties mounted. Gorbachev's dilemma was how to reverse a policy enthusiastically endorsed for nearly a decade by the Soviet Communist Party without losing face or endangering the strategic balance on the southern USSR borders, not to mention detracting from the sufferings and honour of the casualties and their relatives. Glasnost had already begun to expose cracks in public morale. Letters had been published from parents complaining bitterly about the refusal of local authorities to allow gravestones to carry any reference to death in Afghanistan because of a regulation designed to disguise casualty figures. The father of a dead soldier complained, 'One might think he was killed in a drunken brawl.' An article in the party daily *Pravda*, caused outrage by exposing the callous attitude of a housing official in Alma Ata who dismissed a war veteran with the words, 'I didn't send you to Afghanistan.' This phrase ran through the growing debate about the physical and psychological damage done to a generation of young soldiers, often subject to callous indifference at home. The first sign of a change in policy came in the reporting of the war in the Soviet media. Casualties had been almost a taboo subject until 1987 when television began to show pictures of fighting between Soviet troops and the *dushmani*, the Afghan rebels, and reports first appeared in the press of the regular shooting down of Soviet planes. The Soviet Foreign Ministry also decided in 1987 to lift the ban on Western correspondents visiting Afghanistan. This was partly because Moscow wanted to prove to the world that the supply of US sophisticated weaponry to the rebels was prolonging the war and causing civilian casualties. Moscow also felt compelled to show that the Afghan army had the ability to hold on to strategic positions so that when the eventual Soviet withdrawal took place, it would not be seen as a defeat. The latter was certainly one of the reasons I had been invited by the Soviet Foreign Ministry, shortly after I came to Moscow, to travel to Afghanistan to visit Kabul and the city of Khost, which had just been relieved by Soviet and Afghan troops in a rare victory for the Moscow-backed revolutionary government.

The most immediate impression I now received on my return to Kabul after eight years was how little impact the Soviet occupation had made on the fiercely independent Afghan people. Afghanistan airlines used Russian-made aircraft and the passengers on my flight were mostly Soviet citizens, fraternal visitors to Kabul – like Gori Marchuk, president of the Soviet Academy of Sciences who was sitting behind me. The airline, however, made no concessions to the Russians. The 'No Smoking' and 'Fasten Safety-Belt' signs on the plane were in English and Dari, a form of Afghan Persian. The pilot made his announcements in the same two languages and he wished passengers 'all the best' in English as we left the plane. In the Mailmapal Hotel in the Afghan capital, the signs and the brochures were in English and Dari. Most of the staff spoke Dari, Pushtu (the language of the Pathans of eastern Afghanistan and northern Pakistan), and a little English. They did not speak any Russian, though most of the hotel guests came from the Soviet Union. In the lobby kiosk, a few old paperback books were displayed for sale. They included *The Saint Meets his Match*, by Leslie Charteris; *Alfred Hitchcock's Mystery Magazine, 1973*, and *John F Kennedy, A Political Profile* – but nothing in Russian. The shops and street stalls in the 7,000-foot-high central Asian city were well stocked with Western imports – Kodak film, Toblerone chocolate and Old Spice shaving lotion. 'The Afghans are natural traders. You can buy anything here, even a Mercedes if you want', said a resident diplomat. Money-changers in a tiny courtyard of glass-fronted offices traded afghanis for dollars. The money-market was legal, despite the proclaimed socialist nature of the regime. A brief-case was needed to carry fifty dollars' worth of Afghani notes, but the carpet sellers in the lantern-lit shops by the Kabul River were glad to accept dollars. The Russian rouble was nowhere to be seen.

In atmosphere, Kabul was much the same city I had visited in January 1980 as Soviet troops were pouring in. There was little Russification in the way US troops Americanised Saigon. Soviet soldiers and government officials did not mix readily with the civilian population. For one thing, the Soviet servicemen had no dollars to spend; for another, it was too dangerous, so great was the antagonism towards Russians, expressed even sometimes by officials of the Soviet-backed government. The Soviets lived mostly in special four-storey apartment blocks in a compound near the airport. There were a few Soviet goods in the shops, like the dark blue packets of Kosmos cigarettes stacked beside piles of Winstons and Marlboros, and Soviet-made Volga taxis jostled with rounded, old Mercedes sedans on the chaotic streets; however, Russian taxis and buses and tobacco had been imported by Afghanistan long before the revolution. There was one new Soviet-Afghan joint venture: a factory to make bicycles. The management gave a free bicycle to any Afghan boy whose father was killed fighting in the army. Three dozen fatherless boys rode past the reviewing stand at the end of a military parade staged by the government in Revolution Square the week we were there, waving flowers. The military vehicles were all, of course, manufactured in the USSR.

Moscow's strategic interests in Afghanistan went back more than a century. Afghanistan was a buffer state in what Rudyard Kipling described as the 'great game' between tsarist Russia and the British Empire. London's colonial ambitions and the threat of Russian expansion led to British invasions and the Anglo-Afghan wars of 1839–1842 and 1878–1880. After the last war with England in 1919, Afghanistan gained full independence and became a kingdom.

Since then, links with Moscow had steadily developed. Afghan students began attending Tashkent University in Soviet Uzbekistan after a treaty of friendship was signed with Lenin in 1921. A grand assembly of Afghan tribes decided in 1955 that the king should turn to Russia for economic and military aid to strengthen his hand in a long-running dispute with Pakistan over Pathan tribal homelands. The Royal Afghan Airforce was shortly afterwards equipped with Soviet fighters. The great game continued in the form of patronage. United States and Canadian construction teams built roads and dams in the south and west; Russian technicians worked on irrigation and road projects in the north and east.

But revolution was brewing, fuelled by a newly emerging intelligentsia and an urban class centred on Kabul who wanted to speed up reforms. Feudal conditions prevailed in the countryside. Only 3 per cent of the fifteen million people could read. A man could expect to live for only forty-two years, a woman for thirty-five. Women had no rights. Dissent had first expressed itself in the 1920s when a few officials' wives put aside the Islamic *chaudris* covering their faces by permission of the progressive King Amunulla. Amunulla was subsequently forced to abdicate by outraged Moslem tribesmen and the crown given to a relative. The People's Democratic Party, founded in 1965 and led by an army officer, Mohammad Aslam Watanjar, infiltrated the armed forces and staged its coup in 1978. At the military parade we watched in Kabul, Watanjar appeared in a Fidel Castro-style fatigue cap and recounted how he had started up his tank and driven to the Royal Palace in Kabul, his heart 'fluttering with excitement'. The palace fell and the revolutionaries were able to seize control of the country when seven key garrisons threw in their lot with the People's Democratic Party. One of these Watanjar garrisons was in the town of Khost, near the Pakistan border.

We assembled in the darkness at Kabul airport for the flight south to Khost. Accustomed to commercial flights, I had brought along a book to read, a source of some amusement to the other Moscow correspondents in the party. It turned out that the aeroplane was a propeller-driven Antonov-26 troop-carrier which we entered by a ramp at the back and in which we had to sit on metal seats in total darkness during the hour-long flight. No planes flew to Khost during the day because of guerrilla rocket attacks and they were blacked out at night so they couldn't be spotted from the rocket emplacements in the mountains. The city had been cut off by road in 1982 until the previous week when a column of supply lorries had got through. We landed at 4.00 a.m. in complete darkness at Khost airfield, a strip of baked earth with a Nissan hut where the only navigation light was a hand-held torch at the end of the runway.

The chilly dawn in Khost soon gave way to a cloudless day as we sipped sweet tea with the local People's Democratic Party chairman, Saadat Gul Ahangar, a tall, brown-skinned man of thirty-five in a Western suit, blue shirt and paisley tie. 'On behalf of the people of Khost, I welcome you', he said, as attendants refilled our cups at the open-air tables outside the office of tribal affairs. He showed us black-and-white photographs of the bodies of victims of rebel bombardments. 'Our history is of revolutionary struggle', he said. 'Our region of Khost has a 162-kilometre border with Pakistan. After the revolution the counter-revolutionaries intensified their attacks on us. They have railways and asphalt roads, and hundreds of thousands of sophisticated weapons came to their area. We have only poor roads. And we have no road out.' Khost was indeed an underdeveloped rural settlement. From the adjacent streets came the sound of roosters crowing in backyards. A pony and trap clipped along the road, stirring up dust clouds as it swerved to avoid potholes. A donkey with panniers ambled past while a camel haughtily plodded by. Young men whirled along on tall, Chinese-made bicycles. Policemen appeared with peaked hats and traffic indicators like table-tennis bats. We walked down the narrow main street where *shashlik* sellers were preparing wood fires on the pavement under clay awnings held up by roughly cut wooden poles. *Samovars* were being boiled up for the old men who sat all day drinking tea. Piles of oranges and mandarins were arranged on stalls beside heaps of nuts and spices. The apothecary opened his door beside a shopfront covered with colour photographs of Pakistani film stars. The air grew heavy with the smells of cooking and manure.

But the Khost streets were also full of the sights and sounds of war. Young soldiers in ill-fitting khaki wool uniforms, who had been on duty with their *kalashnikovs* all night, sat down on their hunkers and lit cigarettes under the mulberry trees as the sun warmed the air. Some had the slanted eyes and wispy beards of Hazaras, others the blue eyes and fair skins of Pathans, or the delicate features of Tajikhs. Armoured personnel carriers which had been sitting about the town throughout the hours of darkness rumbled back to barracks, and fresh crews took them out again. As the shadows shortened, the daily barrage of rocket fire and artillery directed against the rebels in the mountains began: rapid, single bangs which made the ground tremble alongside the prolonged whine of *katyusha* rockets going off in quick succession in sets of eight, making red streaks in the sky. 'We get a fix on the firing point when a rocket comes in and we strike back hard', said the party chief as we walked through the town. The firing only stopped when Soviet-built M-24 and M-18 helicopter gunships clattered low overhead.

Khost, whose population was 40,000, lay eighty miles from Kabul by air and 140 miles by road. It had been garrisoned by the Afghan army since the revolution and was situated in Paktia province, part of the austere and beautiful land of the Pathans, the largest tribal society in the world, which spreads across the border into Pakistan in the area around the Khyber Pass. Gunfire had for centuries been a familiar sound, marking rivalry and intrigue among the tribes, such as feuds over *zar*, *zan* and *zamin* (gold, women and land). The people were dedicated to Islam and fiercely independent, never really coming under the control of either the Afghanistan or Pakistan governments. War with a godless revolutionary government in Kabul had been inevitable. The largest tribe in the Khost area was the Zadrans who lived in the mountains, cutting down and selling wood from oak, beech and cedar trees on the high slopes. In 1979 the Zadrans attacked and wiped out an army supply-convoy on the way to Khost and it seemed the town would soon be overrun. Support in the army was draining away from the revolutionary government whose leader, Hafizullah Amin, was busy imprisoning, torturing and executing opponents in a Stalin-like purge inside and outside the party. In December that year, the Russians moved in and Amin was killed in the process. A new leader, Babrak Karmal, was installed. Thousands of prisoners were released and Khost and similar garrisons were strengthened by Soviet troops. But the Islamic tribesmen now had an invader to fight – the *Shuravi*, as the Russians were known – evoking the memories and passions of the nineteenth-century wars with Britain. The Zadrans joined the Hesbi-I-Islami rebel group, one of seven counter-revolutionary bodies which formed and set up headquarters in Pakistan. Arms began to flow in from the West. The Zadrans erected heavily mined fortifications on the Satu-Kandall Pass on the Khost road. The only way in and out for the Soviet and Afghan armies was by air.

We had been brought to Khost not only to testify to a victory against the rebels but to hear the other side of the story: the case of the revolutionary government. This was put forcibly at a political rally staged for our benefit outside the bullet-scarred Palace of Culture and attended by a few dozen old men in turbans, a group of mawkish young soldiers and dozens of pretty, brown-skinned children. They were addressed by twenty-seven-year-old Mahbyba, a slim woman with dark hair combed down to her eyelashes who condemned the 'war-mongering imperialistic circles in the West' for supplying weapons to the rebels. As chairwoman of the Women's Council of Khost she described the repression of women under the tribal system and the part they would play in the construction of a new society in Afghanistan. She invited people to take part in the national reconciliation programme, but the rest of her speech was drowned out by a sustained burst of rapid outgoing rocket fire.

We were also there to learn about the suffering caused by weapons supplied by the West to the Islamic rebels. We were driven out to a village to see the wreckage of an Antonov-26, one of four civilian aircraft shot down by a stinger missile near Khost two months previously. Its intact tailplane and burned out shell lay beneath a cypress tree where it had slewed to a halt. The front wheels lay one hundred yards away, and the twisted propeller a little further along. As we examined it, four Soviet helicopter gunships roared low over our heads and moments later four plumes of brown smoke rose from the foot of the hills a few miles away. A forty-year-old peasant, Merza Ali Khan, described how he had pulled the two pilots alive from the Antonov but could do nothing for the women and children screaming in the burning body. 'I cry every time I think of it', he said, tears in his eyes. A few miles further on the liberated highway, Soviet army officers had also laid out for our inspection some of the 4,500 mines they had removed from the road to Kabul, displayed on tables beside a wrecked bridge like goods in a bazaar. There were round and flat mines, like shortbread tins, made in Pakistan and Italy; bulky pressure bombs from Britain; and Chinese and French explosive devices.

That night we were ourselves at the receiving end of weapons supplied by some of the 'war-mongering imperialistic circles'. As we arrived at the airstrip, again in darkness, to board the Antonov which had come back for the return flight to Kabul, a rocket struck the ground 500 yards to our left. A second rocket exploded a minute later in a fountain of red streaks a hundred yards to our right, and bits of earth rained down on top of us as I stumbled behind Robin Lodge of *Reuters* and Chris Walker of the London *Times* towards the plane whose propellers were already turning. The ramp was pulled up as the Antonov roared across the baked mud and began climbing steeply with all lights out. Hanging on to the parachute wire above the bucket seats as the plane circled upwards, Robin and I could see the exploding star of a third rocket landing on the air strip. We estimated it had hit the exact spot where the plane had been standing.

I wondered if those firing the rockets had been among the Afghan rebels I met some years previously when I travelled across the

Baluchistan Desert from Pakistan to live for a short spell with Afghan rebels in the Mujahideen camp in Afghanistan's Zabul province, south west of the Khost region. The experience left me with no illusions about the fighting spirit and religious fervour of the Islamic rebels and what the Russians were up against. The guerrillas, divided into warring factions as they may have been, were far from the 'bandits' the Soviet media had long called them. The rebels with whom I stayed in the wild countryside near Kandahar belonged to the Hesbi-I-Islami group. They were a disciplined fighting force, under the command of a former Afghan army colonel, Zafaruddin Khan, distinguished from his turbaned warriors by a tall *astrakhan* hat, neatly-pressed fawn trousers and manicured nails.

Khan was a graduate of Kabul Military College and was regarded with awe by his followers, not least because he was reputed to have personally killed thirty-five communists during the successful mutiny he had led the previous year at Zabul military base. Zafaruddin Khan had started his life in the mountains by taking up arms against Amin's communist government in Kabul. Now he had committed himself to fighting a holy war – a *jihad* against the occupying Soviet troops. He had captured several Soviet armoured personnel carriers and mortars. In the evenings he led the 150 fighters at his camp to prayers in an open mosque. They prayed in unison, bowing and rising together with military precision. (I often saw individual warriors kneeling in private prayer among the rocks and thornbushes in the 9,000 foot-high mountain camp. They were Sunni Moslem rebels, backed by America, but extolling the greatness of Ayatollah Khomeini, the Shi'ite leader of Iran.) Around the walls of the commander's sunken tent hung green Islamic banners. 'When the Russians are defeated – and they will never succeed as long as there is one Moslem in Afghanistan – then we will have a pure Islamic state here', said Zafuruddin Khan. The Russians, he assured me, had come to destroy Islam, 'but we have the faith; we believe in our holy religion – we will win', his men boasted around the camp fires on the evening of their killings. Mahtat Hakim, a full-bearded twenty-four-year-old Mujahideen with a reputation as a fearsome assassin in Kabul, described how he shot his eight victims. 'I go up to them and I do this', he said, emitting a roar and violently shaking his cheeks and curly black beard as if having a fit. 'Then I do this.' With his fingers he imitated the squeezing of a revolver trigger. His victims had been Afghan supporters of the Kabul regime, but for him the Russians had given the war a new intensity. 'I am very happy here killing Russians for Allah', he said.

The failure of the Soviet army to pacify Afghanistan had one tangible result. The leadership in Kabul was forced to admit it was impossible to build socialism by force in a Moslem country with tribal relations. With Moscow's encouragement a new leader, Najibullah, replaced Karmal and introduced a policy of national reconciliation in an effort to arrange truces and cease-fires with as many tribes and tribal factions as possible and to consolidate his position before a Soviet withdrawal. Najibullah put the revolution into reverse, cancelling socialist plans for the economy. New slogans appeared on the streets idealising the Afghan leader, who fought the British in 1919, as a symbol of unity. Most importantly, the revolutionary government embraced Islam. President Najibullah began regularly attending the mosque on Fridays. Government meetings began with readings from the Koran. In the army, regulations were rewritten to allow soldiers to pray according to Islamic custom. On the road outside Khost at dusk, we saw forty Afghan army soldiers on their knees, their foreheads touching the ground, praying in a mosque which was no more than a circle of stones on the barren earth, just as the Hesbi-I-Islami guerrillas with whom I had stayed in the mountains had done.

In Kabul we spoke with Najibullah. 'You dared go to Khost; you saw for yourself what the situation was like', he remarked. 'I can give a full assurance that the valorous Afghan armed forces are capable of patrolling the country and providing for the peaceful life of the people.' That was on 20 January. The road to Khost was closed again by the rebels on 26 January, though government troops were to hold on to the town with the help of Soviet military hardwear long after the Soviet army had finally withdrawn from the country on 15 February 1989. It finally fell in the spring of 1991.

Only in the final days was the Soviet public told that at least 15,000 Soviet soldiers had been killed in Afghanistan and 37,000 maimed fulfilling their 'international duty'. Russian people began to learn how the war had brutalised soldiers. In Afghanistan, said writer Gennady Bocharov, young soldiers found themselves doing things in a matter of fact way that they would never have dreamed of at home. Where the enemy showed no mercy to the *Shuravi*, the Russians replied in kind. 'War made them kill, burn and destroy', Bocharov said. He described one incident in which Soviet soldiers shot at a car. When it stopped they found the injured driver, a dead young woman, two other women, a teenage boy and two children. The commander, Sharayevsky, contacted his superior officer by radio for instructions. 'I don't need prisoners', came the reply. The Afghan family was shot; the car and the bodies were buried. Returning soldiers later told horror stories of torturing Afghans with electric wires attached to their genitals, and of reconnaissance units regularly killing anyone they encountered in contested areas after beatings to extract information. The collapse of discipline and the revenge psychology was similar to that which affected the American army in Vietnam where it had resulted in the My Lai massacre and other atrocities. Andrei Sakharov, who had been exiled to Gorky in 1980 for his opposition to the war, confronted the Soviet parliament in 1989 with the unpalatable truth that widespread atrocities had been committed. As in America, veterans formed peace movements, led by victims of the war like poet-singer Alexander Karpenko, who was scarred for life by a mine.

In the tradition of Vladimir Vysotsky, Karpenko chronicled in ballads the terrible experiences of the Russian soldiers. 'Naturally people try to forget,' he said, 'but the job of the poet is to keep those memories alive, without bitterness.'

4

'On Thursday I got some flour . . .'

IT TOOK me a while to figure out the rules of shopping in Moscow and how the system worked in the Tagansky supermarket over which I lived. The basic rule was not to take a shopping list but always a shopping bag. Shoppers crushed through the single door of the store not knowing what was going to be available, clutching empty carrier bags of all shapes and sizes. Plastic bags or wrapping paper were rarely provided at the thirteen checkout counters. People travelled hundreds of miles to shop in its gloomy recesses, which smelled of fish and slightly rancid sunflower oil where it had spilled on to the stone floor from a dispenser in the corner. Old village women in scarves with red faces and large pimples jostled with smartly dressed city bureaucrats carrying rectangular metal-lined brief-cases.

The Tagansky was one of Moscow's newest stores, opened only months before, and it had the merit for customers of being near three metro stations. It had only about seventy-five different items in the wire cages and switched-off freezer units which served as shelves – I did an inventory one day – but even so it contained many products not available in the village shops. The longest queues were always at the waist-high freezer units stretched along the back wall beneath the glass windows of four tiled rooms where women in white coats weighed and packaged food in cellophane. A loud, thudding noise filled the store when a glass pane was pulled back and one of the women started to hurl large lumps of chicken or cheese or sausage on to the grills of the freezer, the bundles sometimes striking the hands and wrists of people dipping into the trough. 'What are they giving out?' shoppers would ask, pushing forward. Bang, crash, thud: another window would open and bundles of hake would cascade on to the wire to lie for a few brief seconds beside the unwanted *mintai*, the cheap, frozen fish which people associated with Thursday – fish day in factory canteens. In those days before rationing and panic-buying, there was always milk, potatoes, apples, peppers, cabbage, cucumbers, rice, flour, pancake flour, sugar (mainly in concrete-hard lumps), eggs and porridge oats known as *kasha*. The supermarket sold bread too, laid out on wooden shelves with spoons hanging on a string for customers to test the freshness of the loaves. Outside the supermarket women in white coats would sometimes take up positions in the square with a table, chair, weighing scales and boxes of produce. Queues would form before people knew what they were selling. At first I thought this was private enterprise, an extension of the peasants' markets where one could always get fresh vegetables, but at a high price. They were, in fact, shop assistants sent into the streets by the store to sell perishable goods quickly, like tomatoes or oranges. It wasn't always possible to judge how serious the periodic shortages were as the street sellers would appear and disappear without notice, and people were used to buying up on the spot what was available. There was also a *stol zakazov* around the corner from the supermarket – a little office for ordering goods in advance through trade unions. Many people were entitled to order, once a month, a tin of caviar or of condensed milk, a half kilo of sturgeon, a Hungarian chicken or a packet of coffee. It was the first level of privilege in a country where hidden privileges were a way of life. For the sweating peasants from the country, with their heavy coats and bulging bags, staggering towards the metro, such delights belonged to another world. They were for Muscovites only.

Near the supermarket was a wine shop with a sign in blue plastic letters above the door saying *vino*. In the small window, a notice informed the public that wine, champagne and cognac were sold from 2.00 p.m. to 8.00 p.m., and vodka from 4.00 p.m. to 8.00 p.m. Even without the sign it was easy to tell that this was a wine shop by the steel crush barriers on the pavement outside. Long before 2.00 p.m. a lengthy queue formed, consisting predominantly of men and sometimes stretching fifty yards down the footpath and doubling back on itself. I joined it one day half an hour before closing time. People kept coming up to the head of the queue to ask those leaving what was available. 'Everything', said an elderly man triumphantly clutching a bulky carrier bag. By 8.00 p.m. I was still a block away from the door. A plump, blonde woman in a white coat, who had been letting people in a few at a time, announced that no one else would be admitted. There was a brief mêlée, with men pushing and arguing, and two youths managed to squeeze past her ample figure. Shouting abuse, she hauled one back by the collar. The rest of us drifted away. Some hung around to do a deal with the speculators who had been in the shop earlier and were now offering vodka at black-market prices.

Such scenes had been common in Moscow since Mikhail Gorbachev restricted alcohol shops to shorter opening hours and cut the production of vodka and other drink by a third shortly after he came to power in 1985. The abuse of alcohol, the Communist Party leader had decided, was one of the main impediments to the reconstruction of the Soviet economy. To cut down morning drinking, restaurants were also forbidden to serve alcoholic drink until after 2.00 p.m. The central statistics board claimed that the number of accidental deaths among Soviet citizens of working age in 1986 fell to 680,000 from 799,000 in 1984 because of the 38 per cent cut in hard-liquor consumption. The authorities also claimed a 25 per cent fall in road accidents. But the antidrink laws had produced a host of new problems. The week I stood in the vodka queue, the Soviet Ministry of Internal Affairs held its first ever briefing for journalists as part of the new policy of openness. Officials frankly acknowledged that the wine and vodka queues were a particularly ugly sight in the Soviet Union. They caused intense frustration to people who simply wanted to buy a bottle of cheap champagne for a party or birthday celebration. Things were made even worse, they said, by profiteers – sometimes workers who should be at their jobs. They queued to buy vodka at the standard price of ten roubles a half-litre bottle (about a fifth of the average weekly wage), then sold it at a higher price to people in the queue. Moreover, the manufacture of *samagon*, home-brewed spirits, was causing a shortage of sugar. In 1986, some 11 per cent more sugar was sold than in the previous year, and a full-scale campaign against *samogon* distillers was launched. Television news showed pictures of militiamen breaking down the door of an apartment. The camera followed them inside and found a contraption with all the characteristics of an Irish poteen still. The press also carried some horror stories about people turning to other dangerous liquids. The *Literaturnaya Gazetta* coined the word 'eau de coholics' to describe the hardened drinkers who had taken to tossing back toilet waters and colognes. Swigging perfumes 'explained why the metro trains are full of such heavenly smells in the mornings – and women have nothing to do with it', the paper said.

The one place where drink was almost always guaranteed was a state restaurant. One night a few of us set out for the Russian Izba, a country restaurant about twenty miles out of Moscow. It was a damp January night with the temperature hovering just above freezing point. At the end of a narrow country road our headlights picked out a rather squat militiaman in a grey coat and white belt on duty at a lonely crossroads. I pulled up and asked him if he could direct us to the Russian Izba. Without a word he pointed his traffic stick towards a pretty two-storey log structure nearby. It was a quiet night at the restaurant. Ours was the only car in the park and when we left late in the evening, the same militiaman was standing at the crossroads. This time he raised the white stick to wave us to a halt. 'I think there's something wrong with your headlights', he said gruffly, his round face poking halfway through the side window. I got out and we walked round the car. The lights were working normally. He asked officiously for my documents. These too were in order. Shortly his manner changed. 'What did you think of the restaurant, then?' he said. 'Was it expensive? Which room were you in? Ah, that explains it. Well now, let me tell you a better road back to Moscow . . .'

I knew, of course, what he was really about. He was looking for any sign that I might have been drinking in the restaurant – an unsteady walk, a fumbling with papers, a whiff of sweet champagne. But I had been living in Moscow long enough by then to know that not only was it forbidden to drink and drive in the Soviet Union, but that as part of the anti-alcohol campaign, the militia had become even more vigilant. A colleague learned the hard way. He was parking his car outside our building when a passing militiaman asked him if he had been drinking vodka. 'No, just a glass or two of champagne', he replied cheerfully. The militiaman promptly took him to a police doctor. He lost his licence for a year. So, as my party sipped champagne in the Izba Restaurant – and as the portly militiaman standing out in the damp mentally calculated how many drinks we might be consuming – I stuck to fruit juice.

At least there was alcoholic drink to be had in the Izba. During a visit to Vilnius in 1987, I went with my colleague from the London *Independent*, Rupert Cornwell, for an evening meal in a state restaurant near the city centre. As we entered through a large foyer, an elderly attendant in a brown jacket and peaked hat pulled down over a rough, weather-beaten face asked us in a conspiratorial manner if we wanted to buy a bottle of vodka. The offer was politely declined. We would order a drink with our meal.

'Have you any wine?' we asked the waitress.

'None left', she replied.

'Champagne?'

'No.'

'Vodka?'

'All finished.'

'Anything?'

'Yes, mineral water.'

We recalled the old attendant and I slipped out to the foyer.

'Do you still have a bottle of vodka?' I asked him.

'Yes, for fifteen roubles.'

'Okay.'

The money was handed over and quickly palmed. He shuffled into an unlit office. Despite the heavy lace curtains on the glass door I could make out two militiamen sitting in the dark having a smoke. The old man said something to them and they disappeared out the back. After a minute he opened the door a crack, beckoned me in and produced a bottle from a drawer. I went to shove it under my jumper.

'No, put it down your trousers', he said, 'And' – he raised his finger to his lips – 'say nothing.'

So we had a drink after all, surreptitiously topping up innocent-looking mineral water glasses from the vodka bottle which we kept on the floor beside the restaurant wall. A little later when bending down to pick it up I saw a vodka bottle at the feet of the diners at the next table. We were not alone. At another table the customers were tipping clear liquid out of a teapot but we couldn't swear to its contents.

As foreigners we did not have to stand in the vodka queues to buy drink. We could go to the *Beryozkas*, the hard-currency state shops whose name meant 'little birch tree'. Most of the dozen or so *Beryozkas* around Moscow were located in tourist hotels and sold Russian souvenirs. There were, however, two grocery *Beryozkas* for the foreign community, one in the international trade centre, the other hidden up an alley along the Moscow River embankment. They provided basic foodstuffs and did a brisk business in Georgian wine, vodka and champagne and, when they had it, Scotch whisky.

Soviet citizens could not use these *Beryozkas* as they were prohibited from possessing hard currency in the form of bank notes, but there were special *Beryozkas* for those Russians who had worked abroad and who had brought home savings in dollars. They were required by law to deposit their hard currency in the state bank as soon as they arrived back in the country and to take, in exchange, coupons which could be spent on foreign goods in the 'Soviet' *Beryozkas*. At least that was the principle. In practice there were complications, as I found out when I came across the thirty-day queue around the corner from the Irish embassy just north of the city centre.

By midnight, Astrakhansky Street, a narrow, built-up road, would normally be deserted, abandoned for the night to the odd foraging crow and the half-empty trams which rumbled by at the top of the road. But in February 1988 crowds of people could be found there standing quietly in the dim lamplight. They remained in position all night in distinct groups, one hundred here, fifty across the road, forty by the corner, blue cigarette smoke swirling round their heads and snow settling half-an-inch deep on their fur hats and on their shoulders. More people could be discovered dozing in cars parked in nearby Grokholsky Street or on a building site across the way. Other figures huddled in doorways or in the halls of apartment blocks. Occasionally these people emerged to join the crowds on Astrakhansky Street. More arrived on foot or by taxi. There would be much animated discussion as the street filled up. Female voices called out names from long lists. People answered and drifted back into the darkness, leaving the original groups stamping their feet and pressing close together in the cold February air.

The centre of this extraordinary activity was a long single-storey shop with curtained plate-glass windows which took up nearly a third of the short street. It was the only *Beryozka* in the Soviet Union which sold foreign-made television sets, stereos and hi-fi's to citizens holding foreign-currency vouchers. Some weeks previously the authorities had announced their intention of abolishing the voucher system and closing the special *Beryozkas* as the vouchers had become too much of a black-market currency. They changed hands at well above their face value – such was the demand for high-quality foreign goods in the Soviet Union. In future, people returning from abroad would have to use closely monitored personal cheques in the shops for foreigners. Although the old system would not end until July, the result was panic among the thousands of people who had accumulated or were saving up vouchers, from engineers who had worked in Iraq to speculators who bought and sold vouchers for a living. They laid siege to the shop in Astrakhansky Street.

There would have been utter chaos were it not for the extraordinary Russian ability to organise a queue, no matter how huge the crowd, with the help of volunteers who always seemed to come forward to boss everyone about on such occasions. These volunteers organised the voucher-holders into groups of one hundred each (they were named *sotniki* after the Russian word for one hundred). Instead of queuing all day, people agreed to come to the street three times every twenty-four hours at 8.00 a.m., at 3.00 p.m. and at 7.00 p.m. to register with the *sotniki*. Anyone who failed to report was struck off the lists. The shop dealt with 130 people a day. It took nearly thirty days to get to the head of the queue. When it came close to their turn, people stayed in the street all night. Strangers who came by were eyed suspiciously. When the shop opened in the morning, no one was allowed in without the permission of the queue. One man who slipped by, God knows how, had his television set taken from him when he emerged, though the *sotniki* arranged for him to get the voucher value and sent him to the back of the thirty-day queue. When I went to enter the shop, a *sotniki* checked my press credentials and two people were delegated to accompany me into the shop where all was quiet and orderly. Other volunteers from the queues monitored container lorries coming from the warehouses. Every hi-fi going in was registered by the masses in the street.

People had come from all over the Soviet Union, taking sick leave and holidays to stand in the crazy queue in Astrakhansky Street. The cars had Ukrainian and Crimean registration plates. A seat at night in an old Volga or Zhiguli cost up to twenty roubles, I was told. Profiteers offered vodka at twice its shop value. Prostitutes had come out from the city centre to conduct business with the richer clients in the queue, according to militiaman Mikhail Kupin who said crime in the district had increased by 50 per cent. Doorways had been used as toilets and hallways as bedrooms. The shop assistants in the adjoining children's bookshop dreaded the mornings when frozen hordes trampled in through the doors to thaw out. Some queuers got fed up and sold their vouchers to the profiteers at the lowest going rate of two roubles for a one rouble foreign-currency voucher. Some had been swindled. A mechanic from Tula, Sergei Sidenko, agreed to part with his 3,000 coupons for 6,000 roubles, but he was fooled by sleight of hand and got only 3,000 roubles. He couldn't go to the police, he said. No crime had been committed; he had got the official rate.

A few months later there were similar scenes across town at the big Elektronika store in Leninsky Prospect. After hours of waiting, a crowd almost rioted, and windows of the shop were broken. There were threats to block traffic before the militia restored order. What caused the disturbance was an announcement by the store manager to the queue outside that a big, new batch of hard-to-get Soviet video recorders due to go on sale would not, after all, be made available. The Moscow City Council's executive committee had decreed, only that morning, that they should be sold through factories and work collectives, with trade-union officials deciding who should get them. This was bad enough and it infuriated people in the crowd who did not belong to trade unions, but the shop had informed video-buyers long in advance that on that day it would start putting people on an official list and would begin supplying them with videos across the counter. In anticipation of this a long queue had formed more than a week previously, based on the same system as in Astrakhansky Street and with, for all I knew, the same *sotniki*. Certainly they looked the same – mostly middle-aged women with frizzy hats and officious voices who called people to order with bossy cries of *tovarishchi, tovarishchi* (comrades). The queue had become so long that the shop manager, Viktor Gusev, had been given permission to open a nearby athletic stadium for the official registration process. Then suddenly it was all cancelled, one of the reasons apparently being that authorities feared most of those in the queue were black-marketeers. The unfortunate people left standing in Leninsky Prospect, after giving up a week of work, were scathing about the true intentions of the officials who had redistributed the goods. 'They'll have no trouble getting videos', said a woman in a headscarf.

What we were seeing in these scenes of disorder and frustration was the beginning of the break-down of the state distribution system. It was becoming impossible to buy anything of value over the counter. The reforms had given people more money to spend and the government had printed billions of new rouble notes, but the industrial infrastructure was practically beyond repair after decades of neglect and lack of investment, and shortages had got worse. Gold was in such demand by people who had no trust in the arbitrary whims of an administration-by-command system – which could wipe out savings at the stroke of a pen – that a couple getting married had to be issued with a coupon by the marriage bureau entitling them to one ring each. Even then there were always jostling crowds around the counters of the few jewellery shops stocking rings for a city of nine million people, and only a few ring sizes were ever available. Prospective brides and bridegrooms had to keep returning day after day until the ring they wanted was available. Out in the provinces the news grew more alarming as perestroika continued. The cut-back in alcohol production meant that by 1988 more than half the drink consumed in the country was *samogon*. Sugar supplies were drying up. Ration books had been issued by the end of that year to people in sixty-seven of Russia's eighty-six territories. Sugar was still available in the Tagansky supermarket but only intermittently. The Communist Party had by then decided to put its disastrous anti-alcohol campaign into reverse, and we thought the rationing might be a temporary phenomenon of the villages. But it was too late, as we were to discover in the hard years ahead. It wasn't just a shortage of sugar, or the fact that vineyards which had been ripped up could not be restored. The system could not cope when people panicked.

When I came to live in Moscow, the only authorised buying and selling not conducted by the state was in the peasant markets. The desire for things of value, and the relaxing of state monopoly laws to allow for 'individual labour' and co-operatives, meant the return of private enterprise for the first time since the 1920s. It was a slow process, obstructed by bureaucrats and the psychology that identified business as *speculatsia*. It started in mid-1987 at Bitza Park, in the suburbs, where amateur artists sold their paintings – always watchful for the militia who had in the 1970s bulldozed away unsanctioned outdoor art exhibitions. These bearded men in parka jackets and ski caps were the pioneers of individual enterprise; the artist, in fact, was to become the barometer of glasnost.

I found the art market beside a sports stadium near the park. 'I'm only showing this for the second time', said Saveyli Yakovlev, pointing to an eight-rouble poster propped against a concrete flower-bed. 'Before now, I wouldn't dare.' I had to look closely at the forty-two-year-old artist's painting on a square of cardboard to see that the king on an enlarged playing card had two different faces. One was of Ivan the Terrible. The other was of Stalin, still almost a prohibited subject even after two years of glasnost. Yakovlev had painted it five years previously. 'I'm not afraid of anything now', he said, glancing round nervously. 'I'm a free citizen.' The theme of his poster, he said, was totalitarianism, highlighting not just the past, but recent Russian history.

Saveyli Yakovlev's exhibit was an indication of how cultural glasnost was percolating down from the intelligentsia to other levels of Soviet society. Two months earlier a daring exhibition of modern art by the city's leading painters, produced over the previous twenty years but never shown before, was staged for a few days at an exhibition hall in the nearby Red Guard district. The Moscow Soviet tried to ban the exhibition, put together by the Moscow Artists' Union, but it went ahead after the personal intervention of Minister of Culture Vladimir Zakharov. It was so hush-hush that when I went to see it with Martin Walker of the *Guardian* he made me swear not to tell his competitors. It contained abstract impressionism, visual jokes, religious themes, some sexually explicit motifs and a striking nude statue of protest singer Vladimir Vysotsky. The most outstanding work was by Grisha Bruskin, called 'Fundamental Lexicon', depicting one hundred miniature icons of Soviet life, including a chessboard, a soldier, a *babushka*, a schoolchild, a prison camp and a Jewish passover.

The Bitza Park artists had first begun displaying their comparatively inoffensive paintings at weekends among the silver birch trees of the forest. Sunday skiers would pause to examine their samples. The police generally turned a blind eye to this private enterprise, said Leonid

Nosov, an elderly, long-haired amateur artist. When Gorbachev came along and the climate changed for small-time entrepreneurs, these artists acquired semi-legal status. By the previous December they had become so numerous they were moved into the stadium forecourt and joined by trinket-sellers. 'Officially we are still illegal and the police move us on once in a while', said Nosov. 'But on 1 May we will become legitimate.' On that date Gorbachev's new private enterprise law came into force, designed not only to legalise but to positively encourage twenty-nine different types of cottage industries and small businesses, from car repairs to hairdressing and toy-making; and from taxi-driving to pavement-drawing.

A by-product of the new law was the street phenomenon of glasnost: the portrait artist. After 1 May these artists began to appear in the Old Arbat, the wide pedestrian precinct running through one of the old quarters of the city. Muscovites took to them with great seriousness. I counted sixty-seven, one Saturday afternoon, sketching with chalk, crayon, pencil, charcoal, oils and water-colours. All along the pink brick-paving the subjects posed solemnly – an old woman in a heavy coat with a bag of tomatoes at her feet; a youth with a cigarette hanging from his lips; a girl in a leather jacket and lace scarf, her friends watching critically; a child holding its face as still as could be – while the street artists sketched and painted, surrounded by jostling crowds of onlookers. The artists had to be thick-skinned too as passers-by were not slow to pass judgement. Many were professional artists who liked to play the part, dressing in flowing capes and broad-brimmed hats.

The Bitza Park artists came from the suburbs and invaded the street. They set out their pictures, most of them tiny oil paintings of Russian churches, on the low window-ledges along the Old Arbat, whose apricot, pistachio, yellow and pink buildings once housed the artistic community of tsarist Moscow. As far as the artists of the Old Arbat were concerned, what the ordinary Muscovite wanted for his living-room, and the tourist as a souvenir, was a picture of a Russian landscape, preferably snow-covered, with a pretty Orthodox church in the foreground complete with golden domes. The Old Arbat had always been a lively street with small cafés and shops selling books, posters, paintings, watches, pastries and second-hand bric-à-brac. It quickly became a major attraction, crowded to overflowing at weekends. Photographers got in on the act, with Mickey Mouse and Donald Duck models for children to pose on and, later, life-size cut-outs of Mikhail Gorbachev. One found a hansom-cab and dressed his tiny customers in drummer-boy uniforms.

Trinket-sellers came with their jewellery and crucifixes and wooden carvings.

The art market became so popular that artists were given permission to use part of Izmailovo Park, one of the city's biggest forest parks where the tsars once had a summer residence. At first they offered mostly the familiar junk paintings at hugely inflated prices, propped against poplar trees on the paths around a seventeenth-century baroque church. But within a few months the park also began to attract immense crowds and became one of the world's biggest open-air art fairs. Here in the new atmosphere of daring, the Russians began to indulge in one of their favourite pursuits: political satire. Hundreds of stalls were erected on Saturdays and Sundays along the grass verges of a mile-long pathway, selling everything from caricatures in oils of Gorbachev holding hands with a buxom wench named perestroika, to plaster money-boxes in the shape of Brezhnev. Matryoshka egg sets were painted with the faces of Lenin, Stalin, Khrushchev, Brezhnev and Gorbachev. One stall-holder attracted the crowds by playing Brezhnev speeches on his *Elektronika* 302 tape deck. Crowds stood around grinning at the words in the familiar gravelly voice – 'Our party (applause), the party of Lenin (applause)'. Muscovites found this very funny. The tape ended with the sound of prolonged rhythmic clapping. 'Great beat for a disco if you speed it up', said the vendor. I bought an old cast-iron bust of Stalin for fifteen roubles from a man with thick glasses who specialised in old party portraits. 'There's Stalin', said the innocent voice of a little girl, pointing to a work showing Stalin, Khruschev and Brezhnev gloating over Russia, depicted as an impoverished old woman. The real boom industry along the artistic mile, however, was that Russian passion, the lapel badge. Yelena Yagavitsa, a bespectacled girl from a state souvenir shop, was one of dozens of sellers who made satirical badges in their spare time. Her slogans tapped a deep vein of cynicism. One criticised the reform programme with the words, 'Perestroika: two plus two equals five'. Another said, 'The enemy is not AIDS but indifference and callousness' (a reference to a recent hospital scandal). There was a run on badges proclaiming, 'I am a KGB agent', or, 'Victim of the Cold War', and on lapel pins declaring in English, 'I love sex' and 'Sex-master'.

Amid the junk, Izmailovo proved that competition did improve quality. The people who came to the park had money to spend, especially foreign tourists, and they became more discriminating in their tastes. Some of the art work improved. There was an explosion in the home-produced souvenir industry. Beautifully carved giant chess sets vied with painted eggs for the attention of the promenading customers. It was only when I had shuffled and pushed my way to the far end of the path from the metro one Saturday afternoon that I discovered that Izmailovo also had an antique market – a new and exciting development in a city with no antique shops other than shabby 'commission' stores offering second-hand furniture at high prices. 'You can't buy these anywhere in Russia except here', said a man selling old glass bottles at ten roubles each. His colleague at the next stall was offering an antique brass *samovar* for 120 roubles. Across the path the prize exhibit was an ancient Ericcson wall telephone from Sweden in full working order for 250 roubles. One could buy a tobacco tin with the tsar's insignia, marked 'G Lantrin; Petrograd, Moscow and Riga', for seventeen roubles, or a 1950 matchbox for two roubles. Old and new foreign coins were being snapped up. (They don't count as black-market currency.) An English fifty pence cost eight roubles, about sixteen times the exchange rate. Among the antiques were some bric-à-brac and more modern artifacts like an empty Tuborg lager can at twenty-five kopecks. Even here politics of a sort intruded. An old man was doing a brisk business selling bank-notes dating back to the turn of the century and displayed in albums which he had acquired from collectors around Moscow. As I bought a 1909 five-rouble bill with the tsarist crest and crown for fifty kopecks, he commented, 'Some young people will buy anything made before 1917 – anything to do with the prerevolutionary times.'

It was inevitable that antiques would mean antique auctions, a capitalistic activity which had been forbidden for seven decades in Russia. I found Moscow's antique auction-room by chance. It was in a 'commission' shop where second-hand goods were sold in Oktyabrskaya Square. To my surprise, a full-scale auction was in progress when I dropped by one day. Participants paid three roubles for a large piece of cardboard with a number printed on it, used for bidding. There would be no twitches of an eyebrow here, I thought, no raising of a forefinger to the nose to signal a bid. But I saw after a few minutes that the regular buyers had developed a knack of signalling to the auctioneer with the slightest quiver of their cardboard sign.

The first rule of any auction is to inspect the goods beforehand. One should never bid on impulse. I should have remembered this when I saw, from the back of the room, what looked like a beautiful butter dish being held aloft by a female assistant. While the auctioneer, all flailing arms, was taking bids for this object from the one hundred or so people present, I impulsively held up my rectangle of cardboard and suddenly found myself in possession of what turned out to be a cracked soap-dish, for which I had to fork out 160 roubles, the equivalent of sixteen pounds at the tourist rate of exchange. The lid, I discovered, had been broken and glued together again, but it said Dresden on the bottom. I found out that the antique auctions were taking place twice a week. When I called in again on a viewing day, I spotted a beautiful old ashtray among the copper *samovars*, painted boxes, antique cutlery and old lamps. It was made of china and was about eighty years old, with Russian lettering advertising Martel brandy. Beside it was a sign saying that the starting price for bidding would be twenty-five roubles. I arrived for the auction with 290 roubles in my pocket, much more than I thought I would need. I waited for an hour while the auctioneer tried with little success to sell off two or three dozen beautiful, big *samovars* at about one hundred roubles each. Many had to be withdrawn for lack of interest. Then the ashtray came up. 'Early twentieth century', said the auctioneer, 'some letters faded, slight damage, who will bid twenty-five roubles?' I waved my number but the auctioneer didn't notice as several pieces of cardboard were held on high. I got in a bid as the price reached one hundred roubles, and again at 160. The ashtray went for 450 roubles, knocked down to the woman at the back.

It was then that I began to take stock of what was happening in the auction-room. It was full, not with casual buyers, but with dealers, private collectors and tradespeople vying for business. The people who ignored the *samovars* and bid for the ashtray and several other antiques which fetched high prices knew exactly what they were doing. I recognised a couple of faces from among the sellers at Ismailova Park, but clearly a lot of high-price private dealing was going on in the city. Antiques had become big business and buying them was a way of putting surplus money to use. They were taking trade from the black market, absorbing some of the billions in bank-notes lying idle, and enhancing the value of the rouble. To stop foreigners from snapping up the country's old treasures, the authorities had, however, imposed a ban on exporting purchases. A sign in the auction-room said, 'Nothing sold here may be taken out of the country.' Strictly speaking, I could not take the old ashtray out of Russia, nor the cracked Dresden soap-dish.

In the summer of 1988, the best of the avant-garde artists came in from the cold when Sotheby's arrived to hold Russia's first ever international art-auction. Over 2,000 art dealers, private collectors, diplomats, foreign businessmen and Soviet onlookers crowded into a conference room at the Moscow Trade Centre to bid, in hard currency only, for 119 contemporary works. One of the first lots was 'Fundamental Lexicon', the collage of scenes from Soviet life which I had seen at the furtive exhibition in the suburbs. It had been estimated by Sotheby's at 20,000 pounds sterling. After hectic bidding, it was knocked down for 220,000 pounds. Bruskin was suddenly a rich man. His five paintings sold for a total of half a million pounds, though he was to wait many long months before the Soviet authorities gave him access to any of the money. Under a deal worked out between Sotheby's chairman, Lord Gowrie, and the Soviet Ministry of Culture, each of the artists, whose works had, in total, fetched two million pounds that evening, was to receive 10 per cent of the sale in sterling and 50 per cent in roubles. The ministry, which held on to the sterling equivalent of that 50 per cent, also received 30 per cent of the sale outright. The remaining 10 per cent went to Sotheby's as a commission. The ministry struck gold with the profits of the artists they had suppressed for so long.

While government ministries and international auction houses could engage in such profitable business, *speculatsia*, however, with state property was still officially discouraged; nevertheless, as the shortages worsened it became easy for young people to avoid shift-working and to engage instead in buying and selling anything in high demand, from bottles of vodka and car parts, to cigarettes and hi-fi sets. The real market-price became what an article cost on the street.

The pro-independence Lithuanian authorities were the first to rename *speculatsia* as business. In Lithuania the black market became the open market. I found it one Sunday morning on a tarmacadam arena in the open countryside a few miles outside Vilnius. More than 2,000 vendors who had come from as far away as Moscow, Tashkent and Yerevan stood in twenty lines, one hundred to each row, stretching up and down the hard surface and forming corridors of people like a human *souk*, their wares cradled in their hands or piled at their feet. You could buy a pair of West German jeans for 300 roubles, an Italian leather jacket for 2,000, a French edition of *Playboy* for 90 and a video of *Rambo* or *Emmanuel Goes To Cannes* for one hundred. There were electric train-sets and fan belts for Ladas in this capitalist baazar, as well as packets of Marlboro cigarettes, which were almost an alternative currency.

Back in Moscow I noticed crowds outside the Tagansky supermarket door one Thursday evening – it usually stayed open until 9.00 p.m. – but I thought no more of it at the time. Crowds always gathered when something scarce appeared like coffee or chocolate or ketchup from Bulgaria. I had been covering a Supreme Soviet debate in the Kremlin. The prime minister, Nikolai Ryzhkov, had earlier in the day announced the government's long-awaited plan to raise prices as part of a move to a market economy. The date was 24 May 1990. His speech was transmitted live by radio and listened to all over Moscow. 'Prices of meat will rise by 130 per cent', he said. 'Prices of fish will go up by 150 per cent, prices of milk and sugar will double. The price of bread will treble. Retail prices of separate kinds of non-food consumer goods will grow by 30–50 per cent . . . the government proposes to increase retail prices of bread and bakery products as of 1 July this year.' Ryzhkov went on to explain that bakery products meant flour and anything made from flour.

People literally poured out of their apartment blocks into the shops after Ryzhkov's announcement. July was only thirty-seven days away. You had to listen to the prime minister's speech very carefully to grasp that other price increases were several months away and that wages and pensions were to rise too. By Thursday evening there was not a single kilogram of flour left in the Tagansky supermarket. There was no flour on Friday and none on Saturday. Throughout the city, shelves were emptied fast. Hundreds of buses brought waves of shoppers into town from outlying suburbs. The big GUM store on Red Square shut its doors as the crowds became unmanageable. People bought everything they could find. 'Who knows what the price of clothes will be soon', said a woman laden down with three new coats and plastic bags full of packets of macaroni. 'This government wants the people to pay for years of incompetence', said a young man standing in a queue to enter a shop to see what they had, or hadn't, for sale. 'All they do is talk, talk, talk. The whole country is a talking shop', said a woman in the bread shop angrily. Stores sold more flour and vegetable oil on that Friday than they normally sold in an entire month. People were not starving in Moscow. Some quite clearly couldn't get into their kitchens because of stocks of flour and cooking oil. But those without were suddenly facing hunger. 'The situation in the city is getting critical', said Mayor Gavriil Popov in a press conference on the following Saturday. 'There is a real danger of things getting out of control.' Moscow authorities had been taken completely by surprise by Ryzhkov's speech, which had not made clear that the measures had not yet become law. The government had placed the city authorities in a 'ridiculous, humiliating position', Popov declared. 'If someone thinks that a suit costing 2,000 roubles will soon cost 3,000 roubles, he'll go out and buy it now. It's a natural human reaction.' The anecdote people were fond of telling about the absent-minded shopper who found himself outside a supermarket with an empty bag and couldn't remember if he had done his shopping or not was suddenly no longer funny.

Ryzhkov's speech started a chain reaction. The Moscow Soviet introduced identity cards for shoppers to stop country people from stripping the shelves. Inevitably, enterprises in the provinces retaliated by refusing to send products to the capital. Under popular pressure, the governments of outlying republics decided to hold on to food stocks to keep their own populations supplied with basic foodstuffs. It used to be said that Moscow was in a valley and that everything in the country flowed into the city. Now the process was suddenly reversed. The privileged city was a victim of a paralysing break-down of the centralised planning system.

I went shopping that Saturday, or rather, I went panic-buying. I called into the supermarket to see what was in stock. In the West you might look for special offers in a foodstore. In the Tagansky self-service supermarket, you took what was going, and that was precious little.

There was a fat woman in a soiled, white coat sitting on a stool near the metal entrance door. She never stopped shaking her head in response to questions from the pushing, heaving mass of people crowding through the doors.

'Is there flour?'

'No.'

'Any cheese in here?'

'No.'

'There isn't any macaroni, is there?'

'No.'

'Is there pancake flour?'

'No.'

'Do you have cooking oil?'

'No.'

'What about porridge oats?'

'No.'

'Semolina?'

'No.'

'Are they giving out rice?'

'No.'

'Onions?'

'No.'

'What did you buy?' I asked a woman as she came out.

'What did I buy? Nothing', she cried. 'There's nothing to buy.'

'What did you buy yesterday?' I asked.

'Nothing.'

'On Thursday?'
'On Thursday I got some flour.'
'How much?'
'Six kilos.'

For foreigners life continued as normal. At Stockman's hard-currency store, one of the two foreign delicatessens allowed to open in Mocow in competition with the *Beryozkas* and only a ten-minute walk from the Tagansky supermarket, people unhurriedly stocked up for the weekend from shelves laden with cheese, ham, salami, grapefruit, bananas, flour (several varieties), spaghetti, muesli, espresso coffee, confectionary, French wine, Italian ice-cream – everything, in fact, one might expect in a Western delicatessen or grocery store but unthinkable luxury for the Muscovites politely turned away by a sign saying, 'Credit Cards Only'. 'Thank you, come again', smiled the Finnish assistant at the computerised check-out as customers went through their shopping lists and reached for the high-quality Stockman's plastic carrier bags, supplied free of charge.

In the Soviet Union, the image of a classless society was a distant dream as the populace divided itself into several social strata: rich and poor; town and country; privileged and unprivileged; foreign and Soviet. It wasn't until the middle of 1991, after steep price rises and currency reform, that the shops began to fill again and the Soviet Union began to move towards the market norm: plenty to buy – if you had the money to buy it.

5

Crime and Punishment

AT NINE A.M. one freezing March morning, not long after I had moved to Moscow, Mikhail Rabzonov, a nineteen-year-old army deserter, and Oleg Drobotov, a convict on the run and just a year older, kicked in the door of my office. They spent an hour rummaging through drawers and sorting out goods they had stolen from another apartment ten floors below. Around 10.00 p.m. they left, taking three blank video-cassettes, one Citizen pocket calculator, one black leather wallet (empty), an old jacket, a pair of shoes in need of repair, six Duracell long-life batteries, three packets of Marlboro cigarettes, four lapel pins and a handful of soft-centred chocolates.

Rabzonov, a skinny Jewish boy from a village in Byelorussia, and Drobotov, a thick-set, dim-witted Russian from Dnepropetrovsk in the Ukraine, hardly knew each other. They had met by chance the evening before in the entrance to my apartment block in Taganskaya Square. Both had found themselves in Moscow without money, food or a place to sleep. They had spent the night in the seventeenth-floor attic among the hot-water pipes. It was Drobotov who suggested breaking into an apartment to look for food and something to sell. They began ringing doorbells. When someone answered they apologised and said they had come to the wrong address. They found a Turkish diplomat's flat unoccupied on the sixth floor, broke open the door and stole thirty-six cassettes, a tape recorder and an assortment of smaller items, but they missed a bundle of 12,000 roubles sitting in a drawer. They had rung my doorbell on the way back to the roof space and got no answer. I was in Irkutsk in eastern Siberia at the time. Later, as they stuffed themselves with sweets and smoked Marlboro cigarettes in the attic, the broken doors were spotted and the alarm was raised. When the two miscreants strolled casually out of the building around midday, they walked straight into the arms of the militia. They were caught with the stolen property and their fingerprints were everywhere. The teenage soldier had even left his army jacket in my office with the name of his construction unit on it.

I thus became one of the first victims of crime in Moscow following the relaxation of the policy of confining foreigners to closely guarded compounds. Rabzonov and Drobotov didn't even know they were in a building where foreigners lived. I had been half-expecting something like this to happen. Because of our location beside a busy city-centre square and at the back of a supermarket which sold vodka, men would sometimes gather around the entrance to drink, and at night teenagers roamed up and down the fire-escape. We would sometimes meet them when both lifts were out of order and residents had to use the ill-lit stairwell. A man called at different apartments one night, posing as a plain-clothes militiaman, and asked to 'borrow' a few roubles. He collected over a hundred roubles from residents afraid to turn him down. Two men once rang my bell and tried to walk in, one pulling out his lighter with a threatening movement as if producing a flick-knife. I immediately slammed the door. Along with my neighbour, a Finnish banker, we fitted a security door to the entrance of our tiny corridor, with double locks and a re-inforced glass window, and rewired the doorbells so that we could see who was calling before opening the door. The situation, we were sure, would get worse when Moscow's first all-night shop was opened just yards away on a corner of the building – another example of Taganskaya Square being used as a seedbed for experiments conducted under the reform programme. It sold vodka and champagne and attracted crowds of alcoholics. The shop turned out to be of long-term benefit, however, as militiamen were posted on the street outside to keep order throughout the hours of darkness. They stopped drinkers and anyone else using our entrance hall and would themselves sometimes congregate in the *dezhurnaya*'s glass-fronted cabin just inside the door for a smoke on cold and wet evenings – in effect, providing protection like that found in the foreign compounds. The foreign ministry, which acted as our landlord, also fitted a special lock to the main entrance door which could only be opened by pressing three numbers on a code box. The prowlers ceased coming by and there was less vandalism to the foreign cars parked outside.

The general law-and-order situation steadily deteriorated, however, in the climate of political unrest and chronic shortages, and the crime statistics grew steadily worse. Foreign businessmen, journalists, diplomats and tourists attracted by the reforms became increasingly prone to robbery and sometimes to violence. Foreign cars were regularly broken into and radios and tape players ripped out. Brand names were pulled off the body work as souvenirs. Malice appeared to be the only motive when all four tires of my Volvo 440 were slashed one night while it was parked at Domodyedovo Airport outside Moscow. Foreigners increasingly became a target for thieves since they possessed items which were in great demand in the underworld and on the black market – videos, video cassettes, tape recorders, computers and hard currency. Moscow had always been a relatively safe city for foreigners. Perestroika made it more dangerous.

I received an urgent phone call one evening in February 1990 from Steve Crawshaw, who was on short-term assignment in Moscow for The London *Independent*. He needed the Moscow equivalent of 999 – in the Soviet capital it's 02 – to ring the police. The Crawshaws had also been living outside the complex of guarded diplomatic compounds. They had borrowed an apartment from Russian friends in a residential block where only Muscovites lived. That evening, Steve's Polish wife, Eva, had been attacked in their apartment on the Sadovoye ring road, about three miles away, by two intruders who had broken in, one armed with a kitchen knife. They had just left and Eva had rung Steve in great distress. After telephoning the militia, we raced round the ring road and found a scene of devastation in their third-floor flat. Kitchen furniture lay overturned and broken where Eva had struggled with one of the attackers, a vicious, thin man smelling of alcohol, while his comrade searched the rooms for valuables. There was blood on the smashed chairs and on the white telephone receiver. Blood was still dripping from a deep gash in Eva's hand caused by the knife when she had tried to push it away from her throat. The two men had got into the apartment by ringing the doorbell and answering *svoi*, meaning a friend, or literally 'one of us', when Eva called out who was there. They had pushed her back and rushed in wearing plastic carrier bags over their heads with holes for their eyes. The thief with the knife threw her to the ground. The other went to a cupboard in the bedroom and took bank-notes to the value of 1,000 pounds sterling, the equivalent on the black market to 20,000 roubles. Eva managed to wriggle free from her captor and to scream for help. A neighbour passing by on the landing heard her cries and rang the doorbell. The intruders panicked – one opened the door, pushed past the startled neighbour and rushed downstairs; the other dashed to the balcony door. As the door wouldn't open out because of a deep snowdrift, he smashed the glass and disappeared down the fire escape, leaving a trail of blood from where he cut himself.

Crime against a foreigner is rated a very serious matter by the Russian authorities. Two militiamen had arrived in a patrol car before we got there. Then came a couple of detectives, and hard on their heels a senior militia officer. Three important-looking men in plain clothes arrived next, and as friends of the Crawshaw's crowded into the small living-room, two 'scenes-of-crime' men turned up to look for clues.

They took away bits of the broken glass and the corner of a snapshot that one of the men had handled. The senior officer ruminated aloud that the thieves belonged to a gang which operated around the nearby Leningrad railway station. The courageous neighbour who had frightened them off was convinced that word had got around that there was a foreigner living in the building. They discounted a theory that it might have been an attack by anti-Semitic Russian extremists. The apartment was usually occupied by a Russian poetess who was an outspoken opponent of anti-Jewish racism, and two weeks earlier the Crawshaws had been upset to find a petrol-soaked rag left outside their door. But the consensus was that robbery had been the motive. Some people have no luck. On her last day in the Soviet capital before returning to their home in London, Eva went shopping in the central fruit and vegetable market. When she emerged from a crush of people and reached for her money, she found her pocket had been picked.

I wasn't long in Moscow before I became aware, again at first hand, that the reforms were also breeding another type of crime. One October night after dinner in the Vysotsky Bar, I set out to walk back to the apartment with a few friends. It was almost 1.00 a.m., dark and frosty. There were few people about as we walked across Taganskaya Square. As we passed the end of Great Communist Street on the eastern side of the square, we heard a screech of tires, and a car with two men inside drove out from beneath an archway in an old two-storey house one hundred metres down the street. As it disappeared across the square, we noticed a flickering, yellow glow in a downstairs window of the building. Within seconds flames were curling round the upper edge of the window and black smoke began to fill the roadway. There was a public telephone at the corner and one of us ran to call the fire brigade. Minutes later two fire-engines arrived. A command table was set up in the centre of the road. Firemen climbed ladders and disappeared into the smoke enveloping the roof of the building, which by now was blazing from end to end. The chief fire-officer barked orders through a megaphone from his kitchen chair, behind the command table, as firemen broke the roof tiles, unrolled long hose pipes and began spraying heavy jets of water on to the flames. Within an hour the fire was out and the road was covered with slippery sheets of ice.

Just over a year later I went for a walk in the opposite direction from my apartment, this time to get a breath of fresh air after a day confined to the office. It was almost midnight, it was again cold and clear with a few crystalline snowflakes drifting down from a starry sky, and again there was no one about. I strolled down by the Novospassky Monastery and turned up Sarinskaya Street, past a solid stone apartment block fronted by two shabby second-hand furniture stores and a shop which had just opened and sold jeans and denim jackets, most with imitation Western labels. Beside the shop was a heavy wooden door with a semicircular fanlight from which the glass was missing. Again I saw a flickering, yellow glow, this time from behind the door, and once more I watched in astonishment as flames suddenly began spurting fiercely through the fanlight and a thick column of oily, black smoke rose up in the air, engulfing the snowflakes. I hurried round to the back where the entrance to the apartments was located and shouted a warning to two men standing talking in the doorway, then ran up the hill past the white, castellated walls of the monastery, my breath coming in little puffs of condensation, to a tiny police station opposite its main gates. The militiaman on duty grabbed the telephone and called the fire brigade. By the time I got back to the shop, there were three engines on the scene and firemen were breaking down the door with an axe. Behind it they found the remains of a pile of burning rags which had been soaked in petrol. They managed to put the fire out before it spread out of the hallway and nobody in the eight-storey building was hurt.

Both fires were arson attacks and the target on each occasion was a co-operative enterprise. The introduction of co-operatives was one of Mikhail Gorbachev's earliest reforms and the first co-op ventures began to appear in my early months in Moscow. The law stated that each co-operative should be managed by a partnership collective and should provide competition for the poorly run state stores, cafés, restaurants and workshops. They brought back private enterprise for the first time since the 1920s. The building set alight in Great Communist Street had housed a co-operative tire-repair business. The shop behind the fanlight in Sarinskaya Street had been the first co-operative clothes store in the neighbourhood. The co-operatives had from the start attracted the attention of the Moscow underworld, where the activities of extortionists and gangsters who profited from the vast shadow economy had already given to the Russian language the words *rakyet* and *mafiya*. The mafia moved in on the co-ops, demanding protection money from this new source of wealth in the city streets. There was no law to protect the new entrepreneurs. When the director of the newly opened co-operative *Khachapuri* reported to the militia that he had received an anonymous letter demanding that 300 roubles be left in a certain hiding place, the police set up a hidden video camera and caught red-handed the three extortionists, two of whom turned out to be members of the *Komsomol*, the

Young Communist Movement. The case was thrown out of court, even though they made full confessions, as there was no *corpus delicti*: no article in the law which made it a crime to rob a co-operative. Private businesses did not exist when the criminal code was drawn up in the 1960s.

The militia were also hampered in their attempts to fight organised crime by a severe lack of equipment and by the poor quality of recruits, many of them village boys who joined the force simply to get a *propiska*, a document entitling them to live in the capital. Petty corruption was rampant. In Taganskaya region, the year after I arrived, eighteen militiamen were dismissed for sex romps with an attractive thief called Lyudmila who was so well known to the men on point duty that she would borrow a walkie-talkie radio and say, 'One, two, three, four, five, here comes a hare for a walk', and the little patrolling Zhigulis, recognising her code, would converge from every direction. A corruption investigation revealed that her diary contained details of dozens of militia lovers and of wild card-parties with pistol shooting and sex. The militia were also discouraged from protecting the co-operatives by party bosses opposed to the new laws for ideological reasons, or because their total control of the local economy was threatened. When they did go into action they were tough and uncompromising. One sultry July afternoon I saw the end of a car chase on the Minsk highway, when a police car closed on a white Lada and the two vehicles collided. As a young man climbed from the Lada, three militiamen set upon him, one striking him with a long black baton, the others thudding boots into his side. As I edged my car past he was lying face downwards on the hot tarmac with a boot firmly planted on his back. Other militiamen lifted his half-conscious comrade by a mop of curly hair and flung him across the bonnet, beating him from behind.

The members of the new class of restaurateurs and retailers were faced with the choice of paying protection money or refusing to co-operate and therefore suffering the fate of the two premises which I had watched burn near Taganskaya Square. They could also employ their own guards. Militiamen began resigning from the force to join little private armies which appeared in districts where co-operatives were concentrated. Some co-operative ventures became part of the gangsterland structure. It wasn't untypical to witness minor bacchanalian scenes in the Silhouette Restaurant, a glitsy co-operative in a deceptively shabby nineteenth-century building on the western corner of Taganskaya Square. Tipsy European businessmen would carouse there with hard-currency prostitutes. One evening when I called in, a plump Italian salesman was fondling the breasts of a heavily made-up girl while his friend pawed a scantily clad young woman perched on his knee; meanwhile music played and a dozen tough-looking young men lounged nonchalantly in an anteroom. The city seemed to be slipping back to the days of the early 1920s when the mafia, controlled by the legendary Russian gangster Mikhail Kutyapy, lived high on profits extracted from the *nepmen*, the traders and owners of co-operatives which flourished in Moscow under Lenin's new economic plan. Prices in the co-operatives, already high because the directors were forced to buy produce in the expensive markets, were forced up further by the racketeers, putting them outside the reach of the ordinary Muscovite; as a result, the regular customers of the best co-operative restaurants became foreign diplomats, businessmen, prostitutes, and *aferisti*, those who made their money by shady means. By the early 1990s, the mafia had gained control of, or even initiated, some of the hundreds of joint ventures with foreign companies set up under the reforms. They even tried to muscle in on the first commercial club to be opened in Moscow since 1917, located in a two-storey, nineteenth-century mansion in Great Communist Street, right across the road from the burnt-out building which had housed the tire-repair co-operative near Taganskaya Square.

Like clubs the world over, the Moscow Commercial Club did not advertise its presence. Rather, it hid behind heavy black-metal gates and iron doors leading into a quiet courtyard, bordered by three wings of the mansion which belonged, until 1917, to the Krestovnikov merchant family. Behind the brass-handled doors were three restaurants, two bars, a casino, a room for bridge and poker, and a number of private dining-halls and conference rooms. Heavy red curtains on the ground floor were kept constantly drawn to prevent people on the pavement from peering at the relative opulence inside. Having restored the two-storey mansion and hung oil paintings of bearded tsarist merchants with stiff collars on the walls, director Vladimir Semago told me, shortly after it opened in October 1990, how one of his major problems was keeping the local mafia off his back. Semago, a wiry Muscovite with a blond moustache who used to run a karate club until the mob tried to take it over, confided that the mafia had already been round a few times looking for a cut of the profits. 'I told the mafia, if they want to do business they've got to do it cleanly', he said frankly. 'I know these guys. They sometimes put their money into legal businesses. They organised American football teams for this reason. I told them, we don't have any black-market profits and I personally have no money.' The fact that a powerful state body, Intourist, was a partner in the Commercial Club also acted as a deterrent, he believed. He did not want the club to become a playground for the Moscow mobsters looking for a place to spend their dollars and to entertain their mistresses, otherwise the respectable clientele he was trying to build up would not materialise. Helen Svetina, his tall, elegant assistant, said, as she showed me the blue-cloth roulette and blackjack tables imported from Holland in the basement casino, 'We want to protect our members from unnecessary contacts with members of the mafia. We usually inquire about the quality of our guests before admitting them. We don't want to lose the prestigious face of the club and we want to provide members with some security.'

In the same week as the Commercial Club opened, the head of the KGB, Vladimir Kryuchkov, claimed that some joint enterprises and private co-operatives were being used as fronts to smuggle valuable Soviet goods abroad, such as caviar, in exchange for computers and other scarce Western equipment. In the official Soviet mind, however, there was still confusion between exploitation – the crime of profiteering on the black market – and business – a legitimate activity which amounted to the same thing in a market economy. This led to an anti-business psychology, illustrated by one case of exploitation which I came across three years into Gorbachev's reform programme. The 'crime' was punished with all the severity of the law. A seventy-year-old villager living in the Rostov region sold three bags of potatoes belonging to his crippled neighbour, a widow woman, in the peasants' market. She gave him something for his pains. The old man was heavily fined and stripped of his pension for 'exploiting' the woman by acting as a middleman, forbidden in the communist state since the 1920s.

The growing power of the mobs worried the authorities so much that Kryuchkov admitted that after five years of perestroika, 'organised crime has assumed a scale we could never have expected a couple of years ago. Brutality, violence and sadism have become widespread.' This would have been evident to anyone watching television news, which after decades of official silence on crime was by the 1990s showing gruesome pictures nightly of murdered bodies in 'scene-of-crime' reports. There were places in Moscow where ordinary citizens were afraid to set foot because of their association with organised crime. One of these was the Sevastopol Hotel in the suburbs, a six-storey modern building with a dozen banqueting halls. Wealthy mafia leaders sported themselves there at tables laden with champagne and caviar. Once, taking refuge in the second-floor snack bar, I found it full of their minders, tough young men in leather jackets whose job, I was told, was to collect protection money and to drive their bosses around. Late at night the Moscow mafia dons played cards in inner rooms for thousands of roubles. A waiter said the militia kept clear for their own safety. If there was a fight, 'At best they enter the dining-hall, ask everyone to maintain order and leave right away. No one is prepared to risk their life, because you can't defeat the mafia. We waiters no longer call the militia. Even if someone is lying bleeding and unconscious on the floor we walk by.'

The gangsters were directly responsible for the failure in Moscow of one of the first reforms introduced by Gorbachev. This was the legitimisation of private taxis. In the Soviet capital private cars often cruised the streets to pick up taxi fares and make some extra money. When a law was passed in 1988 allowing 'individual labour', hundreds of Ladas and Chaikas appeared with tiny green lights, signifying they were official private taxis. The mafia moved in, demanding a cut of the profits, threatening to wreck cars and beat up family members if drivers didn't pay up. In November that year, 1,000 private taxis converged on Vnukova Airport to form an association to fight back against the racketeers. They made brave speeches in the car park and called on the militia to take action. But they were helpless. The militia could not protect them and within a year all the little green lights had practically disappeared and the old system reasserted itself. A 'private' taxi driver once dropped me off a few hundred yards from my destination, a busy railway station, informing me apologetically that he did not want to be identified as an unofficial *taxist* by the mafia members hanging out in the station square.

In the traditions of the real mafia, when a gangsterland boss died he could expect a lavish funeral. I went along to the Vagankovskoe cemetery on the occasion of the burial of a Georgian drug-dealer, thief and swindler with a twenty-five-year jail record known as Kuchuloria, who had died of throat cancer. The funeral was followed through the streets by countless cars with Moscow, Tbilisi and Baku number plates as the elite of the crime world, clutching roses, came to pay their respects. They took fifteen minutes to file through the gates and past the monument erected to poet-singer Vladimir Vysotsky, and to proceed into the the maze of metal cages shrouded by beech and fir trees enclosing tombstones on which were engraved the names of many of the city's writers, scientists and historians. They left a seven-foot pile of pine branches and flowers draped with black-fringed ribbons on the gangster's grave. The heap overshadowed a headstone a few yards away with a photograph of twenty-year-old Alyosha Kushnin, a soldier killed in Afghanistan on 29 January 1988. 'Our pride and our shame are here, only a few paces from each other', remarked a Russian journalist.

To many Russians the mafia had become synonymous with the officials they corrupted. *Blat*, the practice of doing and receiving favours, had always been a major part of everyday business and shopping in the Soviet Union, but it frequently degenerated into corruption. Students in Armenia, for example, could secure places at colleges by paying large bribes to the president of the institute. Restaurant directors could guarantee regular supplies of caviar by providing banquets for shop managers. Things had got out of hand in the Brezhnev era, and corruption had penetrated the top leadership. A Russian friend with some inside knowledge took me on an 'alternative' tour of Moscow one day to show me the sites associated with the major scandals of the stagnation period. We started at 164 Kachalov Street, a block of residential apartments not far from the garden boulevard. There, in apartment 9, Semyon Tsvigun, first deputy chairman of the KGB, was found dead with a bullet wound on 19 January 1982, a deed connected with a major anticorruption probe called 'operation cascade', whose origins lay in Kremlin infighting. It had been launched partly to discredit Brezhnev. Tsvigun, married to Brezhnev's wife's sister, was said to have taken massive bribes to protect racketeers. His visitors at apartment 9 used to include a flamboyant figure wearing a gold cross and driving a yellow Mercedes called Boris Buryatia, otherwise known as Boris the Gypsy. The expensive car was the property of his mistress, Galina Brezhnev, the Soviet leader's daughter. Both Boris and Galina were later to be hauled in for black-market currency and jewellery dealing.

We then went to look at the long sandy-coloured building in Ogaryov Street where the interior ministry was located. The minister, Nikolai Shcholokov, dressed in full uniform, shot himself in his top-floor office one day in 1984. He was about to be exposed for embezzling 700,000 roubles. His deputy then was Yuri Churbanov, Galina Brezhnev's husband. Not far away, on the side of Red Square, my friend pointed up to the tenth floor of the west wing of the Rossiya Hotel. In 1975 the rooms there were converted into a secret subsection of the interior ministry, responsible for investigating high-level corruption. On 26 May 1976 the tenth floor was burned out in a fierce and unexplained fire, killing fourteen officers from the Moscow and Georgian intelligence forces and twenty-seven residents. We passed by the giant GUM store whose manager was shot a few years previously for bribe-taking before arriving at the prerevolutionary mansion on

Sadovo-Sukharevskaya Street, which acted as the headquarters of the fraud squad. Every racketeer arrested eventually arrived into one of its converted drawing-rooms or ball-rooms for interrogation. 'Operation Cascade' was launched from this building.

All these places were associated with the profligacy and iniquities of members of the elite in the prereform days, and Mikhail Gorbachev found himself with the task of restoring confidence in the country's rulers. Two senior investigators, Telman Gdlyan, an Armenian with a sharp face and narrow, penetrating eyes, and Nikolai Ivanov, a dour, bearded Russian from Leningrad, were assigned the task of unravelling the webs of corruption, much of which centred on Uzbekistan. They soon had Galina Brezhnev's husband, Yuri, in court. Churbanov was convicted along with eight senior police officers of amassing millions of roubles in bribes and in December 1988 was sentenced to twelve years in labour camp. In Uzbekistan dozens of party officials were imprisoned and Sharaf Rashidov, Uzbekistan party chief and a crony of Brezhnev, was posthumously stripped of his honours and expelled from the party after evidence accumulated that he had masterminded a vast network of official corruption. The investigation was wound down, however, in controversial circumstances after Gdlyan and Ivanov began probing allegations against members of the *Politburo*. Ivanov named *Politburo* conservative Yegor Ligachev on Leningrad television in 1989 as someone whose name had come up in the investigation. This was political dynamite. Gdlyan and Ivanov were sacked. Many of those in prison, because of confessions they had extracted, were released. The two prosecutors alleged that a cover-up had started; the prosecutor's office accused them of using illegal means to obtain confessions. Confidence in the country's leadership was so eroded, however, that the people believed the two investigators, and when they stood for election to the Congress of People's Deputies in March 1989 – Gdlyan in Moscow and Ivanov in Leningrad – both were returned with huge majorities.

The affair spilled on to the streets, with protest meetings at metros and outside shopping centres by supporters of Gdlyan and Ivanov. Banners calling for the protection of the two investigators against prosecution for their methods dominated at the big street rallies which shook the Kremlin in 1989 and 1990. The stakes were high. I got a tip-off one day in January 1990 to go to the social club of the Red October Factory where Gdlyan would be speaking. I found it packed, with hundreds more people crowding into the hallways and cloakrooms and dozens standing on the stairs leading to the balcony. I could just see Gdlyan's bald head from the back of the hall, but his high-pitched, spell-binding voice rasped through the building, relayed by special loudspeakers, as he cited charge after charge of high-level corruption against middle-ranking members of the leadership. Eventually, as the audience almost held its breath in anticipation, he came to Gorbachev. After a dramatic pause he said simply, 'Gorbachev took money.' There was an audible gasp throughout the hall, then a ripple of applause and a loud murmur of voices. Gdlyan went on to say he had no proof that the Soviet president had taken bribes but that as a lawyer and a deputy he could no longer remain silent about what he knew, which was that charges had been made against Gorbachev in the 1970s of taking money from the mafia in Stavropol in south Russia where he was first secretary, and had never been investigated. The 'material' lay in the files of the party, the Soviet Ministry of the Interior and the KGB, said Gdlyan. 'I'm not saying he took money', he exclaimed, 'what I'm asking is why some people are investigated and some are not.' The audience, which included some military officers in uniform, rewarded the speech with loud applause. It was an extraordinary demonstration of how far glasnost had gone that such claims against the party leadership could be made in public, and also of the readiness of Russian people to believe that there was corruption in high places. A parliamentary commission under the chairmanship of historian Roy Medvedev held hearings on the Gdlyan-Ivanov affair and concluded there was no substance to the charges against Gorbachev. The USSR parliament meeting in the Kremlin decided not to press for criminal charges to be laid against the two investigators as a small but determined crowd of supporters staged a vigil on the edge of Red Square outside. Gorbachev himself told members of the *Komsomol* who quizzed him about Gdlyan's allegations during a Young Communist Congress that the mafia in Stavropol had been trying to blacken his name and there was nothing more to it than that.

Undoubtedly, many of the most corrupt villans in Soviet history escaped punishment in the high political intrigue surrounding the Gdlyan and Ivanov affair. Nor could the militia or the KGB do much about the gangsterland bosses whose writ ran through so many layers of Soviet society. They had networks of contacts and friends in high places. As in every country in the world, the small criminal could expect no such protection when caught.

Rabzonov and Drobotov, who had stolen the cigarettes and sweets and pocket calculator from my apartment, appeared before a military tribunal in Moscow a few months later. Both young criminals came under military law because one of them was a soldier. They had made full confessions. The hearing, in an old merchant's residence converted into a courthouse in the Kuntsevsky region of Moscow, was conducted by a uniformed colonel and two lieutenants sitting in high-backed chairs under the fluorescent lights of a yellow-painted room with a linoleum-covered floor. The two robbers sat slumped forward in a dock along the left-hand wall, with two equally young and pimply faced soldiers standing guard at each side. They hung their heads so low at times that only their cropped hair was visible. Below the bench two female defence lawyers faced the prosecutor, also a colonel in uniform. Half-a-dozen witnesses and several soldiers occupied the four rows of wooden benches. The conscript's mother was there, a thin country woman with black hair combed back and a polka-dot print dress. As is the practice in Russian courts, the judge carried out the cross-examinations. He began by asking every witness in the court, apart from myself, their nationality and whether they belonged to the Communist Party. He phrased the question, 'Party or without party?' Alexei, *The Irish Times's* secretary-translator who had been the first on the scene of the crime, gave me a sidelong smile as we learned that he was not a party member. The driver, Valery, was. The two accused were, not surprisingly, 'without party'. The mother of the soldier said she was 'without party' and that she was Jewish. Hearing her voice, Rabzonov lifted his face with its trace of a moustache and put his finger to his lips as if to say 'shh' when it looked as if she was about to cry. Oleg Drobotov had no one in court. His mother, the defence lawyer said, had separated from his natural father, who was an alcoholic, and married again. His stepfather had refused to let his mother make the 1,200-mile round-trip to be in court that day. It wasn't the first court appearance for the dark, thick-set Drobotov. On 9 September 1986 he had been given three years in jail for stealing car parts. This was commuted after a year to construction work in the far eastern Buryat region. He had run away on 6 March and had managed to get to Moscow eight days later.

Drobotov was terrified of going back to jail. He told his defence lawyer that if he was put back inside, 'it will be the end of me'. He had decided the best form of defence, despite the advice of the lawyer, was to feign insanity. She had heard that he had discussed his tactics with fellow prisoners the previous evening and tried to talk him out of it, to no avail. Drobotov refused to answer the judge's questions, staring with narrowed eyelids at the opposite wall. Several times the colonel asked him for his name. Suddenly he blurted out, 'Ask my double. He did it.' The judge called a ministry of defence psychiatrist, a brisk, young physician (and party member) who announced after a two-hour recess that he had not been taken in by Drobotov's piece of acting. The colonel proceeded to ignore Drobotov and turned his attention to Rabzonov who stood to reply, head bowed and his body swaying like an embarrassed schoolboy. His father had also been an alcoholic, he said. When he was a child his spleen was removed. There was something wrong with his head. Since the sixth class he had attended a mental clinic once a week as an out-patient. When he received his call-up papers he had not mentioned the clinic.

'Why not?' asked the judge.

'I wanted to be a normal person', he replied.

He had served thirteen weeks in the army with a construction unit in Gorky, 1,000 miles from his home village. Six of those weeks were in hospital, suffering from a respiratory illness.

'Why did you run away?' asked the colonel.

'I wanted to go home', he replied, almost inaudibly. 'I missed my mama. I had no letter from home for two months.'

'What were you doing when you met Drobotov?'

'Looking for empty bottles to sell to buy food.'

'What if somebody had answered the door of *The Irish Times*'s office?'

'We had planned to say we were looking for Valodya or Vanya or somebody else and go away.'

'Who kicked in the door?'

'Drobotov. I couldn't.'

Drobotov gazed at the floor and said nothing. Rabzonov's mother stood up to give evidence, leaving her shopping bag on the floor beside her bandaged leg. She had written letters, she insisted. The judge sympathised. He knew the problem with army post. Her son had an infection of the nervous system when he was a child, she said. It had affected his brain. He often said he wanted to die. He could only be himself with one person at a time. He could hardly open a door for himself.

'I know he is guilty', she said with simple dignity. 'Before the victims, I say forgive him. He will be broken mentally and physically in prison.' Her son's head sank from view in the box. 'Be merciful. It is the only way he will be useful to the state.'

As the victim of the robbery, I was summoned to the stand and asked my opinion on the conduct of the court and the appropriate sentence. As a foreigner, one of the lawyers had told me, my words would carry extra weight. I said the only thing possible in the circumstances, that the two accused had not acted like professional criminals, they had done me no personal harm and I had got my property back. The colonel responded to the mother's plea and dismissed Rabzonov from the army with a three-year suspended sentence. Oleg Drobotov, who had no one to speak for him and whose desperate tactic of pretending to be mad had failed miserably, got three and a half years in prison for escaping from a construction camp and for breaking and entering two apartments in Taganskaya Square.

6

The First Christmas

O NE SUNDAY when working in my office on the seventeenth floor of the apartment block on Taganskaya Square, I became aware of the sound of church bells coming faintly through the window. I went out on to the balcony. Other people were doing the same. The chimes came from among the spires and onion domes of the Russian Orthodox churches which I could see here and there among the maze of apartment and office buildings of the city. It was an historic moment, the first time the church bells had been permitted to ring out over the capital of communist Soviet Union for decades, and they carried the sound of a spiritual rebirth.

Seventy years of communist rule had left the Russian church in a state of physical and spiritual devastation. Almost every large village and town still had an Orthodox church, usually a beautiful rectangular building with a bell tower and five domes surmounted by a Greek cross. As I discovered when driving through the countryside, however, they were, with few exceptions, either permanently locked, used as storehouses or empty and vandalised. Great monasteries lay in ruins. Before the revolution there had been 54,174 Orthodox churches and 1,025 monasteries throughout greater Russia and, according to the 1897 census, eighty-seven million believers. Accounts of the early days of the twentieth century spoke of a religious fervour characterised by the number of times people crossed themselves and by their obeisance or prostrations before every church door. The Bolsheviks believed in a new, godless society. The first major wave of church closures and the dissolution of the monasteries came under Stalin in the 1930s. After a respite during the war when the state sought to use the patriotic potential of the Orthodox church, the onslaught continued under Krushchev. From 1958 to 1964, two-thirds of churches and almost all remaining monasteries were shut down, though some were preserved as museums. Other churches were also repressed. The Catholic church was regarded as a rival international organisation by Stalin, despite his famous dismissive remark, 'How many divisions has the Pope?' After the Baltic states were annexed in 1940, hundreds of churches were closed in mainly Catholic Lithuania. The church of eastern-rite

Catholics in the Ukraine was dissolved in 1946 and its members forced to join the Russian Orthodox church. Clergy who refused to do so were imprisoned. Barely sixty synagogues were left open to serve the Jewish community, half of them in Georgia, and the number of mosques in the southern republics was drastically reduced. The closures virtually ceased under Brezhnev, leaving 7,000 Russian Orthodox churches still working, but believers were intimidated from openly practising their religion. It wasn't until Gorbachev had been in office for two years that the process started to go into reverse.

It began in a controlled manner with the symbolic re-opening of a small number of churches and monasteries. One of the first monastic foundations to be returned to the church, in early 1988, was the Tolgsky Monastery, situated on a bend of the wide Volga River north of Yaroslavl, about 250 miles from Moscow.

The first glimpse I got of the monastery across the flat landscape of northern Russia was of bell towers and domes silhouetted against the sky. It was only when I got close to it, after driving along a narrow pot-holed road through pastures and clumps of elm trees on the eastern bank of the Volga, that I discovered the onion domes were black and the buildings in ruins. It had been used as a prison camp. A complex of two-storey concrete buildings with barred windows had been constructed on the lower part of an orchard garden sloping down from the red castellated monastery walls. The penal colony had only recently been closed, leaving empty watch-towers and double rows of rusting barbed-wire. To get into the grounds I had to pass through the metal doors of a guard-room. In a dark hallway a young bearded deacon with lank, shoulder-length hair and a black soutane was extending a languid hand to a queue of old women who knelt, one by one, before him to recite their troubles. He had been sent by the Moscow Patriarchy to prepare the way for a new religious community. Though it was less than a week since the announcement of its re-opening, a couple of monks had already taken up residence in an old stone dormitory building in the inner gardens of the monastery where the stillness was disturbed only by flitting wagtails.

One of the monks took me into the biggest church, the Vidyensky Cathedral. It had a notice over the door saying, 'Danger Zone'. The orange bricks of the walls were loose and some were missing. Inside, the stone floor was broken and the once-rich frescoes on the huge square pillars and vaulted ceilings had degenerated into sad patches of blue and yellow amid the damp squalor. The church had been flooded once and used as a swimming-pool. 'You could have driven a tractor in and out, no one cared', said the quiet-spoken monk, surveying the ruined interior and the graffiti on the lower part of the walls. Wooden scaffolding, rotting and black with age, clung to the outside of the cathedral, a relic of a half-hearted state attempt to prevent it from falling down. A smaller church nearby had been used as a cinema; a wooden strut had got in the way of the projector beam, said the monk, and when it had been removed the inner walls had caved in. Tombstones outside had been taken away as house foundations. The monastery itself was founded in 1314 by Bishop Prokhor, who saw a pillar of light at the spot, and destroyed 300 years later in the Polish-Lithuanian intervention when forty-six monks were killed. He showed me the stone monument commemorating the massacre. We strolled beneath twelve rare stone-pines, umbrella-like conifers that had been brought over from the Mediterranean in 1602 and planted near the duck pond. After the Polish invasion, the monastery had been rebuilt and had became a centre of religious art, one of the finest in prerevolutionary Russia and grand enough for Tsar Nicholas II to stay in overnight when the monastery was preparing to celebrate its six hundredth birthday in 1913. The celebrations never took place. The First World War came and then the overthrow of the tsars. Tolgsky was run down and eventually closed in 1929.

As I walked around the ruins that chilly May day, I came across dozens of women in headscarves from the nearby villages already working to clear the rubble from the gardens, many of them old, bending double to pick up debris and to cart it away on hand-barrows. One raised her two arms to heaven, grinned widely to expose a gold tooth in a blackened mouth and praised God for his goodness. Under Soviet laws, no religious associations were allowed to give material aid to their members. To the old villagers, Tolgsky symbolised a return of the social work of the church, with its plans for a community of nuns. People had brought back some of the bells, hidden away for sixty years in villages and working churches. They were hung from a wooden scaffolding, waiting for the old bell-towers to be brought into use so that they could once more ring out over the plains of northern Russia.

A year later I returned to Tolgsky and found the monastery re-opened. The medieval concept of the self-sufficient religious community had once again been established on Russian soil. The watch-towers and rusting wire had gone. A community of eighty sisters had moved in. They had begun farming forty acres of land with ten cows, ten goats, fifteen beehives and seventy-two hens. The nuns had planted potatoes and carrots and blackcurrant bushes. In the garden beneath the monastery walls, a 400-year-old moat lined by lime trees had been restocked with carp. The smallest of the four churches had been reconsecrated even as new floorboards and roofing were being installed. Every Sunday the services drew hundreds of people, mainly old women from the clusters of wooden *izbas* along the Volga. The main cathedral was still in disrepair, but the domes and spires gleamed with fresh green and gold paint. Restoration was being carried out by church artists and volunteers. Teenagers from local schools, chattering and play-acting, tossed bricks from hand to hand in a long line to help the builders. Nearby a mechanical digger was hard at work. Among the volunteers were one or two foreigners from Moscow to whom Tolgsky had become a symbol of hope, including Lady Jill Braithwaite, wife of the British ambassador, who spent more than one weekend with the nuns. Groups of Russians with state guides picked their way over the rubble. Beside the scaffold for the bells sat an immense 3,000-pound bell cast in 1685, rescued from its hiding place in a village church.

Mother Valentina invited me into the restored residence – it had been used by the prison guards as dormitories – and poured coffee into tiny china cups at a polished table in the parlour. The fronds of a huge potted palm filled a corner of the room. In another stood a table with a picture of a female saint. A clock ticked loudly on the wall. 'When the soul is aching, a person turns to the church', said Mother Valentina, a slender young nun from Moscow, her thin face framed in the oval aperture of a simple black habit. 'They come here for spiritual healing.' The nuns came from Russia, the Ukraine, Moldavia and Uzbekistan to establish Russia's first convent since the revolution. Aged eighteen to forty, almost all had a medical education. Seventeen were graduates. 'There are three stages in a nun's life', said Mother Valentina, fingering her *sotka*, a black silk cord with one hundred prayer-knots. 'At first when nobody knows what sort of a person she is, she just works and lives normally. Then after a time she is given a special habit and behaves as a nun but can still leave. The third stage is ordination.' New postulants arrived all the time. They were preparing to open an old people's home for the clergy and had already made ready a small hotel for pilgrims and acquired cars for visiting sick believers in hospital. The nuns rose each morning at 5.30 a.m. and retired at 11.00 p.m. Little had changed since 1914 except that they now had a television. 'But our first duty is to pray', said Mother Valentina. 'The monastery exists on donations from people, and we pray for them.'

With churches, monasteries and convents re-opening, it could only be a matter of time before the state ended another abuse of church property, the conversion of places of prayer into museums of atheism.

Almost every city had such a museum. The first one I came across was in the Catholic church of St Kazimieras in Vilnius, the capital of Lithuania. It was situated on the edge of the old part of the city, a warren of narrow, cobbled streets where women in black shawls sold medals and holy pictures beneath wrought-iron balconies overflowing with geraniums. Parties of school-children were taken every day for a tour of the exhibits, which started with a stained-glass memorial to Liscinskis, described as the seventeenth-century founder of Lithuanian atheism, and which was inscribed with the words, 'Man is the creator of God. God is the creature of man. Therefore God does not exist.' Inside the 200-year-old baroque edifice were glass cases with exhibits ranging from mass vestments to iron torture instruments from the Inquisition. A replica of the first manned space-capsule was on show, with the words of Yuri Gagarin, 'I didn't see any God up there.' I sought the opinion of the local Catholic clergy about the use to which St Kazimieras Church had been put. In those days official interviews with priests could still only be conducted under supervision, and a foreign ministry official sat in on my conversation with Monsignor Juanas Tunaitas, secretary to the Lithuanian Catholic church in Vilnius. His reception room could have been the parlour of any parish priest's house in Ireland, with a picture of St Joseph on the wall, a potted aspidistra on the polished wooden floor and a crucifix over the sideboard. Monsignor Tunaitas was the persecuted church personified: thin, rather dry, extremely careful in discussing church affairs and relations with the state. He acknowledged uneasily that several priests and bishops were in prison or in exile for 'anti-Soviet activity'. As for the museum of atheism, he gave a slight cough. 'Everyone has the right to believe or not to believe', he said.

In Lithuania, however, the process of liberation, which had so cautiously begun in Russia with the return of Tolgsky Monastery and a few churches, came with a rush. A reform-minded Communist Party leader, Algirdas Brazauskas, came to power on a surge of nationalist fervour. On 23 October 1988, the founding congress of a new popular movement, *Sajudis*, was marked by the first Catholic mass in thirty-eight years at Vilnius Cathedral, a classic building with six Doric columns in the city centre, which had been an art gallery and concert-hall since 1950. Tens of thousands of Lithuanians crowded into the square and filled the streets of the old city with flickering candles. The mass was celebrated by Cardinal Vincentas Sladkevicius, an elderly, diminutive cleric who had been living in internal exile in the village of Kaishadoris. As if the elements were in sympathy, the snows of winter did not come that year to Lithuania, and the following

January the highway was damp and the fields green when I drove the twenty-five miles from Vilnius to Kaishadoris to visit the cardinal. He lived in a mustard-coloured wooden house with a tiny wicker fence and an apple and cherry tree in the garden. Slight and silver-haired, he was the first prince of the Catholic church in Lithuania for 400 years. 'This has been the year of rejoicing, the year of St Mary, the year of blessing for Lithuania', beamed the cardinal, sitting in purple-fringed robes at his drawing-room table beneath a coloured picture of the Pope. On a bookshelf behind him stood a miniature green, red and yellow Lithuanian national flag.

Kaishadoris, situated on the edge of a tulip farm, had elements of the world of Don Camillo, the Italian village where life revolved around the communist mayor and the parish priest. The burly Communist Party leader, Algirdas Brazauskas, was a native of Kaishadoris, and his father, a practising Catholic, still lived in the village but was too ill to attend the high-steepled red-brick church located a hundred paces from the cardinal's home. 'Brazauskas comes to see his father, then he comes to see me', the cardinal said, grinning widely. Perhaps the party leader was also a Catholic? 'In his heart, maybe', he beamed, pointing to his chest. 'There are changes in all spheres of life now. We don't sense such dictates as there were before. We can now settle questions independently.' Since the war the number of working churches had been reduced to 630, and the collegiate of priests to 665, with a quota of thirty on the annual intake in the seminary in Kaunas where professors could only be appointed with Communist Party approval. All that was about to change. A few weeks earlier five students had been prevented by a party official from beginning their studies at the Kaunas Seminary. 'I intervened', cried the cardinal. 'All were admitted. There are now forty-six in the first-year course.' Leaders of *Sajudis* also dropped into the cardinal's little house to discuss affairs of church and state around the purple-draped parlour table. Priests came from as far as the United States to share in the pleasure which the cardinal radiated. The old man greeted them in slow, accented English, 'which I learned from the BBC', he confided mischievously.

The cardinal was able to disclose that the cathedral in Vilnius had since been re-equipped as a Catholic church and was about to open for regular services. The church of St Kazimieras, which had been a state museum of atheism since 1966, had also been returned to the church and the offensive exhibits taken out in preparation for reconsecration. The first Catholic newspaper in the Soviet Union, the *Catholic World*, was about to print its inaugural edition of 200,000 copies. People could now practise their religion more openly, said the cardinal. 'In the past there were some cases where teachers would lose their jobs for attending mass. Now schools have started inviting priests to talk to the pupils – I was even invited back to speak at my old school.' Lithuanian priests in prison for anti-Soviet activities had been freed. Bishop Julijonas Steponavicius, the seventy-seven-year-old prelate whom everyone believed to be a secret cardinal, had been welcomed back to Vilnius with flowers and hymns at the railway station. In future, 25 December, officially a working day up to now, would be a Lithuanian state holiday.

But paradoxically, there was a doubt in the cardinal's mind about the long-term benefits of freedom from Soviet rule. 'The Catholic faith is losing ground in Europe', he said. 'The situation is deplorable. They have lost the precious things of the past. The crisis in the Catholic church is there, not in Lithuania. We are afraid of close unity with Europe . . . of pornography . . .', he slapped his hand on the table in disgust. 'If the values of the permissive society are imported into Lithuania, they will do more harm than good. We are thankful to God that we are isolated from bad influences. All things in God's hands have meaning.'

Two years later I called in to see the cardinal when passing Kaishadoris. It was 6 May 1990, just after *Sajudis* had won a general election and declared independence. The cardinal was not there. He had gone to live in the official cardinal's residence in Kaunas. A new bishop, Josef Matulaitis, had taken up his duties in the diocese. I found him in a twenty-room red-brick mansion on the other side of the village, a pleasant middle-aged man surrounded by priests. In a high-ceilinged reception-room overlooking a meadow of dandelions he told me religion was now being taught in the schools again. The mansion, the largest such building in the village, had been used as a branch of the state library, but had been restored to the church. The days when the cardinal received guests in a cottage belonged to the past.

The unique relationship between the prince of the Catholic church and the communist leader of a Baltic republic set the pace for change and for a new relationship between church and state which was to become a model for the whole of the Soviet Union. The flame of religious revival was slower to ignite in areas where repression had been most severe. It suddenly blazed into life in the old city of Lvov in west Ukraine on 15 September 1989 when the banned Ukrainian Catholic church emerged from the catacombs and filled the cobbled streets of the ancient capital of Galacia with a human river of hymn-singing and flag-waving people, demanding official recognition of their church and an end to four decades of imprisonment and exile. Priests and bishops more accustomed to saying secret masses in forests and cemeteries and old women ringing little bells led the multitudes past the town's nineteenth-century merchants' houses to the huge, gold-domed edifice of St George's Cathedral to demand that it be returned to them.

The Ukrainian Catholic church had broken with the Russian Orthodox faith in 1596 under the influence of Catholic Poland, but retained the Byzantine rites while giving allegiance to the Vatican. After it was banned in 1946 by Stalin, its 3,000 churches were transferred to the Russian Orthodox church. Many believers refused to accept the union and went underground. Priests who defied the will of Stalin were executed or imprisoned. The date for their re-emergence coincided with the fiftieth anniversary of the Soviet annexation of west Ukraine, which had between the wars been part of Poland. The suppression of the Ukrainian Catholic church made religion and nationalism as indistinguishable as in Ireland during penal times. Home rule in west Ukraine meant Rome rule.

The giant demonstration was led by a Ukrainian Catholic activist, Ivan Ghel, who had spent eighteen years in prison. He was chaired through the streets. Important guests, including Vyatautas Landsbergis, soon to become president of Lithuania, applauded from a balcony. 'Look how powerful our church is when we are united', he said to me as dozens jostled around to listen. 'There are five million of us. We have not been terrorised; we can now achieve victory.' Ghel led a movement to take back their churches by simply moving in and occupying them. Without the repressive apparatus of the state to help them, the Orthodox hierarchy in Moscow could do nothing to stop the crumbling of their spiritual empire.

The next Christmas was celebrated as a public holiday in Lvov for the first time since 1940. On Christmas Eve, 6 January in the Eastern-rite calendar, I was invited to the home of Roman Krypyakevich, a retired engineer, and his artist wife, Lesya, both fervent believers. I set out to find their house in Engels Street in the suburbs of Lvov. It was quiet, apart from the rumbling and scraping of the wheels of occasional trams. As I peered at street numbers in the dim light of electric lamps, I heard singing in the distance; suddenly, from around a corner came an assorted group of figures in cloaks and masks. They were led by the grim reaper, wearing a skull-mask and carrying a scythe over his shoulder, and the devil, with horned head and forked tail, followed by Roman legionaries, angels, knights, shepherds and witches, all singing hymns. They disappeared into the darkness, heading towards the city centre. Ancient Christmas customs such as the masked strollers had been revived in Lvov, whose origins dated back to the thirteenth century. Lvov had been part of Poland for 400 years before being taken over by the Austro-Hungarian Empire in 1772. After the First World War, it reverted back to Poland. Because of its history and architecture, Lvov always felt less like a Soviet town than a medieval centre in an enclosed corner of old Europe, suffering from the claustrophobia of closed borders all around. The Polish frontier was a two-hour bicycle ride to the north. Czechoslovakia and Hungary were just over the western horizon and Romania lay to the south. Transylvania, whose ancient folklore included Dracula, was not far away, I thought to myself as the strange figures passed by.

With their two daughters, also artists, and other family members and friends, the Krypyakeviches celebrated Christmas Eve in the traditional Ukrainian manner. The book-lined living-room was lit by two candles set on a large dining-table, at one end of which were arranged a sheaf of corn and a brown, twisted loaf lying in a bed of straw. By tradition, no meat was served. There was instead deep-purple Ukrainian *schi*, made from cabbage, and a sweet, soft Christmas pudding of honey, cereal and nuts. They laughed, talked and sang hymns and national songs. At 11.00 p.m. the television was switched on for interviews with church leaders on the Ukrainian state channel, interspersed with Christmas carols. Such a programme would have been unthinkable before. The leader of the Ukrainian Catholic church, Archbishop Vladimir Sternyuk, a white-bearded priest with black eyebrows, a gold robe and a tall white hat, said a few words to the camera about peace and reconciliation from his tiny apartment. For the Krypyakevich family this was state acknowledgement that their church was no longer outlawed or their priests and bishops forbidden to perform religious rites.

After midnight we boarded a tram and rattled through the dark streets to the Church of the Transfiguration in the centre of Lvov. We passed hundreds of people walking to different churches for all-night services as well as occasional groups of more masked carollers. The Transfiguration Church had been repossessed by Ukrainian Catholics ten weeks previously. Waves of emotion passed through the packed congregation, many of them young people, as Father Yaroslav Tuchnin, a former Orthodox priest, sang the liturgy in a loud, rich voice. The galleries along the side were filled with honoured guests, poets, writers, leaders of proreform groups and former political prisoners. Television crews pushed through the congregation. One took over the ornate pulpit. There were representatives from the Ukrainian Orthodox Autocephalous church, another nationalist faith whose congregations had also begun to oust Russian Orthodox priests from the churches. The atmosphere of national fervour that night left no one there in any doubt that the people had lost patience and were prepared to sweep all before them.

The next morning, Christmas Day – 7 January – was grey and bitterly cold, but thousands took to the streets again and crowded into the central boulevard of Lvov where a Christmas tree had been erected. Candles burned in jamjars and people jostled around notice-boards in what had become known locally as 'Hyde Park', pronounced 'Guide Park'. A crib with cardboard figures of the Holy Family under the leafless chestnut trees attracted an admiring crowd. Officious old men ordered people to stand back, but young parents kept pushing forward to lift their children high to see their first street crib. In the middle of the milling crowds a burly, gap-toothed country woman began singing hymns. Soon the whole boulevard joined in. The sound of thousands of voices drifted over Rosa Luxemburg Street and Mitskevich Square throughout the afternoon. All the time, around the boulevard and in the cobbled streets, people parted like waves to make way for masked processions which appeared and disappeared, like actors in a dozen different pantomimes, led by centurion guards with silver-coloured shields and wearing blond wigs from women's hairdressers under their tin helmets. Angels cavorted with devils, and the grim reaper kept appearing and disappearing, grinning maniacally.

In Moscow the new concordat between the Communist Party and the Russian Orthodox church was given official blessing in May 1988 when Mikhail Gorbachev met Patriarch Pimen in the Kremlin, during ceremonies to mark the 1,000 anniversary of Christianity in Russia. The return of churches and monasteries became more frequent and included the ancient Monastery of the Caves in Kiev, the Pecherskaya Lavra, which overlooked the Dnieper River where 1,000 years earlier Prince Vladimir of Kiev had ordered mass baptisms to convert Russ to Christianity. The monastery had been preserved as a tourist attraction, with a warren of man-made caves containing the skeletons of seventy-three saints laid out in rotting, but once costly garments. In the Soviet capital, the Danilovsky Monastery, once a reception centre for delinquent children, had been given back to the Moscow Patriarchy in anticipation of the centenary, and the complex of buildings in south Moscow became its headquarters just in time for a visit by US President Ronald Reagan on 30 May 1988.

The finishing touches for the restoration of the fortress-monastery, first built in 1272, included a little *potemkin*ising, the Russian practice of impressing the visitor, named after Prince Potemkin who was reputed to have built artificial villages to impress Catherine the Great. When Reagan and his wife Nancy arrived, they found young birch trees gracing a courtyard lawn which had been empty wasteground a few days before. Wooden brackets held the nursery trees erect on rolls of turf. The peace of the monastery, nevertheless, was rudely disturbed during the president's tour by an unholy row between Russian and American security agents over who should be allowed into the small room where Reagan would be received, and which was already crowded with a dozen pool-reporters, of which I was one, and a US-army recording unit. A White House agent with a red face and an earpiece shouted at a heavily built Soviet security man with a mole on his cheek that they must put American TV-network crews in as well. 'Tell him that', he screamed at an unfortunate interpreter. The man with the mole shook his head. Eventually a CBS crew was allowed to squeeze in just before Ronald and Nancy Reagan appeared. By now the room had filled up with sixteen arch-priests wearing tall black hats from which black cloth hung down their backs. Reagan told the audience that, 'Americans feel it keenly when religious freedom is denied to anyone, anywhere.' They remained expressionless as Reagan added his hope that Ukrainian Catholics, as well, would soon be able to practice their religion freely. Quoting Alexander Solzhenitsyn that religious faith was at the heart of Russian life, the US president said, 'In our prayers we may keep that image in mind, the thought that the bells may ring again, sounding throughout Moscow, clamouring for joy in their new-found freedom.'

Reagan's wish was granted. The restriction on ringing church bells was lifted exactly a year later. The day that I heard them on my balcony was 9 April 1989. Among the chimes were those of the little Church of the Assumption off Taganskaya Square. This church reflected the revival of faith in Russia. I noticed that young people, not just old women, had begun openly to cross themselves in the street in front of the icon, an unusual depiction of the Virgin with three hands, two clasped before her, the third holding the infant Jesus, which was attached to the outside wall. It had become almost impossible to get into the blue-and-gold domed church at Easter services. On weekends old *babushkas* squatted in whispering groups on camp stools beside the icon-covered walls and younger people milled about beneath the low, vaulted ceilings. Many worshippers stood outside in Volodarsky Street where the smell of incense filled the evening air. I dropped in during the day a few times and found weddings and baptisms going on. Priests said they could hardly cope with the queues.

I also noticed that from the centenary year of 1988 onwards, the supermarket at the base of my building began selling the traditional Russian Easter cake – tall, feather-light currant loaves – for a religious festival which it previously ignored. The state tourist stores, the *Beriozkas*, started to display crucifixes and to offer cassettes of church music recorded by the choir of the Moscow Patriarchy. The re-opening of churches accelerated. One of the temples given back was the seventeenth-century church of St Michael the Archangel, a pretty little building with five coloured cupolas in a built-up corner of south-west Moscow. Once a state storehouse, it became for the thousands of students living in nearby hostels a jewel in a landscape of high-rise apartment blocks. This brought the number of working Orthodox churches in the Soviet capital up to fifty-one, still a long way from the forty times forty churches which prerevolutionary Moscow boasted. Throughout the country, 3,000 churches were given back by the end of the 1980s. Patriarch Pimen died in 1990 and the bishops of the Orthodox church, symbolising a break with the past, rejected the interim 'pope', the hard-line conservative Archbishop Filaret of Kiev, in favour of the more liberal Patriarch Alexei. Political radicals including Boris Yeltsin, the Russian president, and Anatoly Sobchak, the Leningrad mayor, were among the congregation when the Patriarch rededicated St Isaac's Cathedral in Russia's second city. In a rerun of the scenes in Vilnius when Cardinal Steponavicius returned to Lithuania, the Patriarch had been met at the railway station in Leningrad by Sobchak and city officials bearing bunches of flowers. On the streets radical priests, like Father Gleb Yakunin, regularly addressed political demonstrations. In October 1989 the Orthodox church was readmitted to the Kremlin with the rededication of the 500-year-old Cathederal of the Assumption where the tsars were once crowned, and a year later a service was held in St Basil's Cathedral, the little chocolate-box cathedral with twisting onion domes at the edge of Red Square which had come to symbolise Russia itself. The choral singing from the church was broadcast over Red Square where crowds of city people and tourists gathered to listen. It surprised nobody that the same week a priest was on hand to bless the official opening of Moscow's first commodities exchange since 1917.

The day had come too when priests could be interviewed freely on television. In 1988 a current-affairs programme caused a sensation by showing Father Alexander Men, a well-built, handsome priest with a neat grey-black beard, talking to children about religious faith. Young boys with the red scarves of the Pioneers, the Communist Party Youth Organisation, spoke freely to him about why they believed in God. Father Men and a few other radical priests started Sunday schools in 1989 in defiance of the still-existing law which stipulated that religious teaching should be confined to the home, legislation which was eventually scrapped when the Supreme Soviet passed a bill on freedom of conscience in October 1990.

I sat in on one of these classes, which was conducted by a young priest, Mikhail Dronov, in the parochial house attached to the pink-coloured Church of the Resurrection in Moscow, not far from the Kremlin. Before the class began the children took part in the church service, singing the liturgy in quavering voices and standing on tip-toes to kiss the icons like the adults. Some of them queued with the old women for whispered confessions in the ear of a priest, Father Gennady, a huge, florid clergyman who administered forgiveness by placing a lace cover over the penitent's head as he gave the blessing. After the service the five-year-olds trooped across the yard and took their places in a classroom with ten rows of desks. Father Dronov, dressed in a long soutane with wide sleeves which drooped like black wings when he raised his arms, began the lesson by asking each child to kiss a brass crucifix he brought around the noisy classroom. He then put the children through their biblical paces. 'Who knows who Adam and Eve were?' he asked. Several little hands shot up. 'They were the first primitive people', called out a little boy. 'They were *dopotopniye* people', said another, causing the priest to smile at the use of a derogatory word for 'ancient', literally meaning 'before the flood'. 'And where did they come from?' 'Out of the earth.' 'What happened to them', asked Father Mikhail, wandering through the desks and shooing some of the more restless children back to their seats. 'They ate the forbidden apple and God sent them away from paradise and said they would live badly', replied a little girl in pigtails who had been gnawing pickled garlic. 'And who was Abraham?' A freckled boy with huge spectacles said, 'God told Abraham he would have a son and would call him Isaac and his wife started laughing and God said why are you laughing and made her silent until the day the child was born.' 'Who can tell me about the Tower of Babel?' asked the young priest, lifting a stray child back on to its form. 'Was it bigger than Ostankino?' called out a little girl, referring to Moscow's television tower. She was assured that it was. 'They wanted to build it to make themselves glorious but God didn't allow it', said a boy. 'He mixed up their languages. One said let's build it and the others couldn't understand him.'

'Strictly speaking, Sunday school is still forbidden', said Father Mikhail as the children tumbled into the next room for bread rolls and fruit juice, 'but where people were afraid, now there is less fear.'

Among the parents waiting outside were a couple in their thirties, Alexander and Vera Shishkin, whose child Angelina was in the class. 'I want my children to go to school where religion is taught because the Communist Party ideology in the state schools crippled me when I was a child', said Vera. Both are believers. 'She believes through the heart and I believe through the head', said Alexander, who recalled that his mathematics teacher had been expelled from his institute for being a believer in the days before perestroika. The state used to keep a close eye on those attending church. Priests were required to register a parent's passport number and place of work when a child was baptised.

One of the priests who would carry out secret baptisms in the days of stagnation was Father Men, who after his television appearance with the children had become a regular television personality and a major radical figure in the church. During the Brezhnev years, parents would come from Moscow, a forty-minute drive away, to his pine-wood Church of the Purification, with its tiny blue onion domes adorned with gold stars, located in the village of Novaya Derevnya on the Zagorsk Road, arriving sometimes in swirling snow with a child swaddled in warm clothes. Father Men would drop whatever he was doing to conduct a quick baptism. Born in Moscow in 1935, he had acquired the reputation of a priest who refused to compromise with the communist state, a spiritual father to those who spoke out on human rights. He was frequently brought in for questioning by the KGB. Father Men was also pastor to many of the Moscow intelligentsia and had officiated at the funeral of the protest singer and Russian folk hero, Vladimir Vysotsky, in 1980. He embodied for many all that was good and progressive in the Orthodox church as it emerged from its long and painful subjection to the state: a beloved parish priest and, at the same time, a formidable scholar and ecumenist.

There was a dark side to the revival of the Christian churches. Passions were unleashed which recalled the rivalries and enmities of prerevolutionary days when the church was controlled by the tsar, whose procurator general presided over its synods. A small number of physical battles for control of churches erupted in Russia as the Russian Orthodox church in exile and the Orthodox church in the catacombs, both of which had always rejected the collusion of the hierarchy with the state, emerged to assert their claims. And amid the joy and optimism among believers at the revival of religion, tragedy struck. Father Men left his two-storey wooden house in Semkhoz village at 6.40 a.m. on Sunday, 9 September 1990 and set off along a narrow tarmacadam path through damp woods to the railway station.

The priest, dressed in an overcoat and carrying his robes and a cross in a briefcase, was on his way to catch a train to his parish church. As he reached a grove of oak trees, he was struck on the back of the head with a small axe. The blow made a four-inch gash and severed the artery carrying blood to the brain. The fifty-five-year-old priest died within minutes. For days, during which the rain never ceased, people came to place flowers on that dank path in the woods. Father Alexander Men was no ordinary Orthodox priest; he was a Jew, as were a great many of his congregation, and a target for extreme nationalists outraged at the prominence of a Jew in their church – the very citadel of Russian nationalism. His friends believed he was the victim of a religious or racist murder, possibly carried out by someone from an extreme branch of the nationalist society *Pamyat*, or a political assassination like that of Father Popieluszko in Poland in 1984. Father Men's last published words appeared in an article he wrote in the newspaper *Sovetskaya Kultura*, which concluded, 'Chaos growing out of tyranny will not endure. No matter how long the darkness, the night cannot be endless. God's word teaches us to believe in the victory of the light.'

7

Peredelkino

IT IS hard to believe that the sleepy village of Peredelkino is less than half-an-hour's drive from the centre of Moscow. It lies just off the Minsk highway and down a narrow, winding country road which turns off a few miles from where the city apartment blocks and traffic lights abruptly give way to forests, meadows and roadside *izbas*, the painted wooden cottages of the Russian countryside.

I first discovered Peredelkino one Sunday afternoon when the low sunshine of an Indian summer had dispelled the cloud and rain which had hung over the city for several weeks. I found large *dachas* half hidden around the village among elm, oak, sycamore and fir trees, and a tiny Orthodox church with golden and blue domes on a wooded hillside. A path from the village led to a little river and across a wooden footbridge to an old beet field. Beyond it was a recreation zone, a scattering of benches around a lake and a reading-room constructed from logs as well as a tea house, permanently locked, with a notice exhorting visitors to enjoy themselves and not to set fire to the forest or to get drunk. In winter it was possible to ski along the river paths for hours and not meet another soul. It was particularly peaceful around the church and the hillside graveyard. Boris Pasternak, the poet and author of *Doctor Zhivago*, was buried there among the gloomy maze of caged graves and Orthodox crosses, where the only sound was the cawing of the hooded crows in the branches overhead. Pasternak lived across a meadow from the graveyard in one of the fifty-seven *dachas* hidden away around Peredelkino which belong to the literary fund of the Soviet Writers' Union and which have made the village a writers' colony. Pasternak's grave lay near the top of the hill, sheltered by two Scots pines and marked by a simple stone slab on which the gaunt features of the poet had been hollowed out. Every weekend pilgrims came to the cemetery to lay red carnations at the headstone. An elderly Jewish man, Emanuel Libschits, made the long trek every Sunday from his apartment across the city to tend the grave and to put some of the flowers in jamjars at each corner. His shoes were cracked and his suit worn and shiny. His declining years were devoted to Pasternak whom he had never met, but, he told me, 'When I first heard his verse at school when I was young, my life changed.' He was a source of information about comings and goings in the graveyard. 'Yevtushenko was here an hour ago', he would tell me when I arrived on one of my many visits, or, 'You just missed the American ambassador.' He often recited Pasternak for visitors with a passion and energy which lit up his face. When he discovered I was Irish, he launched into Yeats's 'The Second Coming' in Russian.

On my first visit to the writers' village in the summer of 1987, I learned that all was not well in Peredelkino. Paint had been splashed on Pasternak's gravestone one night, and an arsonist had tried, unsuccessfully, to burn down his *dacha*. Pasternak had not yet been officially rehabilitated following his disgrace in the late 1950s when he was vilified and thrown out of the Writers' Union. It wasn't so much because of the anti-revolutionary sentiments in *Doctor Zhivago*, but because he won the Nobel prize after publishing the novel abroad, thus shaming the Russian authorities for banning it at home. After his death in 1960, the Writers' Union had hesitated to reclaim the *dacha*, however, because of Pasternak's stature at home and abroad, and the family were allowed to maintain it as a museum to his memory. The upstairs room with the bay window was kept just as it was on the day he died, with his cap on the wall and his boots beside the door. But the bureaucrats had long and unforgiving memories. In 1981 The Writers' Union began court proceedings to recover twenty-two *dachas*, including Pasternak's, from widows and heirs who had stayed longer than the two years allowed after a writer's death. This party-controlled organisation could thus claim that its desire to recover the Pasternak *dacha* was not motivated by spite. After a long legal battle, the bailiffs arrived on 7 October 1984, loaded all the furniture and possessions of the *dacha* museum on to lorries and locked the doors. The *dacha* was left empty, grass growing wild over the strawberry beds which Pasternak once tended in the front garden. No writer could be found to move into such hallowed ground. This is how I first found it three years later. There was a notice attached to the gate saying, 'Here there will be a museum', but this had been put up more in hope than in anticipation by Pasternak's friends.

Pasternak's son Yevgeny, also a writer and scholar who bore an uncanny resemblance to his father, lived in a book-lined apartment in the centre of Moscow. He told me when I called one winter afternoon that he considered the house where Boris Pasternak wrote most of his verse and his famous novel to be a sacred place and that it should be a permanent museum to his memory. Under Russian law the family could become curators of such a museum. Their pleas were not being listened to, however, despite the promise of rethinking under Gorbachev. 'Nothing has changed; visitors are not allowed, the house is empty', said Yevgeny Pasternak, sitting at the kitchen table with a suede waistcoat over a woolen cardigan to keep out the cold. The one sign of hope was that the journal *Novy Mir* had promised to publish *Doctor Zhivago* for the first time in the Soviet Union, and forty prominent Russian writers had signed a petition asking that the house be restored as a museum.

Everytime I visited Peredelkino over the next three years, I called at the *dacha* out of curiosity and rang the doorbell. The response was always the same. A caretaker would appear and shake his head and say, 'Sorry, I'm not allowed to let anyone in, even to look around.' We got to know each other quite well. One day he told me that there was another *dacha* museum nearby which had been at the centre of a similar struggle with the authorities and which might be worth a visit. I found the two-storey wooden house where Kornei Chukovsky lived on a forest road five minutes walk away. It was an April day, but winter lingered on in the gloomy snow-covered garden, resisting the advances of the tepid sun which had turned the paths into mud. Kornei Chukovsky was a writer of children's fairy tales, as famous and as well loved in Russia as Hans Christian Andersen in Europe. Since he died in 1969, his *dacha* had also been preserved as a museum to his memory. There was no sign on the gate, however, and I had to call at neighbouring houses to find out where it was. Nor was the museum mentioned in any official guidebooks, though about 200 pilgrims a day managed to find it during the summer months. Despite his enormous popularity, the shadow of official disfavour had also hung over this house in the woods since the day Chukovsky died. The museum was unofficial and maintained by his daughter Lydia, then eighty-one, his granddaughter Yelena, his former secretary, Clara Lozovskaya, and other family friends like the student Anna Sosinskaya who showed me round that afternoon. They had preserved the rooms exactly as they were. The living-room, the stairway and the upstairs study were crammed with the mementoes of a full literary life, dating back to the Silver Age of Russian culture when Chukovsky rubbed shoulders with Tolstoy, Blok, Gorky and Mayakovsky. The last letter Tolstoy ever wrote lay on the desk. Kornei Chukovsky received it the day of Tolstoy's funeral in 1910. Beside it were branches from a birch tree hung with toy objects, like the miracle tree from one of his best-loved stories. The crowded shelves contained a unique library of 5,000 volumes, including his children's books and translations of Walt Whitman and a row of Penguin paperbacks in English for a thesis on the art of the detective novel. Ellery Queen sat beside Anton Checkhov. Among these books were to be found the first clues as to why the Soviet authorities had maintained a cold attitude towards the memory of so beloved a writer. There were several volumes by the most reviled Russian writer of the previous two decades, Alexander Solzhenitsyn, author of *First Circle* and *Cancer Ward* and several other works exposing the evils of Stalinism.

Solzhenitsyn lived here on and off just prior to his exile to the West in 1972. Despite the author's growing unpopularity with the party leadership, Chukovsky not only invited him to take refuge in the *dacha* for several months, but left him enough money in his will to live on for three years. In his last six months in Russia, Solzhenitsyn returned to the *dacha* as a guest of Lydia, herself an important writer. Solzhenitsyn later described how he was kept under surveillance at Chukovsky's *dacha* museum, but still managed to smuggle his manuscripts to Western contacts. 'Instead of going out through the front gate as usual, I would go by way of the backyard, where no one set foot in winter, through snow-covered ways deserted at night to the next road.' In those days the telephone on the carved oval table in the dining-room rang with threatening calls, and strange men came by to make estimates for repairs which were never carried out. The authorities finally decided to get rid of Solzhenitsyn and summoned him from the *dacha* for a meeting with the public prosecutor from which he never returned. He was stripped of his citizenship and put aboard a plane for West Germany. The room where he worked during his time in the *dacha* was now the nearest thing to a Solzhenitsyn museum in Russia. The desk still had the ink stains he left. With a mischevious grin, Anna Sosinskaya took a three-pronged pitchfork from behind a cupboard and said, 'This is what he used to carry when walking the roads around here, in case anyone should think of attacking him.'

The powers that be took their revenge on the family. Lydia Chukovsky was thrown out of the Writers' Union in 1973 for her defence of Solzhenitsyn. She said that the writer had not betrayed his native land or his people, rather he had revealed to the public how millions had perished under Stalin. Somehow, however, they could not bring themselves to close down the unofficial museum, such was the great love of the people for a writer whose stories had enchanted generations of Russian children. On the other hand, the official owner of the *dacha*, the literary fund, did not provide a single kopeck for a major renovation needed in 1983, despite having received twenty million roubles from its 10 per cent commission on every Chukovsky book sold. A series of official bodies passed contradictory judgements on the *dacha*'s future. In 1973 the Board of Moscow Writers said the museum should be made official. They were overruled three years later by the Writers' Union. Moscow Regional Council then listed the *dacha* as a protected building. It was taken off the list in 1983, but a government commission unexpectedly recommended the museum be preserved. The Writers' Union, ever loyal to its Stalinist traditions, promptly started, and won, criminal proceedings to repossess the house for another author. But nothing happened; the shadow of eviction was simply left to hang over the *dacha*, letting the family know of their doubtful standing even two years after the introduction of glasnost. They actually preferred it that way. If the museum became official, said Anna, the authorities might take the Solzhenitsyn books away and install a portrait of Lenin, which would not really be in keeping with the spirit of the museum.

But things were changing, and the clouds began to lift not just for the Pasternaks and the Chukovskys but for all the writers, musicians, poets and playwrights who had been suppressed under Soviet rule. A cultural counter-revolution was emerging, which was to reach its climax in 1990 with the restoration of citizenship to Alexander Solzhenitsyn himself and the publication of his message that 'the clock of communism has struck its final hour'. Vladimir Vysotsky, the singer, poet and actor, was among the first to be rehabilitated. In 1987 he was awarded a state prize and the state recording company, Melodiya, began publishing the most outspoken of his songs, which it had so shamefully declined to produce during the years of stagnation. On 24 January 1988 thousands packed the Lenin stadium in Moscow for a memorial concert where actors from the Taganka Theatre appealed for support for a museum dedicated to the singer with the gravelly voice who had articulated the despair of the Russian people throughout the 1970s, once writing:

> Because I disturbed the peace
> Because I croak out my words across the land
> Organisations, instances and individuals
> Have declared open war upon me.

Hardly a week passed during the latter part of the 1980s that some poet, playwright, actor, producer, singer or musician was not being rehabilitated or invited back from abroad, so wide had the KGB and the state cultural bodies cast their disfavours. *Novy Mir* did eventually publish *Doctor Zhivago*. Anatoly Rybakov's novel *Children of the Arbat* about the Stalin years was put on sale twenty years after Soviet officials had first turned it down. Joseph Brodsky, the exiled Nobel prize-winning poet was given back his citizenship and his poems were published. Theatre director Yuri Lyubimov, dismissed and exiled in 1984 for staging productions displeasing to the Kremlin, was given back his old job at the Taganka Theatre. His long-time disciple at the Taganka, the actor Nikolai Gubenko, was appointed minister for culture in November 1989.

It was Gubenko who organised one of the most emotional of the homecomings, that of the cellist and conductor Mstislav Rostropovich, on 13 February 1990. The culture minister – whom I had seen a few nights previously playing the title role in *Boris Gudunov* at the Taganka Theatre – introduced Rostropovich to the press at the foreign ministry in Moscow, on the maestro's first day back in Russia since being stripped of his citizenship and forced into exile sixteen years previously. The Soviet journalists gave him a rapturous round of applause. 'When I left the Soviet Union it was a big island of lies', said Rostropovich, a slight, balding man with a mischevious smile and a strong resemblance to his hero, Andrei Sakharov. 'But now the Soviet Union is cleaning itself of lies. Everything is permitted to be said.' His wife, the Bolshoi opera-singer Galina Vishnyevskaya, her eyes flashing, recalled the 'barbarous act' of Leonid Brezhnev in revoking their passports. The return to Moscow was a particular triumph for Galina, a village girl who almost died in the siege of Leningrad during the war and had risen to become a dinner companion of Soviet President Nikolai Bulganin, who tried to make her his mistress, and of Khrushchev and Brezhnev. As with the Chukovsky family and so many others, it was their friendship and defence of Solzhenitsyn, a touchstone for the integrity of his artist friends, which brought about their official disgrace. Rostropovich befriended the author of the *Gulag Archipelago*, and gave him a small guest-house beside their *dacha* at Zhukovka, outside Moscow, protecting him with their famous names. He moved there for a while from the Chukovsky's house in Peredelkino.

Getting to Rostropovich's concert the following night in the great hall of the Moscow Conservatory was another matter. The first militia checkpoint was half-way along Hertzen Street. We had to show our tickets before being allowed along the darkened roadway. After two more checks we came to a final row of crush-barriers where, for some inexplicable reason, several militiamen were holding people back. 'We have tickets, look', concertgoers cried. Tempers became frayed and the militia lost control. A diplomat fell on the frozen snow and an elderly woman cried in pain as a metal barrier struck her back. The encounter, a reminder of the days when Rostropovich fans could expect to be harried and bullied, left us trembling with

anger, but for all the security every corridor and balcony, every stairway and exit door, was crammed with people who had somehow
managed to get in without a ticket. When the bespectacled figure
of Rostropovich appeared on the stage, the hall erupted in waves
of emotion. Leading the applause was Galina, in a box beside the
stage, jewellery glittering defiantly on her black costume. Beside
her, clapping enthusiastically, was Raisa Gorbachev. The last time
Rostropovich had played in the conservatory was in 1971 at a
concert to mark the sixty-fifth birthday of the composer, Dmitri
Shostakovich, once derided in *Pravda* for his 'crude, primitive,
vulgar music'. That night two decades earlier, the high-ceilinged hall
had tingled with electricity as a bearded figure appeared and people
whispered 'it's Solzhenitsyn', 'there's Solzhenitsyn.' The electricity
crackled again through the great hall as we listened to the haunting
music of Dvopăk's cello concerto, delivered as a hymn of triumph
for those who had longed for the day when Rostropovich would
come back.

The story of the Pasternak *dacha* also had a happy ending. The
leadership of the Writers' Union dropped its objections to the
museum on 18 May 1988. 'It is a victory for the policy of glasnost',
said the poet Andrei Voznesensky, chairman of a commission set up
to rehabilitate Pasternak. The notice on the wicket gate predicting
'Here will be a museum' came true on Saturday, 10 February 1990,
just a few days before the Rostropovich concert, and at last on
that bright, mild winter's day we were allowed to go inside.
Everything was restored as it had been. The spacious room
where *Doctor Zhivago* was written was sparsely furnished, as
he had preferred. On a parquet floor stood a plain wooden desk
on which lay an unfinished letter. In a bookcase by the wall were
works by Kafka, a few dictionaries and a bible. There was a coat,
a grey tweed cap and a pair of boots standing by the doorway.
The black grand piano once again filled the living-room. Nearby
squatted a 1950s television set with a tiny screen framed in a giant
radiogram. The walls were covered with pencil sketches, including
a series of nude figures by Pasternak's father, Leonid. The *dacha*
has become not just a memorial to Pasternak but to the lifestyle
of the Russian literati of the first half of the twentieth century. A
marble and bronze plaque was unveiled that morning beside the
veranda. The occasion was, as Voznesensky put it, a 'victory of
spirit over obscurantism'. Yevgeny Pasternak spoke at the opening
ceremony. 'For twenty-five years after he died, nothing was changed
in the house, not a single thing', he said. 'We kept it as an unofficial

museum, retaining the inviolability of the atmosphere. The ruthless power of the state intruded, like it did on the fate of Boris Pasternak during his life, and even after his death. But now the museum is open again. It is a true victory for the keepers of cultural values.' Poetry readings are now held regularly at the house, though the last time I was in Peredelkino, Emanuel Libschitz was still keeping his loyal vigil at the grave on the hillside.

8

Stalin's Ghost

HUNDREDS of people came running down the boulevard, their faces grief-striken. A hat fell off in front of me and was trampled into the ground. A young man tumbled fifteen feet from a wall with a sickening thud. Then an amplified voice shouted, 'Cut', and we all stopped. 'Everybody go back', the voice said. 'We have to do it again.'

The scene was Trubnaya Square on the garden boulevard in Moscow on a Saturday morning in February 1990. We were playing the role of film extras at the request of the poet Yevgeny Yevtushenko who had asked for volunteers to make up crowd scenes in a film he was directing, to be called *Stalin's Funeral*. I was curious to relive a fragment of the history of Stalin's times. Since I had come to live in Moscow, I had been made aware of just how dark a shadow the former dictator still cast over political and cultural life in the city. To get into the spirit of the thing, I had dressed in an ancient greatcoat and a hat with old-fashioned ear flaps. Yevtushenko had made it a condition that we wear the type of attire Muscovites would have used on 9 March 1953, when Stalin's burial took place in the Soviet capital. The boulevard had a strip of park running down the middle with trees and benches. When I arrived it was already crowded with women in padded jackets and shawls, elderly men in *gulag*-type hats, teenagers in army uniforms taken from old trunks and smart girls in 1950-style wide-brimmed hats. The boulevard and Trubnaya Square had been closed to the public by Mosfilm, the state film studio, and transformed into a street scene of the Stalinist time. On occasions such as this film directors were quite happy that not much of Moscow had been modernised. To enhance the set, however, shop fronts in the yellow, two-storey buildings had been given postwar signs advertising: 'Beer and Water', or *'Papirosi'*, the cardboard cigarettes of the 1950s which were still smoked by some. Black and red mourning ribbon hung around busts of Stalin in shop windows and from lamp posts. Parked by the footpath were several wooden-frame lorries, the Zil F5, mass-produced during the war and equipped with only one headlight, so desperate were shortages at the time. Alongside them were one or two Pobedas, the 1940s sedan modelled on the English standard Vanguard and whose name meant 'victory'. There was also a sinister-looking 1939 Gas M1, the black saloon car with cloth seats in which Stalin's secret police used to cruise the city. Yevtushenko, a very decisive film maker in a black beret, told me his film was about the fate of his generation – the young growing up at the end of the Stalin period. An anti-Stalinist all his life, the poet had decided to combine a tender love story with an apocalyptic epic, making his heroes the teenagers who happened to be in the huge crowd in Trubnaya Square at the time of the funeral, the contemporaries of the men now running Russia along with Mikhail Gorbachev.

He sent us back up the hill for another take. Long columns formed up again on each side of the boulevard. I was shunted into a side street with about 200 other extras and told to wait for the signal to run as fast as I could into the boulevard and down the hill again. A youth beside me in an old-style peaked cap was making valiant efforts to smoke a *Papirosa*. 'I want to feel authentic', he grinned. The man whose hat had come off on the first gallop down the boulevard pulled it tight on his head. We all readied ourselves to dash out of the side street, but the lot of a film extra, I discovered, was like that of a journalist: endless periods of waiting, followed by short bursts of excitement. It was an hour before the loudspeakers barked and we were off again. The young man once again dropped fifteen feet from the wall with a thud. He was not hurt, of course. As a professional stuntman he was used to falling safely – on this occasion on to a pile of cardboard boxes stuffed into a huge canvas bag. We streamed into the boulevard and joined the thousands of 'mourners' running pell-mell towards Trubnaya Square. The man's hat came off again despite all his efforts and was trampled underfoot at the same spot. There was no stopping, however. We were almost a mob. It was a slightly unnerving experience re-enacting the hysteria when hundreds of people died in the Moscow streets, trying to get to the funeral.

The experience was also a profound one for some of the extras there that day; it had become an emotional recreation of a chapter in history in which they themselves had participated. As we rested I fell into conversation with a retired theatre technician, Gennady Monakov, who turned out to be one of dozens of Muscovites there who had seen the real thing. He told me how he had queued to glimpse Stalin's body lying in state in the Hall of Unions. 'Everybody cried that day', he recalled. 'There was mourning throughout the city. You must realise that Stalin was a leader to us, he was a legend.' Like many old men, he was reluctant to acknowledge, as did most people in Russia by then, that Stalin was a tyrant who sent millions to their death. His companion, an erect old man, interjected, 'There's a saying in the church – don't speak ill of the dead.' One of three men who regularly worked as extras for Mosfilm recalled filing through the Hall of Unions almost at a trot and seeing Stalin's daughter Svetlana standing near his body as it lay in state, sorrowful Georgian music playing in the background. 'There are three reasons why Stalin was a great leader', he said, counting them off on his fingers. 'Stalin was afraid of no one, he imposed discipline, and he supported the working class.' One of his comrades interjected, 'And you could get everything in the shops.' An old woman with silver teeth said, 'We had a radio announcer in those days called Levitan. He always gave out the bad news. I'll never forget hearing him at six o'clock in the morning of March 3rd. "Stalin is dead", he said. I started to wail and cry.' Other contemporary accounts describe a city in the grip of hysteria. 'I have never seen such sombre, demented faces as that spring', wrote Nadezhda Mandelstam, writer and widow of the poet Osip Mandelstam who was driven to an early death after being denounced by Stalin. 'People were constantly snarling at one another in queues, in buses and offices.' The poet Joseph Brodsky, then thirteen, was told about Stalin's death by a weeping teacher who ordered the class to go down on their knees to receive the news that the nation had been orphaned. But at home, amid general weeping, his father had winked at him.

As the old Muscovites among the extras showed, Stalin still had his admirers. While people like Yevtushenko tried to lay the ghost of Stalin to rest, a few rushed to defend his name. Just a couple of months before, a society had been formed to defend the dictator's memory. One of its instigators was the Leningrad teacher, Nina Andreeva, known throughout Russia for her pro-Stalin manifesto published in party newspapers when Gorbachev was out of the country in 1988, and thought for a brief spell to represent a return to the old days. It held a founding congress in Stalin's home town of Gori in Georgia in December 1989. On the same day, members of the Russian nationalist society *Yedinstvo* (unity) held a meeting at Moscow University to mark Stalin's birthday.

We buried Stalin again that day on the Moscow Boulevard, but he was still a long way from dead. I gained an insight into the extent to which he had poisoned generations of Russians when I went looking, one cold day in November 1989, for a woman called Vera Antonova-Ovseenko. It began as a search for the descendants of a famous Russian revolutionary and ended in the discovery of a whole family carrying the weight of seven decades of Soviet history, sons and daughters scarred by repression, bitterly divided and dogged by the shadow of Stalin's *palachi*, his executioners who still walked the streets of Moscow, pensioners with good state pensions. The quest arose from a fragment of film I saw on television showing the storming of the Winter Palace in Petrograd in 1917. The scene froze at the historic moment when a young Bolshevik leader, Vladimir Antonov-Ovseenko, triumphantly arrested the provisional government and proclaimed power in the name of the revolution. Antonov-Ovseenko was no ordinary revolutionary. He was a former tsarist officer whom John Reed described in *Ten Days that Shook the World* as 'thin-faced and long-haired, a mathematician and chess player'. He went on to fight in the Russian Civil War and to represent the Soviet Union abroad as a distinguished diplomat. In 1937, however, Stalin recalled him from Spain and had him shot on trumped-up charges. His crime was a past association with Stalin's exiled and murdered rival, Leon Trotsky. The television commentary mentioned that the children of Antonov-Ovseenko were still alive. They clearly had a fascinating tale to tell.

For son Anton, then sixty-nine and a noted historian and author of books about Stalin and Beria, it was a bitter one. He had been arrested in 1940 as the son of an 'enemy of the people' and spent most of the next thirteen years in five different prison camps. He lived on the Frunzenskaya embankment in Moscow. By an irony of fate, this secluded region of nine-storey apartment blocks, set among birch groves, was largely inhabited by former investigators, camp commanders and prison guards. One of them was General Leonid Raikhman, who had been in charge of Anton's investigation. Some of them could be seen on warm evenings, old men sitting on benches in the little parks playing dominoes. Stalin's former deputy, Kaganovich, born in 1903, lived there too. He shook his fist at any journalist who came near. They said that Stalin once asked Kaganovich if his brother should be shot on some charge or other. 'It's up to the police to decide', said the loyal henchman. The brother saved everyone the trouble and shot himself. Such family divisions were not uncommon in Stalin's time; the price of survival was high.

The Antonov-Ovseenko family were no exception. Anton Antonov-Ovseenko had only bitter words for his brother Vladimir and his sister Vera. 'I do not want to denounce anyone, but being an historian I am convinced the truth must be told', he said bitterly. He accused Vladimir, party secretary in a power plant, of denouncing his father.

His older sister Vera, he maintained, did not suffer either, as she denied her father in 1937. I found Vera Antonov-Ovseenko living in a ninth-floor apartment in Dmitrovsky, alleyway near Dynamo Stadium in the northern suburbs. A black-and-white photograph of her father dominated one wall of the living-room. Born in 1917, she was as old as the revolution itself, but she was plump and healthy with a soft smile. Her hair was still blonde and she was busy working as a Russian-German translator. 'My first memory of my father was during the Civil War', she said, as she sorted through old photographs and newspaper clippings. 'My mother and I were on an armoured train. It was covered with hoar frost, and big snowflakes were falling. He was wearing a huge greatcoat and an *astrakhan* hat. He was a dedicated man, always working. We lived with him for a while in the Metropole Hotel in Moscow. Lenin once held me in his arms, or so I was told. I remember watching the funeral of Lenin from the hotel window on 27 January 1924.' Life in the Metropole came to an end when her father was sent abroad as ambassador, first to Czechoslovakia, then to Lithuania. Vera was placed in a boarding-school. In 1929 disaster struck; Stalin had her mother arrested. It was a common trick of the dictator, detaining a spouse while the husband remained in high office. He held Mikhail Kalinin's wife in a prison camp while the tiny, vain, white-bearded Bolshevik was president of the Soviet Union, refusing his occasional tearful pleas for clemency.

Vera described how it happened. 'My father was abroad and we were in Odessa. My mother went out to buy butter and honey. We simply never saw her again.' She fetched a death certificate from a pile of documents. It said Rosa Antonova-Ovseenko had hung herself in prison camp on 22 February 1936. Vera was sent to a children's home. Despite the terrible fate which had befallen her mother, however, she had still retained a zealous faith in communism. She was twenty-one when the second blow fell. Her father was recalled from Spain in 1937. 'We spent an evening together', she said. 'When I tried to telephone him two days later there was no answer. They had taken him away.' After that life for Vera, then a leader of the *Komsomol*, the Young Communist League, and a teacher of German at the Aviation Institute with ambitions to become a pilot, was never to be the same again. 'I was summoned to the NKVD [Stalin's secret police] and they told me that I would not see my father for fifteen years. I was then summoned to a party meeting at the institute and asked to account for myself. I said, "It cannot be that my father is an enemy of the people. I believe that the party and government will definitely clear

up this question and clear his name."' This statement of faith in the
party apparently saved her from the same fate as her brother, but
she said, tears in her eyes, 'I never denounced my father; it was a
lie. I don't know what it is with Anton. It is terrible what he did,
saying those things. He is a very angry person.' Being the child of
an arrested person was in itself an offence, a social stigma. Vera
was expelled from the committee of the *Komsomol* and refused
permission to participate in the athletics parade in Red Square. 'But
I managed to slip in unnoticed and perform all the same.' Vera was
banned from fighting at the front when the Nazis invaded in 1941.
She was, however, recruited for the defence of Moscow and proudly
boasts of the medal received for her bravery.

Nevertheless, the surname she carried plagued her wherever she
went. 'My friends deserted me. They said it was too dangerous even
to talk to me. No one would give me a job when they saw my
papers. So I stopped using the name Antonov-Ovseenko. I wrote on
application forms that I was an orphan. But they always found out.
I had to change jobs thirty times.' If this was betrayal, denying her
father's name, it was clearly not for an outsider to pass judgement.
She continued to believe in the state and even in Stalin. When he
died, she wept. 'I thought it was the end of the world', Vera recalled.
She saw things much more clearly with the passage of time. 'They
took away my youth', she said. 'They persecuted me as the daughter
of an enemy of the people right up to the twentieth Party Congress
in 1956 when I heard Mikoyan say on the radio that my father was
rehabilitated.' The name Antonov-Ovseenko was inscribed on a roll
of honour of repressed Soviet diplomats, just inside the main doors of
the ministry of foreign affairs in Moscow, placed there in 1989 at the
behest of Foreign Minister Eduard Shevardnadze. Anton, along with
the sons of other repressed revolutionaries, Yuri Bukharin and Yuri
Tomsky, meanwhile continued campaigning for the full rehabilitation
of their fathers in the absence of a pardon in writing or evidence of
where the body lay.

Such bodies could be found in any one of dozens of mass graves
of Stalin's victims which were exposed in different parts of the Soviet
Union in 1989 and 1990. The first one I visited was in the forest of
Bykovnya, just outside Kiev. Tens of thousands of bodies had been
unearthed there with bullets in their heads. It was a warm Saturday
afternoon when I dismissed the taxi I had taken from the Ukrainian
capital and walked into the forest. It was damp and deserted and
deathly quiet; it felt like a place of evil. There were humps on the forest
floor where thousands of skeletons lay just beneath the surface. The

bodies had first been located during the war when rich grass began to grow in formerly arid sandy soil. Local people said a strange mist used to rise from among the stunted fir trees and a smell of decay lingered for years. When some of the corpses were dug up after the Nazi occupation of 1941–1943, a Soviet commission concluded, to no one's suprise, that the victims had been killed by Germans. Dozens of witnesses had now come forward to tell the true story of what happened in Bykovnya. I talked to one, Mikhail Geolospalivza, a wizened and articulate survivor of Buchenwald. He lived in a nearby village. Mikhail described how he saw the forest being fenced off in 1937, at the height of the NKVD repressions. Lorries began to drive in every night. Shots were heard throughout the hours of darkness. They never had any doubt what was going on.

Mass graves began to be found closer to home than I would have liked, two not far from my apartment in Moscow's Taganskaya Square. This part of town is close to the Lubyanka Prison where the NKVD used to shoot their prisoners at night. The bodies had to be disposed of somewhere. The first indication I got that our district was the dumping ground came from journalist-historian Alexander Milchakov. I watched him late one evening on the current affairs programme *Before and After Midnight*; he had discovered that many thousands of bodies had been buried in a secret grave in the Kalitnikovsky Cemetery beside Moscow's pet market, a ten-minute walk from *The Irish Times* office. Two years earlier, I had got to know this quiet-spoken investigative reporter, who was in his late fifties, at the founding Congress of the Soviet Memorial Society, set up by radicals to commemorate the victims of Stalin's repressions. He had taken it upon himself to track down the people who were eliminated by the NKVD, the predecessors of the KGB – the Committee for State Security.

Milchakov was driven by the memory of his father, Alexander Milchakov, who was head of the Young Communist League, the *Komosmol*, when he was arrested on Stalin's orders in 1938 and disappeared into the camps, only to be rehabilitated after the dictator's death. The more Milchakov found out, the more old people who had been afraid for years to speak out came forward to help him, including retired NKVD officers. That evening on television, Milchakov explained that some of his witnesses had told him that for several years in the 1930s, lorries with their bloody cargoes from the Lubyanka, passing through Taganskaya Square on their way, had driven regularly to Kalitnikovsky Cemetery. I went down the next day to have a look. Beyond a set of metal gates, I found an ancient, wooded graveyard covering several acres. It was a dense, gloomy maze of monuments and metal crosses, enclosed by waist-high railings. It was November 1989 and the first snow lay heavily on the mourners' benches and on bunches of frost-blackened marigolds. The flakes clung to the domes of the 150-year-old Kalitnikovsky Church, inside which people were pushing backwards and forwards as a funeral service took place at one end and several christenings at the other. The news of the secret of the graveyard, where the bodies had been buried in a secluded corner, was being passed on by word of mouth. Visitors – Yevgeny Yevtushenko, camera around his neck, among them – arrived and held whispered consultations with the *babushkas* in the graveyard to find out where the mass grave was located. They gossiped about the witnesses, who included an old woman who described how, as a young girl, she and her sister used to hide in the trees of the cemetery in the summer evenings. They saw lorries arriving from the direction of Taganskaya Square along Skoto-Progonnaya Street. The name meant 'the street along which cattle are driven'. At the cemetery two soldiers in uniform would open the tail gate of the trucks, men in rubber aprons would throw naked bodies of men and women into a gully, and the soldiers would cover them with a thin layer of earth. They saw this happening during the summer nights of 1934, 1935, 1936 and 1937. Her father told her the bodies came from the Lubyanka Prison and never to say what she had seen. Regular but mute witnesses to the terrible nightly activity were the sad-faced icons of Christ and the Mother of God, staring out over the scene from the wall above the high, black, metal doors of the church, which was known as the Church of All Sorrows. I went to see Milchakov and asked him who lay buried in Kalitnikovsky. Their names are not known, he said, but they were thought to include thousands of party members purged following the murder of Leningrad party chief Sergei Kirov on 1 December 1934.

What we were unaware of was that some of the lorries did not go as far as the cemetery beside the pet market. As the terror continued into the late 1930s, new sites were sought out by Stalin's *palachi*. The night-time traffic from the Lubyanka began taking a different route. Some of the lorries skirted Taganskaya Square, turned down by the Moscow River and pulled up at the ancient Novospassky Monastery. This was one of my favourite places in Moscow. Its green onion domes could be seen over the poplar trees and apartment blocks across the road from my apartment. I wrote once in my newspaper that it was part of a hidden Moscow of derelict but still beautiful buildings which could only be found by going for long walks through old parts of the city. I would take visitors there and tell them the history of the monastery – how it was first built in the fourteenth century as part of a ring of fortified churches which protected Moscow's southern flank from Tatar raids. The turreted walls dated back to the sixteenth and seventeenth century and its bell tower had been added in 1762. It had not been used for worship for many decades and the gardens were dank and filled with rubble and the brickwork was in disrepair; none of this, however, was evident from the outside. The most beautiful view of the Novospassky, or 'New Saviour', Monastery was from across an ornamental lake on the southern side, near the river embankment. From here there was a magnificent panorama of whitewashed walls perched on top of a very steep bank which rose about forty feet above the water. Trees covered the bank, except for a broad stretch about one hundred feet long, where nothing but weeds grew on the grey earth. Above this patch, rising aloft over the centre of the monastery wall, was a six-sided tower with a pointed roof made of wooden strips in the old Russian style. In the winter it was a magical sight, with children skating on the ice. In warmer weather, people strolled along the path which surrounded the pond, or sunbathed at the foot of the bank. I would occasionally walk down from my office with a book and sit by the pond.

In May 1990, Milchakov began to expose the secrets of the Novospassky Monastery. The bank where no trees would grow contained, he told me, layer upon layer of bodies, the remains of thousands of people executed during the terror. This time he could state the names of the victims with greater certainty. They were leaders of the *Comintern*, the International Communist Organisation, set up to spread communism throughout the world and which, in the late 1930s, was ruthlessly purged of 'the enemies of the people'. The people whose bodies were buried in the bank came from all over the world. One of them was John Penner, an activist of the American Communist Party who disappeared when studying in the Soviet capital. They also included Charles Johnson, John Bennet and Max Goldfarb from England, and the skeletons of Herman Remmele, Fritz Schultke, Herman Schubert and Leo Fleig, leaders of the 842 German anti-fascists arrested in April 1938 in Moscow and never seen again. Also dumped in the bank was the body of Bela Kun, the legendary communist figure who led a short-lived Hungarian Soviet Republic in 1919. Here too among the victims of the death chambers of the NKVD were Hungarian party leaders Dezhe Bokan and Laiosh Madyar; the secretary of the Yugoslavia Communist Party, Vladimir Chopich; Romanian Communist Party figures Marcel Pauker and Alexander

Dobrodzhanu; Polish Communist Party member Vera Kostysheva; and leading Italian communist Edmondo Peluso, one of 120 members of the Italian Communist Party wiped out by Stalin. Several thousand foreign communists involved in the *Comintern*, the *Profintern*, the Peasants' International, the Young People's International and the Women's Organisation were living in Moscow at the time. Historians believed 90 per cent were eliminated. Their crime in Stalin's eyes was that they represented a threat to his domination of the communist world, or were inconveniently opposed to fascism at a time when Stalin was doing a deal with Hitler.

One who survived was Leopold Trepper, the famous Polish Jew who spied for the Soviet Union in Nazi-occupied West Europe. He recounted in his memoirs, *The Great Game*, the terror of those days. 'At night in our university, where militants from all countries were living, we used to stay awake until three o'clock in the morning. At exactly that hour, headlights would pierce the darkness and sweep over the facades of the buildings. "They're here." "They're here." When we heard that cry a wave of anxiety would run through the dormitories. Standing at the windows, stomachs knotted with insane terror, we would watch for the cars of the NKVD to stop.'

Milchakov discovered what nobody had guessed before, that the Novospassky Monastery had been a prison and place of execution for those *Comintern* members rounded up in the predawn hours. A NKVD man called Petrovich had testified to him how the prisoners were taken to shower baths which had been rigged up in the Znameny Church within the walls. There they were individually washed and measured and then told to sit on a slab. Behind them a tiny hatch opened and they were shot through the head. According to Petrovich, the NKVD men used an ingenious scheme to disguise the burials from the public. Deep trenches were dug round the monastery. Water pipes were laid alongside as if ready for laying. At night the bodies would be lowered into a trench, attached by the throat and legs to planks of wood so that they could be arranged in compact rows. The pit would be filled in, the pipes moved to a different place and a new trench dug.

I went down to the monastery after Milchakov made public this catalogue of horrors. It was a warm Sunday afternoon, but there were less people around than usual. Three old women seated on a bench outside the nearby block of flats – where I had seen an arson attack on a co-operative shop a few months earlier – refused to discuss the revelations. People who minded their own business in Stalin's time didn't get into trouble said one. A middle-aged woman carrying a handbag was standing alone on top of the bank. The truth about the past must be told, she said, otherwise perestroika was meaningless. She felt keenly aware that the evil still lived on. She had a ninety-year-old neighbour who had worked with Beria, Stalin's secret police chief. The old lady had remarked to her once, 'Many mistakes were made in those days. Now we've got to make sure that perestroika means we should only shoot the right people next time.'

I will never lose my attachment to the Taganskaya district. For me it was my home and the heart of Moscow. But there was a shadow over it now. A visit to the pet market would never again be such an innocent pleasure, and it would be impossible to walk in the Kalitnikovsky graveyard without thinking of the dead bodies and the men in rubber aprons. As for the Novospassky Monastery, the magic of the view across the pond to the castellated walls and the six-sided tower had gone forever.

Ironically, on the eve of these discoveries, the legacy of Stalin was officially removed from my neighbourhood. The administrative district in which I lived in Moscow was known as the Zhdanovsky region, named after Stalin's cultural commissar of the 1940s who enjoyed, among other things, a reputation for anti-Semitism. As glasnost revealed how unpleasant a character he was, people began more and more to resent living under his name and agitated for it to be discarded in favour of the old name of Tagansky. I learned one day that a meeting was to take place in the hall of the meat factory club, just beside the Kalitnikovsky Cemetery, to discuss whether or not to drop the name Zhdanov. The announcement was a hand-written notice stuck on the door to my apartment block and on other buildings nearby. Many of the pieces of paper were torn down shortly after they appeared. Inside the hall half-a-dozen young organisers had pinned a banner across the back of the stage which said, 'Get rid of the name of Stalin's side-kick from the map of the city – give Zhdanov region a worthy name.' Most of the 150 people who squeezed into the rows of tip-up seats clearly approved of this call, but Zhdanov, or Stalin, still had some support in the area, mainly in the form of a few angry, thick-set middle-aged men and a couple of noisy women, egged on by a handful of members of *Pamyat*, the anti-Semetic Russian nationalist organisation. From the start they cat-called and heckled as the bespectacled young chairman in a blue sweater said that people like Zhdanov had yet to be called to account for the massive repressions under Stalin. 'What evidence have you? Where are the documents?' they shouted. A fat woman in a black plastic coat cried, 'I've lived here forty years. What right have you to take away the name of Zhdanov, an historic figure?'

Eventually the meeting got underway with a vote to restrict speeches to three minutes. A succession of people began trooping up to the microphone on the stage. In typical Russian fashion, many veered far from the topic of discussion. One man was wildly cheered when he finished an oration with the words, 'All power to the Soviets, and I mean all, and I mean power, and I mean Soviets.' Then the figure of Andrei Voznesensky, in a white polo-neck jumper and grey jacket, made his way to the stage. A roar of approval and foot-stamping greeted the sight of one of Russia's most beloved modern poets. The man in front of me shouted to his friends, 'Make sure those bastards don't interrupt him.' At first Voznesensky was heard in silence. 'Was not Zhdanov a member of Stalin's circle during the repression', he asked, 'just as Himmler was one of Hitler's acolytes. Thousands of victims were shot and are buried in Kalitnikovsky Cemetery. How many death warrants had Zhdanov himself signed?' Suddenly a voice cried out, 'How do you know all this?' It belonged to a red-faced, bald *Pamyat* member, who called himself Smirnov. 'It's all in the archives', replied Voznesensky. Other shouts came from the centre of the hall. 'What documents have you? What proof?' People everywhere stood up in their seats and shouted at each other, and the fifty-five-year-old poet left the stage, almost tripping and falling in confusion. A black-bearded lawyer then took the microphone. 'What documents do you need? In Minsk there are dead bodies, corpses. That's the evidence.' Smirnov was then allowed to take the stage. He theatrically produced papers from inside his jacket and waved them in the air. 'I have documents here, they have none', he shouted, and began a tirade against Jews. The chairman shoved him aside and grabbed the microphone. 'The constitution forbids stirring up racial or national hatred', he said loudly. Smirnov trotted off the stage. As he passed Voznesensky, he poked the poet in the chest and waved the documents in his face. There was pandemonium. Everywhere people were shouting in outrage at the assault on the poet. There was pushing and shoving round the *Pamyat* group in the centre of the hall. A young man, trembling with rage, was pulled away by the organisers. 'It's just what they want', they shouted. The chairman called for a vote to throw Smirnov out if he continued with his provocations. It was passed by a show of hands and the hall began to calm down. A grey-haired, dignified old lady took the stage. 'I'm not in my first youth', she said. She had lived in Leningrad when Zhdanov was party boss there. He had sent many

people to Siberia, great writers and scientists. Who was Zhdanov?'
she asked. 'We know who Gagarin and Kutuzov were [other names
on Moscow maps]. But Zhdanov was only a functionary. Why keep
his name?' There was loud applause. Another speaker reminded us
that Zhdanov had insulted the great poet, Anna Akhmatova, calling
her 'half-nun, half-harlot'. An old man, who had to pause for breath
with every phrase, said, 'I am ashamed that my generation supported
Stalin. He suppressed twelve million people. One of the tsars repressed
only forty people in his whole life.' He added to laughter, 'The only
thing Zhdanov is known for is that in this region named after him
sausages have only 2 per cent meat.' There was more confusion when
the fat woman in the plastic coat took to the stage and would not
leave. No one could make out what she was saying. Eventually two
resolutions were passed, with only a dozen or so dissentions. The
meeting recommended that the government should drop the name
Zhdanov and throw out all the other city names associated with
Stalin. As people filed out I went over to Smirnov, standing in a
corner surrounded by his mob with sweat dribbling off his bald
pate on to beetle-dark eyebrows. I asked Smirnov what was in
the documents he had been waving about. He pulled them out
and showed me a long lists of names. 'Look at those surnames',
he hissed, stabbing the paper with trembling fingers. 'These are the
names of the NKVD men who did the killings', he said. 'They are
all Jews.'

Smirnov become a regular, menacing figure at such meetings around
Moscow. Eventually he went too far. The last time I saw him was at
10.00 p.m. on Friday morning, 12 October. He was standing in the
dock of the courtroom on the third floor of the Moscow district
court, with five armed guards facing him. He was not Russian but
Georgian, and his name was not Smirnov, but Ostashvili, the court
heard. He was charged with inciting racial hatred by leading a gang
into the Writers' Union Club in Moscow the previous January and
breaking up a meeting of the proreform *Aprel* group of writers while
screaming threats against Jews. He was sentenced to two years in
prison camp. Six months later, on 26 April 1991, his ignominious
career came to an end when he was found hanging in the Tverskin
prison compound north of Moscow. The authorities said he had
committed suicide.

On 17 January 1989, the Communist Party Central Committee
announced that the name of Andrei Zhdanov was to be removed by
decree from all streets, districts, institutions and cities throughout the
Soviet Union named in his honour. Our district was named Tagansky

once more. Many of the relatives of the millions exterminated by Stalin, furthermore, were at last able to lay their dead to rest. A memorial stone to the victims of the 'totalitarian regime' was unveiled outside the KGB headquarters in Moscow's Derzhinsky Square on 30 October 1990, the day of the political prisoner. Thousands of people heaped bouquets of carnations and roses on to the memorial, a grey stone four feet high on a plinth of polished granite which had been brought from the Solovetsky Islands in the White Sea, the scene of a forced labour camp. Many were middle aged and elderly with childhood memories of the midnight knock and the disappearance of parents into the grim six-storey Lubyanka, then controlled by Stalin's NKVD. Mourners held up candles and black-and-white family photographs as five robed Russian Orthodox priests led by a former dissident, Father Gleb Yakunin, conducted a religious service to commemorate the countless dead and missing. The sound of requiem music and the scent of incense filled the darkened square, and snowflakes drifted into the lights of a dozen television crews as people crushed forward with bouquets. The ceremony was conducted only yards away from the black fifty-foot statue of Felix Derzhinsky who founded the secret police. It was business as usual in the Lubyanka where several floors were lit by electric light, and no KGB officers looked out at the Russian flags and gold icons held high over the crowd, though some attended in a private capacity. Father Yakunin called for a government founded on Christian principles and asked the crowd of several thousand to pray to God for a better life in Russia.

'We've waited a long time', said sixty-nine-year-old Marina Suslova as she knelt and placed a candle on the shining granite surface of the plinth, placed there by the Memorial Society founded to commemorate the victims of repression. Both her parents had disappeared into the hands of the NKVD in 1938. With tears in her eyes, Yelena Bergavinova, fifty-four, told me, 'I have been waiting all my life to honour the memory of my parents.' Her father, Sergei Bergavinov, head of the political bureau of the Communist Party, was shot in December 1937 on a charge of plotting against Stalin, and her mother exiled to Siberia, where she died. 'I had nowhere to bring flowers to', she said, 'until now'.

'Yevtushenko buries Stalin', said a newspaper headline in Moscow on 27 November 1990. It referred to *Stalin's Funeral*, which was now finished and premiering in the Luzhniky Sports Stadium that day. At last I was able to see the relevance of the crowd scenes in Trubnaya Square in which I had participated (and to view my début in a Soviet film, though if I had blinked I would have missed it). It had starred two brilliant teenage actors, Denis Konstantinov and Marina Kalinichenko, who played the part of young people meeting at Stalin's funeral. The film also featured Vanessa Redgrave as an American photo-journalist and Albert Todd as an American diplomat. It centred on that terrible stampede in the boulevard when thousands tried to see Stalin's cortège passing through nearby streets. It was frightening enough taking part in the re-enactment. Yevtushenko, fifty-seven lived through the horror.

'I was there; I saw every detail of it', he told us before the première. 'People were killed when they were crushed against the sides of lorries and lamp standards. It was an apocalyptic sight.'

There was no documentary film evidence, however, of the scenes the poet witnessed and which he recreated on the screen: girls being trampled to death; a ring being stolen from a woman who couldn't move her arms; people dropping into a sewer full of rats. It was news to many cinemagoers in the stadium that people had died at Stalin's funeral. This had never been officially admitted. The film was a metaphor for a society so mesmerised by Stalin that even after his death it was not easy to breathe, and people continued to fall and die in the faceless crowd. An evil character symbolising Stalinism stalked the screen, turning up as informer, interrogator, grave digger and executioner. In the film's closing scenes, he ran through an alley and suddenly found himself in 1990 Moscow. A demonstration was passing. Radicals were holding up a banner warning, 'Stalin still lives'.

Stalin's Funeral turned out to be the most powerful anti-Stalin film to appear in the Soviet Union. In making it, Yevtushenko, the country's unofficial poet laureat, was being true to the Russian tradition of the artist as political commentator, and the poet as chronicler of morality as well as soothsayer of doom. A flamboyant figure, still slim and good-looking at fifty-seven, he believed that Stalin was a great hypnotist. People in modern Russia turned to doctor-hypnotists like the popular television stars Kashpirovsky and Chumak, he pointed out. In the climate of political apathy of 1990, they might again turn to a political-hypnotist. Yevtushenko was twenty when Stalin died. He described his horror once at discovering, years later during the Brezhnev period, how ignorant young people were about Stalin. When he was talking to students around a camp fire in Siberia, one of them ventured that Stalin had arrested perhaps twenty people, another about 200. Another said, 'It seems to me about 10,000.' 'When I told them the figure is reckoned not in thousands but in millions they did not believe me', he recalled.

Yevtushenko's film was part of a life-long quest to expose the evil of Stalinism. 'If the truth is replaced by silence', said the poet, 'silence actually is a lie.'

9

No Russians Served Here

A JOSTLING mob crowded the pavements; dozens more crushed into a roped-off area behind the plate-glass windows – and this was just the international press corps who had turned up on 31 January 1990 for the world's most publicised opening of a hamburger joint, a McDonald's in Moscow's Pushkin Square.

Nothing symbolised better the submission of the Russian capital to the ways of the vulgar capitalist world, and revealed the changing face of a city which had for seventy years rejected advertising and neon, than the establishment of this high-street symbol of fast-food. It wasn't just another McDonald's, either. It was the biggest of the 10,000 McDonald's in the world, seating 900 people, a gleaming arena of Americana grafted on to a square dominated by a bronze statue of Russia's most famous lyric poet, Alexander Pushkin. Mayakovsky, a twentieth-century Soviet poet, predicted before he died that he would join Pushkin in the square with the words, 'After death we'll stand, almost side by side, you under "P" and I under "M."' The 'M', however, was to be the golden arches of McDonald's. Before the ribbon was cut that mild January morning (the newly installed eighteen by thirty-six foot Coca-Cola sign across the square had flashed up one degree centigrade on its electronic thermometer) US television crews assembled dozens of bright, shining young Russian employees in peaked maroon caps, smiling hard as instructed, and got them to chorus 'Good morning, America', waving in turn for ABC, NBC, CBS and CNN breakfast shows. They had been chosen, said George Cohen, president of McDonald's, for their adherence to 'QSC and V'– quality, service, cleanliness and value. Human-size Donald Ducks and Goofeys paraded outside while smiling executives inspected the twenty-seven checkout tills and the milk-shake machines. Some smiled into walkie-talkies. The four Soviet managers smiled as they had been taught at the Institute of Hamburgerology in Canada, from which they had graduated before completing post-graduate courses at Hamburger University in Oak Brook, Illinois, where all four made the dean's honour's list.

The company didn't just have a café; McDonald's also had a farm, outside Moscow, where it had already grown 1,200 metric tonnes of russet burbank potatoes, the variety best suited to the *kartofel fri* which accompanied the *gamburger* or *beeg mak*. It had also set up a plant, owned jointly by the Moscow City Council, equipped to process each week 32,165 kilograms of local beef, one million buns and 20,350 litres of pickles. The first fifty customers that day were boys and girls in the care of the Soviet Children's Fund. As they filtered past the smiling executives, an American voice called out from the press enclosure, 'Are they orphans?' A smiling McDonald's woman smiled back, 'If they're orphans, I'll let you know.' They were.

The establishment of a McDonald's in Moscow was the logical conclusion of a process which had begun in Moscow a couple of years earlier. When I arrived in the Soviet capital it had changed hardly at all from the city I first saw in 1980. The shops and offices were as shabby as ever, the restaurants as impenetrable and the cafés few and far between. Service was slow and quality was mediocre. The Communist Party slogans, which had decorated the city for years, were still in place, proclaiming: 'Workers of the World Unite', and: 'Forward with the Communist Party'.

As if anticipating that such exhortations would sit uneasily with free enterprise and capitalist neon, the signs were taken down one day in early 1988 without any fanfare. A mural of a smiling Soviet family on the gable end of a building across Marksistskaya Street was suddenly no longer visible from my apartment, only bare brick. Workmen came with a lorry and dismantled a metal billboard held up by four poles on the opposite side of the road, on which square-jawed mechanics in spotless overalls had urged discipline in work. Driving round the city during the following week, I found that the *Slava Kommunismu* signs had gone except where they had been carved in concrete.

The co-operative cafés, the first to encroach on the culinary desert of Moscow Streets, began appearing in the city in growing numbers around this time. One of the first had opened under the windows of our apartment block, on the corner of a side road in Taganskaya Street. I spotted a notice one day above a newly installed wooden door, saying *Skazka*, the Russian word for fairy tale. I pushed it open and found inside a clean little café offering hot dishes of chopped mushrooms with onions in long-handled metal dishes, Georgian bread stuffed with melting cheese and small fat pancakes called *oladyi* on to which customers were ladeling sour cream at chest-high tables. The girl behind the counter was taking orders quickly and efficiently. The prices were about four times those of a state café, a fact which, after the first rush of curious customers, kept the numbers down and engendered some ill-will among people used to fixed prices. Once or twice when I was having a late breakfast at one of the tables, someone would walk in off the street, look at the menu and shout a few insults at the staff. Thus I learned the Russian word *obdiralovka*, meaning rip-off. Many Russian people were convinced that the co-operatives bought their produce not in the markets as they were obliged to do, but from the back doors of state stores at subsidised prices, leaving the shelves bare for the ordinary shoppers. Indeed, as time went by I spotted workers from another co-operative calling at the back of the Tagansky supermarket for some suspicious-looking transactions. The *Skazka* went through several experimental phases, its menu reflecting what was available on each day and on the state-of-the-art technology on which the co-operative could lay its hands. The *oladyi* machine broke down and was eventually thrown out and an Italian ice-cream machine took its place. After a couple of months the director, Sergei Kutuzov, a slender businessman in a neat suit, opened a thirty-two-seat restaurant upstairs, specialising in traditional Russian fare, with an evening floor show, including a scantily clad contortionist to compete with the Vysotsky Bar down the road.

For the city's foreign community, the appearance of such restaurants signalled a culinary revolution, a chance to eat out without having to endure the pop groups and drunken brawls which characterised Moscow's state restaurants. The cost of an evening meal of pickled garlic and cucumber followed by *pelmeni*, or meat in mushroom sauce, was beyond the pockets of ordinary Muscovites, however, and the *Skazka's* upstairs restaurant quickly became one of the most up-market establishments in Moscow. I noticed one day that a handwritten sign had been affixed to the restaurant door to say that it was closed for 'sanitation purposes', but this, like the name *Skazka*, turned out to be a convenient fairy tale. Shortly afterwards, a fleet of black limousines pulled up and the then US secretary of state, George Schultz, stepped out. He was taking a break from disarmament talks to see a little of the new private enterprise at work. Afterwards Sergei had a picture of himself and a well-fed Shultz put on the wall, and raised the prices on the menu still further.

All around the city centre co-operative restaurants were established in the following months. A Jewish café, the first since before the war, was opened at Dubininskaya Street beside the Paveletskaya railway station, specialising in stuffed fish and strudel. A Georgian restaurant, the *U Pirosmani*, opened beside the Novodevichy Monastry, selling Georgian *hachapuri* and *satsivi*.

Then the co-ops went a step further. After a year in business,

I noticed a new, brightly lit sign outside the *Skazka* one snowy evening. It advertised Gold Fassel lager. Foreign alcoholic drink was unknown in these restaurants. The *Skazka* had broken new ground by entering into a contract with Austrian suppliers to provide lager with its meals. However, it could be ordered only by customers with hard currency, and as the *Skazka* was not licenced to handle dollar bills this meant payment for the beer had to be made separately by credit card, even if only for one tin, which was delivered luke-warm to the table. There was suddenly an apartheid among the customers, between those who could buy beer and those who couldn't. The *Skazka* began to encourage payment by credit card for everything in order to secure hard currency, and set about discouraging Russian customers. Soon, as far as local people were concerned, it was a restaurant for foreigners only.

This apartheid was to become a symbol of perestroika for most Muscovites. It resulted from state laws under which Soviet citizens were prohibited from possessing foreign currency. At least in the *Skazka* the customers were not segregated. This was not the case in Moscow's most celebrated co-operative restaurant at 36 Kropotskinskaya Street, once the town residence of Prince Trubyetskoy, situated across town in a well-preserved nineteenth-century street near the foreign ministry. Written about in almost every newspaper in the world as the first private restaurant in Moscow since the revolution, its back rooms were inevitably reserved for hard-currency customers who could enjoy their veal cutlets in regency-decorated rooms with marble fireplaces and wash it down with French wine while Russians peered in, fruit juice in hand. The Russians were eventually barred altogether in January 1991 when the whole restaurant became 'credit card only'. The segregation policy was formalised by joint enterprises, businesses set up by Soviet and foreign partners which brought a new wave of restaurants to the city, most aimed at the hard-currency customer so that the foreign partner could repatriate a share of the profits. The first was the Delhi, an Indian restaurant which opened near the Moscow Zoo in July 1987. The two shareholders were the Soviet Foreign Trade Ministry and the Indian Tourist Authority. The restaurant had two sections, one for people with roubles, the other for foreigners with credit cards. The Delhi at least introduced higher standards and new culinary experiences for Soviet customers who had never before heard of *rogan josh* or *murgh tikka* and provided the stimulus of competition, which is what the reform allowing joint enterprise was intended to do.

The same could not be said for the Glazur Restaurant which opened on the ring road. The finest restaurant in Moscow, it had stickers on the front door telling passers-by that payment should be made with foreign-currency credit cards issued by Visa, Access, Eurocard, *Kultakurtti*, JCB, Diners' Club or American Express. There were more extreme examples. A joint venture 'British pub' with a dimly lit interior, old wall engravings and a dart board opened in the Soviet Trade Centre on the river embankment and advertised itself in the English language edition of *Moscow News* as 'helping to bring the John Bull spirit to the Soviet Union'. But practically no residents of the Soviet Union could get near the hard-currency Red Lion. The entrances to the trade centre were guarded by burly attendants who admitted only foreigners or people on official business. The US firm of Baskin Robbins opened an ice-cream parlour at the front of the Rossiya Hotel near Red Square in July 1988, but any Russian child attracted by the prospect of an almond or rum-raisin ice-cream found a notice on the glass door saying *valuta* (hard currency) only. As roubles were not convertible into foreign currency, foreign companies mostly looked for their profits from tourists or resident foreigners. Some got round the ethical problem by working both markets. Louis Piancone of Roma Food Enterprises, whose mobile Astropizza became a familiar summer sight on the river embankment, agreed with the city council to sell pizzas for hard currency three days of the week, and for roubles three days. McDonald's was the exception to the apartheid system. It charged roubles and became part of the life of the Soviet capital.

To revive and modernise the city, foreign restoration firms were invited to restore some of Moscow's crumbling hotels. One of the first to disappear behind a forest of scaffolding and hoarding was the Metropole, a grand five-storey edifice built between 1899 and 1903 across Sverdlovsk Square from the Bolshoi Theatre. It was already shut when I arrived and in a dangerous state of disrepair. The Metropole was home, up to the Second World War, for many of my foreign correspondent predecessors. Harrison Salisbury of *The New York Times* described life in the Metropole in the 1940s as 'a little like living in a prison run by a mad hatter. We had adjoining rooms; we ate together, travelled together, drank together, we suffered together and fought together, we knew who slept with whom and who didn't and when the partners changed. I used to say that you could put a blindfold on me and set me down anywhere in the Metropole and I could say where I was by sniffing – which floor, which corridor, which room. I knew the rank humanoid smell of the fifth-floor dormitory; the scent of the raspberry-tinted wax put to the floors by the polishers (they did it with soft rags tied around their old carpet slippers); the wood smoke of the courtyard; the doggy odour of food being cooked by the Uzbek couple on the third floor; the vodka fumes seeping around the locked door of the Japanese consul; the gaseous cabbage-cooking on the fourth-floor back corridor; the acid polish applied to the brass rails of the second-floor skywell; the rancid grease of the elevator shaft. The Metropole was a museum of smells and I knew each one.'

Muscovites loved the old hotel, the upper part of which was decorated with coloured ceramic panels designed by the artist Mikhail Vrubel on the theme of 'the dream princess'. One of the finest pieces of turn-of-the-century art nouveau, it was considered a world-class hotel in prerevolutionary days when Tsar Nicholas I would occasionally grace the fourth-floor tea-room with his royal presence. The Metropole was fought over during the Bolshevik rising. A high relief depicting the advance of revolutionary forces was mounted on the side facing Karl Marx Prospect, with the words, 'Here in November 1917, Red Guards and revolutionary soldiers led by M V Frunze engaged in fierce fighting against the cadets entrenched on the approaches to the Kremlin.' For a time the hotel was used as the second house of Soviets. Lenin made speeches there, reported by the American journalist John Reed. Lenin's comrade Yakov Sverdlov worked from one of the rooms overlooking the Bolshoi in 1918–1919. In those days the following slogan was mounted over the whole width of the facade: 'The dictatorship of the proletariat alone can emancipate humanity from the oppression of capital – Lenin.' In later years the Metropole became an Intourist Hotel and was rebuilt inside several times until repair work became almost a permanent feature. *Smith's Guide to Moscow*, written in 1974, notes that, 'Intourist has been trying to modernise the place, but inside, among the patchwork of renovation, you can still enjoy some of the old splendour. In the great dining-room are crystal chandeliers with plenty of sparkle, cut-glass mirrors, art nouveau lamps and lots of palms.'

The patching up could go on only for so long. The Soviet Foreign Trade Association contracted the Finnish firm Petrusyuktyume in May 1986 to carry out a sixty-million dollar reconstruction. Most of the top floor was unusable because of damp. Some rooms were infested with mice and cockroaches. The cellars were stuffed full of rubbish, mostly old bones, and were crawling with rats. I called in one day to see the work in progress. There was a curious inscription above the second floor, in all probability placed there by the Englishman William Walcot who built the hotel. It read, 'The old story again – on completing a house, you discover that you've learned something.' What that was he did not say, but the words were found particularly apt by project manager Kalevi Hyvunen who, on completing the restoration, had learned something about Soviet bureaucracy. The contract stipulated that the internal floors and walls be stripped out and replaced while the facade be retained, along with the tea-room and the dining-room, with its huge, domed glass roof. But coinciding with perestroika was a growing campaign to preserve historical Russia. Preservationists became interested in the unique character of the art decoration in the old rooms, the pattern of the stucco moulds, the cornices, handles, hinges, wall colours, old plaster work and wooden cross beams. The inspector of restoration work, architect Leonid Nenaglyadkin, intervened, complaining that while the new hotel would be modern and comfortable, 'It will be completely out of the style of the Metropole. Instead of the oak parquet there will be a synthetic floor cover. The window sills made of a rare, valuable marble will be exchanged for identical ones of artificial material, while the old marble is smashed with hammers. The cast iron staircase with the famous *Kaslinsk* casting has already been thrown on to a dump.' He didn't blame the Finnish company, which he said was honestly following the contract – the oak parquet was only discovered when they had stripped away several layers of parquet flooring – but the lack of foresight and control exercised by the city's cultural authorities. 'What I've learned too', said Kalevi in his portable office beside the Metropole, 'is that it is normal in the Soviet Union for a client to change his mind.'

The work was delayed by endless arguments involving the Soviet Ministry for Culture, the Foreign Trade Association and the Historical Monuments Department over such matters as whether or not to restore the cracked 'dream princess' ceramics or to send them to a museum and install a copy. 'The biggest problem is to find some one person who can make a decision. Very often we get many responsible people together talking, talking, talking', said the project manager. Nenaglyadkin protested, 'The Metropole is a unique and outstanding masterpiece of history and architecture. As such it will cease to exist and become just an average good hotel.' The hotel was due to re-open in early 1989. The scaffolding only came down in the summer of 1990 to reveal the restored 'dream princess' and didn't finally open until the spring of 1991.

No such problems attended the reconstruction of the Berlin Hotel across the road by a joint venture formed by Intourist and the Finnish airline, Finnair. It was renovated by the Yugoslavian company, Sipad, and opened in 1989 under its original name – the Savoy – to become the first Western hotel in Moscow with international standard services.

Visitors could wander around peering at the erotic statues of Grecian women in various states of undress or sit in the bar and sip French champagne with shrimp salad while listening to the voice of Bernard (emphasis on 'ard') Shaw from Washington, accompanied by advertisements for Kentucky Fried Chicken on the first TV set in Moscow to receive cable news network from the USA. Hundreds crowded into the hotel for the sumptuous buffet at the opening ceremony, performed by Anatoly Lukyanov, speaker of the Supreme Soviet. For those of us there it contradicted the old adage, 'There is no such thing as a free lunch.' For many of the Soviet guests it was, however, their first and last meal in the Savoy. From that day on it was hard currency only.

Out on the streets one of the only comforts the reforms were bringing the people were co-operative lavatories. The city's 343 public toilets had fallen into an 'unspeakable' state, according to the Moscow Soviet which decided in December 1987 to let co-operatives take some of them over. They were not only allowed to renovate them and to charge fifteen kopeks admission, but they were given coin machines from the underground metro to control the flow of people. Soon these co-op lavatories with their mirrors and potted plants became a feature of airport terminals and railway stations.

Otherwise things didn't change much in the railway stations during perestroika. They were the hub of Russian life, crowded and noisy, smelling of cheap tobacco and wood smoke from the boiler systems on the trains. Three of the busiest stations were located in Komsomolskaya Square and were constantly filled with provincial people arriving, departing or endlessly waiting. Men sat on cardboard boxes, old women with bulky shopping bags tried to rest in draughty corners, young men in imitation leather jackets and baggy jeans stood smoking in groups. Soldiers with shaven heads and overcoats like blankets waited around with the timid resignation of conscripts. Day and night hundreds of people poured out of trains from Smolensk or Ryazan or Torzhok. They trudged through puddles to board trams which rumbled and shrieked towards the city centre, or set off on foot under the railway bridge to Kalanchovskaya Street.

Even before they left the square they could see, beneath the metal bridge, a new neon sign on the far side of the road above a doorway of the Leningrad Hotel. It gleamed brightly on to the bleak pot-holed roadway and said simply in English, 'Casino'. Through that doorway, only a few feet away, was a different world. Soft music played. Men and women in elegant dress sipped cocktails around roulette tables. Pretty girls murmured, 'last bets please' in London west-end accents. One-hundred dollar chips clunked on to numbered squares and white balls clipped around roulette wheels. Waiters in black ties glided beneath crystal chandeliers and around potted plants to bring gin slings to gamblers seated at black jack tables where 'dealer will stand on seventeen, draw to sixteen', according to house rules printed on the baize cloth of the table, made by John Huxley, London. I watched a man one evening lose 1,500 dollars in two minutes at one of these tables and win back 3,000 dollars five minutes later, much to the delight of his woman companion who wore a tiny black dress which exposed long legs and hugged her generous contours. The casino, which opened in January 1990, was the ultimate symbol of how the modernisation of Moscow was tied to the pursuit of the dollar. Official gambling houses had been banned as an expression of Western decadence since the 1917 Revolution. Not only Westerners patronised the casino. Many of the players were from a tiny Russian elite to whom a whole new world had opened up which was never envisaged by the twenty-seventh Congress of the Communist Party when it endorsed Mikhail Gorbachev's reform plans. Some of the Russians playing roulette were, I discovered, returned emmigrants whose foreign passports allowed them to hold hard currency. Others, a waiter told me out of the corner of his mouth, were members of the Russian mafia who ran Moscow's protection rackets and who had access to everything, from dollars to Western cars.

Gambling itself was certainly not foreign to the Russian soul. The upper classes, according to *Baedeker's Guide to Russia*, published in 1914, 'are known for reckless gambling'. Russian literature abounded in tales of profligate wagering. The theme of Dostoevsky's *Igrok* (*The Gambler*) was possession by gambling and the fever to possess large sums of money which afflicted high society in tsarist Russia. Soviet children were brought up on such stories, like Pushkin's *Queen of Spades* in which an army officer sought to discover from a countess the secret of the three winning cards which saved her from bankruptcy. Only after she died did her ghost tell him that the secret numbers were three, seven and ace. He staked his savings on a three and then on a seven and won, but in the final round received not an ace but the queen of spades, lost everything and went mad. In the Moscow casino, a Japanese diplomat was often to be found, unaware of such cautionary tales, trying to find the winning sequence which would make him a fortune at the thirty-six-figure roulette table, where players were offered thirty-five-to-one for a winning number, or seventeen-to-one for a split number. I found him perched on his stool, peering through spectacles held slightly away from his face at sheets of paper on which he had scribbled hundreds of figures. Each time the wheel was spun, he would consult his columns of numbers and cover the table with a mosaic of chips. 'Good luck to him', said casino director Peter Maier from West Germany. 'It's perfectly normal for people to write numbers to try to find a system. But there is no system. You just need good luck and patience.' On the third night after the casino opened, Maier said, a 'very prominent' Turk found just such a combination of good luck and patience and won 35,000 dollars. The casino was jointly run by Moscow state restaurants and Modern Games of West Germany, which had two casinos in Hamburg and twelve in Yugoslavia. The croupiers were professionals on short-term visits; they were mainly from England where the continental code protecting professional secrets which penalised croupiers who moved from casino to casino did not apply.

For the masses passing through Komsomolskaya Square, the bright casino sign indicated only forbidden territory. 'It could make this area a breeding gound for communism', said a Russian friend with a cynical smile. Another place where a Russian could only be a spectator was the Soviet Union's first golf course, nine holes laid out over 2,200 yards along the banks of the Setun River whose natural hazards were a small lake, birch trees and an old Orthodox church on a hill overlooking the second tee. This also was for *valuta* only, though the forty-five-year old professional Ivan Chistyakov, who had never seen or walked round an eighteen-hole course in his life, was given theoretical training as a teacher of golf and put in charge of a class of young Russians in a school gymnasium with nets and patches of green carpet to produce the first generation of Soviet golfers. They would emerge in the 1990s to take on the world, according to the club's five-year plan. By 1995 the best of the bunch, by then in their late teens, would be sent to a professional school in La Menga, Spain. 'I know the road we have chosen is very difficult, especially to penetrate world golf', remarked Chistyakov, 'but the youngsters involved are very highly motivated and interested.' A former trainer of the USSR's alpine-skiing team, he was given instruction in golf coaching by Lars Hofwander, a Russian-speaking Swedish professional. The golf course was run jointly by the Moscow Sports Committee and a Swedish firm, Tumba International, headed by Swedish hockey veteran Sven 'Tumba' Johansson, who persuaded the footballer Pelé and the heavyweight boxing champion Mike Tyson to attend the opening ceremony. The company imported special turf from Finland and Sweden to replace the Russian pasture, which became a glutinous bog after a summer thundershower. The enterprise 'links perestroika with elitism'; so the club director, Viktor Visotsky – a sports official who had never played golf – told me in the wooden chalet which served as a clubhouse pending the completion of a proper two-storey clubhouse with locker rooms and bar. Perestroika meant encouraging Soviet children to learn the game, he said. Elitism meant making the club an almost exclusive reserve for the rich and influential. A membership gold card to gain access to all the club facilities cost 20,000 US dollars. Honorary members included Mikhail Gorbachev, Sean Connery, Prince Bernhard and Arnold Palmer. 'When you consider our climatic conditions', said Visotsky, gesturing helplessly towards the expanse of frozen snow covering the first fairway as we chatted one January morning, 'it can only ever be a seasonal sport in Russia, like football. But the main problem in getting golf established is equipment. No socialist country manufactures clubs or balls. We have to buy them for hard currency, and that's very expensive.' He sighed and added, 'Making golf clubs is not high on the economic agenda right now.' Tumba Johansson was reported to have said, tongue in cheek, 'Professional golfers abroad have asked me to slow down the club's activities; they fear the Russians are coming.'

Apartheid also affected the world of sex. Elite call-girls in Moscow were known as hard-currency prostitutes. They plied their trade outside the Intourist Hotel in Gorky Street and at the National Hotel around the corner, haughty blondes with red lipstick, thick face powder and a black spot on the cheek who would accept only foreign clients. Their very existence was denied before the emergence of glasnost. Totalitarianism has historically been marked by an official prudery towards sex or sexual displays in public. Counter-revolutions also tended to bring about a liberalisation in public attitudes to sex, accompanied by a flood of pornography. It happened in Spain after Franco and it took place in Russia under perestroika, though at a slower pace. It was different from the 1960s sexual revolution in the West, a quarter of a century earlier. In private, Russian attitudes towards sex tended to be exceedingly liberal.

The Russian cinema – open to all – led the way in pushing back the boundaries of prudery. The longest queue in Moscow, one Saturday, was at the 700-seat Burevestnik Cinema on the ring road where the film *Little Vera* was to be premièred the following day. It took us five hours standing in line to get a couple of two-rouble tickets. *Little Vera* was said to be a sensation. It was an artistic work, but had been attacked in the press as the first ever Soviet porn film, with the sex act shown on screen for the first time in a Russian-made production. Appropriately enough, it had an XX certificate, a rating for over sixteen-year-olds. Films dealing with adult themes and popular foreign imports like *Diva, Tootsie* and *Rear Window* were all branded XX. In the Soviet cinema there were no certificates indicating frank sex scenes or violence among the sixteen classifications which ranged from K for comedy to V for war. They were not envisaged in the scale of things with which the communist censors dealt. *Amadeus*, playing at the Enthusiast Cinema, had been given an E (screen version of a literary work), though the earthy story of Mozart's life could easily have merited I (history), N (morality), M (music) or even MD (melodrama).

Before the lights dimmed in the cavernous cinema with its rows of hard seats, one of the actors, Yuri Nazarov – a popular veteran of over one hundred films – walked on in front of the screen to tell us that the film had been the subject of much gossip because of its portrayal of sex. When it was shown to a trial audience in the remote far-eastern town of Komsomolsk-On-Amur, he said, someone had complained bitterly afterwards that there was only one sex scene, and not seven as he had heard. 'I assured him that there had only been one sex scene and that there had been no cuts', said Nazarov as the audience laughed politely. People had become accustomed to looking for something positive in a film, he said, but he warned, 'Everything in *Little Vera* is negative, except for love of people for each other.'

The film is set in Zhdanov, an industrial port full of noise and pollution where Vera, a brassy, bored teenager, lives with her hard-drinking father and down-trodden mother in a tiny apartment. Her life changes when she meets Seriozha at an open-air disco which degenerates into a vicious gang fight, broken up by vodka-drinking militiamen. The pair escape to Seriozha's room in a men's hostel and begin a passionate relationship. The scene showing their lovemaking is brief and would easily have passed the film censor in any West European country. But portrayal of sexual passion was new and the Moscow audience watched in total silence. A few left immediately after the sex scene. They had, after all, been told that was it.

Nudity itself was not unknown in the Soviet cinema, nor in the theatre. In Mikhail Bulgakov's classic work, *The Master and Margarita*, on stage at the Taganka Theatre not far from the cinema that same week, the actress playing Margarita appeared topless for ten minutes, an event which provoked no press comment. What did fill the newspapers, however, was news of the import of the most glitsy of Western shows which exploited sex, – the beauty contest. The first ever to be held in the Soviet Union was the Miss Moscow competition in April 1988. Soon every city and republic was staging parades of scantily clad young women, many attracted by the prospect of world tours to international beauty contests. The foreign press turned up en masse to report the first Moscow contests, where a priest, invited to join the judging panel, turned out to be a local confidence trickster. They soon became a regular feature of city life, along with erotic shows in the theatres as a cabaret atmosphere developed in the city, much like Berlin before the war.

Interestingly, Article 228 of the criminal code of the USSR stated, 'The production, advertising or spreading of pornography, or trading in pornography, is punishable by up to three years imprisonment or a fine of 300 roubles, with confiscation of the pornography and the means of production', but by 1990 Article 228 had been suspended. A walk through a Moscow metro underpass became a venture into a down-market sex shop. Life-size naked girls pouted at commuters from wall posters put up by street traders. Little huddles of people in fur hats crowded round trestle tables to flick through crudely produced booklets. One of the most popular was *300 Poses and Positions*, a dense collection of gymnastic line drawings. It competed with *Brezhnev's Lovers, 12 Word Portraits*; *Max David Sex Technique*; *Sex-Glasnost*; *Sex Digest*; *Kama Sutra*; and *12 Sex Rules for the Revolutionary Proletariat*. The October Revolution in Russia had been replaced by a sexual revolution. A preoccupation with sex pervaded all levels of the media, as the taboo on discussion of the subject evaporated. Even the party, desperately anxious to make contact with the people again, got in on the act. D H Lawrence's *Lady Chatterly's Lover*, unavailable among his collected works in Russian, was published by *Politizdat*, the party organisation which printed political speeches. An erotic show, one of many in Moscow theatres, rehearsed regularly in the house of culture belonging to *Pravda*, the party newspaper. The seamy Moscow underworld of perverted sex was exposed for the first time. *Theme*, a news sheet for sexual minorities registered with Moscow Soviet, revealed to horrified readers where people went to find fresh bodies for necrophilia and to acquire young boys for paedophiles. In the ensuing debate, people learned of cases where small boys were murdered after being 'stolen' by procurers.

With the unquenchable thirst for hard currency, prostitution also became big business in Moscow. Militia officers estimated in 1989 that there were 1,126 'elite' prostitutes in the city who served foreigners. Nine hard-currency prostitutes were killed in Moscow that year in gang wars over territory. A debate began about legalising brothels. The Moscow militia came to the conclusion that if there were brothels, or 'public houses' to use the precise Russian translation, it would be easier to control prostitution and reduce associated crimes. They pointed out that prostitution was legal in prerevolutionary Russia when public houses were governed by rules drawn up on 29 May 1844 by the Soviet Interior Ministry. These were reprinted in *Komsomolskaya Pravda* and included the following.

Brothels can be opened only with the permission of the police.

The manager of a brothel may not keep children on the premises.

Women in brothels must be over sixteen.

Students or under-age males are not allowed to enter.

Beds should be separated by a light partition or a screen.

The manager of a brothel is responsible for the exhaustion of a woman by immoderate use.

Women who contract venereal disease will be given free treatment in hospitals if admitted voluntarily. If treatment is required as a result of a complaint, the manager must pay.

Abortion is strictly forbidden among public women.

Sex was for sale in one Moscow co-operative which advertised a new service in November, the artificial insemination of women whose husbands were infertile, at a charge of eighty-six roubles. It also offered the natural method – for 300 roubles – and guaranteed 'elite descendants'.

The first erotic television programme, *Shock-Show*, was shown after midnight on 26 November 1990, though it revealed little more than the fact that Tsar Nicholas II was a nudist. That same week foreigners found that Stockman's, one of two foreign department store branches which had opened in Moscow, began offering *Playboy* on its magazine rack beside *Newsweek* and the *Helsingin Sanomat*, the management having decided they would take at face value the new rule, that what was not forbidden was allowed.

Some communist officials tried desperately to hold back the tide of Americana, as the co-operative which set up Moscow's first country-music club found out. Nothing could be more American than the country and western songs of Hank Williams, Dolly Parton, Merle Haggard, Waylon Jennings, Dwight Yoakam and Ricky Skagga, whose most devoted Moscow fans came together as co-operative partners to renovate a tiny basement cellar in the Moscow Perfume Factory, making it into a version of a wild-west saloon. The saloon was complete with half doors and kerosene lamps, featuring cowboy hats and spurs hanging on the walls, where fans could play the songs and ballads of their American stars and listen to the Russian groups which imitated country music. While the local party officials had no objection to the playing of the music, they drew a line at calling the club the Tennessee. It was too American, they said. 'They recommended that the name should be Folklore', said Vadim, one of the venture's seven partners who had just finished national service as a submariner. 'We'll call it among ourselves, "One-Eyed Joe."'

That had been in October 1988 and this petty edict was one of the last gasps of the party ideologues who had used names throughout Soviet history to propagate and solidify their ideals. Every city and town in the Soviet Union contained districts, streets, avenues and parks named after communist figures. Since St Petersburg had been renamed Leningrad in 1924, thousands of old Russian names had been replaced with the surnames of party bosses. The main street of every provincial capital was called after Lenin. Moscow was no exception to this urban Sovietisation, but under perestroika a period of reassessment of these Soviet leaders began. It started with Leonid Brezhnev, blamed for the period of stagnation during the 1970s when he was the country's leader. The Kremlin ruled on 29 December 1988 that Brezhnev's name should be dropped from the south-west Moscow district named after him. Shortly after that, the name of Zhdanov, who had been Stalin's cultural commissar, was banned. I had been living in Moscow's Zhdanovsky region and found myself, instead, in Tagansky region as it had originally been called. The town of Zhdanov, where *Little Vera* had been filmed, was renamed Mariupol again.

The process reached a climax when Moscow elected a radical council in the spring of 1990 which decided that the modernisation of Moscow meant turning the clock back. Gorky Street, the main thoroughfare of the capital where Pushkin Square and McDonald's stood, was given back its old Russian name of Tverskaya Street, which it had been called for centuries because it ran north to the city of Tver. Tver was where the map showed the city of Kalinin, on the road to Leningrad. Kalinin was changed back to Tver at the same time. Kalinin Prospect, which cut through the centre of Moscow, was renamed the New Arbat. Mikhail Kalinin had been president of the Soviet Union from 1921 to 1946. Portrayed for forty years as a statesman, he was recognised now as a brutal, weak and vain figure who helped suppress the peasants, allowed Stalin to throw his wife into a camp while he remained president, and renamed Tver after himself in 1931.

Another character, Maxim Gorky, the great writer and father of socialist realism, was acknowledged to have been a spiritual advocate of Stalinism and an apologist for the hated secret police of the time. 'The work of the *chekists* in the camps clearly demonstrates the humanism of the proletariat', he once wrote. Stalin rewarded him by giving his name to the capital's main street while he was still alive, and then (so it's said) murdered him with poisoned sweetmeats in 1936 when the old man become an embarrassment. The town of Gorky to which Andrei Sakharov was exiled in the early 1980s was given back its historic name of Nizhny Novgorod. The bitterest blow for the Communist Party finally came on 12 June 1991 when the people of Leningrad voted to change the name of the city, which had been the cradle of the revolution, back to St Petersburg. Moscow ceased to be a necropolis as the blue-painted metal signs with the names of dozens of dead generals were unscrewed from street walls. Dzerzhinsky Square, named after the founder of the secret police, was renamed Lubyanka Square. The square of the fiftieth anniversary of the October Revolution became the Manezh again. A new square was called after US civil rights activist Martin Luther King, and another after Charles de Gaulle.

And so Moscow tarted itself up by taking off its communist clothes. De-ideologisation became appropriate for a city which boasted a McDonald's and a stock exchange – opened on 16 November 1990 at 500,000 roubles a seat – but it was a nightmare for the publishers of guide-books and maps, and those who drew up railway and bus timetables. All contemporary guide-books to Moscow were made redundant, their street indices referring to names found only in history books. The 1914 edition of *Baedeker's Russia* became, once again, the only reliable manual for the traveller of the 1990s. Its maps indicated where Tver and Tverskaya street could be found. One might have expected that as communist terminology disappeared, Red Square itself would be renamed. The word red however, which in Russian can also mean beautiful, goes back to the seventeenth century and has nothing to do with the Bolshevik revolution. It is found in *Baedeker's* and therefore permissible in modern Moscow.

10

Conscience of the Nation

TWO VEHICLES moved through the centre of Moscow on a bitterly cold December day, drawing little attention from passers-by. The first was a yellow police car with flashing red lights, the second a white station wagon with ambulance markings. As the little convoy sped at a steady forty-five miles-per-hour along the river embankment, past the Kremlin and down Kalinin Prospect, policemen halted traffic so that the convoy did not have to slow down or stop. Only by sticking close behind the station wagon in *The Irish Times's* car was I able to keep up. We drove along Kutuzovsky Prospect, out the long, straight Minsk Highway, and after three miles turned right on to the Rublyovskoye Chaussee. Shortly, the two vehicles veered left down a quiet side road, and then, kicking up a little cloud of powder snow, drove into a secluded enclosure surrounded by birch trees. In the middle stood a white marble building. The station wagon backed up to the door and a body in a green bag was taken inside on a stretcher.

The building was the Kremlin's private morgue. The body was that of Andrei Sakharov, the human rights campaigner, who, up until three years previously, had lived in exile in the closed city of Gorky. He had died the day before, on 15 December 1989 in his tiny apartment at 48B Chkalov Street near Taganskaya Square, where he had held court over the years, dressed in a cardigan and slippers, for anyone persecuted by the authorities. No one was told where his body was being taken when it was carried from the apartment block past the mourners who had gathered with lit candles in the falling snow outside. The police had blocked the road to prevent anyone following the cortège. Only by chance had I come across it a few streets away and was able to discover how the state honoured the former dissident – for years reviled as a traitor – by admitting his body to the morgue reserved for the highest in the land. One of the last bodies to be brought to that marble building had been former Soviet President Andrei Gromyko. It was a measure of how the Nobel prize-winning physicist, who never flagged in his fight for human rights, had emerged from his years of isolation to become a figure honoured not only by the people but by the establishment he had castigated.

When Dr Sakharov had returned to Chkalov Street after six years in exile on 24 December 1986 with his wife, Yelena Bonner, few imagined that within the short time left in his life a largely peaceful revolution would take place on the streets of Moscow, inspired by the ideals of justice, human rights and democracy which Sakharov represented. Nothing much changed at first. Mikhail Gorbachev, already in office for twenty months, had introduced perestroika, but the control of society exercised by the Communist Party and the KGB was still absolute.

Soon after I arrived in Moscow in 1987 I saw for myself how tight a grip the security organs had on law and order. Street protests were then still banned. I got a tip-off that a demonstration was planned for the evening of 30 October at the Engles statue near the Kropotkinskaya metro station, organised by the dissident Group of Trust, a small body of human rights activists, to call for the release of all remaining political prisoners. I arrived to find an eerie scene under the yellow street lamps of the square where the towering black statue stood. Dozens of KGB men in jerkins and ski-caps strolled around eyeing the few passers-by. Police cars were parked in every side street. More agents in ski-caps mingled with militiamen around the statue. It took me a few seconds to realise why the atmosphere was so spooky. Despite the big numbers of people around, there was absolute silence. Cars and buses drove by, but in between there wasn't a sound. Nobody spoke aloud. I heard afterwards that thirty-six people on their way to the square were detained in the metro stations. The demonstration, needless to say, did not take place. On the surface it looked as if nothing had changed from the stagnant years of Brezhnev, when opposition on the streets came from a few activists willing to risk arrest, and when all attempts at outward manifestations of dissent were quickly suppressed.

But political opposition was stirring, and in the most unlikely of places. A few days later, an astute Irish post-graduate student at Moscow University, John Murray, a fluent Russian speaker, dropped by my office and mentioned some very unusual political discussion-groups which he had come across in Moscow's notoriously apathetic academic world. Political meetings outside the control of the party were unheard of. Nothing about such gatherings, organised by socialist groups called Club Perestroika, had appeared in the press, but they were now causing a stir, John said, in the colleges. On a foggy evening a few days later, we went to the Institute of Mathematics and Economics, a large, modern block of steel and concrete where the next meeting was to take place. A portly doorman examined my accreditation card suspiciously but allowed us to go to the fifth-floor conference room where about 150 academics and students had gathered. The discussion among the people wearing pullovers and leather jackets was like that at a fringe meeting of a Liberal Party conference in Britain, but given the repressive political context of the time, and with the benefit of hindsight, it clearly represented the rebirth of independent political activity in the modern Soviet Union. It was a cautious process, the organisers feeling how far they could go, suspicious that they were being manipulated by the party itself.

Apart from a few heated accusations that some speakers were in the pay of the KGB or the CIA, or both, the debate in the lecture room, with its potted plants and purple rows of seats, was little more than a seminar on economic reform and how to achieve it within the existing system. The activists pressed a number of basic demands, however. They wanted the erection of a memorial to the victims of Stalin, freedom of movement throughout the country, the release of political prisoners, and the freedom to criticise Gorbachev. Without a memorial there was no prospect of eradicating Stalinism from Soviet society, and therefore no hope of real reform, said Dmitry Leonov, an earnest, bespectacled thirty-nine-year-old engineer, one of the organisers whom we met afterwards. They were unsure how far they could go. 'Would this meeting have been possible a year ago?' I asked Dmitry. 'I don't know if it's possible now', he replied laughing. He explained, 'We are legalised to the extent that we are not illegal. Our movement is growing from the bottom up, whereas Gorbachev's perestroika is from the top down.' His long-haired, bearded colleague, Igor Mintusov, a twenty-nine-year-old scientist, smiled and said, 'It's like a game of cat and mouse. The mouse runs and the cat plays with it. The regional party committee gave us tacit support but we have no guarantees that the meetings won't be stopped and that people will come and find a closed door.' They did not see any point in objecting to the leading role of the Communist Party. In 1987 it was almost unimaginable that it could be changed. 'To talk now about challenging the existence of the party is political utopianism', said Viktor Pavlov, a thirty-year-old bearded economist and an active party member. 'People, on the one hand, are afraid to speak out. We only voice our opinions openly in our kitchens. On the other hand, they are fed up with being afraid.' 'Unfortunately, we express the view only of the intelligentsia', said Igor Mintusov. 'The masses of the people do not understand that the problems of democracy and goods in the shops are very closely related.' He was a pessimist, he said. 'A pessimist is a well-informed optimist', retorted Pavlov to laughter. 'Next Saturday', Dmitry Leonov said to me before we left, 'you should go to the Old Arbat early in the morning. You will see that we are serious.'

The pedestrian walkway in the centre of Moscow, known as the Old Arbat, was crowded as usual when I arrived, despite the heavy snow which coated the tiled surface and fringed the pictures of the pavement artists. The only traffic noise came from a cumbersome, yellow snow-plow, its horn blowing as it cut lazy swathes between the passers-by. I sensed immediately, however, that there was something in the air other than snowflakes. There were an ununsusal number of militiamen about. The crackle of police radios could be heard from the pockets of overcoated men strolling watchfully through the crowds. My old KGB friends in their jerkins and ski-caps were lounging about. At 11.00 a.m. the bespectacled figure of Leonov appeared. The scientist unfurled a large poster and held it up on the steps beneath the stone pillars of the Yakhtangov Theatre, half way down the street. Two other men detached themselves from the crowd and joined them. A couple of dozen people quickly gathered on the roadway to read the hand-printed messages which called on citizens to sign a petition for a memorial to the victims of the Stalin era as part of the campaign of the Memorial Committee of the Group for Social Initiatives, which was apparently the umbrella organisation for informal left-wing political clubs like Club Perestroika. Dmitry had a resigned look on his earnest face as he waited to be detained and taken away. Half a dozen militiamen converged on the scene, but instead of making immediate arrests began to reason with the demonstrators. One militiaman was almost apologetic. 'Why do you come here; there are quieter places', he said. The men in overcoats also gathered around quietly, one taking pictures with a zoom lens camera. A few girls defiantly went up to the pillars to sign the petition. Then came the 'beep-beep' of a lorry. 'It's the old snow-plow trick', someone said. The yellow vehicle came lumbering by the theatre steps, scattering the supporters and on lookers. Twice more it came past within a couple of minutes to sweep already clean paving tiles, ignoring stretches of trodden snow across the way. After the third pass, when Dmitry and his colleagues were alone on the theatre steps, the KGB men moved in and without any fuss led them up the Arbat and into an alleyway where a police vehicle was waiting.

This ended the first street demonstration by the group in their campaign for a memorial to Stalin's victims. A full account of the action was read to the next meeting of the Perestroika Club in the Institute for Mathematics and Economics. Dmitry Leonov and his colleagues had been held for six hours and fined fifty roubles, a sum which was rapidly collected from the audience. But a new issue had arisen which overshadowed the memorial protest and electrified the meeting. Boris Yeltsin, the proreform Moscow party leader, had been sacked from the Politburo. The fifth-floor conference hall was buzzing with rumours about a speech he had made attacking Ligachev, the Politburo hardliner. 'How can we talk about democracy when our whole movement is threatened', shouted an excitable forty-nine-year-old lawyer, Oleg Lyamin. Everyone knew that Yeltsin, as Moscow party boss, had given the political direction which had ensured informal groups like Club Perestroika were able to hold their meetings. Every mention of Yeltsin's name was greeted with applause. By being sacked for trying to accelerate reform, Yeltsin had instantly become a cause célèbre for the cautious academics, someone whom they could rally behind without appearing to be dissidents. They voted to demand publication of Yeltsin's speech.

There had been other attempts to hold demonstrations for human rights around this time, mainly staged by the Democratic Union, which issued a radical manifesto on thirty-four pages of crinkly paper at its first conference in a crowded eighth-floor apartment in April 1988, calling for a multi-party democracy. But it was the treatment of Yeltsin more than anything else which began to bring people out on to the streets of Moscow. The masses identified with Yeltsin, a heavily built, sometimes ponderous Siberian with small pig-like eyes and a strong-boned face who, in appearance, could have passed for a typical Brezhnevite; he had articulated, however, the well-founded suspicions of the ordinary Russian, of the rank-and-file party member and of the factory worker that they were getting a raw deal while an army of hated bureaucrats led a comparatively comfortable and privileged life. Yeltsin was a member of the Party Central Committee, so it was not 'unpatriotic' to support him. For months after his sacking, the issue of Yeltsin simmered on the surface of Russian political life. It was this, more than anything else, which turned the streets of Moscow in the spring and summer months of 1988 into a series of debating chambers. Political discussions began to spring up in busy streets and at shopping centres. Small crowds gathered in the Arbat to listen to debates about Yeltsin, and they quickly broadened to include shortages, Stalin, injustices and all the major and petty grievances which people had been unable to express publicly throughout their lifetime. People were losing their fear.

By mid-summer Pushkin Square had become a Hyde Park corner on Saturday afternoons, a forum for the people's unhappiness. I went there one afternoon with my notebook. It was one of those sultry, hot summer days when the air was full of *pukh*, the white, fluffy seeds of the poplar trees which swirled round the city in early summer, drifting against the kerbs like snow. A few people were milling around, some deep in argument. An old woman wearing a print dress and carrying a plastic shopping bag cried to no one in particular.

'Look at me; what have I got out of life? My husband died in the war. My pension is no good. I have nothing. My life is ruined.'

Tears mingled with sweat ran down her lined nut-brown face. She was surrounded by about four dozen people. Other small gatherings formed and broke up in front of the 108-year-old bronze statue of Alexander Pushkin, Russia's favourite poet. Men in short-sleeved shirts and women in summer frocks crowded around anyone prepared to speak his or her mind, interrupting, shouting, arguing about everything from personal misfortunes to Mikhail Gorbachev's reforms, forming a very Russian street parliament, a forerunner to the explosion of political debate about how Russia should be governed. The militia, trained for decades to arrest demonstrators on sight, stood around uncertainly, occasionally asking people to 'Move along, please', through hand-held loudhailers.

A tiny, frail woman with a high-pitched voice insisted on telling her story too, the words tumbling out as if releasing a life-time of pent up frustration.

'I was born in Riga', she said, looking up at the circle of impassive faces. 'I work in a *stolovaya* [a cheap café], fifty hours a week on my feet. My husband is ill. He lies in bed all day. My son is in the army. What sort of life have I? Things get dearer. Where can I buy sugar? I can't say I'm behind Gorbachev; what they write and what they do – it's always different. We are suffocated.'

'Am I suffocating you?' said a militia officer who had pushed through the crowd.

'Enough now, old woman', he remarked, not unkindly.

'I'm not afraid of him. Write down my telephone number', she retorted, seeing my notebook. 'Ring me; I'll tell you my whole story.'

I wrote it down. The people waited. The officer waited.

'Finished?' he asked.

'I've got the number', I replied.

'OK, clear the pathway, please.'

In another group behind the statue a man in a check-shirt was reading from the minutes of a party committee meeting which had voted eight-to-one to support a proreform candidate for the Communist Party conference in Moscow on 28 June. He read every statement recorded in longhand in his notes. Voices interrupted.

'A moment, please', he kept saying.

He came to the point. Party bureaucrats had telephoned to instruct the committee to reverse its decision.

'They even wanted us to change our thoughts', complained the speaker.

'Terrible', 'Not right', said voices from the crowd.

Nearby, a red-faced countryman in a cheap brown suit had got carried away with excitement.

'The bureaucrats have ruined everything', he shouted.

'Give concrete examples', said a man wearing glasses. The speaker looked crestfallen as he racked his brains in vain. Then he muttered something.

'They weren't bureaucrats, they were criminals', snorted the heckler, turning away.

Snatches of conversation came from other knots of people.

A middle-aged woman in a fashionable suit said, 'We should all support Mikhail Sergeevich [Gorbachev].'

A man with a brief-case replied, 'We're behind Gorbachev.'

'I fought in the war. You don't know how well you are living', exclaimed an old man.

A young man pulling out a photograph of tanks added, 'I also fought in the war, in Afghanistan. You live well. I don't.'

'Never mind him, he's an old fool', asserted his elegant woman companion.

The bureaucrats had a champion in one group, a man in a striped suit, every inch a party *apparatchik*. Beside him stood a bearded student. They traded insults. The student waved a copy of the 1977 Soviet Constitution, heavily underlined where Article 50 guaranteed 'freedom of speech, of the press and of assembly, meetings, street processions and demonstrations'.

'I'm not against demonstrations', said the bureaucrat. 'All I'm saying is this isn't the way to go about it. I'm not in favour of provocative slogans.'

'He's been planted here by the KGB', replied the student.

Everyone laughed, except for a girl beside him who was in tears. Some of her friends had been among twelve people arrested earlier when they raised placards demanding the release of Valeriya Novodvorskaya of the Democratic Union, jailed for a week the previous day for demonstrating illegally. As far as the militia were concerned, the Democratic Union was comprised of good, old-fashioned dissidents whom they could still rough up and arrest.

Many people drifted up Gorky Street later that afternoon for an officially sanctioned demonstration on the grey-brick piazza outside the twelve-storey offices of the government newspaper *Izvestia*. I recognised some of my friends from the Institute of Mathematics and Economics. The meeting was organised by the informal groups campaigning for a memorial to the victims of Stalin. Under growing pressure, the authorities had begun sanctioning their gatherings. A young man in a leather jacket addressed the crowd of 500 through a megaphone. He warned about people in power trying to return to the old ways.

'They got rid of Boris Yeltsin', he said. 'They must be stopped.'

'Yel-tsin, Yel-tsin', chanted the crowd, fists in the air.

The street debates got bigger and more political as the months went by and elections to Gorbachev's Congress of People's Deputies approached. To the stranger coming across such open-air meetings, they could appear threatening and disorganised, with people milling around, shouting and gesticulating. But the more I observed them and mingled with the pushing, straining crowds, the more I came to understand that an unwritten set of rules was always observed.

I watched a typical political meeting develop one lunchtime on the Old Arbat among the dense crowds of people who promenaded through the narrow street, attracted by the portrait painters, amateur artists, musical groups and coffee shops. Two men standing near the Arbat's famous hunting shop, where a stuffed wild boar peered out the window, began raising their voices.

'In Canada', said one with a weather-beaten face and flat cap, 'a man, his wife, two children and a dog can run a farm of 120 hectares. Here that would be a collective farm with 200 workers.'

'The problem', said his companion, dressed in the gear of the typical street politician – jerkin, beard and ski-cap – 'is that the reforms are all illusions. Nothing is really changing.'

'Speaking of dogs', said an impish little man in a black leather coat. 'A Soviet dog was asked by a foreign dog how the reforms were going. "Well", said the Russian dog, "my chain's a little longer but the dish has been pushed further away. However, I can bark all I want now."'

A passer-by interjected. 'Yes, right, they move a manager here and a bureaucrat there, and say – please look – we have perestroika.'

His wife chimed in. 'It's a disgrace. There's nothing to buy and the prices are going up.'

A young man moved into the circle. 'So what do you want, to go back five years to the time of stagnation?'

Within a few minutes there were fifty people gathered round, most just listening; soon one hundred appeared. Side arguments began and the nucleus divided up into molecules of noisy discussion. Three hundred people were now assembled and another free-wheeling political debate had got underway. The unwritten code dictated that no matter how vigorous the debate, people never lost their temper; no one pushed or shoved or threatened, everyone could have their say. A torrent of debate had been unleashed after decades of repression, but no one knew the extent of the tensions and the potential violence which lay under the surface. A blow struck could have unimaginable consequences.

That weekend the street parliament was the focus for debate about the Soviet Union's first multi-candidate elections, to be held on 26 March. Official, glass-framed posters had appeared all over the city, showing photographs of candidates with the message: 'You must decide which will become deputy.'

But the name on everyone's lips on the Old Arbat was that of Boris Yeltsin, a candidate for Greater Moscow and a symbol for reformers throughout Russia. Many of the orators in the crowd wore Yeltsin badges. Nearby a group of men collected signatures for his 'political rehabilitation' beneath a somewhat overdramatic poster saying:

> All who care for the country's fate,
> All to whom honesty and dignity are precious,
> Must rally around now.
> Let not ice paralyse the heart,
> Go to the end and vote for Comrade Yeltsin.

Across from the video saloon where two American movies were showing – *Red Police* and *Time Patrol* – one of several political poetry sessions had also got underway. In these sessions, amateur versifiers stood on boxes to deliver impassioned political messages in doggerel verse, some of them epics in Pushkin-style, others a few couplets with a joke at the end, such as one recited by an old man and translated roughly as:

> We were lucky in our generation,
> No one can say I am wrong,
> We worked in the time of stagnation,
> And we loved before AIDS came along.

However much they might have wanted to, the city Soviet, still ruled by the party, could not stop the weekend political theatre without a return to the old repressive ways of arrest and detention which had become politically unacceptable.

One of the new cries to be heard in Pushkin Square and the Old Arbat that summer was for a *Narodny Front*, a People's Front, uniting opposition groups. I learned one day that there was to be a gathering of People's Front organisers in the ancient city of Yaroslavl on the banks of the Volga, several hours drive from Moscow. I found the meeting taking place in a modern building near the river which served as the local artists' union headquarters. There, in a room resembling a village hall, with tsarist and prerevolutionary flags propped against the back wall, the first all-Russian Popular Front was founded on 29 October 1988 to campaign for greater democracy and freedom in the Soviet Union. It was a ragged, rancorous start, in contrast to the huge, well-organised rallies which marked the setting up of popular fronts in the Baltic republics where they had become powerful mass-movements for reform. There were only ninety-nine delegates, two foreign correspondents – I found a colleague from the *Financial Times* there – and one Soviet television crew to witness the launching of what became for a time the most influential force in Russian street politics. Delegates from thirty-five Russian cities, fourteen local popular fronts, fourteen political clubs, five religious groups, four patriotic movements and four other groups declared themselves united on the need for fundamental reform in Russian political life. The lack of political experience led to ill-tempered and sometimes malevolent arguments in the hall, and exposed a deep division between those who wanted to strive for reform in the whole of the Soviet Union and the rapidly emerging minority of Russian nationalist groups, promoting exclusively Russian culture, religion and politics. The former waved the blue and red flag of the Russian federation, the latter a black, yellow and white tsarist flag on a pole topped by a cross. Some youths wore blue, red and white jumpers representing prerevolutionary Russia. The most extreme right-wing views were put by one of four intense, bearded men with glowing eyes and black shirts, belonging to a religious sect; they were dismissed amid laughter by the chairman, Alexander Obolensky, with the words, 'If a person wants to be blue, let him be blue', a colour used in Russian to denote both conservatism and homosexuality.

There was also a clear split between the Moscow delegates and the rest, resulting from a deep resentment in provincial Russia over the dominance of the capital city and the privileges of those who lived there, a jealousy which was to find expression in the economic wars between town and country of the 1990s. They feared that Moscow would try to take over the Popular Front. The general theme of the discussion was that events then stirring in Eastern Europe were about to engulf the Soviet Union. There were calls for a fundamental change in the system, including the creation of opposition parties. The programme that was adopted condemned chauvinism and called for democracy, the right to organise, freedom of speech, press and religion, separation of legal and executive power and the altering of the constitution by referendum. One of the Moscow activists there was a small, conspiratorial and rather nondescript man in a flap cap called Yuri Chernev, a middle-aged former camp inmate who promised to let me know what they were planning in the capital in the months ahead.

The tsarist ensign, which I first saw in Yaroslavl, began to make its appearance at demonstrations in Moscow. With the ideology of communism in tatters, people began looking back at prerevolutionary history with nostalgia. One day I went to the Donskoi Monastery in Moscow where I heard that suporters of the Romanov dynasty planned to gather to commemorate the anniversary of the death of the Russian tsar and his family at the hands of the communists on 17 July 1918. Such a gathering would have been unthinkable before the era of demonstrations. They had chosen the monastery gardens because of the patriotic significance of the huge Romanesque sculptures set in the high monastery wall, commemorating Russian heroes who had fought the Tatar hordes. I found a scene from a madhouse in the gloomy, dank corner beneath the huge wall statues. Men with blazing eyes strutted about in jackboots and peaked military caps, taking turns to bark exhortations to the people milling around. A man with a horribly disfigured face and voice – his mouth was twisted into his chin – occasionally shouted something unintelligible. Women moved around slowly, crossing themselves elaborately. A huge, florid Orthodox priest with greasy black hair towered over them, now and then imparting an indulgent blessing to a bowed head. On the fringes of the fervent little crowd, traders sold momentoes of the Russian monarchy, the most popular a glossy black-and-white photograph of Tsar Nicholas posing with his wife, the Tsarina Alexandra, his son Alexei and daughters Olga, Tatiana, Maria and Anastasia; there were also lapel badges with portraits of the

Tsar, the Virgin Mary, Boris Yeltsin and the Beatles. After a prayer service for the soul of the murdered Romanovs, they lit candles and placed them in crevices in the wall, along with hand-written slogans, among which was one saying, 'Smelt down the statues of the murderer of Sverdlovsk', a reference to Lenin.

The Romanov family were believed slaughtered on Lenin's instructions in the Urals mining town of Ekaterinburg, later called Sverdlovsk, though some historians argued that the children were taken away and executed in another place and that Anastasia escaped. Yeltsin was party boss in Sverdlovsk when Ipatiev house, where the crime took place, was levelled in 1980. He said it was done on secret orders from the Politburo to counter a new stirring of curiosity about the Tsars. Knowing that the commemoration in the monastery gardens would be taken over by *Pamyat* – the extreme Russian nationalist group – the new royalist political party, the Orthodox Monarchist Union, had stayed away. Led by Sergei Engelgardt-Yurkov, whose noble ancestors included Pavel Engelgardt, a hero of the 1812 Battle of Borodino, the memorial was dedicated to the restoration of the monarchy through parliamentary means, though Yurkov maintained, 'Democracy is leading our country into chaos. The great transformations facing our country can only be carried out under the unifying leadership of a ruler.'

The men in uniform strutting around showed fascist rather than democratic sympathies. Their leader was Igor Sergeevich Sichyov, an artist by profession. His burly frame was clad in the green uniform of the tsarist army, with leather straps and blue-and-white shoulder flashes. When I asked him to write his name in my notebook, he was shaking so much from the emotional effort of an impromptu oration denouncing Zionism, delivered with jackbooted feet wide apart and cap held at arms length, that he had to order a uniformed youth to provide his back for support, which he did with a snapping of heels. Their antics were watched with approval by a few dozen people, one of whom, a middle-aged engineer, said, 'I am here because I am a Russian. I am a monarchist. Look at every monarchist government in the West, Great Britain, Sweden, Spain; these countries are very prosperous and very strong. Russia was strong and peaceful when she was a monarchy, but for seventy years the communist government has repressed it.' This mild-mannered man with tight, black, leather gloves then added, speaking in English, 'The newspapers say Russians are lazy-bones. Just like the British newspapers say the Irish are lazy-bones. Why?

Because here they are controlled by Jews and Zionists. I'm talking about *Pravda* and *Izvestia*. They want Russians and Russian culture repressed.'

The right-wing patriotic organisations were divided in their support for the Soviet Union, which they saw as Russia's empire, and for reforms which gave Russians more independence. They stayed on the fringes of the great political demonstrations which began sweeping Russia in 1989, resulting in the ousting of party leaders in dozens of towns and districts. Occasionally, however, they emerged to assert themselves. They turned out on Marksistskaya Street in Moscow one Saturday afternoon, beneath *The Irish Times's* office window. A mass meeting of workers had been summoned, ostensibly to discuss reform in the manner of the Arbat gatherings. What was unusual about this event, organised by the hard-line Tagansky Region Communist Party, was that the militia obligingly diverted traffic to allow it to take place in the middle of the six-lane carriageway, right beside an empty park, and shift workers in local factories were given time off to attend. It soon became apparent that far from being a meeting to back reforms, it was a show of strength by a party faction which claimed to support perestroika, but in reality was against radical changes in communist society. The bureaucratic empire was trying to strike back. The banners declared support for the United Workers Front, an organisation opposed to the democratic movement. Among the crowd applauding speeches against privately owned co-ops and a multi-party system, I saw Alexander Samsonov, congress deputy and director of the first Moscow watch factory, a glass-fronted building further down Marksistskaya Street. Samsonov, a burly figure with a voice like that belonging to Northern Ireland's Ian Paisley, had the distinction of being the USSR's most unpopular parliamentarian, coming last in a poll organised by the mass-circulation journal *Argumenti i Fakti*. I had tried to interview him once in his office, but his language was so full of street colloquialisms I found him difficult to understand. He told me that most of the 7,000 watch-factory employees backed the United Workers Front and had been encouraged to take part in the demonstration. Samsonov made no secret of his support for the widely discredited administration-by-command system of management. 'It works well in my factory', he said.

The meeting might have ended as a small victory for the conservatives but for one incident which had an unwelcome sequel for the organisers. A man named Mikhail Kriger produced an 'unauthorised' placard. It stated, 'The United Workers Front is a Child of the

Apparatus'. He was jostled by some youths and arrested by the militia. A few weeks later I got a telephone call from Yuri Chernev, the political agitator I had met in Yaroslavl. He said Kriger's trial was about to take place in the Tagansky courthouse, also on Marksistskaya Street, and the hearing would be worth attending.

The court room was packed. The trials of people 'lifted' by the militia on public-order charges were usually a formality, ending with a fine or fifteen days in detention. This time the radical opposition had decided to make a stand. Kriger, a twenty-nine-year-old excavator driver, was accused of 'shouting loud slogans, interfering with the meeting and ignoring militiamen's calls to maintain order'. Evidence was given that Kriger, once awarded a medal as a volunteer Young Communist worker on a new Siberian railway line, held up his placard during a speech made by the first secretary of the Taganskaya Communist Party, comrade Zhukova, a well-known conservative who had opposed the Kremlin decision to remove the name of Stalin's cultural commissar, Zhdanov, from our district the previous year. He testified that he was immediately surrounded by five or six young men wearing the 'George Victorious' badges of a Russian nationalist organisation. They started to pull the placard away from him. A militiaman standing nearby did nothing to stop them. He was then arrested by Major Marksimov, chief of the local sobering-up station, and brought to the Tagansky militia office. For three hours defence lawyer Abushakhmin cross-questioned witnesses and it soon became evident that many of the people attending the meeting, the workers prodded out on to the street by the management, were also outraged by the arrest. They expressed indignation that the militiamen did not deal with the 'hooligans who attacked him'. The defence lawyer asked a witness, 'Would you agree that the militiamen and the young men had clearly defined roles, that the young men's task was to destroy the placard and the militiamen were to arrest the owner of the placard?' People's judge Antipov ruled the question out of order, but the witness replied that it looked as if that indeed had been the case. Judge Antipov dismissed the case. A Soviet journalist, Pavel Gutionov, crossed the road to the party headquarters to ask a few more questions about the meeting. Party secretary Kolominov told him, 'Don't you think it significant that the militia arrested not somebody called Ivanov or Petrov or Sidorov, but Kriger?' He didn't have to explain to the journalist that the first three surnames were Russian and Kriger was more than likely Jewish.

The anti-Semite *Pamyat* agitators, who maintained that Jews were responsible for Stalin's excesses, turned up at the founding conference of the Memorial Society at Dom Kino, the house of cinema, in Moscow on the last day of October 1988, to heckle from the body of the hall. The movement against Stalin had become widespread under the reforms, both in the media and on the street. The historic conference was the first major anti-Stalin manifestation in Moscow since the early Khrushchev days. It was an emotional occasion for the former prison-camp inmates and leading Soviet intellectuals who had opposed Stalinism throughout the years when it was dangerous to do so. In rooms beside the conference hall, pieces of paper were pinned up with the names of prison camps – Taishet, Potma, Karaganda, Magadan and Norilsk – with invitations to delegates to write in the names of people who were held in them. The congress was the culmination of the campaign begun by groups like Club Perestroika. Dmitry Leonov, the engineer from the institute who had submitted himself to arrest in the Old Arbat, was prominent among the organisers. The Communist Party itself had turned its back more and more on its Stalinist past, especially under the influence of Alexander Yakovlev of the Politburo. Yakovlev argued that only when this was exposed and discredited could they dismantle the administration-by-command system formalised by Stalin, which had brought the country to economic and social ruin. The party had even begun to vie with Memorial over the right to erect a monument to the victims of Stalinism.

That conference in Dom Kino also marked the emergence of Andrei Sakharov into the thick of political life in the Soviet Union, less than two years after his return to Moscow. There was tumultuous applause when he appeared. He was almost immediately elected honorary president of Memorial, along with historian Yuri Afanasyev, and took his seat in the centre of the platform. Sakharov the dissident had become Sakharov the political figure.

One could measure the pace of change in the Soviet Union by the official attitude toward Andrei Sakharov. His release from exile in 1986 had been a turning point in policy regarding dissent. Back in Moscow, Sakharov was, however, still a non-person as far as the officially controlled Soviet press was concerned. Then, in mid-1987, the outspoken journal *Moscow News* carried his comments on a human rights play. In November it published an interview with him about Stalin's crimes. In December the same paper publicised his call for the release of all imprisoned dissidents. The greatest sensation, however, was the decision by the foreign ministry to host a press conference for Andrei Sakharov on 3 June

1988, eighteen months after his return; this was to allow him to cope with requests for interviews from hundreds of correspondents assembled in Moscow for the visit of US President Ronald Reagan. The balding, bespectacled scientist faced an audience of 500 Soviet and foreign journalists, as well as curious, and even incredulous officials. In the front row sat his wife Yelena Bonner, officially discredited a couple of years before as a Zionist, CIA spy and evil genius behind her husband. 'I have not compromised by coming here', Sakharov told the journalists. The press conference was 'a witness to the substantive, positive changes that are taking place in our country. It is not Sakharov who has changed, but the situation.' Mikhail Gorbachev, an outstanding statesman, deserved trust and should be given a chance, he said. 'From the bottom of my heart I wish him luck.' He fully supported Gorbachev's summit disarmament policies and perestroika. 'I believe by my activities I am also helping perestroika.' He praised young people who demonstrated for change in Pushkin Square. He accused 'forces representing the past' of still harassing dissidents. 'All persons, all prisoners of conscience should be released immediately from jails, labour camps, psychiatric hospitals and places of exile', he said, adding that there were still twenty prisoners of conscience in the Soviet Union, convicted under Article 70 of the USSR Criminal Code forbidding anti-Soviet agitation. He read their names. Among the twenty was one Milanov who 'was jailed because he took part in a protest when I was exiled to the city of Gorky. He is still there because he refuses to ask for a pardon.'

One American journalist who had come with Reagan was not convinced that Sakharov could use a government platform without compromising himself. He asked the scientist if he had discussed his answers in advance with officials. Did he, for example, support the Soviet line on disarmament talks regarding what the reporter referred to as 'slickoms' – a jargon word for sea-launched cruise missiles. This was too much for Yelena Bonner, a fiery, dark-eyed woman, always a formidable fighter for her husband's rights. She jumped up and turned to face the questioner. Hands on hips she said, 'That is a base question. I'm sick and tired of hearing such accusations. You are trying to suggest Sakharov has compromised. He has not. He remains what he always was. Neither he nor I have been bought.' She was loudly applauded by many of the Soviet and some of the resident correspondents who glared angrily at the American. Sakharov said quietly, 'No conditions were placed on me. If they were I wouldn't be here.'

At the Memorial conference which Sakharov co-chaired in the House of Cinema, much time was spent discussing how to prevent repressions from continuing. The consensus was the establishment of a legally based state as well as a monument to the victims of the camps. The debate had its moment of drama too. Yuri Skubko of the Democratic Union, a tall young man who worked in the Africa Institute and was well known to English-speaking correspondents, said in his speech that KGB headquarters in Dzerzhinsky Square should be turned into a memorial. Later in the room beside the hall, Skubko had an altercation with a conference organiser named Yermakov who called him a provocateur. Skubko slapped his face. I had gone to the room to interview him and found two girls holding on to Skubko's arms while Yermakov was persuaded not to retaliate. Skubko, allowed to take the microphone again in the hall, said, 'I slapped Yermakov because of what he called me. If I say KGB headquarters should become a memorial, and you think it's provocation, what ideals have we got?' Only Sakharov on the platform applauded. There was another moment of high emotion when an ancient figure with a craggy frame hauled himself up the steps on to the platform and said, 'I have been a party member since 1926. You may consider me old-fashioned and conservative, but it is our socialist state which helped us survive and our one-party system that helped us become a superpower.' There was derisive applause, forcing him to leave the platform. The chairman said, 'Shame on you all. He was in prison twenty years. Maybe he has more to say than us.'

After that conference, at which Sakharov emerged as a major force in alternative Soviet politics and a moral focus for progressive forces, members of the establishment took steps to try to prevent him from getting a national platform. When the presidium of the Academy of Sciences met a month later to select their nominees for twenty-five academy seats in the 2,250-member Congress of People's Deputies, they omitted Sakharov. Rank-and-file scientists decided the time had come for direct action. On a cold, snowy day in January, 3,000 scientists held a rally outside the eighteenth-century yellow stucco building which served as the academy's headquarters on Leninsky Prospect. It was an act of courage for many of the participants to defy the bureaucracy which ensured their careers and promotion. The academy president, Gori Marchuk, sat in his office and refused to come out. Sakharov himself stood almost unnoticed behind a crush barrier, his gaunt face hidden by a large fur hat, turned up collar and spectacles. Behind him a banner said,

'We are not Slaves'. A few weeks later the presidium bowed to the pressure and Sakharov was nominated.

Such victories had an important impact on the psychology of the Russian people. Demonstrations achieved their desired result. Totalitarianism was on the retreat in the face of widespread unrest and discontent. This was evident again when the congress was elected and Boris Yeltsin, who won the biggest single mandate of any of the 1,500 elected deputies with his sweeping victory in Moscow, was not given a place in the Supreme Soviet – the 542-member working parliament. His voters took to the streets in large numbers, this time organised by the Memorial Society and the Russian Popular Front. The authorities, fearful of marches on the Kremlin, hastily permitted pro-Yeltsin rallies in Luzhniky Park, a huge carpark beside the Lenin sports stadium in a loop of the Moscow River. It was walled on one side by a high, grassy railway embankment. I remember a commuter train passing by slowly as a rally was taking place. It sounded its whistle and passengers crowded to the windows to wave and to give peace signs. There was no doubt where the people's sympathy lay. A place for Yeltsin was quickly found in the Supreme Soviet when a deputy gave up his mandate, and the party, despite its control of the congress through what Afanasiev called its 'aggressive, obedient majority', did not challenge his gift of the seat to the popular Moscow representative.

For a while the big demonstrations were confined to Luzhniky, but with the people becoming bolder, it was only a matter of time before the radical opposition converged on the centre. It was the Memorial Society which brought them there, a few months later. They organised a human chain, in memory of Stalin's victims, around the massive granite blocks of the seven-storey building in Dzerzhinsky Square which housed KGB headquarters. This building with its high wooden doors and barred windows had come to symbolise terror and repression. People materialised at 6.30 p.m. on 30 October 1989, the day of the political prisoner, as the rush-hour traffic thinned out, to hold a thirty-minute vigil of remembrance. They stood, some in tears, in a long, silent line, holding candles which formed flickering pinpoints of light in the early evening darkness at one end of the vast square, a few hundred yards east of the Kremlin. Widows in black coats and fashionable hats, old men muffled against the cold, youths in windcheaters, stood with their backs against the harsh stone. For many relatives of those who were repressed, it was a sad, bitter moment, evoking memories of the days in the 1930s and 1940s when their fathers and mothers, husbands and wives where hauled into the Lubyanka, as it was then known, never to be seen or heard of again.

The evening of the human ring around the Kremlin, I got another telephone call from Yuri Chernev, my conspiratorial friend from the Yaroslavl conference who had become an invaluable contact. He told me that on 7 November, the anniversary of the Bolshevik revolution, there would be a counter-parade of anti-communists. Only half believing that such a blasphemy would be allowed, I forfeited my usual place in the press-box beside Lenin's tomb, from which we watched the tanks roll by each year, and went at dawn to the Dynamo Stadium in north Moscow, as advised by Yuri.

Groups of people were arriving in the dawn light with flags and banners, their breath emerging like smoke in the frosty morning air. They assembled and set off towards the city centre, the first anti-revolution parade to be seen in the Soviet capital. It was organised jointly by the Russian Popular Front and a new body, mostly made up of Yeltsin election workers, called the Moscow Elector's Club. A small figure walked in front carrying the club's new blue flag. It was Yuri. At 9.30, half way along Novoslobodskaya Street, we could see in the distance – moving slowly across a flyover – the tail end of the official Revolution Day parade, a line of red flags carried by invited factory workers and their families on their way to Red Square. Any of them who looked in our direction would have seen the twelve-lane Moscow artery filled from pavement to pavement with thousands of people carrying tsarist flags and anti-Soviet placards. All around people chanted, 'Down with the October Revolution', 'Down with communism', and 'KGB out'. They carried posters with slogans saying, '72 Years on the Road to Nowhere', 'Revolution 1917 – Our Tragedy', and 'Workers of the World – forgive us', a parody of Marx's famous rallying cry, 'Workers of the World Unite'. 'We wanted to join the Red Square parade but they wouldn't let us, so we decided we didn't want to go there anyway', said Yuri as he laboured under the weight of his flag pole. The authorities gave permission instead for a five-mile march from Dynamo Stadium to Olympic Stadium, taking in part of the wide Moscow ring road. Thousands turned up to express their weariness with life under the Soviet system. Militants from the Popular Front wanted to hijack the demonstration and take it to Red Square. At the first junction, they headed towards the city centre crying, 'Follow us, comrades', but abandoned the attempt when few paid any attention.

On Novoslobodskaya Street, the ranks swelled from 5,000 to more than 10,000. There were retired army officers in uniform, former political prisoners in camp uniform and several Ukrainian and Baltic nationals with their flags. Startled residents came to their balconies to gaze down on the mass of red, white and navy blue flags of independent Russia. Some flags were decorated with black ribbons or exhibited the white Russian naval emblem with a blue cross; there was also the occasional black anarchist flag with a red star. We proceeded to the ring road, led by youngsters who kept up a chant of 'KGB out', 'Shame on Ligachev' (the Politburo's leading conservative), and 'Down with Communist Power'. A new slogan also appeared for the first time that day: 'Down with Article 6'. This article of the USSR's constitution gave the Communist Party a leading role in Soviet society. As the sound of distant ceremonial cannons boomed out in the grey light, an old woman called out to me, 'We want to live like people in the West.' At the wide ring road, the marchers found Chekhov Street, leading directly to the Kremlin, blocked by double lines of police. Behind them lorries and buses had been pulled higgledy-piggledy across to block the road. The young radicals made another attempt to storm the Kremlin, calling on people to follow them up a flyover instead of turning off towards the Olympic Stadium. 'You are sheep', they called down from above. 'You are goats', people called back. Only a few dozen went with them. Sheepishly, their leather-jacketed young leader, Vladimir Ivanov, brought them back. The march ended peacefully. The authorities were learning how to cope with the rising tide of anti-communism, conceding ground step by step. Few of us thought then, however, that within a year the same people would be carrying their banners through Red Square.

I knew something fundamental had changed when I went to Pushkin Square later in the day where about one hundred members of the Russian Young Democrats held an unofficial meeting almost within sight of the giant Lenin banners in Red Square. One young man with the tsarist flag shouted repeatedly, 'Long live the White Guards'. Katherine Lemmerman, a seventeen-year-old Moscow University student, addressed the crowd, which included army officers and people from the official parade, with the words, 'They ask us to return to Lenin principles. Lenin started the terror.' She raised a black-gloved fist and shouted, 'Down with Lenin'. The crowd of onlookers laughed and applauded at this audacious heresy. The few militia standing nearby did not interfere. 'Isn't that the fascist flag?' said an old man standing beside me.

The death of Andrei Sakharov occurred suddenly, not long afterwards; it was apparently a heart attack. The enforced exile and a long hunger strike had taken its toll on his physical health. He had been busy with parliamentary work and had retired to write a speech. When word spread through the city, people came to the apartment block at 48B Chkalov Street to keep vigil in the falling snow. They instinctively felt the enormous loss to the country and its people of a man who could not be replaced as a touchstone of morality and integrity. 'He was the conscience of the people', said a woman shielding a candle-flame from the large snowflakes. A long black Zil limousine without registration plates drew up, and Yevgeny Primakov, alternate member of the Politburo, hurried in to pay his respects and, as chairman of a special funeral commission, to help organise the burial ceremonies. Radio Moscow broadcast tributes throughout the morning, praising his role as dissident leader. The official Soviet news agency, *Tass*, which had done its share to discredit Sakharov as an enemy of the people during the Brezhnev era, announced his death and, seconds later, offered its English-language service subscribers a video on Sakharov's last days for 1,500 dollars. The insult was compounded by the publication of a potted biography of Sakharov which completely ignored his period of exile in Gorky.

The next day tens of thousands queued in bitter cold for several hours in a massive, dignified tribute to Sakharov, who had been taken from the Kremlin morgue, where his brain had been removed for scientific purposes, to lie in state in Moscow's Youth Palace. The slowly shuffling queue outside the building was ten deep. It included former camp inmates, serving army officers, students, factory workers, writers and government officials, and stretched for a mile along Komsomolsky Prospect to the entrance of the Park Kultury metro station beside the Moscow River. They waited in temperatures of minus thirteen degrees centigrade, and at times in driving snow. Many cried and crossed themselves as they walked slowly across the mable-floored hall, past the foot of the raised bier holding Sakharov, his face exposed and framed by red carnations. The flowers were occasionally rearranged by Yelena Bonner, who sat beside the red-draped coffin, dressed in black and with her grey hair tied back, occasionally stroking his face with her knuckles. An honour guard of four Congress Deputies changed every few minutes and kept vigil on each side of the bier. Haunting movements from Bach and Brahms were played by the Borodino string quartet, invited by the new minister for culture, actor Nikolai Gubenko.

Boris Yeltsin, who with Sakharov led the opposition faction in the Congress of People's Deputies, stood for ten minutes, a black-and-red mourning band on his sleeve. He gazed sad-faced at his colleague as people moved by at the rate of sixty-a-minute to a continuous whisper from ushers, 'Hurry along citizens, please; there are many people waiting.' The mountain of red carnations grew steadily. The wreaths included one from the Nobel Committee in Norway and another which declared simply, 'Andrei Sakharov, conscience of the intelligentsia'. Among the mourners were dozens of members of the Moscow intelligentsia, including Yuri Lyubimov, just reinstated as director of the Taganka Theatre. There also was the former editor of *Pravda*, Viktor Afanasyev, under whose editorship articles were published calling Dr Sakharov and his wife anti-Soviet traitors. An elderly woman broke the silence with the cry, 'Who killed Sakharov? – Those who dictate and the usurpers of power.' She was gently urged to keep moving.

The following day the body was moved to the Academy of Sciences. Mikhail Gorbachev arrived to say his last farewell along with five Politburo members. The Soviet leader said, 'We shall all feel his absence, but *perestroika* will go on.' At his funeral service the next day in Luzhniky Park, the cold snap broke and tens of thousands of people stood in ankle-deep slush. Among their placards was one which said, 'Forgive us, Andrei Dmitriyevich; we should have gone into the streets and squares in 1980.' There was no clapping or shouting, but thousands of clenched fists were raised in the air as Sakharov's favourite music, an Italian adagio, was played over loudspeakers before the body was driven off. Many in the crowd carried flowers. As people drifted away in the fading light, a woman handed a bunch of carnations to a man who had climbed a tree for a better look. He carefully arranged them around the branches. The Communist Party newspaper *Pravda* published lines from Yevtushenko that day. They declared:

> The heart is on strike, like a coalmine.
> Only yesterday, whiter than the snow,
> He came out of the Kremlin without a hat, unsteadily,
> Through ghosts of *boyars*, tsars . . . Beria,
> and that pocked hangman,
> The last words to his wife and the world were
> Tomorrow there will be a fight . . .
> He has left a frighteningly yawning moral void.

11

Ten Days that Shook the Kremlin

Those ten days, in which almost the whole country watched the desperate debates of the congress, unable to tear themselves away from their television sets, gave the people more of a political education than seventy years of stereotyped Marxist-Leninist lectures ... almost the entire population was awakened from its state of lethargy.

Boris Yeltsin

I N a propaganda booklet issued to journalists in 1987 by the *Novosti* news agency, former Soviet president Mikhail Kalinin was quoted as saying that single-candidate elections were 'a sign of socialism; a sign that the working masses have no internal antagonisms, nor can they have any'. The Soviet Union's last single-candidate parliament, the Supreme Soviet, certainly showed no signs of internal antagonisms when I attended their two-day, twice-yearly session in the Kremlin Palace in July 1987.

The twilight of this rubber-stamp parliament was marked not by debate, but by a series of set-piece speeches applauded by the whole assembly. At issue were some significant changes proposed by Mikhail Gorbachev as part of his reform programme, including a new law to make public servants more accountable to the courts. Given the hard-line opposition to the Soviet leader's policies inside the Communist Party, one might have expected the press gallery to be packed for 'the divisions'. It wasn't. *The Irish Times* was the sole representative of the foreign press in the pinewood gallery, a narrow observation platform like an elongated theatre box high above the deputies, who sat at shiny, black walnut desks as if in a gigantic classroom; they were mostly men in brown suits and women in smart hair-dos, with here and there the coloured headscarves and square caps of members from the southern republics. I soon found out why my colleagues hadn't turned up.

Everything was preordained. Behind the podium, the members of the presidium, drawn from the leadership of the Communist Party, sat with folded arms on rows of elevated seats. They were so far away that I had to use field glasses to see who they were. I was able to make out the round puppet-like face of Andrei Gromyko, the titular Soviet president, and the restless features of Mikhail Gorbachev, his eyes never ceasing to flick around the hall. Nine hundred diplomats and guests stifled yawns in a back gallery as the voting began. A motion was proposed to wind up the debate. 'Who is in favour?' intoned the speaker. All hands were raised to shoulder height, as if hinged on elbows resting on the surface of the desks. 'Who is against?' There was a pause. 'None.' 'Abstentions?' Another pause. 'None.' All this took five seconds during which the speaker hardly glanced up to see if any hands were raised in opposition. The law on public servants was proposed next. All hands went up. Again there were no votes against, nor any abstentions. Then came the climax of the session, a vote on a law on economic reform. Surely here a hardliner or a radical reformer among the unpaid deputies would make a stand. It passed in another twinkling of an eye, the automated hands swinging up to face level. 'Against? Abstentions?' None. And that was that. The result was a rubber stamp for anything proposed.

Things could not be allowed to continue in this way if Mikhail Gorbachev was serious about reform and democratic renewal, and the building of a state based on proper laws and legislation. He brought this system of sham democracy to an end, however, with his announcement, late in 1988, that as an experiment in democracy the Supreme Soviet was to be replaced by a Congress of People's Deputies of 2,250 members, 1,500 of whom would be elected in multi-candidate elections. The congress would, in turn, elect a smaller, permanent parliament, with paid-up members as in Western democracies.

The onset of the election campaign turned the ad hoc street demonstrations, which had become a regular feature of Moscow life, into impromptu election rallies. Suddenly Yeltsin badges appeared on sale in the Old Arbat. For the first time real electioneering was introduced into Soviet political life. The announcement came as a shock to party officials used to selecting a single candidate for whom everyone would turn out to vote. Local party committees were told they had to make halls available for formal question-and-answer sessions and selection meetings involving several candidates, many of whom did not belong to the party. The one-party system still prevailed, but now any individual could be nominated by work collectives or large gatherings of electors without party supervision.

One of the first selection meetings was held in a crowded hall in the Gagarin district of Moscow. There were ten would-be candidates, among them Yuri Chernichenko, an outspoken agricultural commentator on Radio Moscow with a brittle, homespun way of talking. The atmosphere was charged by the arrival in the hall of the enormously popular Boris Yeltsin as an observer. His presence appeared to give encouragement to people normally subservient to the presidium, made up of party officials who ran the meeting from a table on the stage and who seemed determined that their rulings should be law. Each candidate said in an opening speech that all ten names should be put on the ballot paper in order that the electors could decide which one they wanted. The presidium had other ideas. They raised countless procedural objections in a patent attempt to ensure that the most radical candidates were eliminated. The meeting was to have ended at 10.00 p.m. It went on until 2.00 a.m. Afterwards the elated electors poured out into the freezing night air, furiously lighting up cigarettes. They had won. All ten candidates were on the ballot paper.

The capital was divided into several constituencies, with a separate seat set aside for the whole city, called the Moscow Number 1 constituency, for which the population of nine million could also vote. Whoever won it would have the most powerful single mandate in the country. Yeltsin was nominated by several groups of electors. Again there were ten candidates, of whom only two others counted, Yuri Brakov, general manager of the Zil automobile factory, and Georgy Grechko, a cosmonaut. Both were backed by the party *apparat*, which planned that only their two names should appear on the ballot paper. Each candidate was allowed to bring twenty of his nominators into the hall where the selection meeting was held. The rest of the audience was made up of 'electors', but the 800 or so packed into the hall had clearly been carefully filtered by the party. They included individuals openly hostile to Yeltsin. This became clear from the tone of some of the questions on anonymous bits of paper passed from row to row and handed up to the stage and which the candidates themselves had to read out. One addressed to Yeltsin asked, 'Why did you let down the Moscow Party organisation by your cowardly failure to face up to difficulties?' His answers were slow, measured and appeared self-effacingly honest. The more antagonistic the questions, the more sympathy seemed to swing his way. His platform was clearly popular: the end of the administration-by-command system; the end of privileges; the subordination of all ministries and the party to the congress.

The meeting adoped the suggestion of the presidium to put only two candidates' names on the ballot paper, but their plans to squeeze out Yeltsin were thrown into disarray by the popular cosmonaut. He sat through the questions, then, at the very last minute, withdrew his name. In a secret ballot the hall chose Brakov and Yeltsin as the two candidates. The wily Siberian disclosed afterwards that Grechko had approached him privately before the meeting and said he did not want to stand in his way. Yeltsin asked him not to declare his hand until the voting was about to begin. The cosmonaut played his part to perfection. The *apparat* was out-smarted.

The burly Yeltsin, with his thick white hair and voice like a foghorn, emerged during the campaign as the darling of the people, and the scourge of the party and its privileged elite. The party itself added to his mystique by making sure he remained officially a 'non-person'. His name did not appear in the party-controlled newspapers; he was not shown on state television. The media, furthermore, did not give details of his election meetings in advance. A more effective telegraph agency was at work on his behalf, however – the rumour circuit which had for decades been the conduit of hard news in the Soviet capital. I learned one evening that Yeltsin was about to make a public appearance, one of his first since being fired as Moscow party chief in 1987, in a lecture hall at the Moscow University in Gertsen Street. I raced the two miles by car but found the meeting had already begun. The corridor leading to the hall was packed with students straining to hear his voice. I fought my way in and heard him castigate party members who clung to old dogmas, but it was impossible to write down his words in the unbearable crush of bodies. The people were packed so tightly around the entrance door that I could not take my notebook or tape recorder from my pocket. A pale, dark-haired student passed out and was lifted over people's heads behind me on a forest of hands. I saw another girl in glasses standing nearby with eyes fluttering in a faint, but unable even to fall as she was held up by the crush of bodies. There were no stewards to control those pushing to get in or to help people trying to get out. Those of us who escaped after a while stood dazed in the corridor, while others continued to suffer inside, students and academic staff unwilling to miss a chance to hear Yeltsin or to get his words on the tape recorders they held high in the air.

Things were less hectic in the Tagansky district where I lived and where ten candidates fought for one seat. The best known was Alexander Samsonov, the hardline communist director of the Moscow watch factory and a powerful force in the Tagansky Party

Committee. Hardly anybody knew his opponents, four of whom held an election meeting one evening in a hall on a narrow side street running down to the river embankment. It had been advertised on little, typewritten notices stuck on the wall of the Tagansky supermarket. I went along out of curiosity. There were sixty-one people in the room, most of them men in their fifties and sixties. They didn't quite fill all the fixed rows of hard wooden chairs. Two young men and a woman lounged by the side door next to a framed copy of the Soviet Constitution. At a table on the stage, before a larger-than-life bust of Lenin, sat an official of the Tagansky Communist Party Committee, a self-assured, sharp-faced young man with a neat suit and condescending smile. Beside him were ranged the four election candidates. He sighed audibly as, in typical Russian fashion, loud arguments about procedure broke out before the meeting could get underway.

'Comrades, comrades, pay attention', said the official crossly, tapping his pencil against a tumbler. 'I have a proposal. Quiet please, comrades – please. I suggest each candidate speak for five minutes, then we'll have questions.'

We heard the four candidates in relative silence after this proposal had been debated, amended, thrown out, restored and eventually passed by a show of hands. The first to speak was a party veteran, his peroration full of clichés about perestroika. The second speaker was a flashy young man who turned out to have little to say for himself. He had not prepared a speech and people began to converse out loud before he finished. The third was better prepared. An electrical engineer, his platform included referendums on key national questions, nation-wide presidential elections, the stripping of state power from ministries, and sweeping defence cuts. It sounded very like the election proposals of Boris Yeltsin, and he was rewarded by a few cheers. The fourth candidate was an elderly, bespectacled writer, an invalid with a crippled leg who wanted independence for local Soviets, human rights for all, and military cuts to finance the economy. But he was campaigning first and foremost as an invalid, fighting for better conditions for the twenty million sick and disabled in the Soviet Union. 'You are all potential invalids', he warned us. We then had another noisy procedural wrangle, the outcome of which was agreement that each candidate should in turn submit himself to ten questions from the floor, and limit himself to one minute in replying to each. The questions revealed the main preoccupation of the voters in the hall. Several times the candidates were asked what they intended to do about crime, speculators and corrupt officials, and about the protection rackets and mafia gangs in Moscow.

A man in a heavy overcoat and glasses suddenly stood up and bellowed, 'The only mafia was the party organisation in this region for many years.' There was uproar and cries of 'shame'. The woman at the door burst into giggles. The party secretary primly smacked his pencil against the glass.

A thin man in a blue raincoat arrived late in a bustle of self-importance and immediately fired questions at each candidate. What did they think of a multi-party system? Did they support the end of conscription? Would they vote for the return of private property? The first two candidates gave standard non-commital party replies. They would do everything which promoted the cause of perestroika. The second was suddenly asked by a heckler what he thought of Yeltsin. 'He's okay', came the reply. 'His programme is all right.' His lack of enthusiasm clearly condemned him in the eyes of the Yeltsin fans at the meeting. The two radicals said cautiously they should not be afraid of competition from other parties. The engineer went so far as to say he had no objection to private property.

'Are you a party member?' called out a thick-set elderly man, sitting straight up on his hard chair, his outstretched hands leaning on a walking stick.

'I am', he replied.

'Ah!' retorted the heckler, as if this had deep significance.

'Gorbachev is a member of the party', replied the candidate defensively.

'So was Stalin', shouted another bemedalled old man at the back, his face purple. Three of his comrades clapped loudly.

Uproar developed and subsided again. All the troubles and woes of the people got an airing: price rises, housing shortages, the impossibility of buying a car. No one had a clear idea of what a deputy should do. A woman called out that they should not be bothering with local issues, the deputies must settle national questions; but the writer was cheered when he promised he would meet constituents once a month.

During the campaign, state television showed a nightly programme in which candidates faced each other. After the selection of Yeltsin, he could not be passed over, and two weeks before election day a televised debate was arranged between Yeltsin and Brakov. The streets were deserted that evening and telephones stopped ringing for ninety minutes as millions tuned in to see Yeltsin make his first television appearance in eighteen months. I watched the debate in the spacious, book-lined apartment in central Moscow of Zoya Zalubina, vice-president of the state-sponsored Women's Committee and a member of the circle around Raisa and Mikhail Gorbachev, where there was little love for Yeltsin. Both candidates were given ten minutes to speak, and then asked to answer questions telephoned in by members of the public and read out by the presenter. Zoya, a motherly woman who spoke excellent English, poured scorn on Yeltsin. 'Look, look, he's dodging the question, he won't answer that', she said angrily as Yeltsin was asked about his 'impetuous' style. Yeltsin accused the Moscow party apparatus of being used to promote his adversary. 'Nonsense', she cried. Brakov, an articulate but uninspiring technocrat, doggedly supported the party line. Yeltsin called for a secret vote for every top position, including president, and for an end to privileges still enjoyed by some people in power 'who have been robbing the population'. 'Oh, listen to him', said Zoya. He demanded major cuts in military spending and the shelving of some space programmes, and said that Gorbachev's promise that everyone would have an apartment by the end of the century was unrealistic. 'We too often throw out slogans and don't look at the figures', he declared. The 'provocateurs' seemed to be at work again that night. Some of the questions were deliberately aimed at damaging Yeltsin. One viewer rang to ask, 'Why do you always play to the gallery . . . even your regular visits to the doctor are reported by journalists and television cameras.' Yeltsin came to life as he responded. When taken to task by one viewer for the way he had confessed to incompetence on 'resigning' from his position in Moscow, he explained that he had been brought from his hospital bed, a sick man, to apologise for his over-ambition at the Moscow party meeting which sacked him, and wasn't quite aware of what he was saying. Now he was a changed man, more principled, and devoted to the slogan, 'All power to the Soviets'. 'Oh do you hear that?', snorted my host.

A couple of days later I turned to an ,evening current affairs programme on television and saw a report in which a reporter approached an apartment door in a Moscow suburb. He rang the bell and a diminutive, nervous man opened the door. His name had been given during the Yeltsin-Brakov television debate as the person who had asked the question about Yeltsin's visits to the doctor. He had never telephoned the television station, he told the reporter, nor had he asked any questions about any doctor. He did not know anything about such things. Moreover, he supported Yeltsin, and the reporter was to please tell him not to worry as he was going to vote for him. Yeltsin later claimed that the dirty-tricks campaign against him was so well organised that all party committees in Moscow had received ten typescript pages of advice on how to discredit him with loaded questions at election meetings. If this was true, the campaign was backfiring.

On the morning of polling day, Sunday, 26 March 1989, the clocks were put forward to summer time. An old palace near the Lenin hills was converted into a polling station for the area where most of the leading party members were registered. Gorbachev's thirty-year-old daughter Irina arrived before her parents on the arm of her doctor husband Anatoly. 'Whom did you vote for?' a journalist asked. 'It's a secret', she replied trimphantly. Yeltsin's sworn enemy, Yegor Ligachev, bustled in and out early. 'Did you vote for Yeltsin?' called a reporter. Ligachev's eyes narrowed. 'I voted for the most worthy candidate', he said, 'and anyway, the vote is secret.' Ordinary city voters trickled in: an old couple helping each other up the long path from the road; a trendy father and mother in denims holding the hands of a child in a jump suit, trying to ignore the media circus camped on the palace steps. Nobody under the age of ninety in the Soviet Union had had more than one name to chose from in an election before. One man spread his arms wide. 'How do I feel? Wonderful. I'm sixty-three. For the first time I have a choice.' Would he vote for Yeltsin? He winked. 'Of course.' Others arriving at the polling station were equally forthcoming. 'Yeltsin speaks our language, he is for the people', stated a woman, huddled under an umbrella with two companions as a cold rain began to fall. Mikhail Gorbachev arrived with Raisa like any other voters. They strolled through the empty grounds from the roadway, accompanied only by a couple of security men, and on past the hundred or so reporters at the door. How easy it would have been to have waylaid him on the pathway, I thought. I positioned myself beside some bushes to try to snatch a few words with him on his return journey to his long, black Zil limousine. With his love for an audience, however, the Soviet leader decided, when he emerged, to give a long, impromptu press conference to my colleagues while I stood in the rain on the empty pathway. When he finished and approached me, one of his two security men, the familiar burly figure with a mole on his face who accompanied him everywhere, simply pushed me and my notebook into the bushes and the small party swept by.

Yeltsin voted at the Palace of Pioneers in Frunze district, arriving in a mêlée of microphones, tape recorders and video cameras. As soon as he had voted and headed for the exit, there was a mad scramble in the polling station as journalists tried to follow him on. One of the voting booths was knocked over. Yeltsin was trapped outside like a hunted animal and conceded to answer the questions hurled at him. His eyes intense and staring, his voice slow, Yeltsin accused the party of a dirty-tricks campaign against him. 'One could write not a novel, but a thriller about it', he said. The latest ruse had been the decision to give Soviet citizens living abroad, most of whom could be expected to vote for the party-backed candidate, the right to vote in the Moscow Number 1 district.

Yeltsin's campaign headquarters was a small office in the construction ministry on Pushkin Street. People came in and out all day. In an upstairs room plastered with posters showing Yeltsin's craggy, peasant features with their distinctive Y-shaped eyebrows, fifty-six-year-old Vladimir Bunin twitched his moustache, banged his stick on the floor and barked, 'We are on the alert.' Bunin was typical of the helpers Yeltsin attracted. A disabled steel-worker with a red badge showing he had won a state prize for labour, he had been a loyal party member all his life but was completely disillusioned with the incompetence and corruption he saw all around him and the worsening shortages in the shops. Yeltsin represented a return to the ideals of Lenin and fair treatment for ordinary people. The main concern of the election team was not conveying supporters to the polling booths – the idea of a fleet of cars to get out the vote was foreign to Moscow where everybody travelled by bus or metro – but what happened after the votes were cast. They were afraid the bureaucrats might somehow fiddle the results. 'We got together here to make sure that the law is observed', Bunin told me. 'There must be openness in the way the count is conducted. There are are 3,393 polling stations in Moscow. We wanted all the ballot papers brought to the city electoral commission, but the bureaucrats decided the votes should be brought to the thirty-three city party-district headquarters.' He puffed furiously at his Kosmos cigarette and drew a diagram on a piece of paper, full of lines and dots, to show how the ballot boxes would be rerouted round the city. 'But it's all right', he said. 'Of the thirty-three centres, we have managed to take care of twenty-nine. We will have observers in there. We're working on the other four.' Mikhail Poltoranin, one of Yeltsin's aides who later became minister of the press in the Russian parliament, got a phone call during the day from an acquaintance in a panic who had visited a number of polling stations.

'Look, there are no public inspectors in the polling stations. I thought a large team worked for Yeltsin, but he is all alone, without any help.'

He need not have worried. Yeltsin got six million votes, 89.6 per cent of the turn-out. It was a resounding defeat for the party bureaucrats and the system of privileges they represented. Even the city's executive chairman, a typical *apparachik* in a suit and narrow-rimmed spectacles who arrogantly dismissed questions about shortcomings in the administration during his selection meeting, got his come-uppance. He was trounced in a Moscow district by a humble house-painter, Nina Ageyeva, who campaigned for a better deal for women. 'I have to haul sixteen-kilogram bags of putty', she complained. 'I know even more about our hard lot than my rival. He is given the data but I see everything for myself every single day.' It was a succinct summing-up of the class difference between the Communist Party elite and the workers. But in some city districts the radicals had a harder time, mainly because they were still unknown and had little experience in politics. Having all the names on a ballot was not always a good tactic as many radical votes were dissipated among several candidates. In Tagansky region, Alexander Samsonov defeated all his opponents, wiping out the party veteran, the flashy young man, the electrical engineer and the crippled writer who had addressed the meeting in the tiny hall on the embankment, though he still had to go to a second round with another factory director before he became our deputy and ensured that Tagansky region stayed communist (old style).

The first session of the congress was timed for 10.00 a.m. on 25 May. We assembled at 7.15 a.m. in the foreign ministry press centre for a security screening. We were then taken in tourist buses to the Kremlin through the ancient Borovitsky gate by which Napoleon entered the seat of tsarist rule in 1812. The concrete-and-glass Palace of Congresses sat uneasily beside the domed cathedrals of the Archangel and the Annunciation. Inside, the 2,250 deputies and journalists mixed freely in a huge, airy foyer and at a gigantic buffet, complete with hanging ferns and 140 long tables laden with savouries and attended by 280 waiters in identical white suits and bow ties. For the first time we encountered a phenomenon which was to become a familiar part of Soviet political life. Camera crews and posses of reporters were permitted to roam the concourse to interview everyone coming in and out, from country deputies to Gorbachev himself. The Kremlin, once one of the most secretive political institutions in the world, was suddenly open house. The Soviet leadership became at a stroke more accessible than in most

Western parliaments. The congress hall itself was undoubtedly the biggest debating chamber in parliamentary history. The only figure easily recognisable from the gallery without binoculars was a sixty-foot high Lenin, carved out of white stone and suffused with pink and green lights, a barely visible and mysterious trap-door on the top of his bald head. The gathering brought together for the first time all the opposing elements of Soviet political life. At one point as I peered through my USSR-made Tento field glasses, three personages appeared in line – Lenin, the state founder, brooding over the proceedings; Mikhail Gorbachev, seated at the green biege platform table on which he drummed his fingers impatiently; and Andrei Sakharov, speaking from the podium, less than three years since he was a dissident in exile. A bishop of the Orthodox church, metropolitan Alexei of Leningrad, resplendent in his robes and wearing a porcelain brooch showing Christ as the good Shepherd, chatted amiably with reporters in the lobby. He told us that he was one of three bishops elected to the congress along with an Armenian Catholic prelate and two Muslim *muftis*. A passing deputy stopped and said, pointing to his chest, 'Many of us are brothers here in the soul.' This was communist Russia 1989, whose conversion we used to pray for in school in Ireland.

From the first it was clear things were going to be very different from the old Supreme Soviet, but the officials who organised the new parliament were still 'unreconstructed'. No preparations had been made for proper debate. There was no order paper, no documentation, no arrangements for committees, no microphones on the floor, no plans to make available transcripts of the proceedings, no mechanism for voting or for divisions. None of the rank-and-file deputies had access to offices or secretarial services. The foreign ministry, like everyone else, assumed that the dictatorship of the congress secretariat would still be absolute. They told us the congress would sit for five days with two afternoons free. It would elect a president on the first day and a 542-member legislative chamber, the Supreme Soviet, on the second. The Supreme Soviet would hold its first meeting on the sixth day and we could all go home. It would all be televised to show the new Soviet democracy in action.

But many deputies had different ideas. Immediately the congress opened at 10.00 p.m., a deputy from Latvia walked up to the podium before anyone could stop him and called on all present to stand in memory of those who died when troops attacked a demonstration in Tbilisi in the early hours of the morning of 9 April, two weeks after polling day, killing twenty people. The deputy also requested that congress establish who gave the order for soldiers to attack the protesters. Caught unawares, the deputies had to rise, including the whole of the Politburo. Several army deputies who had been chatting among themselves got to their feet and stood to attention, evidently thinking it was part of the opening ceremony. Mikhail Gorbachev quickly regained the initiative, taking the chair immediately and making up rules as he went along. The first divisions in the history of Soviet parliamentary politics came thick and fast. Sometimes Gorbachev called for a proper count of votes in a procedural division, otherwise he simply counted the votes from the platform himself like an auctioneer, his eyes swivelling round the hall: 'One, two, three, six, ten, fifteen, twenty-nine'. One expected a gavel to fall when he finished. Some deputies, used to the old ways, initially wanted to ensure that the session ended quickly so they could go back to work. One figure with a stentorian voice even proposed that all votes be mandatory and those voting against should be punished. I recognised his voice even before I picked him up through the binoculars. It was my own MP, Alexander Samsonov, the watch-factory director.

The *apparat* had good reason to think that whatever happened they could still control the congress. One third of the 2,250 deputies were not directly elected. They had been chosen to represent public organisations, including the Communist Party, the *Komsomol*, trade unions, womens' committees, cultural unions and smaller organisations right down to the USSR Stamp Collectors' Society with one seat. The total electorate in these bodies was 16,200. They provided places for Mikhail Gorbachev and most of his Politburo colleagues, but also brought in radical deputies like Andrei Sakharov, Nikolai Shmelev and Yuri Karyakin, all chosen by their colleagues in the Academy of Sciences. But the majority clearly deferred to the party leadership. And furthermore, of the 1,500 elected deputies, 399 had stood unopposed in districts where party officials had managed the election in the old way.

The preponderance of conservatives meant that the party would not suffer the fate of the Bolsheviks, who were able to win only 175 of the 707 seats in the last Soviet parliament – the Constituent Assembly of 1918 which Lenin dissolved when his resolutions were not passed. The ten-day congress of 1989 did, however, provide explosive drama and real political debate as the long-standing taboos of political life were swept away, including those prohibiting criticism of party leaders, the KGB and Lenin. It started as soon as

Gorbachev moved to have himself elected president of the congress on the first day. The vast arena of deputies was electrified to hear the guttural southern accent of a member from Kharkov in the Ukraine declaring from the podium, 'I will vote for you, Mikhail Sergevich, if I am sure you are not overly influenced by your wife, Raisa, and people's flattery.' There was consternation. An Uzbek deputy, a woman, jumped up indignantly to say, 'I would despise myself if I didn't defend Raisa Gorbachev's role in helping in international matters by her presence.' No sooner had the hubbub died down than Yuri Karyakin called for the removal of Lenin's body from the Red Square mausoleum, saying, 'Lenin himself wanted to be buried near his mother's grave in St Petersburg; naturally his wife and sister wanted this also.' A nuclear plant foreman, Gennady Bykov, thundered, 'I was outraged to the depth of my heart and offended by deputy Karyakin's speech . . . we must keep Lenin on Red Square forever.' Yuri Vlasov, a former world-champion weight-lifter, was the first to attack the KGB. He said it should be moved out of the Lubyanka and its provincial headquarters – usually the biggest building in the town centre. 'The very extent and inexplicably monumental vastness of these buildings is evidence of who really controls this country', he declared. Yuri Chernichenko, who had won the election in the Gagarin district, savaged the reputation of the Politburo member in charge of agriculture, Yegor Ligachev, in a biting speech delivered with a comedian's sense of subtlety and timing. 'I greatly enjoy watching Yegor Ligachev on television', he snarled. 'He travels around the country and learns a great deal, evidently because he hasn't dealt with agriculture before. I only want to ask why someone who knows nothing about the subject and who has made a mess of ideology was put in charge of such a politically important branch of the economy. How could it have happened?'

Deprived for so long of the right to indulge in or even listen to such criticisms, people outside the congress chamber could not tear themselves away from television and radio sets. The voices of the deputies could be heard coming from the back rooms of shops and offices. They stopped the gossip in hairdressing salons and halted people in their stride in the Old Arbat and on the pathways of Ismailovo Park. Commuters squeezed into trams with transistor radios held to their ears. The arguments crackled over tinny loudspeaker systems at Luzhniky Park where radical supporters held rallies each evening to discuss the progress of the congress. In the Soviet far east, several time zones away, people stayed up until breakfast so as not to miss a second of the drama. Soviet diplomats in Western Europe and America got up before dawn to watch the debates beamed live via embassy satellite dishes.

Gorbachev acknowledged the criticisms of perestroika, admitting, 'I know there are jokes about the state of the economy. I know war veterans travel on the Moscow buses giving out cartoons showing Brezhnev with a chest full of medals and Gorbachev with a chest full of ration coupons.' He added, 'There were and there are miscalculations. I take them to heart. In the framework of the congress we must answer painful questions.' His election as president of the congress was assured when Andrei Sakharov declared that he did not see anyone else who could lead the country, adding, however, 'but my support is conditional'. The writer Chinghiz Aitmatov paid for his place as a Communist Party nominee to the congress by proposing Gorbachev as the man who came from the depths of the system to disturb 'the enchanted kingdom of Brezhnevite stagnation'. A deputy replied to loud laughter that one should not heap praise 'on such a great man'. Alexander Obolensky, a soft-spoken deputy from Karelia whom I saw chairing the meeting of the Russian Popular Front in Yaroslavl, proposed that his own name be put on the ballot paper in the election for presidency in the interests of giving a democratic choice, though he said disarmingly, 'I do not doubt that Gorbachev shall win, and I shall vote for him myself.' The proposal was defeated by 1,415 to 589, with thirty-three abstentions. It was the first indication of the balance of conservatives and radicals in the congress. Yeltsin was nominated too, but withdrew his name. Gorbachev was elected president by 2,123 to eighty-seven. It was his finest hour.

For the first time, however, the nationalist voice of the republics was heard at the centre, raising the prospect of secession and the break-up of the Soviet Union. We heard, too, the counter demands of the pro-union Russians who lived there. A retired major, Sergei Chervonopisky, won enthusiastic applause by proclaiming, 'I believe the three things we should struggle for with all our might are the state (*derzhava*), motherland and communism'. Marju Lauristin, daughter of a famous Estonian communist, retorted later, 'When you translate the Russian word *derzhava* into Estonian, it comes out as empire.' A little-known professor of music from Vilnius, Vytautas Landsbergis, forecast the rise of self-governing republics who would enter into a new union as nations and states. 'Then, of course, our European home would cease to be like a dormitory controlled by a supervisor who knows best and suspects everyone.' His colleague on the Lithuanian delegation, Kazimiera Prunskiene, won prolonged applause for a closely argued analysis of how the centre kept Lithuania in economic subjugation. For the first time people outside Estonia, Latvia and Lithuania heard the argument expressed openly that the Baltic states had been annexed. The secret protocol to the 1939 Molotov-Ribbentrop pact was read from the tribune by an Estonian delegate to a vast television audience which had never before heard of the conspiracy between Stalin and Hitler that divided up Europe and gave the Baltic states to the Kremlin. The historian Roy Medvedev told the hall his fellow scholars were not afraid to record that Russia conquered central Asia, 'But we still continue to write in our official historical works and elsewhere that Estonia, Latvia and Lithuania voluntarily joined the Soviet Union. This is not true.' The exchanges between the Baltic nationalists and the Russian deputies from the region were bitter. There was no place in Estonia for the majority of the non-Estonian population who did not support the 'cult of the nation', complained factory director Vladimir Yaravoy from Tallinn. Kazimieras Uoka of Lithuania accused him of organising his enterprise so that Estonians could not work there. 'Moreover', she said bitingly, 'The Russians who live in the other republics have their own native land: Russia. But the nations of these republics have no other to go to.'

It was on the evening of the first day that we got the first whiff of the bitter drama about to be enacted over events in Georgia. Eldar Shengelya, a film director from Tbilisi, took the floor to say that as a consequence of 'punitive action' by armed forces in Tbilisi on 9 April, twenty-one people had died (one was shot after a curfew was imposed), and more than 4,000 had applied for medical treatment. 'This action was directed by General Rodionov', he said. 'I do not think that such a deputy should sit among us at this congress.' People in the hall and the press-gallery craned their necks to try to spot the uniformed figure of General Igor Rodionov. He sat, red faced, in the body of the congress chamber, one of twenty-seven armed forces generals elected to the congress and sitting together in the centre of the auditorium, However, he made no move to reply. Late the next day Tamaz Gamkrelidze, director of the Georgian Institute of Oriental Studies, made clear that the Georgians would not let the matter rest. He accused Rodionov of 'a specially planned punitive operation aimed at murdering people'. The troops 'gave no warning of any kind before starting. Soldiers blocked the passages, surrounded the demonstrators and hit them with clubs and sappers' spades. They did not spare the hunger strikers lying in the square, who included young girls and old women ... the reports in the central and military press ... later read as though Georgian men had been killing their own womenfolk and children while the troops tried to save the victims.' For good measure he asked the congress to condemn 'the annexation of democratic Georgia in February 1921 as a gross infringement of the Treaty of 7 May 1920 signed by Lenin.' There was uproar as he ended his impassioned speech by declaring that Rodionov, who had won a seat with the help of military votes in a Georgian constituency, 'has neither a legal nor a moral right to remain a People's Deputy'.

Rodionov at last strode to the podium. The hall went deathly quiet. Here was the embodiment of the power the conservatives trusted and the radicals feared. 'Those who are talking now about the peaceful nature of the rally forget that at the same time vile calls to assault communists were heard', he said, in a tone of cold outrage. 'A mass rally led by the Tseretelli Society on 6 April approved an appeal to the US Congress and Nato countries to support the independence of Georgia ... let me quote some of the slogans disseminated in Tbilisi, some of them in English. "Down with Russian communism", "Russian invaders get out of Georgia", "Down with the rotten Russian Empire."' Some of the radical deputies looked at each other in amazement. Such slogans were not uncommon at meetings in Moscow. 'Out of the sixteen bodies found on the site of the tragedy, not a single one had stab wounds or cuts. It is all rumours and emotion', the general claimed. The more he went on, the more agitated he became. 'We now talk of Stalin's reign of terror in 1937, but today things are harder than in 1937', he cried. 'The mass media can vilify you in any way they please, but they give you no chance to reply.' He disclosed that he had written an open letter to his constituents after the tragedy, but 'we had to distribute it as we did in the last war over enemy territory, dropping leaflets from aircraft.' He concluded, 'In a recent and slanderous article in the Georgian youth paper, the responsibility for the events is attributed to the top political and military leadership of the country. I believe, on the contrary, that it was itself the target of this provocation.' The general stormed back to his seat amid prolonged applause.

Gorbachev announced the setting up of a commission of deputies to investigate the events of 9 April, but there was more to come. Next to the podium came Djumber Patiashvili, who had resigned as first secretary of the Georgian Communist Party the day after the massacre. He said he had been accused of making a mistake in putting General Rodionov in charge of the operation to clear the square. What had in fact happened was this. Patiashvili received a telephone call that night from Defence Minister Yazov to say Deputy Defence Minister General Kochetov, accompanied by Rodionov, would visit him in Tbilisi in the next twenty minutes. The bureau of the Central Committee of the Georgian Communist Party had little choice but to pass a resolution to clear the square and to put Rodionov in charge. Patiashvili had suggested postponing the operation because the crowd had grown bigger. 'The commander assured me that he saw no complication ... unfortunately, instead of dispersing the rally the troops surrounded the crowd and brutally assaulted them ... though their task was to clear the square they pursued and beat people a long distance from it.' He demanded an answer to the questions, 'Who ordered the use of spades and gases? Who determined the extent of violence towards the public?'

The Soviet leadership was badly rattled by the implications from Patiashvili's hand-washing exercise that they bore responsibility. Anatoly Lukyanov, a Politburo member and college friend of Gorbachev's who had been elected first deputy chairman of the congress, announced to deputies the next day that he had located the telegrams received from the Georgian communist leader on that fateful night and would read them to the congress 'to give an objective picture of events'. He waved papers in the air. The last telegram was timed 10.45 a.m., 9 April. It was an urgent account to the Communist Party Central Committee in Moscow of what had happened. Lukyanov put on his glasses and read Patiashvili's cable. It said that in view of growing chaos in Georgia and plans by nationalists to seize power, 'a decision was taken to use force for clearing the square ... but the organisers of the rally called on the participants to sacrifice their blood and lives ... Police and troops did not employ any weapons. The rule on the careful treatment of women and minors was carefully adhered to ... Many provocateurs in the crowd used steel weapons. In the resulting stampede sixteen persons were killed, thirteen young women and three young men ... signed Patiashvili.' Lukyanov concluded, 'I do not want to add any comments to it.' Patiashvili did not respond, but the Georgians were not finished. His successor as Georgian party chief, Givi Gumbaridze, came to the rostrum to renew the attack on Rodionov. 'Deployment of paratroopers for this kind of operation is hard to explain, let alone justify, though some people are trying to do it ... one would think that General Rodionov, who referred to the tragedy as the "Tbilisi provocation", would find in his vocabulary some words of sympathy for the victims.' Again there was an uproar.

Boris Yeltsin took little part in this Georgian drama. He was at the centre of another conflict, a struggle for the reins of real power – the winning of a majority in the 542-seat Supreme Soviet which was to become the USSR's first working parliament. We watched this developing on the floor of the house, and we participated in the heated discussions in the lobby and in the Moscow Hotel, the grim concrete building just off Red Square where the deputies were staying and where late evening meetings were held in crowded rooms, sometimes filled with the acrid blue smoke of Russian cigarettes despite a ban on smoking. Everything was open to the press. The new personalities of Soviet politics carried on their arguments in the presence of Soviet and foreign correspondents and gave lengthy interviews about the latest developments. Gathering every day in the giant foyer of the Palace of Congresses, we became familiar with the rhetoric of Russian political conversation, the invariable habit of ending a long dissertation with the words, 'That's the first point; now the second point', and the use of the hands for emphasis, not in Italian style, but with solid Slavonic movements, fingers of both hands spread out exuding power rather than volubility. The silver-haired Ligachev would make points with his arms outstretched as if holding a small barrel. Inaccessible before the congress, the second most powerful man in the Soviet Union amiably harangued journalists everytime he passed through the lobby. A few feet away another group of journalists might, at the same time, be clustered round his political opposites, young men with moustaches like Arkady Murashev, the enfant terrible of the Moscow council, busy trying to co-ordinate the first ever opposition in a Soviet parliament. It was largely thanks to him that the Inter-Regional Group of Deputies, with Boris Yeltsin as its figurehead, emerged during the congress, though it was Gavriil Popov, the stocky, white-haired Greek economist, who proposed the formation of the group on the floor of the house – a suggestion which so shocked the presidium that they ordered the television cameras switched off for a while. The Inter-Regional Group not only united, but broadened the outlook of its deputies whose alliance was based mainly on opposition to the party *apparat*, the centralised economy, the KGB, and cultural and national repression.

The baby-faced Moscow deputy, Sergei Stankevich, became a target for Western reporters prowling among the aspidistras of the lobby because of his command of English. Soon we found out that he was a tough, brash reformer in his own right who, as an historian, had researched how the parliaments of twenty other countries had worked. His refusal to accept the proposals of the platform earned him the nickname from Mikhail Gorbachev of 'comrade Nyet'. He could often be found in the company of Anatoly Sobchak, a commanding Leningrad law professor with a slightly manic smile who personified the emerging new Soviet parliamentarian, and challenged policies with which he disagreed with a power and articulation that awed the house. In intellect and ability and height, Sobchak stood head and shoulders above his fellow deputies in the Inter-Regional Group. He was also politically ambitious, which may have accounted for the anecdote told about him in the buffet. According to the story, the congress was divided on a vote on whether to support communism or capitalism. Sobchak was indecisive. 'What's wrong, can't you make up your mind?' Gorbachev called down to him. 'The trouble is I want to work like people do under communism, but live like people live under capitalism', replied Sobchak. 'Well then', said Gorbachev, 'you'd better join us on the presidium.'

The urbane figure of Mikhail Poltoranin was prominent among the people around Yeltsin. As editor of *Moskovoskaya Pravda* during Yeltsin's tenure as city party chief, he had led the way in transforming the turgid Soviet press into a campaigning media against corruption, inefficiency and the mafia. In the lobby I also came across Oleg Borodin, a newspaperman whom I had met during the election campaign in Yakutsk, in north-east Siberia. He had defeated his factory-director opponent in a classic David versus Goliath contest. Of the women deputies, Galina Starovoytova rapidly bacame the most prominent and the most provocative, accusing deputies appointed from official women's groups of making a profession out of their sex. She quickly emerged as one of the strategists of the Inter-Regional Group and a passionate advocate of the Armenian cause in the dispute with Azerbaijan over Nagorny Karabakh. Alla Yaroshinskaya, a tall brunette in her mid-thirties, could often be seen deep in conversation with the proreform deputies. She was another victor in a struggle with the right. A non-communist, she had defeated three party-backed candidates in Zhitomir in the Ukraine. She recounted how, after her victory, forty-eight court proceedings were taken against her constituency agents, while others were beaten up, including two lieutenant colonels and a colonel, or expelled from the party.

The stooping, mouse-like figure of former dissident and historian Roy Medvedev also became a habitué of the lobby, though he stayed aloof from the Inter-Regional Group. He was suspected by Sakharov and others of having connections with the KGB. On the second day of the congress, Medvedev was re-admitted to the Communist Party, saying he 'would like to help the party in its work of making society healthier'. Medvedev, sought after by the Western press as a dissident voice in the era of stagnation, did not endear himself to journalists either, sometimes demanding 'presents' for in-depth interviews. (He asked an American correspondent for scotchtape. She brought him all she had in her office. He said curtly that it was not enough.) Some of the hard-line conservatives were regarded by the press as slippery characters, a view which may have been affected by our strong prejudice for the radicals who said what we wanted to hear, but it was hard to feel much empathy with representatives of the old order like Ivan Polozkov, a glowering, tight-mouthed communist secretary from Krasnodar whose main contribution to debate was an attack on co-operative ventures, or the oily Boris Gidaspov, head of the Leningrad Communist Party. One of my American colleagues said after interviewing him, 'I feel like a shower.'

We stalked the generals and the artists too. General Sergei Akhromeev, the slight, wiry military adviser to Mikhail Gorbachev, was quick to voice his opinion. If preoccuppied, he would snap at reporters to leave him alone, but would halt in his tracks to pose for a photograph, whipping out a comb to brush back the few hairs from his tiny, gnarled face. The Siberian writer Valentin Rasputin, with his nut-brown features, could be found sitting on a couch earnestly telling a reporter that it was not Russia that was to blame for the ills of the republic, but the administrative-industrial machine 'that has so degraded and robbed Russia that she is barely alive'. He electrified the congress one day by saying, 'Perhaps Russia itself should leave the union . . . we're fed up with being a scapegoat and putting up with insults and abuse.' Like so many statements considered outlandish at the time of the congress, these words were to echo through the Russian federation a year later when the Russian parliament declared sovereignty. Russia's unofficial poet laureate, Yevgeny Yevtushenko, a deputy representing the Writers' Union, appeared in the poet's garb of a coloured neckscarf to fulminate against the monopoly of Communist Party members in high office. 'Search as you may, you will not find one non-party factory director', he exclaimed, 'and there is only one non-party minister in the republics, Raimond Pauls in Latvia, and one, only one, non-party chief editor, Sergei Zalygin (of *Novy Mir*). They should be registered straight away as endangered species.'

Sakharov was always a favourite with the press, though not with the hard-liners in the congress hall. In his last speech to the congress, he was constantly interrupted as he called for a federal structure to replace the Soviet Union in order to end the oppression suffered under the Stalinist model. 'Certain dangerous developments are taking place', he said. 'One sympton is the universal crisis of public confidence in the country's leadership. If we just drift along, comforting ourselves with the hope of gradual changes for the better in the distant future, then the growing tension may erupt with the most tragic consequences for the future.' As he began to speak about the equal rights of Soviet nations, the microphone on the podium was cut off. People watching on television were outraged. They believed that Gorbachev controlled the sound system. Many never forgave him for this one arbitrary act of censorship.

When it came to elections to the Supreme Soviet, the silent majority, inherited from the recent past, saw to it that most of the radicals were excluded. This prompted historian Yuri Afanasyev to say, 'We have again chosen a Stalinist-Brezhnevite Supreme Soviet', adding, as the hall filled with cat calls, 'I am specifically addressing you, those I would call the aggressive obedient majority.' Each region put forward nominees for places they were allocated in the Supreme Soviet, except the Moscow delegation of 197 deputies. This was a conservative group, with only twenty-seven elected deputies, the other 170 being nominated by public bodies, including Gorbachev himself. Thus they avoided including Boris Yeltsin, despite his overwhelming mandate, and some of the most able deputies. Yeltsin was later nominated in the list of thirteen for twelve seats allocated to the Russian federation. He came last, though all got more than half the congress votes. The crowds came out on to the streets of Moscow in spontaneous protest. There were calls for a political strike and further demonstrations. The next day the situation was saved by a deputy from Siberia, Alexei Kazannik, who gave up his seat on the list of twelve to Yeltsin. Congress was obliged to approve what Yeltsin described as this 'castling' measure.

The high point for opposition unity in the congress came when Tatyana Zaslavskaya tabled a motion protesting against a special decree which banned demonstrations near the Kremlin during the congress. On the first evening, 1,500 mostly young people had gathered to cheer radical deputies and to boo the hard-liners, but they had been surrounded by interior ministry troops – tough young men with long batons and dark blue berets who stared aggressively at the protestors, cradling their batons as if straining to bring them crashing down on people's heads. She was backed by Sakharov who made the long trek up to the microphone to say, 'This is our youth, our future, our people. We cannot surround them with the divisions which were used in Tbilisi.' The vote united the radicals in the Moscow Group, the Leningrad Group of Young Radicals, the Baltic Bloc, and the Georgians and Armenians, as well as dozens of individuals from other areas. They lost the vote by 1,261 to 831, but the figure of 831 was the maximum they could rally. It was also the first and last coalition of the anti-conservative forces of the whole Soviet Union. Within a year most of the Baltic deputies had stopped taking part in proceedings as they pursued outright independence. In 1990, Georgia also declared independence. The congress showed how fragile the USSR was, and exposed the fissures which ran through its structures. It revealed the unbridgeable gulf between factions in the Communist Party, to which more than 80 per cent of the deputies belonged. Boris Yeltsin pointed out that if party membership could include Yeltsin and Ligachev, Samsonov and Vlasov, then 'we have altogether forgotten what a political party is'. Yeltsin, Popov, Afanasyev, Stankevich, Sobchak and many other radicals all left the Communist Party in the following year. Polozkov became leader of a new, right-wing Russian Communist Party. The congress was also the high point of Gorbachev's flirtation with the radicals, who gave him credit for personally deciding that debates should be televised and for ensuring fairness in the composition of the commission set up to report on the Tbilisi affair (its report was an inditement of Rodionov, who was relieved of his command the following September and transferred to the Staff College in Moscow). After the congress, the radicals came to regard him more and more as an obstacle to further reform, a feeling which found full expression just a year later on May Day 1990, when the Soviet president was whisked off the Lenin Mausoleum by workers on the annual parade through Red Square.

The final irony was that all the battles for seats in the Supreme Soviet faded into insignificance when new elections took place a year later for local and republican bodies. Yeltsin would play little part in the deliberations of the Supreme Soviet, hardly ever taking his seat and devoting all his time instead to the parliament of the Russian federation of which he became president. Popov became leader of the Moscow City Council, with Stankevich as his deputy. Sobchak was elected leader of the Leningrad Soviet. Nikolai Travkin quit the Communist Party and formed the Democratic Party of Russia, which by 1991 had become the country's second-largest political party. Medvedev travelled in the opposite direction, becoming a member of the Central Committee of the Communist Party.

Yeltsin said, 'On the day the congress opened they [the deputies] were one sort of people. On the day it closed, they were different people. However negatively we assess the final results . . . the most important thing was achieved. Almost the entire population was awakened from its lethargy.' But many remembered as well the warning of Ukrainian writer Vladimir Yavorivsky that if they did not succeed in setting an example of greatness and principle at the top, 'the people would turn their backs on them and retreat into silence and vodka and anecdotes – about you, Mikhail Sergeevich, and about us deputies.'

That warning appeared to be coming true by the time the fourth and equally dramatic congress took place in December 1990. It also lasted ten days. By then the high hopes of the reformers had been dashed as the conservative forces in the country overwhelmed the democrats in a bitter struggle for power which left the people exhausted and demoralised. Few will ever forget the hammer-blow which came on the fourth day of that congress when Eduard Shevardnadze stood up to speak in the stadium-like auditorium of the Kremlin's Palace of Congresses. The foreign minister had submitted a text for his scheduled address. He delivered a different one.

'This is the shortest and most difficult speech of my life', he began. The hall went deathly quiet. UPI correspondent Gerry Nadler guessed immediately what was happening and sent a colleague out to open a phone line to his office. The speech was full of emotion and very dignified. Shevardnadze's voice shook a little, and here and there he had to search for the right words. But the end, when it came, was quite definite. 'Comrade democrats, you have scattered. Reformers have taken to the hills', he said. 'A dictatorship is on the offensive. I tell you that with full awareness. No one knows what this dictatorship will be like, what kind of dictator will come to power and what kind of order will be established. I cannot reconcile myself with what is happening in my country. I am resigning.'

Half the members of parliament burst into applause and the rest sat in slack-jawed stupefaction. Some Soviet journalists in the gallery had tears in their eyes. It was an attack on Gorbachev himself. One of the last people to leave the hall when the session broke up for lunch shortly afterwards was Alexander Yakovlev, one of the three reformers at the top during the five years of perestroika, along with Gorbachev and Shevardnadze. The heavy-jowled Yakovlev, then sixty-seven, had been sidelined from the Politburo in the summer of 1990 after harsh attacks from the right. He walked slowly, almost unnoticed, through the foyer, limping slightly, and continued down a few steps to the cloakroom where he donned an overcoat and a flat cap. 'Is it the end of perestroika?' I asked him. 'Well, it doesn't depend on one person, but there are signs that the extreme right is holding its head high and has a glint in its eye', he replied, speaking slowly and heavily before walking out into the cold air. Back in the foyer the bespectacled, bald-headed Nikolai Petroshenko, the personification of the extreme right, showed no intention of leaving. He went from group to group, flushed with excitement. Usually to be found scowling, he now looked, in his brown colonel's uniform, like a cheerful Sergeant Bilko. Colonel Petroshenko was one of the two military members of parliament singled out by Shevardnadze in his speech as claiming the credit for getting rid of proreform Soviet Interior Minister Vitaly Bakatin, sacked by Gorbachev a month earlier, and who were now saying the time was nigh to settle scores with the foreign minister. Shevardnadze had said, 'Is it a measure of the boldness of these boys, and I say boys because my age allows me and they are young indeed, with colonels' shoulder-stripes, that they make such statements against a minister. Who stands behind these comrades. What is this? Why does nobody debunk them?'

'What do you say to that?', I asked Petrushenko, who told me his age was in fact forty.

'Shevardnadze did not receive even one millionth of the dirt thrown at Yazov [the defence minister], Bakatin, Kryuchkov [head of the KGB], Ryzhkov [the prime minister] and even Yeltsin', he declared. 'Our foreign ministry would like to be the sacred Indian cow. I use my right to criticise any political department.' Would there be a dictatorship as Shevardnadze had predicted? 'We have a dictatorship already. We have Gamsakhurdia in Georgia; Landsbergis in Lithuania – there's real dictatorship', he cried, referring to the pro-independence leaders of the two republics. Why then had Shevardnadze resigned? 'Perhaps he is afraid that some members of the Supreme Soviet, taking their cue from the French left forces, will question the inadmissibility of ratification of the agreement on Germany.'

Petrushenko was suddenly swallowed up by a rush of several television crews and reporters prowling the huge glass-walled foyer before he could explain what he meant by that. Oleg Kalugin, the former KGB colonel and now a radical deputy, paused in the swirling, excited crowds in the foyer to voice his opinion that Shevardnadze could no longer make common cause with Gorbachev because the president was about to impose a crackdown. 'He would rather flee the field than fight his friend', he said. Where the right was exultant, the left was in disarray. A meeting of the Inter-Regional Group of proreform deputies stayed behind in the congress hall during lunch to plan what to do. Boris Yeltsin didn't join them, nor did Gavriil Popov or Anatoly Sobchak. They decided that editor Foedor Burlatsky should ask for the floor when the session resumed and request Shevardnadze to rethink his decision. In the foyer another mob of journalists surrounded a very sombre Sergei Stankevich, the Ukrainian-born deputy mayor of Moscow. The baby-faced Stankevich, who always wore a worried expression, represented the large body of dispirited radicals who had moved to the centre as the situation in the country came to resemble that in Germany and the Soviet Union before Hitler and Stalin came to power, and, as the newspaper *Rabochaya Tribuna* put it, 'the pendulum of public opinion swings ... from vulgar notions of freedom to a striving for a new order'.

'The obligation of a politician is to see what is inevitable, to see the course of events', said Stankevich. 'The course of events is that our regime will be more authoritarian in the nearest future. Absolutely. Whatever some politicans may think or do, it's absolutely inevitable; it's the logic of the historical process in this country. This is absolutely clear for me. I prefer not to cry about this but to use pragmatically this course of events.' For this reason he would vote for the sweeping extra powers President Mikhail Gorbachev had requested of the congress and which Boris Yeltsin criticised as greater than the constitutional powers enjoyed by Stalin and Brezhnev. 'I think we really need more authoritarian rule because now we have no power in this country, only several centres of influence, and we need a real centre of power to be created immediately. The only problem for me is what aims these powers will be used for. What direction is the president going to act in using his extraordinary powers? So we need to give him a certain direction. We need guarantees about presidential intentions. It cannot be done blindly.'

Stankevich had found out about the balance of power in the country the hard way. Moscow and Leningrad were subjected to economic blocade by hard-line conservatives to discredit the radical councils elected in the spring of 1990. They were under pressure from their supporters to resign like Shevardnadze, rather than give any more credibility to the communist system which still controlled industry and security. Stankevich said the situation was too dangerous for street demonstrations to oppose dictatorship at the top. 'The crisis in the economy makes us more moderate in our political confrontations', he declared. 'I think any demonstration now in this situation, when a great potential for mutual hatred has accumulated in society, can bring us unpredictable situations and violence. We would have to concentrate all our police in order to prevent riots on the streets, and therefore our criminal elements would be able to act freely. Unfortunately, our newly born democracy is not effective, and self-discrediting of democracy is also a real danger. If you are a politician it's your obligation to understand the political situation in depth and not to be governed by emotions. If you are simply a translator of the street voice, you are not a politician.' The tall, imposing figure of Anatoly Sobchak echoed this view and its sense of fatalism. 'I think this warning [by Shevardnadze] is more than serious', he said. 'This means that the people do not believe any more in the possibility of resolving their problems by democratic means and think that if this is so, only dictatorship remains.'

Soviet journalists huddled in corners, trying to make sense of the affair and looking for the manoeuvre they always suspected when there was an unexplained development in the congress. *Tass*'s political analyst, Andrei Orlov, asked, 'Did Mikhail Gorbachev know about it? If not, Shevardnadze's actions equal betrayal.' The president did not know about it. His spokesman, Vitaly Ignatenko, summoned us in the throng of the lobby to say that Gorbachev had spoken to Shevardnadze, and the foreign minister would stay on until his resignation had been approved by the Supreme Soviet. A shock of jet black hair belonging to Colonel Viktor Alksnis, nicknamed the 'Black Colonel', moved through the crowd. Alksnis was the second of those wearing shoulder epaulettes mentioned by Shevardnadze. 'It's a step in the right direction', he told anyone who asked his opinion.

When the session resumed, the atmosphere was taut. Shevardnadze was nowhere to be seen. Gorbachev sat on the presidium, Yeltsin beside him. Burlatsky took the floor. The situation in the country had reached a critical moment, he said. The latest events meant there was a real threat of a dictatorship coming. Such a turn would mean the end of reforms, of the new thinking in international affairs, and the crash of perestroika. 'In the long road, it could lead to civil war with the loss of life and bloodshed', he declared. On behalf of the deputies who met at lunch time, he said, they should not accept the resignation.

Byelorussian writer Alexander Adamovich electrified the assembly with a chilling speech. 'I suppose we should express our disapproval of this act due to the fact that he was afraid; he showed weakness at the moment when he himself is saying that reaction is coming. So here you are. You, Shevardnadze, together with Yakovlev and Gorbachev, started perestroika. You had no idea that these shoals of bastards would throw themselves at you. You didn't know it then. But what of the fact that the colonels offended you? If a general gave an order to a colonel he would even offend his beloved mother. Those who pushed you into taking this step knew what they were doing. They counted on your honesty and dignity, your dignity as a Georgian. The same techniques were used against Yakovlev. They worked.' To lose Shevardnadze meant that Gorbachev was losing his very face, his authority. 'If this is going to continue, some day very soon we are going to look at our president and we will see only uniforms and the heads and backs of generals. They will circle him as a hostage. The sad thing is that Gorbachev is the only leader in our history who hasn't stained himself with blood, and now' – he turned to Gorbachev – 'they will make you guilty of everything. They will clean their hands on you and arrange everything as if you did it.' He concluded bitterly, 'There will be no coup. We will give all our power to Gorbachev and they will chose the people for him.'

No less extraordinary was the speech which followed from Colonel Alksnis, made with chopping motions of the hand and delivered at machine-gun speed. 'In front of you there is a reactionary; in front of you there is a bastard', he said. 'I understand the accusation. Yes, I'm a reactionary when I'm concerned about a baby being thrown out of a burning building. I'm a hawk when a pregnant woman is thrown out of the ninth floor. I'm a hawk when an old man is skinned alive. They say that perestroika brought us only good things, when there are 600 killed and 600,000 refugees in the country. I simply express my opinion. Yes, I am for the resignation of Eduard Shevardnadze. I am not against foreign policy. No. We should leave Eastern Europe. But I'm against the way it is conducted. Let Shevardnadze go now to the tent cities in the snow in which military people live and look into the eyes of those people, because he signed the agreements on withdrawal timetables.'

President Gorbachev had been sitting silently throughout. He then took the podium and said of Shevardnadze's resignation, 'I personally condemn such an action taken without consulting the president. Now, perhaps, is the most difficult time, and to leave at this time is unforgivable. This must be denounced.' He had been planning to offer Shevardnadze the new post of vice-president, he said. This was impossible now. There wasn't a word of tribute for his foreign minister, with whom he had spent five years travelling the world.

'They say', said Nikolai Ryzhkov in the foyer afterwards, 'that a revolution eats its children. The meal has begun.' Ryzhkov had started perestroika as a cautious reformer but had moved to the right. Under attack from all sides for the collapse of the economy, he himself succumbed to a heart attack during the congress shortly after a stormy meeting with republican leaders.

Few people paid much attention during the ten-day congress to a stocky deputy in a dark grey suit with fine pin-stripes, the uniform of the party official. He had a ruddy complexion and a small lump on his right cheek sprouting unshaven bristles. His thick, greying hair, which badly needed trimming, was brushed forward as if to hide the fact that it was receding. He had large bags under his eyes. This was Gennady Yanayev, the unknown who, on 28 December 1990, became vice-president of the Soviet Union and only a heart-beat away from being its leader. The election of fifty-three-year-old Gennady Yanayev to the post in which he would substitute for President Mikhail Gorbachev in absences, sickness and presumably death, was achieved only after the sort of drama which had characterised the first Congress of People's Deputies. The nomination stunned the 1,900 deputies attending the fourth congress, particularly the republican delegates who had expected a non-Russian to be given this sensitive post. The second shock came when Yanayev failed to win the necessary 1,120 votes, getting only 1,089. The congress hall emitted a confused babble of voices. Gorbachev's fury showed in his steely eyes. There was the usual rush of journalists to the telephones, and the value of the dollar fell immediately in the world's money markets. But nothing was ever as it seemed at the fourth congress and the defeat of Yanayev quickly turned out not, in fact, to be a defeat. Gorbachev took the podium to declare that the deputies would have to vote again and this time it would be a vote of confidence. 'If this leadership fails to break through, we should leave the arena', he said angrily. 'We can see the crystallisation of opposing forces in our country. I want a man I can fully trust at this critical moment.'

'We will keep voting until we get the right result', said a radical figure outside, only half jokingly. Several deputies took the microphone to say that, under the circumstances, they would vote for Yanayev after all. Among them was the Kazakhstan president, Nursultan Nazarbayev. In the foyer a correspondent had asked Nazarbayev for his opinion of Gorbachev's choice. The Kazakh chief had looked him in the eye, then turned on his heel and walked off. His contempt was clear. Yanayev was not elected for his sparkling personality or his parliamentary abilities, or for the confidence he inspired in non-Russians like Nazarbayev. He and Gorbachev represented a 'dream ticket' only for the military and party officials who packed the congress. 'Let's back our president and Communist Party general secretary', cried Marshall Sergei Akhromeyev to rally the predominant party vote in the hall. Yanayev proved to have a raw, crude sense of humour. Asked about his health, the stocky Russian, born in Nizhny Novgorod, replied, 'My wife says I am in good health. I have the same ailments as any normal, real man. I am a red-blooded fellow.' Deputies dissolved in laughter at the obvious innuendo. Like Gorbachev, he was never elected to any post by the people. He had a seat in the congress as the leader of the official trade union movement, an instrument of Communist Party policy. His path to the top was up the classic ladder of a party official, and he was unenthusiastic about market reform. Before a second secret ballot was held at 2.30 p.m., Yenayev reaffirmed to sceptical delegates, 'I support the ideals of perestroika.' He then sat tensely, head in hand, to wait for the result. At 5.40 a.m., an official in a black suit crept down a side corridor of the chamber, caught Yenayev's eye and gave him the thumbs up sign. Gorbachev spotted the movement and smiled expansively for the first time that day. The result – 1,273 for and 563 against – was officially announced at 6.50 a.m., by which time everyone knew that Gorbachev had pulled it off again, and Yenayev had got in on his very long coat tails.

12

Feeding the Children

RYAZAN lies in the heart of Russia, a secretive provincial capital of half a million people. It lies in the plains south west of Moscow, officially closed to foreigners for several decades for unspecified military reasons until opened again in 1989. Even then the road between Moscow and Ryazan still ran through forbidden territory, obliging foreign visitors to make a detour of more than one hundred miles. Its history goes back to before 1237 when it became the first Russian settlement to be attacked by the Tatar armies of Batu, grandson of Genghis Khan, as he swept westwards in one of the early Mongol invasions. Ryazan later became an important principality under Ivan the Terrible, and after the Bolshevik revolution it was transformed into a great industrial centre. Traces remain of prerevolutionary Russia. At the end of its tree-lined main avenue, the bright, blue star-studded domes of the Kremlin and the 1776 Cathedral of the Assumption rise above a high embankment of the river Trubesh. A short walk away is an old two-storey school house with the unique distinction of being associated with two Nobel prize winners, Ivan Pavlov, the great Russian physiologist who sat in the classrooms as a pupil in the 1850s, and Alexander Solzhenitsyn, who taught in the school after coming to live in Ryazan in 1957 on his release from exile in Siberia; Solzhenitsyn was later to be awarded the Nobel prize for literature.

Solzhenitsyn spent ten years living in an apartment at 17 Uritsky Street, a two-storey wooden house in a narrow back-road running between old buildings and modern factory blocks, not far from the centre of Ryazan. Here the author worked on his novels about the prison camps: *A Day in the Life of Ivan Denisovich*; *Cancer Ward*; and *First Circle*. In 1969 he left for Moscow and was later banished to the West as a traitor for exposing the full extent of the camp regime of Stalinist Russia. It was not until 1990 that Ryazan began to acknowledge Solzhenitsyn's role in its civic history. Ryazan's proreform Soviet, elected in the spring, made him a freeman of the city. *Evening Ryazan*, the newspaper of the Ryazan Soviet and edited by a non-communist, Nikolai Molotkov, carried a picture of Solzhenitsyn on its front page on 20 November 1990 with a message sent from the author's home in Vermont expressing thanks and affection. Solzhenitsyn was the last of the great writers and artists to be rehabilitated under Gorbachev, having been left to the end of the queue because of his uncompromising anti-communism. Two major journals, *Literaturnaya Gazeta* and *Komsomolskaya Pravda*, made amends for years of silence about the great writer when they published, around the same time, a 16,000-word epistle from Solzhenitsyn to the Russian people called, 'How to Revitalise Russia'.

When I called at his former home at dusk one frosty December day a few weeks later, I found a plaque had been erected on the green-painted planks with the words, 'In this house lived Russian writer and Nobel laureate Alexander Solzhenitsyn.' His apartment was number 2, the first of two doors on the left in a dimly lit hallway of bare floorboards. Its tenant now was Nina Sergeeva, a peasant woman with a round Russian face who lived there with her husband, her three sons, a daughter-in-law and two grandchildren. They occupied three rooms, two of which had comprised Solzhenitsyn's apartment. A naked baby was sitting on a pot in the room where Solzhenitsyn wrote his powerful masterpieces, its father tending it in trousers and vest. They had never seen Solzhenitsyn, who moved away before they came along, but their neighbour Tatiana Markovnya, a short, plump woman of sixty-seven who lived on the landing upstairs, remembered him. She recalled that the residents knew he was a former camp inmate, but no one had spoken about this in his presence. Solzhenitsyn would never invite anyone in, fearful that an observant eye would discover his writings and that the KGB would come and confiscate them.

In *How to Revitalise Russia*, Solzhenitsyn proclaimed that, 'The clock of communism has struck its final hour.' The proof of the failure of the communist system was evident in Ryazan, and not least in the blue, date-stamped ration coupons in the drawers of the sideboard of Solzhenitsyn's old room. These coupons were issued to everyone in the city in order to ensure that the inhabitants got a minimum amount of meat, sausages, sugar, butter, sunflower oil, margarine, eggs (fifteen a month), macaroni and cereal. They did not have any coupons for flour as there was no flour. Nikolai Molotkov, a fifty-three-year-old worker and poet with a Solzhenitsyn-type beard, remembered the last great hunger in Russia in 1947 when he got sick eating weeds and potato peel. The cause then was the post-war chaos. This time it was the collapse of the centralised administration-by-command economy. Humanitarian aid had begun to flow to the Soviet Union from the West, prompting Molotkov to say, 'I feel ashamed that food parcels are being sent to us when we are such a rich country, and here we are, standing with our hands out.'

The situation was full of ironies for Ryazan, officially classified before perestroika as a 'hungry city'. The rationing, introduced a few weeks previously, meant, in fact, that, 'For the first time I can go out and buy meat in the state shops', said Arkady Gorokhov, a tall, bespectacled surgeon in the Ryazan Children's Hospital who invited me to lunch in his two-roomed apartment. Here he lived with his wife, Lena, a doctor of psychology, their two small children and Arkady's grandmother. They put up a special lunch of meat pie, steak and potatoes, stuffed tomatoes and cream cake. They were deeply troubled by the crisis, however, and like most people in Ryazan had hoarded supplies of basic foodstuffs in their kitchen and little outhouse. Arkady insisted I take a small bag of potatoes back to Moscow where they had heard the shortages were worse. Moscow, three hours away by train, had always been the city of plenty in the eyes of Ryazan people who traditionally took the *elektrichka* to do their shopping there. That summer, as panic-buying swept Moscow, people from the provinces had been barred from using the shops. Some enterprises and collective farms in the countryside had retaliated by holding back food supplies from the capital. One of the effects of this economic war was that there was more milk in Ryazan than normal, and hardly any in Moscow.

One of the paradoxes of Soviet life for Arkady and Lena was that, while they were highly qualified members of the intelligentsia, they were worse off than many of the workers in the huge enterprises based in Ryazan district, the sixth largest industrial centre in the Soviet Union. These were a secondary source of food for the population. They had been given the freedom to earn hard currency by trading surplus production in the West, and much of it went to provide extra consumer benefits for the workers, such as jeans, hi-fi systems and food mixers. The employees also profitted from barter deals which factories conducted with big farms and with each other, exchanging consumer goods for food. In the economic chaos, a huge black market had also developed in Ryazan, as well as a 'grey market' where people brought things to a square to stand in rows and buy and sell. As the old ways disintegrated, law and order came close to breakdown. In the museum of the local Kremlin, a sad-faced middle-aged woman guide showed me the empty stands from which two million roubles worth of precious silver had been stolen two weeks previously. The general atmosphere of instability was enhanced by the unswept streets of the town. 'I got a telephone call this morning asking why Ryazan was so dirty', said Molotkov. 'In the old days a gang of men from a factory would be ordered out to clean the place up. Now we cannot do that. We cannot use the old methods.'

The proreform Soviet came to power full of hope that things would quickly change. Sergei Voblenko, the young vice-chairman, acknowledged sadly that only then did they learn that real power lay with the enterprises and the self-perpetuating system which they controlled. He reflected in his spacious office, overlooking a large statue of Lenin in the square outside, that 'I myself have passed through the infant-school period. After the elections it seemed that with a little bit of work and effort, everything would be destroyed; we would have a new era. Now I know we cannot get it so easily. As soon as the council was elected in May, the enterprises cut off all communications, and I began to understand that with their experience of seventy years of power, they knew the weaknesses of the system.' The industrial plants organised an economic-political isolation of the radical cities, 'making us feel like people who have come with spades to plant trees and have to use them to dig trenches'.

Voblenko and many of his colleagues possessed a powerful sense of history and harked back to the days, centuries before, when Ryazan was an independent principality and a prosperous trading centre. 'The majority of deputies are for free towns, cities and republics', he stated. 'This would not lead to anarchy, but a system such as existed in seventeenth- and eighteenth-century Germany which laid the foundations for a mighty state based on the free development of cities.' Solzhenitsyn's letter 'How to Revitalise Russia' conveyed a vision of Russia also rooted in the past, with Soviets replaced by *zemstvos*, the nineteenth-century land assemblies which worked at four levels: village, district, town and region. It would be a country of small-scale private businesses and farms. The land should be given to peasants with the right to own their plot for life. 'We have destroyed the peasants as a class together with its villages; we have polluted our soil and water', he wrote.

The lament for the lost ways of the prerevolutionary peasantry was not new to Ryazan. In a little park near the city's Kremlin, I came across a gigantic stone head and shoulders rising from the earth to commemorate Sergei Yesenin, born in Ryazan region in 1895 and the last great and tragic peasant poet of Russia. Yesenin welcomed the revolution as heralding the imminent arrival of a peasants' paradise. After a brief and disasterous marriage to the American dancer Isadora Duncan, with whom he travelled the world, he returned to Russia and wrote poems full of bitter anguish about the disappearing countryside, before committing suicide in 1925.

A century before Solzhenitsyn's letter, the same 'big' questions about Russian life preoccupied another of the country's great literary talents, the writer Leo Tolstoy, who lived seventy miles west of Ryazan, just outside the town of Tula, and who, like Solzhenitsyn, wrote with an honesty of purpose which made it seem he alone knew the truth. Much of his estate, known as *Yasnaya Polyana*, or clear meadow, remains as it was when he wrote *War and Peace* and *Anna Karenin*. Since the 1920s, it has been a place of pilgrimage for Russian and foreign visitors, and it has become a custom for newly weds to complete their marriage ceremony with a walk around its paths, the bride still in her wedding dress.

I found a thriving trade in Tolstoy memorabilia at kiosks outside the pillars of the main gateway. The white, two-storey family house with its books and furniture was beautifully preserved and furnished as it had been in the eighteenth century, having survived an attempt by Nazi troops to burn it down in 1942. The wicker chairs and wooden table still stood on the veranda where Tolstoy spent many of his summer days, shaded by a wild vine which fell around the carved wooden balustrades like a green curtain. In the carriage house was the *droshki*, the open carriage from which Tolstoy left the estate, an old and lonely man, on an October night in 1910. From there he went to live with the peasants over whose fate he had agonised much of his life, only to die of pneumonia a few days later in a wayside railway station at Astapovo in the Steppes. He was buried under a green mound in his favourite patch of old forest at the back of the house. Yasnaya Polyana provided the inspiration for much of the social content of Tolstoy's great works. He wove the beautiful surroundings into the fabric of his creations, as well as the character of the estate's inhabitants, their family traditions and scenes from nature. The long, beech-lined avenue leading up to the house was described in the chapter of *War and Peace* dealing with old Prince Bolkonsky. Tolstoy's love of physical labour, which caused him to disappear for days into the fields at harvest time to mow with the peasants, was chronicled in the experiences of Levin, one of the main characters of *Anna Karenin*. The first time I visited *Yasnaya Polyana*, the meadows were thick with wild flowers and butterflies. The descendants of the estate workers who peopled his books were scything and tossing the hay down by the Voronka River under the direction of a farm manager who maintained the estate's traditions, sowing rye and buckwheat, tending the apple orchards and beehives, replanting the oak and birch burrows and preserving the stock of woodcock.

Much of Tolstoy's life was devoted to trying to understand how the people of Russia lived, and how the great injustices of serfdom and inequitable distribution of the land could be redressed. He attempted to manage his farm on collective principles and conducted many social experiments. In later life, Tolstoy engaged in debates on how new technology from abroad – the strange, new harvesting machine – could affect the life and output of Russian farmlands. At *Yasnaya Polyana*, Tolstoy sensed the great changes about to sweep the country in the twentieth century. He could not, however, have foreseen the catastrophic events which did ensue: the enforced collectivisation which destroyed the peasant incentive he regarded as crucial to the proper management of the land; the mass killing of cattle in 1930 by peasants reluctant to hand them over to the state; and the pollution from huge industrial plants which replaced the city's traditional craft industries and caused acid rain to fall over the woods of the estate where Tolstoy himself planted many of the trees, leaving some of them withered and dying.

The great Russian debate on the land was revived after Gorbachev came to power. By then it was openly acknowledged that while enforced collectivisation had given the peasants a guaranteed income, the price was spiritual estrangement from the land. Students and factory workers recruited to help bring in the crops told stories of collective farm workers taking the opportunity to laze and drink at the height of harvest time while they did the work. There was little evidence of caring for the land. Anyone who travelled around the Russian countryside saw decay and neglect. Much of the harvest was lost as it spilled from lorries on pot-holed roads or when fuel or spare parts were not available for tractors. Huge tracts of land lay fallow or poisoned. All this helped produce the potato-gathering crisis in the autumn of 1990.

When I went to the potato fields at Maryino, a village a few miles south east of Moscow in late September that year to see for myself how bad things were, I discovered another impediment to agriculture: the Russian mud. It had been raining for several weeks in central Russia, a miserable, intermittent, dispiriting, cold rain falling from a blotchy grey sky at a time when Russia should have been enjoying the *babye lyeto*, or 'old-women's summer' – the warm, early-autumn spell when the *babushkas* relax in the sun with the harvesting all done. The rain had turned for a while to wet snow that day and settled briefly on the red-brown leaves of the maple trees and on the potato drills of the state farm at Maryino before melting into the sludge. The mud clogged the tires of tractors and clung to the fingers of potato-pickers with a viscuous tenacity. It stuck to my boots as I stumbled across a field, making them heavier with each step. The authorities had panicked at a break-down in the old system of recruiting tens of thousands of potato-pickers, combined with the worst autumn weather anyone could remember. They had pleaded for volunteers. The workers I found there, bent over the cloying earth, wore gloves with the fingers cut out. They had mud to their elbows and were wet and cold. Some had come from the city. 'Fear of hunger has brought them here', said Alexei, a farm engineer. 'For every 400 kilogrammes they pick, they are allowed to keep one hundred. That's two days work. They take as much as they can back to Moscow. There's no guarantee there will be potatoes in the shops this winter.' Coercion had brought other potato-pickers to the countryside to try to save the potato harvest. Teachers, undergraduates, conscripts, factory workers and civil servants had been 'rounded up', even officials from the foreign ministry. Many resented the long journey in uncomfortable buses and the couldn't-care-less attitudes of the farm workers. Despite the food crisis, farm employees still worked a factory-type shift, where their counterparts on farms all over the world laboured from dawn to dusk at harvest time. 'Why should they work more, they don't care', said Alexei. 'It's not their land. They are demoralised. All they want is to drink.' I plodded through a ten-acre field where the potatoes protruded from the heavy rills. They were half-green and those beneath were turning black. Alexei saw no hope of a revival of Russian agriculture until people worked their own land. He was prepared to become a farmer. 'I want to farm', he said, looking out over the fields at Maryino. 'If I had land I would work from morning to night. I've asked for six hectares to become a private farmer, but they won't even give me the bad land they don't use. In the meantime things are getting worse.'

The Russian parliament was the first legislature to take the initiative and pass a law on private property in December 1990 as part of a comprehensive project to revitalise the Russian countryside and villages, which included provisions for buying private property. Ironically, the hard-line communists in the assembly fought the hardest to ensure that it was hedged with the restrictions on which Solzhenitsyn insisted in his letter to the Russians, in particular that there should be no big estates, no speculation and no foreign ownership. The idea of the *narod*, the people, owning all the land, rather than individuals, had deep roots. 'Russians call the land their motherland and it's hard to sell your mother', admitted President Boris Yeltsin.

Traditional village life had been impoverished by collectivisation, and by the 1980s two villages a day were dying. Gorbachev told the Communist Party Central Committee at one of its plenums in March 1989 that, 'The situation is so grave in many regions that people are deserting the land, moving out of villages. Migration of the rural population has reached the critical level in several regions of the country ... sometimes one has to travel scores and even hundreds of kilometres to get the most urgent things done, receive medical assistance, get elementary services or buy primitive necessities.'

These words were fresh in my memory as I drove through endless villages a few days later on the way to Vladimir, one of the ancient cathedral cities on the golden ring which encircled the centre of Russia. I stopped at random in the village of Bardino, which lay about 120 miles east of the capital along a crumbling, pot-holed highway made even more dangerous that day by a white mist creeping across the surface from the melting snows of the woods. As in most Russian villages, almost all the 300 houses were *izbas*, pretty, single-storey wooden structures with carved window frames straggling along each side of the road against a background of flat pasture land, broken by birch groves stretching to the horizon. In Bardino there was no village square, no pub, no doctor's surgery, no veterinary clinic, no post-office. The centre of Bardino was, as in every other village, a single dingy shop with a sign above the door saying *produkti*, meaning simply products.

These state-owned shops were a barometer of the country's economic well-being. They were once warm, welcoming places, if one can believe the description of a village store in a 1950s work, *Country Living*, by the author Efim Dorosh. 'It was semi-dark in the shop and smelt of all kinds of groceries', he wrote. 'Two sales girls were busy at the counter. One was selling salted herring, butter, salt and sausage, the other wine, sugar, sweets and gingerbread.' In Bardino the plump woman behind the counter had no salted herring, no butter, no sausage, no wine, no sugar, no sweets, no gingerbread. Her stock consisted of bread, flour, cereal for *kasha*, or Russian porridge, vinegar, tinned fish, bottled fruit juice, potatoes, salt, a few school exercise books and little else. She had no fresh vegetables or fruit, not even potatoes.

All too clearly, Russian rural life, the inspiration of Tolstoy, Chekhov and Turgenev, had become an adjunct to the cities and towns where the villagers had to travel for practically all their shopping, and where the young people fled to as soon as they could. Three teenage girls in Bardino said there was nothing for young people. An old man with a drooping, tobacco-stained moustache said many people just grew up and left. 'Isn't it the same everywhere?' A stooped woman carrying two loaves said some people came back to live or to maintain a holiday home, but they were very few. The chances of private farming at Bardino, which adjoined a state farm, were remote. No one had taken up Gorbachev's offer of leasing land. 'Sure, all the young, strong men have gone, or they aren't interested. People remember what happened before. Who knows, it might happen again. Understood?' snapped the old man, running the back of his hand over his moustache and walking on. No one in the villages spoke openly about the brutal suppression of the *kulaks*, the well-to-do peasants during collectivisation in the 1930s. I heard the same doubts in every village I visited. People who had tried to lease land found that they were treated as outcasts, a threat to the control of the countryside by the collective farm-managers, and to the subsistence-level existence of the descendants of the peasants who were demoralised by large-scale mechanisation. Father Alexander, the priest at the small Russian Orthodox church on the eastern side of Bardino, asked simply, 'Who is there here to work the land? Where will we get tractors or harvesters?' A year previously when I had driven past the village, I noticed his church had been deserted, the brickwork showing where huge patches of dirty plaster had fallen away, the roof rusting. This time the five miniature onion domes were gleaming with blue and gold paint. Father Alexander, a young priest with shoulder-length hair and wearing a blue robe and silver chain, said, as we picked our way across mud and rubble, that the church, closed since 1936, had been allowed to reopen the previous July. Until then, believers faced a journey of seven miles to the nearest working church. Most were old and none had cars. Inside the church, there was warmth and light, though restoration work had only begun on the blackened walls, once covered with murals of Christ and the Virgin. About fifty old women were chanting, bowing and crossing themselves as another priest walked around with a smoking incense holder. Just inside the door, two old women sold plastic-framed religious pictures from a little counter. One remembered the closing of the church in Stalin's time. It had been used first as a tractor station, then as a storage shed, and for many years had lain idle, she whispered. 'It's a great joy, oh such a great joy for us', said her friend in a cackling voice that made some of the congregation look round. To them the return of the church brought a renewal of spiritual life with warmth, colour, song and faith to counter the shoddy, decaying materialism of the atheistic state.

It also brought people together in a communal activity which was not subordinated to the idea of material gain which, lamented Valentin Rasputin of the Modern School of Village Writers, had corrupted old values. In his story 'Money for Maria', one of the characters asked, 'When did it happen in the old days that village people took money for helping one another? If someone was building a house or putting in a new stove, people would come to help him. If the host had some hooch, he brought it out, if not – never mind, next time I'll come and help you. But nowadays it's all done for money. Ten roubles to dig your allotment. Ten roubles to bring in your hay – they work for money and by money they live. They're looking for a profit all the time.'

As the Russian economy collapsed, and as the rouble lost its value and shortages worsened, cash was again replaced by payment in kind in the Russian village, where currency became a piece of butter, a cabbage, a jar of blackcurrant jam, a sausage, or, most acceptable of all, a bottle of hooch. On another expedition into the Russian countryside when my car got stuck in mud in the factory village of Krasniye Tkachi, or 'red weavers', the preferred payment for the rescue service was a bottle of Georgian wine. The rescue was performed by the local collective tractor whose engine was started with a piece of twine. The main concern of the people in the village, which lay on the ouskirts of Yaroslavl in northern Russia, and of Ira Zakharova, a widowed school-teacher in whose house I stayed for a few days in the spring of 1988, was the introduction of sugar rationing in the village store – a portent of the hard days to come. The immediate reason for the sugar rationing was the cut back in alcohol production throughout the USSR in an attempt by Mikhail Gorbachev to improve work discipline. As vodka shops closed down and half-mile queues formed at those still open, people in every village began making *samogon*, the Russian version of poteen. It was the first great rebellion against communist rule where the whole rural population conspired against the party bosses.

Ira's home was a typical *izba*, with delicate carvings around the windows, a veranda, and white birch logs piled high against the gable, like turf beside an Irish cottage. It had four rooms, all heated by the wall tiles of a centrally located wood-burning stove. It was May Day and the village parade came by the house in mid-morning: a couple of hundred villagers holding red flags, balloons and branches with paper flowers attached, strolling rather than marching behind a small band of three trumpet and two trombone players. The plump parade marshall called out, 'Move to the right comrades', as a black Volga sped by, bearing a military officer to some distant celebration. Perspiring heavily under the weight of the amplifying system around his collar, he called out to people watching from their doorsteps: 'Don't be shy, get into the parade.' In the garden of a shabby wooden house, seven youths wearing dark sunglasses, though it was a cloudy day, sat around scowling and listening to rock music from their *Elektronika* ghetto-blaster, competing briefly with the trumpets and trombones in a cacophony of discordant notes. The little brass band marched twice up and down the road and then led its dwindling number of followers around the back of the village club house and on to a soccer pitch edged with bare trees overburdened with rook nests. On a red-draped trailer, the director of the Red Weavers factory gave a few calls of 'hooray' and made a short speech to the almost empty field before giving way to a football match between his workers and those of the Little Oaks State Vegetable Farm, which was idly watched by a few youngsters lying under the trees.

We didn't realise it then, but it was one of the last May Days of innocence in Soviet Russia. Other villagers spent the holiday afternoon strolling through the neat silver birchwoods, planted after the war to commemorate the 300 local people who died at the front. Beyond the trees a few fishermen dangled their lines in a narrow, fast-flowing river. The quiet was occasionally broken by young fellows on motor-bikes clattering across the metal slats of a suspended footbridge, and by the clink of bottles from the trees where a few men, one already lying senseless on the forest floor, were celebrating May Day in more traditional Russian fashion. The school children went to a disco in the club house where the hallway displayed black-and-white photographs of the village war dead, hollow-cheeked young men and boys with frightened eyes, framed alongside posters with anti-alcohol slogans, including a quotation from Tolstoy about the abuse of drink. Despite the high number of casualties, the war didn't reach Krasniye Tkachi. Sitting on the veranda in the evening as smoke rose straight into the air from neighbouring *izbas*, Ira's father, a dignified, silver-toothed old soldier with a weather-beaten face, described how tank traps had been set in case the Germans came in the garden behind the house where he now grew blackcurrants, rhubarb, carrots, lettuce and tomatoes. They never got that far.

Since the war the village had shared some of the consumer boom of the 1970s. Most people had a television set. Ira's model, attached to a stabiliser to regulate the erratic electric current, sat in a corner of the living-room beside a bookshelf on which rested a slim, well-thumbed copy of Solzhenitsyn's *A Day In The Life of Ivan Denisovich*, his only work published in Russia before his exile. At first glance it was an idyllic life, but Ira, like most of her neighbours, could never hope to get a car. She had been trying to buy a new bed for years in Yaroslavl, but her name had not yet come up on the waiting-list in the furniture shop. She needed a washing-machine but couldn't get one. There were only a handful of telephones in the village. We had to make do that weekend, like everyone else, with a chemical toilet in a back shed, where the temperature in the depths of winter fell to minus forty degrees centigrade. Fresh water had to be fetched half a mile from the nearest well. Two buckets, I discovered, were easier to carry than one. Another rule of village life was that a good *izba* was one beside a well. At least there was electricity in Ira's house. It was hardly surprising that most of the people from the wooden houses in Krasniye Tkachi wanted to move into the five-storey apartment blocks which had been built at the northern end of the village and where Ira's father had been assigned an apartment as a war veteran. His apartment had hot and cold running water, an inside toilet, a shower in the bathroom and central heating.

When I returned to Krasniye Tkachi two years later, when everything was rationed, all basic foodstuffs were in short supply and the country was on the verge of economic collapse. I found that the club house with its photographs of the young men and girls who had died at the front long ago had been burned down in a mysterious fire. All that remained was a gutted, empty shell, a symbol of the end of an era.

The practice of cultivating vegetable gardens to provide food for the winter was not confined to the villages. In the hot summer of 1988 when the temperature stayed in the thirties for weeks and the mosquitoes made life almost unbearable, I went to stay with a family in Torzhok, just off the Leningrad-Moscow Road, a sleepy provincial centre which was once a staging post for travellers between the two cities, but was now bypassed by the main highway and time itself. The family had plenty of fresh produce in the refrigerator of their third-storey flat, located in an apartment block owned by Torzhok's printing-ink factory. Like most of their neighbours, they also rented an allotment. It lay in a field a few minutes walk away, past the factory and past a shantytown of lock-up garages where men spent the torpid evenings fixing their motorbikes and sidecars. Apples, raspberries, blackcurrants, whitecurrants, redcurrants, beans, peas and potatoes grew in rich profusion in a vast jumble of densely cultivated gardens. Tomato and cucumber plants filled hundreds of shoulder-high polyethylene greenhouses. Most plots had little two-room *dachas*. The nearby forests were also rich in mushrooms and wild raspberries which grew along the banks of the river where the whole town went swimming on Sunday afternoons, defying the mosquitoes and horseflies and avoiding the anthills which reached knee-height on the sandy edge of the birch-tree groves.

Seven decades of Soviet centralisation had left provincial towns like Torzhok in an advanced state of decay. It had seen better days. Torzhok was founded in 1139 as a trading centre on the Tveretz River which flows into the Volga. Over the centuries, merchants built fine houses and helped pay for beautiful churches. Flax was cultivated by the river and laid out to dry on the meadows. The town became well known for its fine gold embroideries on velvet and leather. The gentry used to stop off in Torzhok on their way by stage coach or sleigh from St Petersburg to Moscow. One of their number was Pushkin, the great Russian poet of the early nineteenth century who stayed overnight in Torzhok twenty-seven times, a fact carefully recorded in the town's tiny Pushkin museum. The elegant two-storey Pozharsky Hotel, where he stopped over, still stood on the main street but had been converted into a club for young people. Few travellers ever came to stay in Torzhok. The balcony above the entrance was used for speeches during the May Day parade. The old dining-room was a cinema. The Pozharsky Hotel, which was mentioned in Tolstoy's *War and Peace*, apparently produced tasty meat dishes. A plaque on the door quoted two couplets by Pushkin, praising the chef's cutlets. A century later it was impossible to get a cutlet anywhere in the town. Just outside Torzhok was the grave of a local girl, Anna Kern, whom Pushkin admired. On her tombstone were the lines he dedicated to her, perhaps the best known of his love poetry:

> I remember the moment
> When you appeared before me
> You were a momentous vision,
> A genius of the purest beauty.

Half an hour's drive out of town, through fields of flax and past old villages where women carried pails of water from the well on wooden shoulder harnesses and herds of cows sometimes blocked the road, we came to Bernova House, a fine old mansion where Pushkin also stayed occasionally and which had been converted into a museum dedicated to his memory. Recorded orchestra music began to play in the ballroom when the door was opened. In the garden was a grassy mound called *parnassus*, where the poet is said to have composed his verses. Few foreigners ever came by. Torzhok was not included in *Russia's Golden Ring* of tourist towns with state-preserved church museums. Even the invading German army bypassed the town, taking the main road on each side instead, though air raids destroyed 70 per cent of the buildings in the centre. Once there were forty churches; now only sixteen remained. Of these only one was open for worship. The rest were either boarded up or used for state enterprises. Most were falling down. An octagonal, three-tiered wooden church, a unique example of seventeenth-century Russian Orthodox architecture, stood empty above the river, its heavy beam-ends succumbing to rot. The only sign of a revival of the town was scaffolding around the seventeenth-century Borisoglebsky Monastery, a fortified cathedral fort with its towers and cupolas reflected in the river. The monastery was a witness to Soviet history. It had been closed after the revolution, then opened in Stalin's time as a prison and finally converted into a small factory.

I drove by Torzhok several times on my way to and from Leningrad in the following years. Nothing seemed to change. There were still the same queues outside the two alcohol shops serving a population of 50,000. The shops in the deserted, dusty main street had less goods on the shelves and by 1990 there had been no flour or yeast on sale for a year. The only items I could guarantee I would find were salt, bread, juice and frozen fish. Sausage meat and sugar were rationed. The residents could no longer go to shop in Moscow or Leningrad where shop assistants demanded residence cards. A woman said she was haunted every night before going to bed by the thought, 'What will I feed my husband and children tomorrow?'

Not all Russian cities were as stagnant or as bereft of life and provisions as Torzhok. Sometimes being remote from the centre was an advantage. Murmansk, the largest city within the Arctic Circle, had some unexpected benefits to compensate for the bleak existence of its 468,000 inhabitants. The best time to see Murmansk is during the midnight sun. When my plane left Moscow at 10.00 p.m. in mid-May, the capital was in darkness, but when we landed at 11.55 p.m. in Murmansk it was light enough to read the small print of *Polyarnaya Pravda*, the local edition of the Communist Party daily. From 17 May to 27 July the sun does not dip below the Connemara-like horizons around Murmansk, named after the Lapplanders' word for 'the end of the earth'. Even though the ten-week polar day had just begun in Murmansk, there were still old snow drifts lying in hollows and crevices, and blizzards in June were not unknown. Just sixteen weeks previously the metropolis had emerged from the continual darkness of the polar night, which lasted from 21 November to 21 January. The sixty-day night caused psychological problems and depressions, relieved sometimes by hard drinking, admitted Galina Podobedova, the motherly deputy-president of the city's executive committee. Sun lamps were in big demand. Children were brought in relays to the Olympic-size winter swimming-pool and given sunray treatment. In summer they were sent to Black Sea camps to catch up on sunshine. The inhabitants liked to boast that Murmansk had the most northerly trolley-bus service in the world. I was lodged in the concrete-and-glass eighteen-storey Hotel Arctic, where the guests included merchant marine officers with heavily made-up girls in tow, and groups of morose and sometimes very drunk Finns and Norwegians, whose borders lay just over one hundred miles to the west and who had special permission to holiday in Murmansk without the usual visa formalities.

Murmansk escaped from the stifling provincialism of Russian regional towns because of its links with the outside world. When it was built in 1916 to give Russia a sea route to its allies, the first houses were brought from England. It was occupied by British, French and American marines for two years after the revolution. A stone monument in Murmansk the shape of a captain's bridge commemorates the Bolsheviks who fell during the 1918–1920 allied intervention, though there was, in fact, little fighting and most of the casualties were privates from the Green Howards, Royal Scots and Royal Marines who died from Spanish flu. The Germans came to Murmansk in 1939 and 1940 during the short-lived Stalin-Hitler pact, then again when war broke out, returning in bomber planes. The British, too, came back, this time on relief convoys. The day the German army surrendered in Berlin, allied ships in the harbour raised their flags and sounded their sirens in triumph. Behind them, Murmansk lay in ruins, devastated by ninety-seven air raids. I found the graves of twenty-four British and five American seamen who perished in the relief of Murmansk in a carefully tended corner of an old graveyard outside the city, overshadowed by a giant power-station. Rows of small granite headstones recorded the bare details: 'Gunner P J Corrigan, Maritime Regiment, died 4.4.42, aged 22', 'P Murphy, 3rd radio officer, Lancaster Castle, died 24.3.42, aged 20'. Some of the names were Pakistani, others Spanish. Since the war Murmansk's links with the outside world had been maintained through its huge fishing fleet of 1,500 deep-sea vessels which roamed the oceans of the world. The Gulf Stream kept the Murmansk fjord ice-free all year. Eight out of ten people in the city depended on the fishing industry for their livelihood.

As I explored the town, a cold drizzle swept over the six-storey city-centre blocks from the Barents Sea. I decided to buy an umbrella and dropped into a busy general store in a side street. It turned out to be no ordinary shop, but something of an Aladdin's cave by Russian standards. There were expensive French perfumes on sale for five roubles, which then was five pounds at the official exchange rate; quality Italian shoes at fourteen roubles a pair; Swiss windcheaters for twenty roubles; West German mohair sweaters at twenty-five roubles each; and a range of foreign consumer goods, including packs of 200 St Moritz cigarettes for three roubles. None of these were available in ordinary Russian shops at the time, and would not be seen on open display even in Moscow or Leningrad until after the price reform of early 1991. A notice by the door explained that the store was for Murmansk seamen and their families and purchases could be made only with hard-rouble coupons issued to fishermen by the local bank in exchange for foreign currency acquired in overseas ports. Ordinary roubles or foreign banknotes were not accepted, and I couldn't, for this reason, buy the three rouble Japanese umbrella I wanted. For once, the tables were turned on the normally privileged foreigner. The connection with the sea also provided another bonus for the people who lived in remote Murmansk. This was the Neptune fishmonger in Lenin Avenue. Locals said it was not what it used to be, but late on a Saturday afternoon it had fresh mackerel, cod, halibut, perch, whitebait, sprats and pilchards, laid out on spotless tiled counters. I had never before come across a fresh fish shop anywhere in Russia. According to Galina Podobedova, Murmansk had also developed techniques to grow greenhouse vegetables in the dead of the polar night. They had cucumbers in the shops in February, two months before they were in season in Moscow, and they had even started to grow vines and produce their own grapes.

Despite all this, Murmansk was afflicted by the same ailments which made life so raw in Russian cities. There were the same long queues for vodka, fights in the evenings among local youths, and increasing crime and prostitution. To attract workers, pay in the giant fish-processing plant and factories and mines was 40 per cent higher than average and increased each year, but there was a fifteen to twenty year waiting list for apartments. Construction work went on constantly and the city was framed by tall cranes, as row after row of ugly functional apartment blocks appeared on the slopes behind the town centre. No concessions were made to the environment. The structures were identical to those erected in Tallinn, Kishinev, Kiev or Moscow. The all-union enterprises in the capital were intent on the rapid industrialisation of the mineral-rich Kola peninsula on which Murmansk stood. 'I picked cloudberries and mushrooms there just last year', said a fisherman on shore leave, pointing disconsolately at a half-finished factory complex. 'Murmansk is like a permanent building site', said Galina Podobedova. 'The city is growing too quickly and many demand that it stop. We don't have enough shops, goods, schools, kindergartens, cafés or apartments.'

I was reminded of Murmansk when I saw the film *We Cannot Live Like This*, the starkest account of life in Russia ever to be seen in the Soviet cinema. First shown in 1990 and designed to shock, it made the case that turning cities into permanent building sites and exploiting natural resources without regard for the environment or people's health had brutalised people, and that criminality and corruption flourished under the communist system, even more so when the system was destabilised. Law enforcement agencies were not respected or trusted. 'Seven decades of the wrong genetic development of the people could not be cured in five years of perestroika', said director Stanislav Govorukhin in the film's commentary. 'When the country is rich and the people are poor, that is the real crime. Who is to blame? We can't find out but we know the organisers of the crime', he said as the screen filled with a communist banner declaring, 'The Party is the Organiser and Inspirer of all our Victories'. Wherever it was shown, cinema audiences applauded his stark message; after seventy-three years of socialism, the Soviet Union was impoverished, criminalised and morally bankrupt. For the first time cinemagoers saw the stark differences between life in the Soviet Union and life in the West. *We Cannot Live Like This* used juxtaposition to highlight what had been inflicted on ordinary people and Russia by the Communist Party. The camera panned over desecrated churches and polluted landscapes, and over gigantic statues of Lenin. There were shots of endless queues, including one ill-tempered line of 5,000 people in Govorukhin's home town of Bereznyaki in the Urals, waiting to get into a shabby alcohol store. 'We spend our lives looking at other people's backs', he remarked. We then saw comfortable, tastefully furnished apartments and a shopping mall in Hamburg, where people strolled past brightly lit windows. This was West Germany's economic achievement, said Govorukhin, whereas the much-vaunted Exhibition of Economic Achievements in Moscow was no more than a 'deceit'. In a country village, two old women described how they lived on potatoes and vegetables. There was nothing in the nearest shop. Only once in three months could they buy flour. We were shown a better-stocked shop with several basic products and told that it was inside a strict regime camp. How could it be, asked Govorukhin, that people lived worse than criminals. The scene shifted to a hard-currency shop for foreigners in Moscow laden with meats and cheeses, and then to another Aladdin's cave, the Aer Rianta-Aeroflot duty-free shop in Moscow Airport where Govorukhin was seen enduring the ultimate humiliation of Russian people: offering Soviet roubles for, in this case, a box of Russian chocolates and being told, 'Sorry, only hard currency accepted.'

Until 1990 it was illegal for Soviet citizens to hold foreign currency, but this did not deter those determined to get access to Western consumer goods. In Murmansk the port provided a window to the world much like a bank-teller's partition through which foreign currency came in a trickle. In Leningrad, Russia's second city, it came in a flood from the millions of tourists who arrived each year from abroad, many of them Finns on a day trip from Helsinki, only a seven-hour drive away. They provided a steady revenue in hard currency, or *valuta*, to such an extent that by the end of the 1980s the dollar had become a second currency, and the city earned the nickname *Valutagrad*. Taxi drivers would take only *valuta* from foreigners. In Nevsky Prospect I was stopped every few yards by youths speaking only two words of English, 'change money'. Many spent their dollars in one of the string of hard-currency shops jointly run by Aer Rianta (Irish Airports Authority) in the airport and city hotels, one of the channels through which Western clothes and electronics found their way into the Leningrad economy. The dollar had become a second currency for enterprises too. Intourist Hotel managers found they could only guarantee food to their restaurants by paying the Soviet suppliers in hard currency. The proximity to

Helsinki made people in Leningrad even more acutely aware of
the contrast in the standard of living between Russia and Finland.
Leningraders told an anecdote against themselves. They wanted
independence, but only for one day. They would use it to declare
war on Finland, and surrender immediately.

Though one of the great cities of the world, with five million
inhabitants, Leningrad suffered all the ills of decaying Russia.
At first glance it appeared unspoiled, one of the loveliest cities
in the Northern hemisphere – a unique blend of Russian and
European architecture, with streets lined by low classical and
baroque buildings. The city was built by Peter the Great as
the capital of Russia, a status it enjoyed from 1712 to 1918.
Originally called St Petersburg, it was renamed Petrograd in 1914
and Leningrad in 1924. It was partially destroyed during the terrible
900-Day Siege from 1941 to 1944 when German armies camped
on the outskirts, and the only means of supply was in winter, by
what became known as the 'ice road' over a frozen Lake Lagoda.
Leningrad was restored to its original condition soon afterwards,
but the city in the 1980s was a sorry sight. Cornices sometimes
fell on people's heads in the streets. Pollution had eaten away
the faces on gargoyles and stone carvings. Construction standards
were so low that as soon as a new Pushkin museum was opened
in 1988, it had to be closed again for repairs. Academician
Dmitry Likhachev, whose great grandparents lived in Leningrad
and who himself had lived through the revolution, remembered
how the intelligentsia of the city was annihilated under communist
rule, while architectural monuments were destroyed and priceless
treasures from the Hermitage Museum were plundered and sold
abroad. Many people still lived in appalling squalor as deteriorating
old buildings with dank courtyards returned to the conditions
of Dostoevsky's St Petersburg. Residents who wished to change
flats gathered in the evenings in Peace Square where they studied
thousands of hand-written notices stuck to wooden hoardings, as
trams rumbled by through the dimly lit cobbled streets. Some stood
around with pieces of paper pinned to their chests stating 'Will
exchange flat with two rooms in Kalinsky district for one-room
apartment in Kirovsky region'. The city roads were pitted with
enormous pot-holes and criss-crossed by twisting tram-lines which
obstructed motorists like tank traps. Leningrad became known
throughout the country as much for its crime, prostitution and
decay as for its architectural beauty. The city's economy was in
a shambles, said Viktor Yugin, editor of the Leningrad journal,

Smena, when I called to see him one day. 'The people are tired; they have had enough.' The economic plight of the city could be quickly learned from its taxi-drivers. 'There are 7,000 taxis in Leningrad', one said. 'Only 3,500 are working. This one', he said, tapping the dashboard of his old yellow Volga, 'has 400,000 kilometres on the clock.' He sighed. 'Of course, if all the taxis were working, there wouldn't be enough petrol.'

The revolution started in St Petersburg in 1917 in the Smolny Institute, built by Catherine II as a school for young women. John Reed described it in *Ten Days that Shook the World*, his classic account of the hectic events of 1917, as a hive of activity with lights blazing all night as Lenin and Trotsky came and went and the future of Russia was decided. From here the Communist Party presided over Leningrad's affairs, unchallenged behind its Ionic columns, for seventy-three years until March 1990 when a counter-revolution got underway in another building of the tsarist era, this time the Marie Palace – an Italianate mansion built for Marie, Duchess of Leuchtenberg, and situated opposite St Issac's Cathedral. It housed the city parliament, the *Lensoviet*, traditionally a subservient instrument of the party. After the first multi-candidate elections under Gorbachev's reforms, the Marie Palace became a hive of activity, with the 375 deputies of *Lensoviet* meeting in constant session under the blazing electric lights of crystal chandeliers adorned with tsarist eagles. All but twenty of the deputies belonged to the prodemocracy Election 90 group.

When I visited the building six weeks after the election, I found the mosaic-floored hallway where Kerensky presided over the prerevolutionary *Duma* thronged with townspeople lobbying the deputies. There were propaganda posters on the marble pillars. One of these advertised a 'Mission of Spiritual Rebirth', and invited people to a Protestant evangelical meeting. A woman nearby handed out copies of *Dubinushka* (Little Stick), a news-sheet with the slogan, 'Socialism or Death', published by Leningrad's pro-Stalin celebrity, Nina Andreyeva. Election 90 was returned on a platform of opposition to the Communist Party apparatus. It had, however, no other coherence. There was endless confusion in the Marie Palace debating chamber. The Election 90 alliance had rapidly broken down as political parties emerged. They included a Democratic Russia bloc, Social Democrats and Liberal Democrats, and 'even a group with a hard-core of six or seven for those of us who don't know what to do', said Zhenia Bronnikova, editor of *Soviet Teacher*. *Lensoviet* at least knew what it didn't want.

When deputies arrived for the first session they found two KGB men at each entrance. They were ordered out of the building, said Bella Kurkova, editor of the popular *Fifth Wheel* current-affairs programme on Leningrad television, looking triumphantly over her huge spectacles. They didn't want to celebrate May Day and had voted to cancel the parade for the first time since the war. They scrapped that weekend's Lenin *subbotnik*, a time when people normally gave a free day's work in honour of Lenin's birthday, and renamed it Earth Day instead. They also passionately did not want the city to die and had set up a revival commission, whose chairman, history professor Gleb Lebedev, remarked to me, his face breaking into a silver-toothed grin, 'Leningrad was sacked by the Huns, then ruined by the Russian proletariat. But the tragedy is now ended.' The majority of the deputies also did not want to be saddled with the name Leningrad any more and they were preparing for a debate on what would have been unthinkable a few months previously, changing the name of the city back either to St Petersburg or to Petrograd. 'I suggested we have all three names', said Professor Lebedev in his university study, decorated with a pop-star calendar and a stuffed bird. The name change came about almost by default. People simply switched back to the prerevolutionary St Petersburg when they referred to the city. An international telethon to raise money for the city's revival in January 1991, supported by all the official organisations, was called St Petersburg Renaissance. Eventually, on 12 June 1991, the population voted by 55 per cent to make St Petersburg the official name.

In those heady days when the radicals thought they could change the world, warning voices could be heard. 'The situation has its dangers', cautioned deputy Pyotr Fillipov. 'People expect too much from their radical city government. Leningrad is broke, and these people have no experience of bureaucracy in seventy years.' 'I am more optimistic', said Professor Lebedev. 'It's a soviet of the intelligentsia. We will make up for inexperience with specialist knowledge. But we must not repeat the old Bolshevik mistake and destroy the old power structure.' The 'soviet of the intelligentsia' found itself unable to take decisions, even under the leadership of Anatoly Sobchak, one of the most impressive reformers to emerge under perestroika and who was determined to transform the 'cradle of the revolution' into a free economic zone. The party bosses still controlled much of what went on in Leningrad, where the big industries were run by the military or the all-union enterprises whose managers were answerable to the party's central committee. As in Ryazan, the jubilation at the victory of the reformers was soon tempered by the realisation that seventy years of communism had fundamentally affected the psychology of the people, and that the economic system which had brought the country to collapse had a strong grip on the economic life of the city.

The counter-revolution in Russia would not be a ten-day affair like the Bolshevik uprising, but a long, hard struggle to revive a Russia which lay stagnating, from the provincial town of Ryazan, where the country's favourite peasant poet Sergei Yesenin was born, through its villages and byways, to Leningrad, where Yesenin hanged himself in despair in 1925 in a city hotel.

13

Exploding Fish and
Triple Glazing

THE ROAD was blackened in places by coal dust and was unexpectedly bumpy, though not rutted so badly as to slow down the steady stream of cars, lorries, taxis and yellow school buses packed with children. It could have been any road in rural Russia except that it ran along the frozen surface of the wide River Lena, a dual carriageway carved through a vast, grey wilderness of ice hummocks and snowdrifts on the mighty waterway which stretched from southern Siberia to the Arctic Ocean. The ice road, laid out by engineers in the autumn when the ice was a metre thick, opened up areas of Yakutsk in north-eastern Siberia accessible only by helicopter in summer. It was marked by posts and little trees stuck in the ice. Potholes were repaired simply by boring a hole and filling it with water, which froze solid in less than an hour. There were slip roads, roundabouts, signposts, petrol stations, even the odd lamp post, and, at one busy junction, a set of traffic lights among the ice knolls.

After a long drive in a Volga (a constant source of local amusement – the idea of a Volga on the Lena) down the centre of the frozen river which was two miles wide in places, we took a 'side road' where a signpost stuck in the ice said, 'City of Yakutsk'. Yakutsk, situated near the cold pole of the Northern Hemisphere, was, we discovered, one of the most rapidly developing industrial cities in Siberia, whose population had gone from 100,000 to 225,000 during the 1980s. Founded in 1637 as a fortress, it was now the capital of the huge Yakutsk autonomous republic, an area of over a million square miles. It was always a forbidding place. Yakutsk had the greatest extremes of temperature of any city in the world, from minus sixty-four degrees centigrade in winter to thirty-four degrees centigrade in summer. When I arrived on a February evening in 1989, I felt the cold burning my skin as I left the overheated car interior. It froze the moisture inside my nostrils, and breath turned to ice on my scarf. I noticed that people wore shoes with fur on the outside. The windows in the shabby hotel – Yakutsk was not on the Intourist map – were equipped with triple glazing, and even with that the inner

glass in the bedroom had a coating of hoar frost after the temperature
went down to minus forty degrees centigrade outside. Cars as well
had double windshields. Engines were never switched off in winter to
prevent them from freezing up. At night you could hear the murmur
and grumble of cars and lorries parked on the street, and the air during
the day was always thick with their white exhaust fumes.

Nevertheless, I found the still, cold air intensely exhilarating. The
secret of coping with such temperatures, I learned, was to wear long
johns and several layers of thin clothes beneath a heavy coat, two
or three pairs of knee-length socks tucked into outsize boots, and
a fur hat with ear flaps tied beneath the chin. Taxi-drivers made a
show of waiting about bareheaded and jacketless in the open, but I
noticed that they never lingered for more than a couple of minutes.
The snow was pure and white and creaked noisily underfoot, unlike
the frozen slush we had to cope with in Moscow. In the depths of
winter, its texture was like fine sand. You could plow through it up
to your waist and it would not compact beneath your feet. It was
too grainy for cross-country skiing, and the Yakutians only enjoyed
this sport in the early autumn and late spring when the temperature
was not far below freezing. The local Siberians took a perverse pride
in their city's climatic notoriety and boasted that they hated when
it got mild in winter. Mild was minus twenty degrees centigrade.
At this temperature, they said, children started getting colds. Schools
were not closed until the temperature dipped below minus fifty-one
degrees centigrade, at which point metal became as brittle as glass. The
apartment blocks in Yakutsk, mostly four- or six-storied, had plastic
bags hanging from windows stuffed with meat – it was the best way
to keep it frozen – and all the buildings, including the seven-storey
Communist Party mansion, were standing on concrete stilts.

Yakutsk lay right in the middle of the permafrost zone, the only
modern city built on the permanently frozen peat-moss which covered
47 per cent of Russia. The first concrete buildings erected here had
sunk into a quagmire when the heat they generated melted the
permafrost, which in any event thawed to a depth of two metres
in summer. You could still see them here and there, leaning over and
cracked as if an earthquake had shaken them. A special technique
had since been developed to build on permafrost. Pillars of concrete
twenty-inches square were sunk thirty-six feet into the frozen earth and
used to support buildings a few yards above the ground. The empty
space beneath was useful for car-parking, though very few residents
were lucky enough to own a car. To sink the pillars, compressed steam
was piped down into the permafrost. Metal pipes filled with kerosene

were placed inside the concrete piles to draw down the surface cold and to prevent melting. All over the city we could see forests of these concrete stilts ready for new structures as Yakutsk prepared to expand its housing estates even further and add to the 272 enterprises already exploiting the rich coal, diamond and other mineral resources of the region.

This bustling, thrusting, modern city was the epitome of the old Soviet dream to open up and industrialise Siberia. Yakutsk was, however, as we quickly discovered, a city with no future, doomed to exist in a desert of earth which the city itself had made sterile. Having conquered the permafrost, the urban sprawl began to destroy it, and only now were scientists coming to realise the extent of the calamity. Fields and gardens, once fertile, had died. On many building sites, further construction had become impossible in the destabilised permafrost. Some new pillars of concrete already leaned over and had been abandoned. The dream had become a nightmare, and the main villain was human waste. Chemicals deposited in the ground from the urine of tens of thousands of people concentrated in a few square kilometres had changed the texture of the permafrost and lowered its freezing point. Water used for irrigation had left behind all its salt deposits as there was no run-off from the frozen mass beneath the two metres of melted earth in summer. The soil became salinated after ten years to the point where no vegetation would grow. You could see the barren patches of land around the city, testimony to the destructive capacity of man and the folly of the Soviet dream of taming nature. Heat from the concentration of factories and people had raised the permanent temperature of the permafrost from minus five degrees centigrade to minus three degrees around the city. The effect had been to create 'melted' zones which did not freeze properly again, and these patches, called *kriopegi* had begun spreading of their own accord.

This tragedy had been monitored with a feeling of helplessness by Professor Veniamin Balobayev of the Yakutsk Permafrost Institute, the only one of its kind in the world, with 500 scientific workers providing it with data from throughout the permafrost zone. The institute was located outside town. In the driveway stood a statue of a mammoth, the remains of which had been found intact beneath the frozen ground. Inside the building, a stairway led down to caverns dug in the permafrost to enable visitors to see it from below. The walls were suprisingly sandy and crumbled to the touch, unlike the more common permafrost mass which resembles frozen peat-moss. 'We have come to the conclusion that big city conglomerates cannot be erected on permafrost. Nature cannot carry such a load', said the bespectacled, heavily built professor, who had spent his whole life trying to understand the secrets of this frozen land. 'We have to live on permafrost. Our task is to find out some form of interrelation between man and permafrost so as not to create irreversible phenomena.' He feared the effect on the country's climate of building more cities in the permafrost zone as the authorities then planned. 'Permafrost is the result of climate', he said. 'Damaging it will have a back effect on the climate, creating non-uniform temperature fields and new fields of atmospheric pressure.' Even after four years of glasnost he feared no one was listening to his warnings. 'The city should be spread over a large area and not concentrated', he said. 'In fact Yakutsk should be abandoned and people should move to the nearby hills overlooking the River Lena where less damage would be done to the permafrost of the plains. But Yakutsk, unfortunately, is a city of bureaucrats. It is being built like a Western city and that is simply not right.' The grandiose plans of central authority dictated that the population should rise to 300,000 in another ten years. Even the city architect, Fedor Sheshigin, said he thought 100,000 was enough. But no one in far-away Moscow, where the decisions were made, was listening to the ominous prophesies coming from the Permafrost Institute. Professor Balobayev said, 'They tend only to take advice into account when they see the negative results. As the old saying goes, people don't take precautions until they have been burned by the fire.'

When I got back to the city centre from the institute, I saw a youth hurrying through the freezing mist and white exhaust fumes of Yakutsk's main street, every now and then stopping to paste a leaflet on to the wall of one of the concrete-built stores along the narrow roadway. The type-written paper announced that the local branch of the Democratic Union, a proreform pressure group, was backing candidate Oleg Borodin in the March elections to the new Soviet parliament. A few people paused to glance at it, and then walked on. It was too cold to linger. Real electioneering had come to the frozen plains of eastern Siberia for the first time. Borodin was the Yakutsk correspondent for the government newspaper *Izvestia*, a forty-five-year-old journalist whose articles promoted the idea of freeing Yakutsk from the departmental control and environmental vandalism of the all-union ministries in Moscow. His opponent in the constituency, which stretched through the drab apartment blocks, slogan-bearing factories and wooden houses north of the city centre, was Spartak Borisov, fifty-two-year-old director of an industrial enterprise. I met both of them in the director's office, the

Izvestia man balding and earnest, armed with statistics and manifestos, Borisov radiating power, every inch a Russian boss from his broad face and gold teeth to the huge fist with its anchor tattoo from his days as *tankist* in the Soviet army. Both had been endorsed at constituency meetings where several other candidates were eliminated. Both were party members – Yakutsk north would clearly stay communist.

At first they said there was little difference in their platforms. 'I can't speak against Borodin', said the director. 'What would I say to persuade people not to vote for him? Why, that's a Western reporter's question. We respect each other. My opponent has a very good programme – he wants a sports complex and a new trollybus line. I support that. We're all progressive here', he said with a grin. But Borodin, as he well knew, wanted much more than a new trollybus line. The differences between the two candidates, the distinctions which would eventually drive them into different political camps in the Congress of People's Deputies, emerged after a few minutes despite the courteous politics of the Russian Klondike. The director was for cautious change in keeping with the mood of the times. The newspaper man was for radical reform. 'We must decentralise the economy', said Borodin. The director interjected, 'Yes, but we must have a strong centre and strong regions.' 'Gorbachev should subject himself to a nationwide election for president', said the *Izvestia* man. 'He's right, but we're not ready for it yet', said Borisov. Borodin, who was to become a leading member of the opposition Inter-Regional Group of deputies in the Soviet parliament, made ecology his number one issue. His manifesto read, 'An examination of industrial projects must be conducted by regional commissions for the ecology. The zones where the nationalities of the north live should be declared free from intensive development. When constructing cities and towns, referendums should be held on ecological matters. Local Soviets should be given the right to veto projects, proceeding from the principle that there is nothing more precious than a man's health.' The disillusion with the centre had drawn the reformers and some party *apparachiks* together in Yakutsk. 'Gone are the days when everyone just voted yes to everything from above', said the city party first secretary Alexei Artur, a soft-spoken native Yakutian with characteristic Inuit-like features. 'People now want to know about solutions to their problems and about new ideas for the region, such as self-financing and joint enterprises with foreign companies.' Voices were even being raised to suggest that Yakutia become a province of Japan.

Life was tough in Yakutsk. Much of the city population was transient, made up of migrant Russian workers prepared to suffer three or four hard winters for a salary up to four times higher than the average. Hard-drinking, brawling young men and heavily made-up girls packed the hotel dining-room on Saturday nights, where a cartoon-graphic notice in the kitchen gave instructions on what to do if the city was subject to chemical or nuclear attack ('after the nuclear blast, follow the instructions of defence officials to move to uncontaminated areas'). Accommodation was scarce in a city once described as the end of the line, except there was no line. The nearest railway track ended 700 miles away. Oleg Borodin's latest story in *Izvestia* had revealed that plans to build the Amur-Yakutsk railway had been scrapped because of a budget deficit. It was now up to Yakutsk to find the money. The cancellation of the railway was good news for the ecologists who wished to save the permafrost. It meant continuing hardship for the city population, dependant on supplies from more temperate regions of Russia. Almost all produce had to come by lorry or boat up the River Lena, depending on whether it was frozen or not. Meat was rationed to seventy kilos per person a year. It didn't always turn up. Food in the peasants' market was very expensive. Produce on the stalls was displayed by Kazakhs and Uzbeks who flew up from the south with their wares in cardboard boxes and plastic carrier bags.

In Yakutsk South, one of the candidates was Andrei Borisov, a Yakut who was director of the city's theatre. His wife, Stepanida, was his principal actress. They had toured Canada and Mexico with a Brecht play, *The Good Person of Szechwan*, in Yakutian. It was in their apartment in a city block that, along with my travelling companions, Rupert Cornwell of the London *Independent* and Stephen Handleman of the Toronto *Star*, I tasted the other side of life in the remote north-east of Siberia. We were treated to a memorable supper provided from the fruits of the Taiga forest and its rich rivers, including frozen strips of *omul*, the delicious Siberian salmon, brought in from the window-sill and dipped in salt, and carp stuffed with roe and wild hare, washed down with vodka and whortleberry juice. Andrei, a long-haired Yakut with twinkling eyes, was passionately concerned about the decline of the Yakut language. Stepanida sang an ancient song to illustrate its onomatopoeic qualities, a haunting lament with frequent throat-stops. For them the tragedy of the Russian colonisation of Yakutia was the damage to their culture. One Yakut child in nine had lost the mother tongue, and young people needed Russian for a career, they told us. It was a problem which affected all the northern peoples of Siberia, from the Yakuts to the Buryats who lived around Lake Baikal.

I first visited Lake Baikal, 2,000 kilometres south-east of Yakutsk, in 1980, and had been back twice since coming to work and live in Moscow, drawn by its ethereal beauty. There was no place quite like it on earth. It lay an hour's drive from the town of Irkutsk, through the unspoiled Taiga forest of eastern Siberia. Baikal, the deepest lake in the world, was longer than the island of Ireland and contained one sixth of the world's fresh water. It had 1,200 creatures which were not found anywhere else. Fresh-water seals, for example, basked on its islands. Lake Baikal froze over in winter, except at the point where the outflowing Angara River created a small bay of steel-blue water, framed by snow-clad hills and lakeside villages. Occasionally, a little ferry boat chugged across the bay, and behind it, on the white horizon of ice, trucks and motorbikes made their way from shore to shore on the winter ice roads. It was a dangerous way to travel. The lake was so deep that at the bottom the water temperature was always four degrees centigrade. Occasionally huge bubbles of this warm water came to the surface and melted the ice from below. The inevitable then happened. Lorries and cars fell through what looked like safe ice. Sometimes a thick mist formed over the water, and cars moving across lost their way and literally drove off the ice into the bay. I preferred to walk out on to the smooth surface. A few hundred metres from the shore, pebbles could be seen clearly through the metre-thick ice where the dry snow had blown away, as if through the bottom of a crystal bowl. The oxygen-rich water had been filtered from glaciers and 336 rivers in an area of Siberia as large as Western Europe, and held in almost distilled form for millions of years. I was told you could top up a car battery with it. The water was also exquisite to drink. The grandeur and majesty of the lake had been celebrated by Russian writers like Valentin Rasputin, who lived and worked in a *dacha* by the waters for most of the year. 'To go there even for a day is a kind of celebration, like visiting a cathedral', he told me.

But for Rasputin, a quiet-spoken Siberian with a permanent brown tan, the cathedral had been desecrated. On a clear day a thin column of smoke could be seen rising from the far shore, forty miles away. It came from one of the Soviet Union's biggest paper-and-cellulose combines which had been discharging polluted water into the lake for twenty-one years. The people of the villages and harbours up and down the lake shore – clusters of wooden houses with names like Baikalsk, Babushkin and Khushir, and writers and artists who drew spiritual strength from Baikal – had known for many years that their beloved lake was being damaged. They could do nothing. The 1970s and early 1980s were the years of stagnation when public unease counted for little and critical ecological studies could not be published in the press. One of the first results of glasnost was an explosion of public outrage in Irkutsk over Baikal. Courageous local reporters like Alexander Batalin sent articles to the sympathetic liberal journals in Moscow. Openness made public the extent of the problem. Informal groups appeared in Irkutsk to carry their protest to the authorities.

The extent of the damage caused by the pulp mill was explained to me by the director of the Lakeside Museum, Valentina Galkina, a pleasant middle-aged woman whose voice took on a passionate edge as she described how a 'dead zone' had formed around the discharge area at the cellulose combine. Two thirds of Baikal's flora and fauna was unique to the lake, she said. It contained millions of tiny crayfish found nowhere else in the world. These filtered the water and killed the bacteria. Now they were dying in the thirty-five square miles of lake around the pipe which discharged acids and alkalis into the translucent water. A mysterious illness was also killing the seals, though they lived hundreds of kilometres away in the northern reaches of the lake. 'In former times', said Valentin Rasputin, 'you could pour Baikal water into a jug and it would still be fresh after a week. Now it goes stale after two days. There is pollution not only from the mill but from chemical and manufacturing industries being set up on the inflowing Selenga River.' As a result of the ecological outcry, the government in Moscow decided in 1988 to divert the pulp mill discharge through a seventy-kilometre pipeline to the River Irkut and promised that in five years the enterprise would be converted into a harmless furniture assembly. To the conservationists, however, as Nikolai Logachev, president of the Irkutsk centre for scientific research, put it, this would have meant 'the death of the Irkut River, the shores of which abound in settlements and recreation zones'. Moreover, much of Lake Baikal's environs would have been despoiled by huge pipes laid on the surface along a path bulldozed through the forest. The people of Irkutsk staged an ecological rebellion. Mass meetings were held in the town square, with banners proclaiming, 'Save Baikal, our soul'. A permanent picket was placed on the Communist Party buildings, reinforced by big crowds on Saturdays. A petition demanding the scrapping of the pipeline attracted 100,000 signatures. To sign a complaint was no small act of courage in those days and the Irkutsk authorities showed that they had been completely untouched by the spirit of perestroika. On instructions from the Irkutsk party office, police tore down rally notices; schools were visited and pupils warned not to go to meetings; photographs were taken of those who turned up; and the deputy chairman of Irkutsk Council, Yuri Kushkin, warned after one big rally in November that organisers would be 'called to administrative account' – Brezhnevite shorthand for repression. Attempts were made to dismiss a reporter in a youth newspaper and a government inspector in the Baikal area who supported the movement. A police file was opened on a student at the Agriculture Institute and on colleagues who helped him organise the petition. A sympathetic militia lieutenant was publicly warned of punishment by a senior officer in front of people in the square. Workers in enterprises who signed the petition were reprimanded by party committees.

But it was a rear-guard action. Glasnost and the ecology campaign had friends in high places, and in December 1987 the USSR Academy of Sciences came out against the pipeline. The day I talked to Valentin Rasputin in the portrait-lined reception-room of the Irkutsk Writers' Union in March 1988, he said the Central Committee had just decided that it should not be constructed. More convincing evidence came from one of his friends who had seen the giant pipes being trucked away again. It seemed that the people had won an ecological victory of far-reaching consequences in a country where officials were at last being made to recognise that a vast complex of environmental problems had been created by rapid industrialisation, with rivers and lakes throughout the Soviet Union threatened or dying. Deep scepticism, however, remained. 'In former times technocrats didn't let the people speak', said Valentin Rasputin. 'Now they can't express their own views, but it doesn't mean that they are weak.' He used his finger to draw an imaginary map on the polished wooden table to show how the authorities had used sleight of hand in another controversial case. They had agreed not to erect a phosphate factory on a river flowing into Baikal, but the new site would simply mean the pollution would eventually filter to the lake by a more circuitous route. He also had evidence that the new pulp factory was unlikely to be finished within five years, and during that time the poisonous discharges would continue along Lake Baikal.

Rasputin had become famous throughout Russia for his fight for Baikal. He was much loved for his village stories, fired with a sense of loss for a kinder, more humane Russia. He was born in the remote village of Ust-Uda on the Angara River. It was submerged when a hydro-electric power-station was constructed. The villagers lost their spiritual and moral values when uprooted and thrust into unfamiliar jobs, he said. He didn't like Moscow very much and avoided going there – which became difficult when Mikhail Gorbachev made him a member of his presidential council in 1990. 'I get the same feeling when arriving in Moscow as my mother on coming to Irkutsk', he remarked. The first time she left her village to visit the town more than thirty years earlier, her reaction had been to ask, 'Where will they find enough earth to bury all these people?' His passionate views had made him a Russian nationalist, angry at the submergence of Russia in Soviet culture, and he had been criticised for allowing his name to be linked with the anti-Semitic Russian society *Pamyat*, 'memory'. 'I am proud of being Russian', he said. 'When you contacted me and said you were Irish, I had a picture of you. The conflict in your country I know about – your culture. But if you said you were simply from Europe, what would that teach me about you? Just that you were from a political entity. Here the word Soviet denies nationality. Every nationality in the Soviet Union should be respected. The Russian language is constantly imposed. Even in Byelorussia there is no teaching in Byelorussian. Who's to blame? Bureaucrats who want to be seen in a better light in Moscow. When I'm in Byelorussia or the Ukraine, I want to hear their national sayings and national music and folklore, but I'm more likely to hear spoiled Russian.' In eastern Siberia, people had developed a profound distrust of bureaucracy. They remembered what happened to the beautiful Orthodox Kazansky Cathedral, one of the 'seven pearls of Russia', which dominated Irkutsk until local officials pulled it down, stone by stone, in great haste one day in the 1930s to prove their atheism to Moscow. They recalled, too, that three days after it was destroyed a letter arrived from the Soviet capital, in response to appeals from Irkutsk residents, to say it could be spared.

In Irkutsk, which Rasputin described in the city guide-book as 'modestly famous for its glory, past and present, modestly cultured since olden times and traditionally hospitable', functional office blocks in the centre gave way to streets of intricately carved nineteenth-century larchwood houses lined with poplar trees. It had become the regional capital of eastern Siberia, having begun life as a frontier town three centuries previously. The town had been a place of exile. Several leaders of the noblemen's *Decembrist* revolt were sent there in 1825 and played an important role in developing the region. Eighteen thousand six hundred Poles were exiled to the region in 1863. The Irkutsk transit prison became notorious among the tens of thousands of unfortunates who passed through on their way to Stalin's Gulag Archipelago. Unlike Yakutsk, it had been put on the tourist map. It had a large Intourist Hotel and was a stopping point on the trans-Siberian railway. Some of the pioneering spirit remained. Antonov turboprops droned across an eggshell-blue sky on their way to and from the outbacks. The untamed Taiga forest lay all around. Nevertheless, for many of its workers, life was hard and lacking spiritual and moral values. Irkutsk had eighty-two industrial enterprises, but was listed as one of the Soviet Union's twenty hungry cities, though the co-operative movement had brought back some of the atmosphere of the merchant adventurers of the tsarist times. One entrepreneur travelled regularly to Odessa to buy foreign clothes from sailors and to refashion the material into stylish gear. But the state shops were miserably understocked.

Just how desperate people could be to escape from a town like Irkutsk was highlighted by the bizarre case of the Seven Simeons, a singing group made up of members of the Ovechkin family, an event which shook the city of half a million and which coincided with my visit to Irkutsk in March 1988. I found their home on a frozen dirt road with sunken tram-lines between rows of old wooden houses. It could have been a scene from a century ago; figures were moving about in the half light of a bitter Siberian dusk, the only sound the cracking and squeaking of ice underfoot. Here in the 'Workers' Region' of Irkutsk the Ovechkin family had lived in number 22 Detskaya Street, a three-roomed log-house with pink shutters and a tiny wicker fence. Behind it loomed the gaunt skeleton of a derelict Orthodox church and nearby an electricity pylon with skull and lightning warning signs. The family had clearly been leaving for good when they set out for the Irkutsk airport a day or two earlier. They had sold most of their furniture and taken their personal valuables. In one room a broken electronic keyboard lay abandoned on a mattress. In another, two empty vodka bottles stood side by side. In the yard a sheet of music fluttered, left-handed exercises for a string instrument. The neighbours thought they were just going on another of their tours. Four years previously the brothers in the Ovechkin family had formed a traditional jazz band ensemble, the Seven Simeons, and the sound of banjos and skiffle-boards had become familiar in Detskaya Street. They had often been invited to play at concerts around town and to travel further afield. The Ovechkins – the name means little sheep – were aged between five and twenty-four when they started playing and were patronised by the authorities as a unique family group. They appeared on television and starred as the opening act at the 1986 Moscow Jazz Festival. The city council appointed them cultural emissaries of Irkutsk and gave them sinecures in the sports and recreation centre.

When the Ovechkins reached the airport they boarded a plane for Leningrad. The snappily dressed, handsome boys – one of the stewardesses recalled thinking, 'What a lovely family' – waited until they were airborne and then produced shotguns from their instrument cases, ordering the crew to take the plane to London. The pilot brought the aircraft down at a military airfield in Leningrad and the attempted hijack ended with the violent deaths of the mother, Ninel, and the three eldest sons, Vasili, Dmitri and Oleg in an orgy of bloodshed. Witnesses said they turned the guns on themselves as police stormed the aircraft. The initial horror over the hijack quickly gave way to some uncomfortable questioning about how the Seven Simeons came to be the cultural representatives of a town which boasted two theatres (one was showing *Hamlet*), a philharmonic orchestra, and nationally renowned writers like Rasputin.

The Ovechkins had had a difficult history. The father was an alcoholic. The mother, who sold beer at a state kiosk, dealt in black-market vodka. 'Everyone knew they were a problem family', said Valentin Rasputin. Local journalist Alexander Bakatin said, 'The children were underdeveloped. They had a feel for music, but they were not very gifted. But they were a family and so the authorities encouraged them and made them "something of which we could be proud."' The official patronage went beyond proper limits, however. In their eagerness to promote the Seven Simeons, the authorities found the older brothers places in Irkutsk and Moscow music colleges, though they lacked proper qualifications. The Irkutsk Council then sent the Seven Simeons to a Japanese city, where cultural exchange had been organised. The Japanese sent their ballet company. 'Japan clearly fired their imagination and their sense of self-importance', said Batalin, 'while at the same time their popularity in Irkutsk was on the wane and people were getting tired of their programme.' Irkutsk residents believed the glimpse of Western life turned their heads. Some said that they were fleeing from trouble they had got into at home, though others said this theory reflected a desire to avoid the embarrassing conclusion that the whole family found their life in Irkutsk so miserable they had to resort to such desperate measures to escape.

Krasnoyarsk is another Siberian city from which a certain category of people would like to escape. It lies to the west of Irkutsk and some of the survivors of the Seven Simeons may have ended up there; Krasnoyarsk is the prison capital of Russia. It is also a closed city. Foreigners have been banned since it became a centre of the military-industrial complex during the Second World War. Though still officially closed, I was allowed to make a private visit in mid-October 1989, the first Western correspondent to be permitted to walk its streets for half a century or more. As if intent on shrouding its secrets, blue-tinged fog enveloped the sprawling city on the mighty

Yenisey River when I arrived after a four-and-a-half-hour flight from Moscow. I found a modern metropolis of a million people with trams, electric commuter trains, five theatres, a philharmonic orchestra, a university, ten institutes, and pleasant promenades along the river bank – as well as prisons. Krasnoyarsk was a city of jails and work camps. I came across them turning a corner or cutting down a side street – converted barracks with blocked-out windows or corrugated iron compounds topped with barbed wire, armed guards dimly silhouetted in watch-towers. The country's most dangerous criminals were sent to Krasnoyarsk. They said in Krasnoyarsk, 'I live across the road from the prison. It's better than living across the road from home.' The jails were mostly on the industrial east bank of the Yenisey River where murder, too, was common. Dangerous men were sometimes released on to the street when their sentence was completed. The west bank was more pleasant, with a river-boat station and a piazza flanked by the Lenin Museum, the most modern building in town, and the concert-hall. The tarmacadam of the square covered the cemetery of an old cathedral, knocked down after the revolution. Its only memorial was a modern stone bust of Konstantin Chernenko, born in a village 200 miles away and Soviet leader for a few months before his death in 1985. Chernenko had been discredited under glasnost as a neo-Stalinist, but to the disgust of most people in the city, the authorities had not taken away the monument. Some months before I visited Krasnoyarsk, ship's paint had been thrown over the bust and it had been removed for cleaning. Many hoped they would never see it again, but it had been put back, scrubbed clean by the city soviet, a clear signal that the old guard still ran things in Krasnoyarsk. Nevertheless, they had to put a militiaman on guard at night, and proreform groups gathered in the square at weekends to demand that Chernenko be replaced by a statue of a nineteenth-century merchant adventurer, Nikolai Rezanov.

Young people had first started demonstrating for change in a leafy pedestrian precinct in the city centre nearby. Unable to resort to old methods of arrest and intimidation, the authorities ended the rallies by simply opening the precinct to traffic. About then, Mikhail Gorbachev visited Krasnoyarsk and for the first time as Soviet leader came face to face with the harsh realities of Soviet discontent. He was subjected to a barrage of criticism in the streets about shortages and high-charging co-operatives. Some 900 co-operative businesses had been set up by local entrepreneurs in Krasnoyarsk in the two years they had been legalised, but had met resistance from apathy, ideologically stereotyped officials and racketeers. One of the most prominent landmarks in this city where practically no restaurants could be found was the burnt-out shell of what had been a splendid, new log-cabin restaurant on a hillside. Private enterprise had ruthless enemies. After Gorbachev's visit, the local party chiefs lost some of their arrogance. A sixteen-storey building under construction as a new party headquarters was converted into a hospital for children. But the officials did not remove the bust of Chernenko until a year later in October 1990.

Krasnoyarsk had also started to acknowledge its ecological tragedy and for the first time to monitor the pollution which filled the Siberian sky and the lungs of the people with smoke and fumes from chemical factories, shale mines, iron and steel mills, cellulose combines and aluminium plants. Local people called Krasnoyarsk the city of death because of the high infant mortality rate and the unexplained miscarriages and premature births. Every day the radio broadcast pollution levels. The weekend I arrived these were exceptionally high because of the thick haze.

Another popular Siberian author, Viktor Astafiev, of the same village school of writers such as Rasputin, described the mood of the people of Krasnoyarsk at that time as 'irritated'. Speaking in his fifth-floor apartment in the suburbs, the sixty-six-year-old writer said housing and shortages were a big problem – even tea was rationed – but at least they had the Taiga, which was rich in natural food. 'One day in the Taiga is worth a season in Crimea', he said. 'I feel closer to God than to people there.' Like everyone else, he drove out of town as often as possible to the vast, silent Siberian forest, from which he drew his inspiration. Townspeople thought little of disappearing off to the Taiga for a weekend. They would hunt a bear and kill and roast it on the spot, or shoot the ducks which lazily crossed the sky in huge V formations. The scenic route out of Krasnoyarsk lay along the mighty Yenisey, which flowed to the Arctic Ocean through the immense Krasnoyarsk region, four times bigger than France. Passenger ships sailed by, as well as barges pushing huge platforms of floating logs. Families would spend hours gathering bilberries, cranberries, forest strawberries and red whortleberries, and my happiest memories of Siberia are of picnicking among Scots pines and firs near the Yenisey banks, the smoke from a camp fire rising into the still autumn air in columns as straight as the slender Serbian spruces.

The river was the life-giving heart of Krasnoyarsk, founded by Russian traders in 1628. There was an outcry when one of Krasnoyarsk's best-kept secrets was revealed, thanks to glasnost – the existence of an almost-finished cavern beneath the river, twenty miles outside town, designed as the world's largest dump of atomic waste. For fourteen years, excavations had been going on at a secret construction town which did not even have a name. It was called simply *Ploshadka* 27 – site number 27. When the facts became known, an ecological rebellion broke out in Krasnoyarsk similar to that in Irkutsk over the pollution of Lake Baikal. Unsanctioned meetings were held in the streets. In three days, informal groups gathered 60,000 signatures against storing radioactive waste not only beside a major city, but beneath one of the world's great rivers. A commission of geologists and ecologists was set up and concluded that the possibility of environmental pollution 'could not be completely ruled out'. The authorities bowed to the fury of the population. The chairman of the regional executive declared, 'People are against this burial place. They are frightened by Chernobyl. Here, Soviet power is opposed to the project. We will do our best to stop it.' Astafiev, a member of the Congress of Deputies, said the problems of Siberia were at last being redressed. 'The building of the nuclear-waste dump has been frozen until the year 2000. I am more optimistic about the future these days.'

14

The Occupied Territories

BEFORE the nationalities question bubbled up at the end of the
1980s, Western correspondents in Moscow agonised a lot
about how they should describe the way the Baltic republics
and Moldavia came to be part of the Soviet Union in 1940. One
could say they were 'annexed', as did most Western governments
who refused to allow their diplomats to attend functions in these
'occupied territories'. The word 'annexed', however, offended the
Soviet Foreign Ministry, which maintained that the Baltic republics
had all voluntarily joined Stalin's empire. Many reporters wrote that
these countries were 'absorbed' into the Soviet Union, or used the
equally neutral word 'assimilated'. The argument was settled when
the Supreme Soviet in Moscow in 1989 acknowledged, after years of
denying, the existence of a secret protocol to the Molotov–Ribbentrop
pact of 1939, under which Stalin and Hitler carved up Europe, with
Estonia, Latvia, Lithuania and Moldavia falling into the Kremlin's
grasp. Annexation it was.

What we discovered, however, in our frequent journeys by overnight
train to Tallinn, Riga and Vilnius, as the crisis in the Baltics deepened
with increasing demands from Estonia, Latvia and Lithuania for
the return of their prewar freedom, was that any undoing of the
annexation had been enormously complicated by five decades of
Soviet rule. Nowhere was this more obvious than in the frontier
town of Narva, situated in a strategic bay off the gulf of Finland
in north-eastern Estonia.

It took me a good five minutes to climb to the top of the
thirteenth-century castle in Narva, pausing once or twice for breath
in the galleries and banqueting halls which had been converted into
centrally heated museums and art galleries. From the top I found
a magnificent view across the raging torrent of the Narva River to
the ruined fort in the adjoining town of Ivangorod, a cannon-ball
shot away. The castle was in Estonia and Ivangorod in Russia. The
turbulent waters marked the centuries-old border between the two
countries. Local people said the castle was haunted and that at night
groans came from an underground passage. The story was told that

a knight called Indrik von Berengaut lived here with a very beautiful wife and child. The Russians invaded Narva from Ivangorod in overwhelming numbers one day and von Berengaut killed his wife to prevent her being captured. They made off with von Berengaut's infant child instead. Consumed with a desire for revenge, the knight spent thirty years constructing a tunnel under the river with the aim of taking his enemy by surprise. The night before the planned assault, however, he slipped into Ivangorod to warn his son, only to find that the boy, now grown up, had married a Russian and adopted Russian ways and refused to leave. The next evening, when von Berengaut launched his attack through the tunnel, he was met by a Russian force led by his son who killed him at sword point. At that moment the tunnel collapsed, drowning everyone. The unhappy ghost was said to be the young man, begging forgiveness for betraying his father.

The Russification of von Berengaut's son became a symbol of the fate of Narva itself. Narva was an Estonian city in population and character between the two world wars. It was destroyed in fighting between the German and Soviet armies when bombs flattened the Lutheran churches, the steamboat pavilion, the old Lloyd's office and 98 per cent of the medieval houses. Only two people, they said, emerged from the ruins. Narva was rebuilt after the war as a Soviet city in a Soviet republic. New people moved in to occupy five-storey Khruschev apartment blocks, built around the restored baroque town hall. They were practically all Russians, mainly immigrants invited by Moscow ministries to work at chemical and industrial enterprises established near the town. By 1990 only 4 per cent of the population of 85,000 was Estonian, and of these 3,400 inhabitants, half did not know the Estonian language. The museum keeper in a stone-washed denim suit who told me the story of the ghost was a Russian, Valery Kosolapov. So too was the secretary of the Narva Communist Party, a little man in huge spectacles with a tiny moustache called Vladimir Kotlov who gave me the statistics.

Like the Russians in all three Baltic states, the new inhabitants were urban settlers, factory workers, cleaners, retired army officers, and members of the Soviet militia like Ulyana Kuksina, policewoman number 1733, on duty on the narrow bridge between Estonia and Russia. She wanted to be a good Estonian citizen. 'I have a son four years old, and I have been sending him to Estonian classes, though to be honest it means nothing to him because he has no occasion to use it', she said, adding with a smile, 'I think tomorrow there may be a need for it, however.' There was none of the fierceness of the Ulster unionist in this Belfast of Estonia, though the parallels with the settlement of north-east Ireland were striking. The difference was that the people did not have the same attachment to the land. Their roots were shallow. They spoke and thought of Narva as Estonian, not Russian, despite their numerical superiority. There were no defiant gable murals or painted kerbstones. The blue, black and white flag of independent Estonia flapped and cracked over the castle in the breeze from the gulf. There was a joke among Estonians that new Russian immigrants had only one desire: to wake up in the morning and find themselves abroad. Even Kotlov knew that the old Soviet administration-by-command system had failed and that rule from the centre was not the way forward. 'We're all for economic sovereignty for Estonia – within the framework of a new union treaty', he said. The Russian population had already achieved a sense of the advantages of living in Estonia, where conditions were slightly better than in Russia. The process of setting up new barriers between Estonia and Russia started that year when each citizen of Narva was issued an ID card which said, 'Purchaser of Estonia'. It meant, said Kotlov, flipping out his own card, that a Narva shopper could buy items like Estonian cheese, while someone from Leningrad could not.

But there was resentment of Estonian exclusiveness. 'They want us out, they call us occupiers', said a stout woman in Petrovsky Square. 'If they close the border where will we be? My sister lives in Ivangorod.' A Russian man in an imitation leather jacket and cap said, 'If Estonia gets independence, they'll start closing all-union enterprises and the Russian workers will be the first to go.' Many objected to the new language laws passed by the Estonian parliament in Tallinn requiring everyone dealing with the public to achieve competence at one of four levels of Estonian. Said Kotlov in his office above a row of shops with Estonian and Russian names, 'At the lowest level, shop assistants should be able to count; at the highest, managers of factories have to be fluent.' The big all-union enterprises ignored Estonian. 'The trouble is, out of fourteen schools here, there is only one teaching in Estonian and it has only sixteen children in the first class', he said. Kotlov himself didn't speak Estonian and had to rely on interpreters when he went to Estonian party congresses in Tallinn. Estonian is a notoriously difficult language, related to Finnish and Hungarian. 'Imagine, it has fourteen different case endings', said a blonde girl in a food store. 'I've given up.' The language question had stirred a partitionist mentality in the Interfront movement, drawn from Russian speakers from the all-union enterprises. It proposed attaching Narva and two other nearby Russian-speaking towns to the Soviet Union in the event of home rule. In the all-union enterprises in north-east Estonia, there were no blue, black and white flags to be seen, only the Soviet emblem, still flapping in the wind in defiance of the republic's new laws.

The all-union enterprises, with their head offices in the industrial ministries in Moscow, were the great colonial arms of Soviet Russia – states within a state which could build towns and move populations from one place to another to serve their needs. They established in Estonia, Latvia and Lithuania huge textile mills, mines, engineering works, machine-tool factories, chemical plants and factories. They built ugly apartment blocks for the workers they brought in from Russia, Byelorussia and the Ukraine. By the time Estonia began trying to retrieve its independence, 90 per cent of its industry was controlled by the all-union enterprises and 40 per cent of the population was non-Estonian. In Tallinn, the ancient Estonian capital, Estonians were already in a minority. Here in May 1990 the Russian factories held a brief strike to oppose the moves towards independence. I called into strike headquarters in the Dvigatel military enterprise on the city outskirts. A red Soviet flag was flying over the gates where a banner proclaimed, 'Political strike on here'. Inside, all the signs were in Russian. A statue of Lenin guarded a little remembrance garden. There were no Estonian workers to be seen. Not all the Russians were anti-Estonian. Some had been infected by the radical ideas of Moscow's new political movements. The strike had been encouraged by the defence ministry in Moscow, a worker born in Perm told me. 'I support eventual independence for Estonia', said another, 'but prices are going up and my wages stay the same. They are going too fast.' Inflation was happening everywhere, but in Tallinn the Russians blamed the Estonians.

The Estonians could not go fast enough. They were the first to realise that perestroika offered them a chance of regaining their freedom and saving their national identity, language and culture. Estonian history had been one of a long struggle against foreign rule. Estonia, with its beautiful bays and islands on the Baltic Sea, had been fought over by the Teutonic Knights, the Poles, the Swedes and the Russians. It had been governed as a Russian province from 1721 until the Bolshevik revolution when the Red Army took the place of the tsarist forces, but in January 1919 the Estonians drove them out across the bridge over the Narva River. An independent bourgeois republic emerged from a peace treaty with Lenin on 2 February 1920 and lasted until 1940. 'Those twenty years have spoiled us forever', said Maarika Saarna, a broadcaster at Estonian Radio. In the radio building in the centre of Tallinn, the executive staff and journalists were Estonian; the cleaning women were Russian. Many Estonians had no Russian friends. 'I don't have a single Russian acquaintance here, though I have friends in Moscow', said Maarika. The Estonian resentment of Russians who had occupied hundreds of apartment blocks around the medieval capital was expressed in different ways. Shop girls would turn away from a Russian voice. 'We have good relations with the Russians who came here in the 1940s, who were born here, and whose parents are buried here, but the recent immigrants are a social group with few prospects anywhere', said Jack Taam, a founder of the Estonian Popular Front. 'They just want to enjoy higher living standards. They are too lazy to learn Estonian.' For Estonians their imprisonment was made harder to bear by their window on the outside world – the television programmes they could receive from Helsinki across the Gulf of Finland. They had more contact with the West than any other Soviet republic. Every weekend hundreds of Finnish tourists arrived on the Helsinki ferry for humourless drinking sessions in the Viru Hotel. Tallinn was a popular resort. The old town was a perfectly preserved walled city of the Hanseatic league, with a fourteenth-century town hall and an apothecary which had been in business since 1422. Almost all feature films made in the Soviet Union which required European street scenes had been shot in the old town with its *Grimm's Fairytales* atmosphere, dominated by Protestant church spires. But no symbols of Estonia's nationalism could be found there. Even the Estonian crest of three lions above the door of the old theatre had been cemented over. As if in response to such petty colonisation, a new Estonian-produced 1988 guide to Tallinn failed to mention the existence of one of the biggest and most obtrusive buildings in the old city, the Russian Orthodox church.

It was the Estonians who first started the popular fronts for reform which swept all before them in the Baltics. While they had sensed the futility of opposition during five decades of communist rule, they were the first to realise that if reforms meant the end of repression, they could restore all the symbols of their freedom as the first step to achieving it. The Estonian Popular Front was launched on 17 June 1988 at Tallinn's Pevcheskiy field, scene of huge folk concerts, the day after the Brezhnevite party boss Karl Vajno, who spoke Estonian badly, had been replaced by Vaino Vajlas, a highly cultured native speaker. 'The rally was one of the biggest events in Estonia for the last few decades', said Taam. 'It gave people back the feeling that they were a real force. It was a turning point.' With a sophisticated, north European sense of political finesse, the Estonians kept pushing the door further open. Seven months later, on 24 February 1989, the anniversary of independence, they raised the flag of freedom again. At

8.33 a.m., the exact moment of sunrise, the blue, black and white flag was hoisted over the ancient Danish stone tower in Tallinn known as 'big Hermann', to the cheers of tens of thousands of Estonians massed below in the deer park in the grey, chilly light of dawn. The flag of Soviet Estonia, with its hammer and sickle, had been hauled down at dusk the previous evening and consigned to the city museum. Psychologically at that moment, Estonia left the Soviet Union. The rotund figure of Edgar Savissar, who had started the Popular Front by suggesting it on a television programme and who was later to become prime minister, told the multitude, 'The flag taken down yesterday had no respect among Estonians. On our flag we don't have the colour of blood. The raising of the Estonian flag shows we are masters in our land. God save Estonia.' A choir of boys in white suits sang, 'My homeland, my happiness', and men took off their hats and fluttered them in the air, Vaino Vajlas among them. Standing near a placard saying, 'Mary, look down at your land and pray for us', Archbishop Kuno Pajula declared, 'It is very symbolic that there is dark on one side of the building and light on the other. The dark light is behind us. We have survived. It is a holy thing to be an Estonian.' In the Tallinn concert-hall that evening, several hundred members of the Estonian intelligentsia cheered and threw flowers when the Estonian national choir of sixty men and forty women in evening dress sang, 'I want to love you, Estonia, to my death.' Throughout the concert a colour guard of three youths stood to attention in front of the stage with the blue, black and white flag. They clenched their fists in the determined, rigid way I had seen young men do at Provisional IRA funerals in Northern Ireland.

Eduard Berklavs once tried to stop the Russification in neighbouring Latvia. I met him in Riga in the twenty-seven-storey Latvia Hotel, a typical Soviet concrete tower overlooking nineteenth-century German warehouses and the medieval town. To the fury of Latvians, it topped by three feet the previously highest structure, the elegant steeple of the thirteenth-century late Gothic Church of St Peter, patron saint of Riga, thus becoming a symbol of the dominance of Soviet realism over national sensitivities. Berklavs had originally been one of a hard core of Baltic communists working underground before the war. When Stalin sent the tanks into the Latvian capital in 1940, Berklavs, then twenty-four, had been summoned to the Soviet embassy with other party members and presented with the names of the new pro-Soviet Latvian government by Andrei Vyshinsky, the infamous prosecutor in the Moscow show trials of the 1930s. In the next twelve months, 34,000 Latvians were deported. After the war, tens of thousands more were sent into exile and Russian immigration began in earnest. Berklavs was opposed to the influx of Russians. He was a Latvian communist first and a servant of Moscow second. But he kept his counsel until he became Latvia's Communist Party boss in 1958. He then stopped the flow of immigrants, cutting it back from 3,000 a month to 300, and introduced economic reforms. He was, in his way, Eastern Europe's first *Dubchek*, and, like the Czechoslovakian Communist Party leader, a reformer before his time. Berklavs also introduced measures to protect the Latvian language. 'They didn't like this', he said. 'They started a campaign of vilification against me. Letters were sent to the Kremlin saying I had developed bourgeois nationalist tendancies. I was investigated by a central committee commission from Moscow. Then Khrushchev came to Riga in 1959. I met him at the airport. He said, "Where's this Berklavs", and confronted me saying, "are you an enemy or an honest person?" From Khrushchev's tone I knew I was finished.' The commission asked him to sign a document denying that Russification was taking place. Berklavs refused and was stripped of his post and exiled to the Russian town of Vladimir, where he was given the job of procuring films for the local cinemas. He was not allowed to return home for eight years.

I first came across Berklavs at the founding congress of the Latvian Popular Front in October 1988, a national conference supercharged with emotion. Former political prisoners intent on pushing the front towards independence vied with party conservatives determined to hold it back. But the tide of history had turned. Latvia's intelligentsia – learned men with goatee beards – won ovations from the 1,000 people in the packed hall with speeches fired by nationalist passion. They went one step further than Estonia. The proceedings, with subversive sentiments which would have meant instant arrest a year before, were broadcast on radio to incredulous people gathered round wireless sets in cafés and barber shops. 'We want the same rights as independent nations, the same as the Irish people, and we don't want the destruction of our language and culture as happened in Ireland', said Doctor of Philosophy Vilnis Zarens during a break in the debate. In the front of the hall the Catholic bishop of Riga, wearing a purple skull cap, sat beside a Lutheran priest. Invited Communist Party officials in grey suits occupied the row behind. Berklavs sat a few rows further back, now leader of the Helsinki Human Rights Group and the Latvian Independence Party. Janis Rukshans, a long-haired Latvian communist, brought the cheering delegates to their feet with his accusation that the country had been occupied and the economy destroyed by criminals. To cries of 'get up', the first secretary of the Communist Party, Jan Vigris, and the rest of the grey suits slowly rose from their seats, looking around sheepishly as if searching for someone in the crowd. Rukshans, I noticed, was wearing a tie with the letters NIDG. These were the initials of the Northern Ireland Daffodil Growers Association from whose members, he told me, he had bought the best daffodil bulbs in Europe for his private business. How could he, a party member, conduct a private enterprise? He laughed. 'This is Latvia', he cried, 'I'm a Latvian', as if that explained everything.

Not far from the Latvian capital was Riga Strand. I went there one afternoon on the wide commuter train with wooden benches like curved garden seats. Riga Strand had been one of the great beaches of Europe. It stretched for miles along the Latvian coast, a wide promenade of deep, white sand gently curving away to the horizon in both directions between pine trees and an almost tideless sea. I got out at Jurmala, one of seven holiday villages behind the belt of pine trees criss-crossed by avenues of *dachas* and Victorian-style stone villas. These were built by Latvia's resident German barons and by rich merchants from St Petersburg at the turn of the century. Latvia at that time was the tsarist provinces of Courland and Livonia, and Riga was a mainly German city, where fashionable citizens dined at the Frankfurt-am-Main or the Kloster-Keller restaurants and taxi fares were displayed in German and Russian. Riga Strand could have been a watering place in northern Germany. In those days the natives, the Letts as they were known, had no place on the strand. They were a despised peasant race. Latvian-language books and newspapers were banned. Visitors to the resorts only heard Latvian spoken by the kitchen maids and the porters in Horn's Hotel and the Hotel Bilderlingshof, or from the Letts who came to sell strawberries in Karlsbad or to serve tea at the concert gardens in Edinburg or Dubbelin, two of the villages named after Scottish and Irish merchants. After the Great War and the collapse of the exhausted Russian Empire, Latvia gained its independence and the Letts were finally the masters of Riga Strand. The seven-mile beach became a pleasure resort for the newly liberated peoples of the Baltics – the Estonians, Lithuanians, Poles and Finns – and for the Jews who lived along the shore in great numbers. The Irish essayist Hubert Butler, who visited Latvia in 1930, found that practically the only Russians on Riga Strand were lonely emigrés, once the wealthy, proud patrons of the hotels, now forced to seek refuge among a people they looked down upon and to learn Latvian to find a position in life. Before 10.00 a.m., the beach belonged to the men who bathed nude in the chilly water. From then until noon the women had it to themselves. After lunch everyone slept on the sand or under the pine trees until summoned for the evening meal by bells ringing from the pensions.

All this ended in 1940 when Stalin's tanks appeared and barbed wire replaced the beach umbrellas. The following year Hitler's troops invaded. It wasn't until the defeat of the Nazis that people began returning to the strand. This time they were almost all Russians from the east, not emigrés but members of the proletariat. Moscow's all-union enterprises and trade unions took over the merchants' houses and built new concrete *sanatoria* – hydrotherapy clinics and rest homes among the fir trees. Loudspeakers instead of bells called the masses to dinner. I found tennis courts on the sandy avenues with slogans in Russian exhorting Soviet youth to healthy exercise. A Protestant church had been converted into an art gallery. The place names Edinburg and Dubbelin had disappeared. The couples I met on the strand, walking for miles in an endless procession along the edge of the sea, were Russian speakers, pensioners in bulky overcoats, retired military men and factory directors in trilby hats accompanied by their plump wives who were wrapped in artificial furs. They were part of the million-strong community of Russians, Byelorussians and Ukrainians who had come to settle in Latvia since the war, making the Letts almost a minority in their own land. In the summer they would be joined by tens of thousands of Slavs from Moscow, Leningrad and cities as far away as Novosibirsk and Omsk, packing the beach so tightly that there would be little room to move.

In the elections to local councils in early 1990, the first poll under Soviet rule with a choice of candidates, the Popular Front swept to power. It gained an 82 per cent majority on Jurmala Council which controlled the whole area of the strand and its villages. To their astonishment, the new councillors found that they owned all the 1,800 *dachas* and mansions that had been occupied by the Latvian Communist Party Central Committee, the Jurmala Communist Party, the Riga Party Committee, the ministry of internal affairs, the KGB and the army. They had been rented at nominal sums from the council, which for decades had used the borough's resources to maintain them at enormous expense. The most modern had double bathrooms, sunlit bedrooms, telephones and central heating. A conical tower dominated the exquisite old merchant's summer-house, occupied by the commander of the Baltic military district. An elegant *dacha* built in the 1970s and occupied by Latvia's first secretary had an antique fireplace with azure porcelain tiles listed as a national treasure. The chambermaid, Dzintra, lived with her family in a single room in a wooden house on the same street with no central heating or hot water. The scheme under which all the expenses were shouldered by Jurmala while the party bosses enjoyed the *dachas* could only work as long as the party controlled Jurmala Council. The new deputies had no legal problem in deciding in January 1990 to withdraw permits from all organisations and to reclaim the properties. They set up commissions to evaluate the *dachas* and decide whom to give or sell them to. 'Most of the *dachas* will be used commercially and the rent will go to public health and education', said Silvija Viksina of the Jurmala Council. Ten modern cottages occupied by party officials were rented to a US company. Foreigners from the West began to return to the strand, though the big *sanatoria* still legally belonged to their builders, who included the USSR Council of Ministers, the Soviet Communist Party Central Committee, the ministry of public health and other powerful all-union bodies. The holiday-makers from the east could still come to occupy them until the day Latvia nationalised them.

But what concerned the would-be rulers of Latvia more was a catastrophe which had befallen the strand. The heavy industry situated in Riga by the all-union ministries had polluted the waters of the Baltic. In addition, as the population of the Latvian capital doubled and then trebled to almost a million, not a single sewage disposal plant was installed along the shoreline. In 1988 bathers on the strand started coming out in a rash. Health inspectors tested the waters. They decided the pollution was so toxic that bathing in the sea was banned and the Russian parents and children found themselves prisoners on the sand they occupied, unable to swim in the bathing strips between the three natural sandbars which ran the length of the beach.

Eighteen months after the founding of the Popular Front, its candidates won control of Latvia's parliament and declared their intention of making Latvia independent again. For a while nothing happened. Then in November and December, night-time explosions began to ring out over the city as pro-Moscow forces sought to destabilise the republic and create a pretext for direct rule from the Kremlin. In January 1991 the crackdown began.

The Latvians erected barricades to protect their parliament. At 3.00 a.m. on Thursday, 17 January 1991, I was in the Lutheran Cathedral in the barricaded old town. All around were sleeping people, many of whom had been on the streets for three nights already. Some were lying on pews. Others were so exhausted they slept sitting up. A few were stretched out on beds in the emergency operating room in a side chapel. Someone turned up a radio and I recall thinking it was an inconsiderate thing to do. Then others sat up and switched on their own portable transistors. The whole cathedral stirred. The first reports were coming in of the start of the Gulf War. At that moment it appeared to be the worst possible news for the Latvians. 'Moscow has a free hand now', said a weary young man with a gas mask attached to his belt. Everyone was acutely aware of the historic precedent for a Soviet crackdown while the eyes of the world were elsewhere. It happened in Hungary in 1956 during the Suez War. The barricades in Riga had gone up round the eighty-seven-acre old town to protect the parliament and radio building situated among its churches and shaded squares. Double rows of lorries, tractors, snow-plows and fire engines had been parked across all entrances in and out, leaving room only for pedestrians. The old town was ideal for barricades. They would not stop tanks but they symbolised Latvian defiance and raised the cost in blood of a Kremlin coup against the nationalist government. The Riga barricades produced a euphoria which affected all of us who spent night after night behind them in the open. There was a festival atmosphere in the little squares. Pop groups competed for attention with male voice choirs and folk dancers throughout the frosty nights. Thousands of Latvians kept a round-the-clock vigil by dozens of wood-fires which filled the air with sweet-smelling blue smoke. Neatly cut logs were stacked beside the bonfires; tea and snacks were provided free at street corners and volunteers kept the streets clean with brooms. With typical Latvian efficiency, two shoulder-high blocks of granite weighing several tonnes brought in to barricade a narrow street were lowered gently on to wooden rollers so as not to damage the cobbles. A street hoarding was transformed into an exhibition of political satire as amateur artists pinned up savage cartoons mocking President Gorbachev. People threw coins and cigarette ends at a rag doll tied to a chair, labled 'Communist Party soldier'.

The Latvian people were, in fact, united as never before. 'If we don't defend our freedom now, it's the end. Pray for our freedom', said Oswaldi Gasyons, a white-coated retired doctor who had come to Riga from a village ten miles away to volunteer his services. 'Why am I here?' asked a middle-aged man, Andris Mednis, as he squeezed through a gap in the lorries with his wife. 'We need freedom. Where else would I be?' Latvians, almost a minority in their own country, believed they might not get another chance of freedom. In the parliament press-room, exhausted Latvian youngsters recruited from emigré families in Canada, the United States and England put out endless press releases in English. Radio

Riga broadcast around the clock in English, German, Russian and Latvian. It denounced Kremlin accounts of the crisis, saying, 'The Soviet Empire in its last wave of terror is spreading lies.' Behind the sandbags at the radio building, young men with *kalashnikovs* and tin helmets nursed petrol bombs and watched the Gulf War on Sky News. The fears of the Latvians when the Gulf War began were initially justified. While US warplanes bombed Baghdad, the sky over Riga was suddenly filled with red and green tracer bullets as Soviet Interior Ministry troops, the Black Berets, stormed the five-storey Latvian Interior Ministry building near the old town to seize its store of arms. Four people were killed. German Glazov, a remorseful Black Beret, came to the parliament to confess that the 120 Black Berets who had terrorised Riga were given special salaries and fine apartments by the Latvian Communist Party. The plan was to seize key buildings for the party's 'Salvation Committee', but it did not quite work out. Outraged world and domestic reaction to the violence in the Baltics, and the threat of the end of aid and credits from the West caused Moscow to call a halt. Nor did the expected support from the Russian population materialise. Many of the Russians appeared to have little stomach for a return to totalitarianism. Prerevolutionary red, white and blue Russian flags appeared on the barricades. Some of the nurses in the Riga Cathedral were Russian volunteers. 'How do you get on together?' I asked a Latvian and a Russian nurse in a whisper that night as hundreds slept. In reply they hugged each other. Dozens of Russians queued with Latvians at the post-office to send telegrams of protest to President Gorbachev when he attacked Latvian nationalists as 'bandits'. A Russian engineer in the queue, Yuri Teryokin, said, 'Ten per cent of the Russians in Latvia support Soviet rule, 30 per cent are for independence and the rest are indifferent', a forecast borne out in a subsequent referendum in Latvia when the majority voted for independence.

The Lithuanians took the whole Popular Front movement in the Baltics to its logical conclusion. They were the last to found a front, which they called *Saujdis*, and the first to declare independence, which they did on 11 March 1990. The declaration passed by the *Saujdis* majority in the parliament in the capital Vilnius concluded with the words, 'From this moment Lithuania has again become an independent state.' The young *Saujdis* deputies, whom I had seen leading street demonstrations, now sat in the plush parliament chamber in neat suits, deciding measures to make the declaration a reality. The Soviet emblem above the entrance was removed and replaced with a canvas depicting a knight with a sword in hand, the emblem of prewar Lithuanian independence. The new minister of the interior ordered that the silver buttons and badges of the Lithuanian militiamen with their hammer and sickle emblems be scrapped, a decree which was temporarily shelved when it was realised that every militiaman needed at least twenty new buttons. American accents could be heard in the corridors, coming from expatriates returned from Chicago and Los Angeles to help as advisers and translators. An English-language newspaper, the *Lithuanian Review*, was launched. English had replaced German as the desired *lingua franca* of the Baltic nationalists, though when the leaders of Estonia, Latvia and Lithuania met for sessions of the Baltic Council which they set up in 1990, they had to resort to Russian for their deliberations – the only language common to them all. English signs frequently appeared at demonstrations with slogans such as, 'Dear Europe, we want to join your democratic home. Will you open the door?' Russian signs were removed from the streets. At the music conservatory from which the slightly stooped and bearded music professor, Vyatautas Landsbergis, had emerged to become Lithuanian president, the Russian language plaque beside the door was unscrewed, leaving a square of unweathered stone. Having declared independence the Lithuanian government set about creating the illusion and psychology of independence to help bring about the reality. They came to believe themselves that independence had been won.

It was premature. Moscow imposed an economic blockade and threatened tougher action. Army helicopters dropped leaflets over Vilnius – crude messages on recycled paper encouraging members of the 20 per cent Russian and Polish population to join pro-Soviet rallies. Many thousands heeded their call. At one rally attended by 30,000 people, a Russian pensioner complained to me, 'How can I live here; Lithuania will be cut off with no petrol or gas.' The kindly old face of a Lithuanian woman, Mikalina Urbelita, a Communist Party supporter, become contorted with fury when I asked her why she wanted Lithuania to stay in the Soviet Union. 'Before the war there were no factories, there were no pensions, there was unemployment', she said. 'And we had a fascist government.'

Later, when drinking in the almost deserted bar of the Intourist Hotel, two young Lithuanians rushed in shouting, 'The tanks are coming.' Rumours of military action to take over government buildings had been sweeping the city for days. We piled into a car and raced through the empty streets, unlit because of the energy blockade. We turned a corner and there they were, not just tanks but armoured cars, jeeps, marching soldiers and six military vehicles carrying long red-tipped rockets, moving slowly in a line through the darkness. Only when we stopped and approached the lines of soldiers did we discover it was not an invasion but a rehearsal for a military parade, a show of strength in a phoney war in which the Russians hesitated to provoke the Western world into a resumption of the Cold War. The military convoy parked for an hour along the narrow main avenue, with the rockets stopped right outside the parliament door. Landsbergis, the elected president of Lithuania, had not been told of the rehearsal. The message was clear to everyone.

The phoney war came to an end in January 1991 with the seizure of strategic buildings by Soviet paratroopers, culminating in the death of fourteen people as troops stormed the broadcasting tower on 13 January. The crisis in Lithuania had begun on 10 January when 1,000 paratroopers were sent to the republic to enforce conscription into the Soviet armed forces, and President Mikhail Gorbachev warned the Lithuanian parliament to submit to Soviet power. The military draft had been largely ignored in all three Baltic republics after they opted for independence in the spring of 1990. On 12 January a pro-Moscow committee for national salvation announced in Vilnius that it was the legitimate government and that it would take over power in Lithuania. It had the backing of the tiny Communist Party drawn mainly from Russians and Poles. It was this shadowy committee, which refused to divulge the names of its members, which asked the army to seize the broadcasting tower. The paratroopers chose to regard it as the legitimate authority and went in with the tanks. But they too had to draw back in the face of hostile world and domestic reaction, and the Lithuanian government still held control of its modern, new parliament building, which for months to come became a tourist attraction for visiting world politicians, with its antitank earthworks and its forest of wire spikes installed on the flat roof to prevent a parachute landing.

The manoeuvrings of Soviet troops to exert political pressure on Lithuania brought back unwelcome memories to Yousas Urbshis, the last foreign minister of independent Lithuania and the only living link with the prewar Baltic governments. It was Urbshis, then a handsome young diplomat with experience in Berlin and Paris, who had to go to Moscow to face the demands and threats from Stalin which eventually led to the entry of Soviet troops into

Lithuania and its annexation in 1940. On the way to visit him in his apartment in the city of Kaunas the day after watching the tanks rumble through Vilnius, I passed a two-storey wooden house in the open countryside. 'That', said my taxi-driver, 'is where the border with Poland used to be. That was the custom-house.' Between the wars Vilnius and the countryside around it had been seized by Poland. Kaunas had been the capital of Lithuania and the seat of the government of which Urbshis was a member.

At the age of ninety-four, Yousas Urbshis was frail but alert, a tall, dignified man with a crystal-clear memory. He lived in a cramped third-floor apartment at the end of a long city avenue which he had been assigned by the communist authorities. The country he represented had been a classic parliamentary democracy until it became an authoritarian state in 1926, 'which I always saw as a mistake', he said. But it had its own stable currency, a viable economy and good international relations, even with Russia – or so he thought. 'Then, on 1 September 1939, Germany fell upon Poland. On 17 September, Soviet troops came in on the other side. They occupied eastern Poland, including the Vilnius region. Under the Soviet-Lithuanian peace treaty of 12 June 1920, the Soviet Union recognised Vilnius as part of Lithuania, so we recalled this agreement and asked Moscow that Vilnius be given back to us.'

'I was invited to Moscow on 3 October 1939, for what they called "friendly negotiations". The Lithuanian and Soviet flags were flying at the airport. It was 10 o'clock in the evening when I arrived and I was taken directly to the Kremlin. Stalin was there with Molotov.' Urbshis remembered the Soviet dictator as a stocky man of middle height with strands of grey in his hair, prominent ears and a defensive manner. 'Stalin put a map of Europe on the table', he said. 'On it was a line. He told me the Soviet Union had agreed with Germany that Europe should be divided and most of Lithuania would go to the Soviet Union. It was the first time I had heard of the secret pact between Molotov and von Ribbentrop. I was greatly shocked. Molotov said then that an imperialistic state could be expected to simply occupy Lithuania in such circumstances, "But we won't do that. We would not be Bolsheviks if we did not search for another way." At that Stalin produced another map, showing Lithuania with Vilnius attached to it. He said we must sign two treaties, one concerning Vilnius and another on mutual aid. The mutual aid treaty was a diktat. I could see that. Under it we would have to allow 20,000 Soviet soldiers in garrisons on Lithuanian soil. I tried to argue. I said, "Clearly this is the occupation of Lithuania." Stalin and Molotov smirked. Stalin said, "Our garrisons will help you put down a communist rising if there is one in Lithuania", and grinned again.'

Urbshis flew home for consultations, taking a plane to Riga and another to Kaunas. His government was appalled. But some noted it might be the only chance of getting back their old capital. He flew again to Moscow on 7 October to suggest that Soviet troops be garrisoned in Lithuania only in times of war. Stalin's response was *neyt*. Negotiations went on until dawn in the Kremlin, with a break only for a film show for Stalin's entertainment. Eventually a single agreement was signed on 10 October 1939, returning Vilnius to Lithuania and allowing Soviet troops to establish bases in Lithuania with a fifteen-year lease. 'It was the first step to annexation', said Urbshis, though many rejoiced at the return of Vilnius. In the Lithuanian history museum in the town of Trakai, I later saw prewar Lithuanian postage stamps franked 'Vilnius 10 October 1939', and photographs of the dismantling of the old frontier by grinning Lithuanian soldiers.

Pressure on all three Baltic states was stepped up by Stalin in the subsequent months. Latvia and Estonia had also been forced to allow Soviet troops to establish bases on their territories. Urbshis was summoned again to the Kremlin, this time at the stroke of midnight on 14 June 1940. There he was presented with an ultimatum to form a pro-Soviet government and to allow an unlimited number of Soviet troops in Lithuania. 'We were given ten hours to reply', he said. The ultimatum was accepted by the Lithuanians after frantic consultations, but Molotov, now hostile and curt, raised new objections. A pro-Soviet revolution was staged in Lithuania on 15 June and occupation followed immediately. The personal nightmare for the young foreign minister began two days later. 'It was a bright morning', he recalled. 'I glanced out the window of our *dacha*. It was surrounded by Soviet soldiers.' He and his wife Mariei were exiled to Tambov in Russia. They were arrested a year later when Stalin and Hitler went to war. 'We spent the next thirteen years in prison in Tambov, Saratov, Moscow, Gorky and Ivanov, always moved together but kept apart', he said, speaking slowly as the painful memories returned. 'When Stalin died in 1954, my wife and I were released but not allowed to return to Lithuania. I worked part of the time as a baths attendant to make a living. When we eventually arrived home in 1956, I found I had lost my mother, my father, my older brother and other family members.' He stopped talking for more than a minute as tears formed behind his spectacles. 'They had been deported to Siberia and had died there', he said. After a pause he added, 'I didn't know.' His wife, Mariei, died in 1959. He was given his present tiny apartment in Kaunas in 1964 and the minimum old-age pension of fifty roubles. This had been tripled by the new government. The apartment block had no lift, but the sophisticated elderly statesman managed to go for a short walk every day and to analyse the developing crisis as a veteran diplomat. 'In my opinion we must go back to the agreement of 10 October 1939', he said. 'As the Americans and British leave Western Europe, the Soviet troops should leave Lithuania and the number of troops in Soviet bases left behind would be open to negotiation.' Urbshis didn't live to see full Lithuanian freedom restored. He died in April 1991, as Soviet troops began attacking border posts set up to symbolise independence.

The line on Stalin's map which had shocked Urbshis also cut through Romania, far to the south. The Soviet dictator did not bother with diplomatic niceties when dealing with Romania. He simply issued an ultimatum to the Romanian government to return the province of Bessarabia, which had been part of the Russian Empire before the fall of the tsars. The government in Bucharest had no option but to accede to superior force and on 28 June 1940, two weeks after the seizure of Lithuania, Soviet troops moved into Kishinev, which a few weeks later was proclaimed the capital of the new Soviet Republic of Moldavia.

The new border was formed by the Prut River, which meandered through vineyards, cherry orchards and rich pastures on its way to the Black Sea. The river was crossed by a narrow bridge on the road from Kishinev to Bucharest. Like all Soviet border crossings to the west, it was heavily fortified. To get to the bridge from the Moldavian side we had to negotiate a way past the gates, watch-towers, custom-huts and immigration posts which formed the fabric of the Iron Curtain. On Sunday, 24 June 1990, the curtain was pulled aside briefly to allow a human chain to link hands across the frontier in order to symbolise kinship between Moldavians and Romanians. All the way along the sixty-mile drive from Kishenev to the border that day, Moldavians in national dress sold cakes and hot pies at roadside trestle tables to the thousands of Moldavian nationalists on their way to the crossing. The cheerful crowds which gathered on the Moldavian side in hot sunshine carried the blue, yellow and red flag of Romania, their symbol of rejection of

Soviet rule in Moldavia. As the gates opened, people began running, waving and cheering towards the Romanians waiting on the centre of the bridge. The Soviet officials had no choice but to stand aside. The same fate awaited the few Romanian policemen who were holding back their own people, ensuring that the toes of their cheap shoes did not protrude across the red line painted across the tarmacadam to denote the border. As Moldavians and Romanians exchanged embraces, the line broke and hundreds of Romanians romped into Moldavia, disappearing down a long country road.

In the chaos, the foreign press from Moscow – myself and Quentin Peel of *The Financial Times* – were able to to stroll into Romania. There wasn't much to see other than a cow tethered to a tree and a couple of country houses. We returned to find the road was being closed again by border guards, and had an awkward few moments before we were let back and the curtain closed again behind us. It was a good-humoured affair, even when Soviet soldiers pushed reluctant Romanians back to the centre of the bridge. An old peasant woman in a black scarf shouted abuse at them, but a tall guard just picked her up and kissed her and everyone laughed. A military van later toured the roads on the Moldavian side, with a Romanian immigration officer pleading through a loudhailer for Romanians to return to their own side. We saw them struggling back, laden down with purchases, including two carrying a television set in a blanket. Shortages in Romania were worse than in Moldavia. This, and the political instability, had discouraged Moldavians from pressing too hard for unity with Romania. There had been no question of an exodus with the opening of the border from one part of the country to the other in the way East Germans had fled to West Germany. 'They don't want to live here and we don't want to live there', said a Romanian doctor at the scene. The day before the border opening the Moldavian parliament had declared sovereignty and renamed its territory of 4.2 million people Moldova. Most felt they would fare better simply with greater independence from Moscow. 'We want cultural and spiritual union with Romania', said Ion Khadyrka, the leader of the Moldavian Popular Front who organised the human chain. 'But not full unity – not yet. What we want is an independent state of Moldavia, with open borders, like that between the US and Canada.' The frontier had divided families for three generations. 'Why can't we send our children to high school in Romania, ten kilometres away, rather than Kishinev, one hundred kilometres away', said a blowzy woman who had been dancing provocatively in front of the soldiers. An old, bent Moldavian told me, as we walked away from the bridge to where a fleet of buses were parked, waiting to take us back to Kishinev, that he had just met his brother, living only five kilometres inside Romania, for only the third time since the Second World War. He wanted unity and the removal of the border. 'When we were part of Romania, we were poor but we had no fear', he said in heavily accented Russian. 'Then the Red Army came, and in 1946 there was famine. People died by the roadside. I couldn't speak Russian then. I picked it up, one word at a time, just by going to the shop.'

Since the war, the rich province of Bessarabia had been subjected to intense Sovietisation. Russian was made the state language. The Romanian alphabet was changed to Cyrillic script – a romance language forced into a Slavic greatcoat, as they said in Kishinev. Shoddy Soviet architecture and manners despoiled the capital, an old central European city filled in summer with the heady scent of linden trees. The language had been restored in the surge of nationalism which flowed south from the Baltics and which brought to the surface the all-too-familiar East European resentment of Russians who, along with Ukrainians, formed a quarter of the population.

The hatred burst forth during an argument over seats on the bus waiting to take us back to Kishinev. A beautiful young Armenian woman in our company began to explain how there had been a mix-up over places. She was mistaken for a Russian because she did not speak Moldavian and addressed them in 'pure' Russian. The Moldavian passengers began to scream abuse at her. A bald, red-faced man thrust forward his contorted face and shouted, 'These aren't your seats, understand? Get out.' The shouts followed her as we left the bus. Seeing her in tears, other Moldavians offered profuse apologies and later, as we were returning to Kishinev in a different bus with tricolours flying, the driver stopped to pick up a young Russian couple and their baby, whom the passengers passed around to admire.

When bathing at a lake near Kishinev that weekend, a thunderstorm forced us into a pavilion café full of boisterous Jews and Russians. A tipsy Jewish youth imposed himself on our company. 'My friends call me Alec, but I am Aaron', he said. He couldn't wait to get to America. Moldavia was an ethnic powder-keg, he declared. Half the 100,000 Jews in Moldavia had left in the last two years, fearful the population would turn on them as 'collaborators' with the Russians. In Kishinev a poster invited Jews to a lecture on 'Absorption in Israel'. It was history repeating itself, as the certainties of the Cold War unravelled. Jews fled Moldavia before, in 1903, following a pogrom when half the population of Kishinev was Jewish, and again in 1941 as the Nazis approached.

Tiraspol, the second city of Moldavia situated on the east bank of the Dnestr, was the Moldavian equivalent of Narva in north-eastern Estonia; its population was overwhelmingly Russian, with clocks running on Moscow time and the red flag flying from public buildings. Tiraspol, along with the towns of Bendery, Dubossary, Rybnitsa and Grigoriopol, held a referendum to form an autonomous republic. 'The irony is we have no love for communism and want free enterprise, but we fear Moldavian independence will make us second class citizens', said their spokesman Vladimir Solonar. In Tiraspol they told an anecdote (at least before the ethnic violence which began to claim lives in November 1990) that a pessimist learned Moldavian, an optimist English, and a realist how to handle a *kalashnikov*. The experience of Ireland was not lost on the Soviet army commander, Colonel General Vladimir Osipov, who accused the Moldavians of creating an 'Ulster-style' situation by harassing troops, or on Moldavian Prime Minister Mircho Druk, who promised an Ulster if the Russians did not accept Moldovan rule. Druk spoke with the unsophisticated voice of middle Europe. 'The Russians here remind me of the OAS in Algeria, or the white minority in South Africa', he said.

We made that journey to Moldavia on the eve of an encounter between Ireland and Romania in the World Cup Football Championships being held in Italy. Moldavians said they were naturally cheering the Romanian side. The Russians who lived there were not. We fell into conversation with a Russian technician at Kishinev Airport who said, when he found out I was Irish, that he supported every team playing against Romania, he disliked the Romanians that much. 'They come to Moldavia and buy up scarce goods like television sets on the black market', he said bitterly. 'I've been waiting two years for a television and I still havn't got one. They're no good. Good luck to the Irish team, I say.'

15

'. . . it wasn't an earthquake . . .'

I T WAS a Sunday morning early in December and bitterly cold as refugees from Armenia gathered in the snow-covered cemetery of the Armenian Apostolic church in a suburb of Moscow. Dozens of men and women pressed up against the altar rail of the tiny church, some with olive complexions and brown eyes, others fair-skinned and almost indistinguishable from Russians. The priest in a tall, embroidered hat blessed them and prayed for peace. Around the walls, clusters of candles hissed and spluttered on sand boxes, providing little pockets of warmth beside the cold stone of the unheated building. From outside came the sound of scraping as two men with wide shovels removed deep snow from the path to make room for dozens more refugees arriving, seeking news of family and friends.

The date was 4 December 1988. Civil war was brewing in the Trans-Caucasus. A notice on a tree listed the names of forty-five Armenians missing in the panic and confusion gripping the region, the youngest a girl of ten called Christina Badalyan. A thickset man with a Stalin-like moustache regaled a crowd with a story of how the women and children from his Armenian village in Azerbaijan had fled to Armenia while the men patrolled the village at night with guns. Another man told of a priest's house being burned down in Kirovabad and of Azerbaijanis raping a seventeen-year-old girl. A woman described how two days earlier thousands of Azeris had tried to attack Armenians at the railway station in Baku, the Azerbaijani capital.

The trouble had arisen over the Armenian-populated enclave of Nagorny Karabakh in the Soviet Republic of Azerbaijan. A year before, the regional soviet in Nagorny Karabakh had taken Gorbachev's democratic reforms as an historic opportunity to right an old wrong and voted to join Armenia. This had unleashed decades of pent-up ethnic tension. The Armenians of Nagorny Karabakh, or the High Karabakh, had survived centuries of invasions by Turkish Moslems. They considered themselves historically part of Armenia and had a passionate attachment to their beautiful and rich land of sheep pastures and ravines, mountain villages, vineyards and tiny orchards of peaches, apples, plums and nuts. Fighting over Nagorny Karabakh had last broken out after the Bolshevik revolution of 1917. The famous Armenian general, Andranik, was poised to capture it for Armenia in 1918 but was persuaded to wait for a negotiated settlement by a British officer, General W M Thomson, who was administering the British mandate, which at that time ran through the Trans-Caucasus. British policy, however, favoured the Azerbaijanis because of the oil fields near Baku, and the area eventually fell under the control of the new Republic of Azerbaijan. Soviet power was established in both Azerbaijan and Armenia in 1920 and Azerbaijan's communist leader, Nariman Narimanov, offered Nagorny Karabakh to Armenia, but the status of the region was decided by Stalin in 1923. He decreed that it should stay in Azerbaijan as an autonomous republic. That was where it had remained ever since. The Armenians in their Soviet republic, a fraction of their former nation size in the Trans-Caucasus, could do nothing. They were still stunned and demoralised after the worst experience in their history – the genocide of 1915 when Ottoman Turkey slaughtered a million Armenians and uprooted hundreds of thousands more from traditional Armenian lands in eastern Turkey. For the Armenians living in the republic and in the Armenian diaspora, the central issue uniting them was that they had been wrongly deprived of their beloved Nagorny Karabakh, and that a great crime had been committed against them by the Turks which had gone unpunished. Everyday the people of Armenia were reminded of their lost homeland by the sight of their sacred mountain, Mount Ararat, whose snow-capped peak beyond the Turkish frontier could be seen from Yerevan's streets.

In the months after the vote in Nagorny Karabakh, huge demonstrations had taken place in support of their compatriots in the Armenian capital Yerevan. As the Kremlin hesitated about what to do, the outrage of the Azeris, the Turkish inhabitants of Azerbaijan, had taken its traditional form. Twenty-six Armenians were slaughtered in the Azerbaijani town of Sumgait on 28 and 29 February 1988. The temperature rose steadily throughout the year. The bloody history of the Armenian and Azeri peoples taught them that more killings would follow. By November the area was on the verge of civil war and mass movements of people began. Two tidal waves of refugees, Armenians from Azerbaijan and Azerbaijanis from Armenia, broke past each other going in different directions. Many fled to Moscow. It was these Armenians who were in the cemetery and church that snowy Sunday, seeking news of their relatives.

The earthquake came three days later, on 7 December at midday, a massive earthquake which laid waste the towns of Spitak, Kirovakan and Leninakan in the hills north of Yerevan. The capital was not damaged, but in the streets and avenues there was confusion and panic. The Soviet army moved in to seize back the authority the Kremlin had lost in the previous months. When I arrived in Yerevan a few days afterwards, there were tanks in the streets. Massive T-72 tanks with caterpillar treads sat at each of the five intersections around the vast main square, their long 125-millimetre guns pointing up the tree-lined avenues. It was late in the evening and groups of soldiers in battle dress stood around, watching the last pedestrians disappear before the midnight curfew. The next morning I saw more tanks and BTR personnel carriers on the narrow mountain road to Spitak where the first winter snows made driving precarious. There were armed soldiers in metal helmets in Spitak directing the traffic through streets, which were little more than paths through mounds of rubble. The town had literally been shaken apart.

I found a curious lethargy in Spitak, as if it was gripped by paralysis. All the resources of the republic should have been marshalled to help with rescue work, yet here, some days after the apocalypse, there was little activity. I wandered through empty streets where thousands of unclaimed bodies lay beneath the ruins. Corpses were still being brought out by gangs of rescue workers wearing face masks. Here and there small groups of men stood around with haggard, unshaven faces. I climbed up a pile of masonry to speak with three men standing on top. It had been a six-storey apartment block and bits of exercise books, picture frames, parts of refrigerators and torn mattresses protruded through the bricks and lumps of plaster. As I joined them, a green Lada came slowly along the street and stopped. The passenger window was wound down and a loud hailer appeared. 'Comrades, have you any dead here or not?' a voice called. The men shook their heads and the car moved off.

'Are there any people under here?' I asked.

'My mother's down there', said one of the men, pointing to my feet.

Most of the women and children among the survivors had been evacuated from Spitak. The men remained, keeping vigil beside the rubble, wretched, unshaven, melancholy figures, their eyes betraying a deep and weary anguish.

'Everyone lost a mother or a father or a son or a daughter', said Grachik Simonyan, a forty-year-old railway linesman with a stubbled face and heavy, blank eyes.

'And you?'

'My wife and daughter.'

He pointed out the wrecked school where dozens of children perished at their desks. Their black-and-white photographs smiled out of a display board in the yard. A few cranes laboured nearby at wrecked factories and half-demolished apartment blocks. It would eventually be established that 4,000 of the 16,000 residents had been killed in the earthquake. Most had yet to be found. A shout went up from the ruins of the sugar refinery. Four rescue workers brought a body down the rubble mountain and carried it towards the football stadium where the coffins were kept. In a macabre irony, this town of the dead had too many coffins. There were coffins everywhere, stacked in piles of fifty or one hundred on the roadsides, or left in twos and threes outside the ruins of stone cottages. In the stadium I counted about 5,000 coffins at one end, black, red, brown or just plain wood, and another 2,000 on the little terrace where the fans watched the local team *Basum* win the Armenian cup earlier that year. More spilled on to the seven-lane running track.

'We will never use them all', said Dr Bagdasar Givorkyan, a young Armenian physician in a tent for infectious diseases erected beside the stadium. 'They will stop looking soon.'

A smiling youth in the tent offered me Cadbury's chocolate. The doctor insisted on giving me little bottles of Halalone water-purifying pills, made in the USA. No Armenian will allow a stranger under his roof without offering hospitality, and this applied to the hospital tent. The doctor produced little glasses and a bottle of home-made Armenian vodka. We gulped it down. He wanted to know what I thought of the crisis over Nagorny Karabakh. After the earthquake the leaders of the Karabakh Committee, which had organised the giant rallies in Yerevan, had tried to take over the earthquake rescue co-ordination, issuing passes for drivers. When the army moved in they had been arrested and jailed. The people were in a rebellious, truculant mood. This, and deep shock, helped explain the paralysis. Among those arrested was a national hero, Levon Ter-Petrosyan, a highly respected Armenian academic. People would have worked for him to cope with the after-effects of the earthquake, said a medical helper at the back of the tent. The mourning for the dead was mixed with fury. 'The Kremlin has repressed the first genuine democratic movement in Armenia', said the doctor angrily.

All the dead were taken to a bare hillside above the stadium for identification and burial. That day 132 coffins containing bodies were laid out in rows. The lids were lying loosely on top and some had slipped off. A few relatives moved from coffin to coffin, a handkerchief over their mouths. Two volunteer Moscow police officials in plain-clothes waited at the end of the row and registered names in a ledger. A man squatting by the coffin of his wife held open the lid and wept. Walking past, I couldn't avoid seeing inside but quickly looked away again. Earthquakes leave people terribly maimed and broken. Many coffin lids had not been screwed on because the dead didn't always fit. Mass graves were being dug for bodies which would never be identified. Two deep pits had already been excavated. In one there were twelve coffins, including a child's.

'We are left without children and it means without future', said the town party secretary, Norik Muradyan. 'There is nothing to continue our generation.' A tent in the little square beside the market had a sign saying, 'Party Headquarters'. Behind it stood the wrecked party building. Muradyan was in Yerevan when the earthquake struck on 7 December. He lost eleven relatives, including his wife and a son. Another son of four years was buried beneath the rubble of a wrecked kindergarten. The party secretary refused to believe it when told four days later that his little boy had been found alive.

The boy, Masis, said, 'Daddy, the ceiling fell on us and at first I was frightened. Then I saw something bright. I crawled and then I could see the street. I got out. There was nobody there. I got inside and helped a boy out. I wanted to go back for my jacket and pistol but grown-ups ran up to me and wouldn't let me.' Listening to his son, Muradyan cried for the first time.

On the road from Spitak to Kirovakan they were still finding bodies in the wreckage of a giant flour combine, an awesome, bizarre, horrifying sight, standing in a desolate plain against beautiful, snow-capped mountains. A concrete administrative block, as high as a small skyscraper, was left tilting over at a precarious angle. A lorry was parked directly underneath, with a man in the cab smoking a cigarette while waiting to pick up a load of rubble. Men walked nonchalantly by. An army tank, belching clouds of black smoke, pulled slabs of concrete from the masonry. The tank driver couldn't see what he was doing as he faced the wrong way. A worker standing beside him signalled instructions.

'There are still eighteen bodies up there', said a portly militia officer, a volunteer from Kiev in the Ukraine. 'Today we found a girl, aged twenty-two, dead. No one has been found alive for a week.'

On the bare hillside beside the combine, a group of welders from Lithuania had hoisted the yellow, green and red flag of the once-independent Baltic republic over their tents. Soviet conscripts helped unload sacks of flour from a giant store. Bodies had been found there and the flour was to be destroyed. I saw three exhausted young soldiers resting beside a fire some distance away. Two were sitting with heads bent over their knees and a cloth pressed to their faces. They had seen the twenty-two-year-old girl being found.

Much of the town of Kirovakan, an industrial centre and a spa resort of 165,000 people twenty miles further north, was destroyed, though the grey stone four-storey buildings around the elegant city square remained intact. No one knew how many hundreds of people were killed.

Soldiers from another army, whose training probably envisaged combat with, rather than assistance for, the Soviet Union, were in Kirovakan's main square. Israeli military vehicles were parked by the central restaurant, not far from a statue of Lenin. Dozens of curious people were crowded around a jeep with long, waving radio antenna, and a military ambulance marked M-325 and painted the colour of desert sand. The extraordinary sight of Israeli war equipment in a Soviet city had resulted from Israel's offer of medical help as part of the international relief effort. They had flown in a field hospital as well as support vehicles. Colonel Mikhail Wiener, an athletic-looking Israeli officer in his fifties, was dining in the restaurant with other Israeli servicemen. There were fifteen Soviet emigrés among the eighty-eight uniformed Israeli soldiers on Soviet soil. Colonel Wiener wouldn't let them talk to me but said, with some understatement, 'It's a pretty unique feeling for them coming back to the country in which they grew up.'

About 200 yards down the avenue from the square, the area of destruction began. The first wrecked building was the Palace of Culture, a modern edifice of pink stone with decorated pillars soaring up above the entrance. Much of it had collapsed inwards. Further along, Kirovakan was like a bombed city. Piles of rubble tumbled into the street. The damage extended far up the avenues to the left. There were tremors daily. Aftershocks rumbled through the ground, 367 since the earthquake. Practically no one slept in their apartment at night. They lay huddled in blankets on the ground in courtyards and parks in temperatures of minus five degrees centigrade. During the day women cooked and brewed tea over fires in the open. On a long, low wall along the main avenue, bundles of telegrams were laid out for inspection. They were addressed to wrecked or uninhabitable houses and came from relatives and friends every day, seeking news of loved ones. Groups of people sifted through the telegrams. Behind the wall a tent had been set up by Soviet engineers as a temporary post-office.

Occasionally a resident would extract a telegram from a pile and go into the tent to send a reply. At one five-storey apartment block a twelve-wheeled Japanese Kato crane was pulling slabs of concrete from the top floor. Everytime the crane pulled on its cable, part of the building collapsed with bangs and thuds and a clatter and tinkling as hundreds of particles of stone, metal and glass tumbled down in clouds of dust.

The noise could be heard by the crowds in the square where Nagorny Karabakh dominated the conversation.

'The first priority is getting people housed', said a young man in a brown suit when I engaged him in conversation.

'Well said, young fellow', said a voice from the dozen onlookers who crowded round.

'But secondly', said the man, raising his finger for emphasis, 'we must establish our right to Nagorny Karabakh. The Azerbaijanis say it is theirs. We say it is ours. But we have the historical documents to prove it.'

'You know that Raisa Gorbachev is a Moslem', said a man with dark, furrowed brows. 'That's why Gorbachev backs the Azerbaijanis.'

'Gorbachev is her fourth husband', said another.

The Armenians in Kirovakan saw conspiracies all around them, with fate joining in. The week before the earthquake, the 20,000 Azeri inhabitants of the city had fled, fearing for their lives, after a fight in the nearby village of Vartu with guns and knives which left one Armenian and one Azerbaijani dead. Every single Azeri had escaped the earthquake.

I again heard the theory about Raisa Gorbachev's role in Armenian history when I returned to Armenia a year later. In a barber's shop in Yerevan, as a portly Armenian trimmed my neck hair with a razor, a customer assured me that Gorbachev hated Armenians because Raisa was a Moslem and sympathetic to the Azerbaijanis. The barber nodded knowingly, as did the other clients. I kept my head still, partly because in Yerevan it was little use trying to contradict popular folklore. I heard many such absolutes in the narrow oak-lined streets of the Armenian capital, and in the cafés in the elegant squares ringed by solid buildings of pink tufa.

'I know why Gorbachev is under the influence of the Moslems', said a doctor. 'He has a brother living in Turkey. Did you know that?'

This time I shook my head.

'The end of the world is coming', said an earnest-looking young factory worker who gave me a lift through the city.

'How do you know?'

He produced a tiny bible from his pocket. It was in Armenian. He told me that it foretold that a man named Michael with a mark on his head would come to power in Russia just before doomsday.

An editor at the Armenian news agency, *Armenpress*, confided that the massacre in Sumgait was organised by the KGB as punishment of Armenians for demanding the return of Nagorny Karabakh. He prophesied that the population in the disputed territory would soon be dominated by Azerbaijanis because 'they breed like a production line'.

The national paranoia had deepened since the earthquake. They saw new conspiracies all around them. A railway blockade imposed by Azerbaijan had brought the republic to the brink of starvation and halted reconstruction work in the earthquake zone. It underlined how defenceless their land-locked republic was, no bigger than Belgium and enclosed by hostile forces – to the west, Turkey, to the south, Iran, to the east, Azerbaijan.

Levon Ter-Petrosyan had been released from prison after six months and exerted a powerful influence over Armenian politics from his often crowded office, situated at the end of an indoor balcony in an old merchant's palace with a curving, marble staircase. This was the headquarters of the Committee of the Karabakh Movement. Day and night it was the scene of frantic activity, organising defiance of the autumn call-up, plotting ways of getting into besieged Nagorny Karabakh, around which sporadic fighting had continued. Consultations, debates and arguments went on in the street outside and in the hallways and committee rooms. Paradoxically, it was at the heart of this Levantine powerhouse of intrigue that rational voices could be heard to counter the wild rumours in the street, prominent among them that of Ter-Petrosyan, the committee's joint leader. Petrosyan was a handsome forty-four-year-old professor who spoke several languages, including Armenian, Russian, Arabic, Hebrew, ancient Greek and Manchurian Chinese.

'In every republic at this time, there are alternative centres of power', he explained, drawing on a Marlboro cigarette. 'The party has administrative power. We have power over the people. But we have always kept contact with the administrative organs. We thus have been able to avoid a Tbilisi.' The turning-point for the movement came in May when the army left. 'We won a decisive struggle, thanks to powerful support from democratic deputies in Moscow, international public opinion, and not least the desire of Gorbachev for the evolution of a democratic federation as independence tendancies grow in the republics.' The committee had organised the founding congress of the Armenian National Movement which brought together most national factions and representatives of the diaspora for the first time with the aim to struggle for a more independent republic within the USSR. As for the anticonscription campaign, 'Armenians are ready to serve in the army, but here in Armenia only. We had an Armenian division in 1956 and we must have it back. There were two moments in our history when we could have been wiped out – 1918, when Armenians were at the Western front, and 1943, when the Armenian division was at Stalingrad and the Turks were massing on the border. Now we must take into account that in future Russians may be too preoccupied with their own problems to protect us. Demands for independence have grown but our policy is realistic. We want sovereignty within the Soviet federation. We want economic independence and freedom to make political contacts with foreign countries such as France, the United States, Lebanon, Syria, even Iran.'

At the barber's shop there had been a consensus that the best friends of the Armenians abroad were the French, Americans and Lebanese Christians. 'We could learn something from them, the Lebanese Christians', said a customer who had just been shaved. 'Some people say, better a permanent Lebanon here than a permanent Sumgait.'

I heard the most paranoid theory of all after I drove on from Yerevan to Spitak.

'Earthquake? What earthquake? There was no earthquake here', said an old man hobbling slowly across the main square.

'No earthquake?'

'It was no earthquake. It was an explosion. They did it. To punish us for trying to get Nagorny Karabakh'.

There were hundreds of containers in Spitak, giant metal boxes such as those used by long-haul lorries. They nestled among the ruins and lay in rows by the side of the road. Holes had been cut in the sides and fitted with panes of glass. Pipes protruded from the top. Old women emerged to bring buckets to a well. The containers were temporary homes. Throughout the earthquake zone, where the temperature sometimes dropped in winter to minus twenty degrees centigrade, 40,000 families, up to a quarter of a million people, were preparing to spend the winter in these rectangular compartments, thirty feet by fifteen. Red Cross officials feared that many *vagonschiks*, as their inhabitants were called, would die during the winter, especially the old in the containers which became frying pans in the summer and refrigerators in the winter.

Khachik Bidzyan and his wife Anait were *vagonschiks*. They lived in the centre of Spitak in a pair of containers, to which they had added a couple of rooms made of plywood, clapboard and any other materials to hand. It was still incomplete but, like every rural Armenian home, was spotlessly clean, and their hospitality was overwhelming. Within minutes they produced a meal of tea, juice, pastries, fruit and bread, and walnuts gathered from a gnarled tree outside, which had been planted by their grandfather fifty years previously. Like most people in Spitak, Khachik was bitterly critical of their treatment. 'The whole world helps, but we got nothing', he said. 'Nobody has ever come to see us. My back was injured and I spent five months in hospital, but I came home to nothing, just empty containers to live in. I built these extra rooms myself. Gorbachev said Armenian soldiers would be allowed home to help but they didn't come. He promised all the survivors would get a pension. They haven't got anything yet. There is no washing powder in the shops, hardly any meat, only a little sugar, and potatoes are scarce. There is no gas. We will stay here, of course; everybody will. The new town they are building is too far away. It is windy. The graveyard is here and my family always lived here.'

While he spoke, his two daughters, thirteen-year-old Ninish and fifteen-year-old Giane, served the meal with smiles and blushes. They and their thirteen-year-old brother Medesh miraculously lived through the earthquake.

The complaints were overshadowed by Khachik's thankfulness for their survival, however. 'My family's alive. That makes me a millionaire in Spitak', he said.

'But you know it wasn't an earthquake', he added. 'It was some sort of deliberate underground explosion.' They all nodded in agreement.

The faces of the dead looked down on Spitak, row upon row of headstones lined the bleak hillsides to the west of the town, hundreds of flat, rectangular stones, stretching across irregular contours. On each tombstone, etched in white lines on the shiny, black surface, was a life-size image of the deceased, copied from photographs recovered from the ruins. They portrayed the permanently smiling faces of the children who perished as they sat at their school desks, the posed features of the fathers and mothers taken from their wedding-day snapshots, and the stern countenances of grandparents posing proudly for the camera. The sculpting had been done by artists from Yerevan and other cities, working flat out for the year. More were put up every day. The sculptors charged 8,000 to 10,000 roubles, about four-year's income, for the best headstones, said the parents of a little boy at his graveside as dry snowflurries fell from a dark sky. It was the first priority of bereaved families, even before a new home. Nobody helped the survivors with the cost. The money came from relatives or was borrowed. They were not very religious people – there was no church in Spitak – but honouring the dead in this fashion was a way of coming to terms with the tragedy.

Three months after the earthquake, the authorities had announced that a new Spitak would be built on the far side of the hill, about five miles away. Its outlines were visible on the mountain road to the distant capital. Here were two-storey stone houses built by Uzbek workers, and neat rows of bungalows provided by the Italians, whose tricolour flew nearby. Across the road stood a modern single-storey complex just completed by the Norwegian Red Cross. Inside was a little bit of Scandinavia, with wide corridors of hospital-green lino, pine-wood partitions, digital clocks and habitat-style furniture. From the gynaecological ward came the cries of newborn babies. The people, however, didn't want to leave their town or their dead. Generations had been born and raised in the stone cottages of Spitak's streets. Most survivors still dwelt among the ruins. Some had moved into pretty, new chalets, like that just occupied by building worker Gagik Rafablyan and his family on Shaumyan Street. It had carved wood around the windows, three rooms, a coal fire, and a cellar full of cabbage for the winter. It was here that I had stood on a heap of rubble as a car had come slowly by with a man calling through a megaphone for dead bodies. The rubble had been carted away to a gully in the mountains and replaced by rows of Russian village houses donated by different Soviet cities, such as Tambov and Penza. Shops had reopened and there was a videobar, but many buildings had yet to be demolished and their walls and ceilings were pitched at grotesque angles, contrasting sharply with some sparkling, white, prefabricated units beside them. One of these housed the new Communist Party headquarters. Outside, a driver dozed in a white Volga. At the back, standing in a row, were five bronze busts of Soviet heroes, one with the distinctive moustache of Marshal Bagramyan, commander of the first Armenian cavalry brigade in the 1920s, waiting, almost certainly in vain, to be restored to a place of honour.

In the city of Kirovakan, half an hour's drive from Spitak, they estimated that 3,000 had died and half the 100,000 inhabitants had lost their homes. Some of the 1,000 prefabricated houses being erected by Red Cross societies from Bulgaria, Canada, West Germany and the United States stood on the outskirts. Children played in front of new houses built by Estonians and Lithuanians. But local construction work had been almost halted by an Azerbaijani blockade of railcars carrying construction materials. Some even arrived with cement bags ripped open and concrete panels smashed.

In Kirovakan there was a schoolgirl known as the Mute Margarita. She had not spoken since the earthquake. She refused to go to the toilet in case she was trapped inside by another tremor, and soiled her clothes instead. A children's psychological centre catering for 900 boys and girls with behavioural problems had been set up. Red Cross volunteer Sarian Oganyan said 95 per cent of the children were still disturbed. Some couldn't sleep; others were melancholic.

As I walked through the side avenues off Kirovakan's main street, I met Gigik Simonyan, a young unemployed man who lived in a wooden hut among the temporary homes along the centre of the road. Nearby were containers and square tents, some with patches of snow dampening the canvass roof. Their six-storey apartment blocks along the street were so badly damaged that they were uninhabitable, but they still stood and people used them for storage and washing. Gigik invited me in and introduced his mother Rosa and his sister Gohash, a teacher in a local primary school. Within minutes I was again sitting down to a meal, this time of soup and home-baked bread and sweetmeats, and being plied with tea and vodka. They thought they would have to live in the hut for five years before the building was torn down and new houses erected for them. Gigik survived the earthquake because he was on a break from work in the Spitak electricity station. 'The road under my feet rose up like a wave', he said. 'I was certain the ground was going to open and thought, which way will I jump? There was a huge roar and the sky was instantly filled with black clouds.'

I said, 'There are people in Spitak who believe it wasn't an earthquake at all.'

There was a pause. 'Yes, people say that', said Gigik. 'I also don't believe it was an earthquake. Most people don't. It was some kind of underground explosion. It was done to punish us.'

'How?'

'How do I know?' he said. 'I'm a simple person.'

The people of Armenia would have to live with the consequences of the earthquake for a long time, and many would never believe the conclusive evidence of scientists that it had been a natural phenomenon. Events continued to fuel their belief that the world was conspiring against them. Armenia and Azerbaijan became more like Lebanon, with sporadic fighting around Nagorny Karabakh and on the Armenian-Azerbaijan border. There was a fresh massacre of Armenians in Baku in January 1990. Nagorny Karabakh, after being ruled directly from the Kremlin for a few months, was given back to Azerbaijan. Thousands more refugees came to Moscow where they lived in hostels or in small, overcrowded apartments. For a while a few erected tents in front of the Rossia Hotel and camped under the beech trees on the grassy forecourt in November 1990, insisting the authorities had failed to assess the Sumgait and Baku massacres as genocide and should give them refugee status.

Throughout the two years of agony something else happened in Armenia. Whatever loyalty the people felt for the Communist Party disappeared. In the spring of 1990, after elections to a new parliament, Levon Ter-Petrosyan, a year after walking out of prison, became president of Armenia. Administrative power and the power of the people became one, but the Armenians still could do little to right historic wrongs and their paranoia appeared justified when in 1991 the Kremlin sided with Azerbaijan to reward the Azerbaijanis for voting to stay in the Soviet Union. For the Armenians, history has become a conspiracy theory.

16

We Will Have our MacSwineys
and Casements

THERE was a red-painted wooden hoarding, seven feet high, stretching for fifty paces along the footpath of Tbilisi's main boulevard, Rustaveli Avenue. It turned back at each end so that it enclosed an area at the bottom of the steps leading up to the imposing doors of the tall, yellowstone government buildings. Officially, the wooden fencing had been erected so that resurfacing could be done. The stone pavement had been dug up and two statues, one representing a working man, the other a peasant, had been taken away. But no one doubted that the hoarding had been put up to stop people gathering at the steps.

It was here, at 4.00 a.m. on 9 April 1989, that the tanks came crawling up Rustaveli Avenue from Lenin Square, followed by soldiers who gassed and hacked to death twenty people, most of them women, and injured hundreds more who had been demonstrating for Georgian independence. A few weeks had passed and Georgia, closed to foreign journalists during the crisis, had been opened again. I found that on the surface, life had returned to normal in the Georgian capital. The only army presence was an occasional troop-carrier parked outside the officer's club a few yards along Rustaveli Avenue from the hoarding, the driver lounging under the plane trees in the floppy bush hat which Russian soldiers wear in hot climates. Beside the lace-curtained windows, through which retired officers could be glimpsed in animated conversation at dining-tables, a large display board showed photographs of the Soviet army 'on their international duty'. There were pictures of smiling, friendly soldiers helping Afghan tribesmen and assisting with earthquake relief work in Armenia. Across the narrow avenue from the hoarding, near the Museum of Art which once was the seminary where Stalin trained for the priesthood, people wandered in and out of Tbilisi's biggest video saloon, where for a rouble one could watch any of a dozen videos, including *Tragedy, Rock Style*; *King Kong* and *Crocodile Dundee II*. The boulevard had a mediterranean atmosphere, enhanced by the Tuscan-like hills hanging over the city centre. Tbilisi had an air of ease, even prosperity, to someone just arrived from Moscow. There were few queues, and the bars selling Turkish coffee and sweet cakes were rarely overcrowded. There were usually seats available in the *shashlik* cafés and in the restaurants a few minutes walk away overlooking the Kura River, where delicious *khachapuri*, toasted bread and cheese, was served with sweet lemonade.

The day I arrived was the feast of St David. Many churchgoers made their way up the steep, cobbled alleys from Rustaveli Avenue and under the wooden balconies of old houses, past little yards overhung with vines where roosters pecked in the dirt, and on up a precipitous zig-zag lane to the church of the saint, perched high on a pine-covered hill. The patriarch of the Georgian Catholic church, surrounded by chanting men and followed by women crossing themselves with exaggerated motions, walked around the cone-spired church, blessing its walls with showers of holy water. The smell of candles and fir trees mingled in the still, hot air. More people had begun attending services since the surge in Georgian nationalism, especially the young, a priest said. The church had become identified with the national fervour which had gripped Tbilisi. For the forty days of mourning after 9 April, the pictures of the dead had been displayed outside the ancient Sioni Cathedral on the banks of the river. It had become a place where young people in jeans and white, open-neck shirts hung about. They gathered to talk and sit on the walls, in order to be there, a silent commitment to the ideals of the dead protestors. There were also special services for the dead at the Armenian Catholic church.

Tbilisi once had a predominantly Armenian population which, in the previous century, gave it an urban, bourgeois character. In the pedestrian underpasses beneath Rustaveli Avenue, unshaven young men sold plastic lapel badges with the crimson, white and black flag of independent bourgeois Georgia, which existed from 1918 to 1921. The official version of how Georgia became part of the Soviet Union could still be found in the state guide book available in the Intourist Hotel. It declared that 'After the Great October Socialist Revolution in 1917, a bourgeois nationalist Menshevik government came to power in Georgia and ruled for more than three years, supported by the bayonets of foreign interventionists.' It failed to state that the independent government was overthrown by the Red Army, which marched into Tbilisi on 26 February. The still-banned nationalist flag was now defiantly displayed in the window of the Rustaveli theatre, and could be glimpsed hanging from balconeys in the narrow lanes.

The Communist Party first secretary, Djumber Patiashvili, had resigned at the time of the massacre and been replaced by the more nationally minded Givi Gumbaridze. The party-controlled press was filled with detailed accounts of the Georgian Supreme Soviet Commission of Inquiry which confirmed the evidence of the demonstrators of an unprovoked attack by soldiers. In the coffee bars, the shops and the streets, even in the Intourist office, people openly gave voice to their feelings. An official interpreter talked at length about Georgia's historic right to freedom and the need to get rid of the 'murdering Russian troops'. An old woman in a black dress said, 'We need independence now. Gorbachev comes on television and he grins' – she grimaced in imitation, showing a gold tooth – 'but life doesn't get any better.' A woman shopper with a baby in a pram commented, 'Why should we stay in the Soviet Union? Sugar is rationed, meat is rationed, soap is rationed, even cheese is rationed here now. What sort of a life is that? Thank God we have vegetables at least.' There were those in Tbilisi, however, who were apprehensive about the future. An Iranian taxi-driver, who refused to charge me a fare, said, 'We're better off under Moscow. Everyone respects everybody else in Tbilisi; Jews, Moslems, Georgians, Armenians. But if Soviet power was gone, who knows?' He shrugged ominously. Georgians dismissed such fears. Dr Thomas Gamkrelidze, a People's Deputy and professor of linguistics at Tbilisi University with a Lenin prize to his name, told me, 'They say we joined the Soviet Union in 1921. We call it annexation. Next year there will be elections to a new Georgian Supreme Soviet. It must decide our future and give Georgia sovereignty. Nobody has any reason to fear.'

One of the organisers of the demonstration and hunger strike in the square which had ended in disaster was Merab Kostava, a stocky Georgian with thick white hair, looking older than his fifty years. He was evidently a national hero. The waiters rushed to get us a table when we entered a *khachapuri* restaurant on a terrace overlooking the fast-flowing, muddy Kura River. He had just been released from prison after forty days without charge. 'We're seeing the break-up of the Soviet Union – every Georgian wants independence now', he said, adding, 'We'll see independence in my generation. I'm sure of that now.'

The independence movement in Georgia was complicated by the presence of minority ethnic groups on Georgian territory. The hunger strike had arisen directly as a result of a renewed secession campaign by Abkhazians, an ancient people numbering less than 90,000 whose language is believed to be phonetically the fastest in the world and who live in a Black Sea province in the north west. The Georgian demonstrators were protesting against what they suspected was Kremlin encouragement for Abkhazia's sudden campaign to join the neighbouring Russian federation. Apparently, this was because of the alleged failure of the Georgian authorities to protect their cultural development. 'The KGB is behind it', said Tamara Cheidze, a young nationalist who accompanied Kostava and who had also been a political prisoner and one of the leaders of a pro-independence group named after the nineteenth-century Georgian patriot Ilia Chavchavadze. The group had played a large part in organising the protest. 'Abkhazia has always been Georgian, even when Georgia was a kingdom', she said. 'Russia is now trying to bring about the disintegration of Georgia. It always happens when the nationalist movement is strong.' Kostava said he believed the Kremlin was working actively to destabilise Georgia in order to justify a crackdown.

Everytime I visited Georgia in the following months, I was struck by the way the disputes with ethnic minorities preoccupied and agitated Georgian nationalists almost as much as the independence drive itself. As elections to a new Georgian parliament approached, offering a choice of candidates for the first time, the political temperature rose steadily in the Caucasian republic. The nationalists became more confident, and independence flags appeared more frequently. The headquarters of a popular front was established in the House of Cinema on Rustaveli Avenue and became a gathering place for dozens of militant young men. When I returned to Tbilisi the following winter, the city was in turmoil over an influx of a few hundred Georgian refugees who had fled from ethnic fighting in South Ossetia. The 65,000 Ossetians, a Persian people who, like the Abkhazians, occupied an autonomous region bordering on Russia, had also begun agitating for membership of the Russian federation, claiming that Georgian chauvinism threatened their language and culture. Some of the Georgian refugees, old peasant women and children, were sleeping in the entrance to the parliament building, others in the foyer of the House of Cinema. I went to the cinema to arrange to meet Zviad Gamsakhurdia, the most prominent of several emerging nationalist leaders. As a couple of his lieutenants checked my press credentials, a large rat crept down the stairs of the cinema hallway, taking no notice of the people coming in and out. I was taken by car through a series of narrow streets and alleyways to Gamsakhurdia's home, a two storey, red-brick mansion surrounded by a high wall with metal gates. Tough-looking men lounged round the entrance and identified callers through an intercom system. A ferocious dog was tethered inside the gate.

The object of all this protection, Zviad Gamsakhurdia, was a handsome, green-eyed university professor, a fluent English speaker with a full moustache which made him look like a Causcasian general. The fifty-one-year-old Georgian academic was a general in many ways. He could call out an army of men, some armed, and had done so to confront the Ossetians a few weeks previously. He was a controversial figure in Georgia. Gamsakhurdia served short prison sentences in 1954 and 1957 for nationalist student activity. When he became a lecturer in American literature at Tbilisi University in the 1960s, he began protesting about the corruption of communist officials and the destruction of Georgian monuments. In 1972 he telephoned the Georgian interior minister, then Eduard Shevardnadze, about the theft of religious treasures from the Georgian Patriarch. An investigation led to the wife of the Georgian party leader, but no charges were ever brought. Three years later Gamsakhurdia and Merab Kostava founded a Helsinki human rights group and started sending details of torture in Georgian prisons to Andrei Sakharov and other dissidents in Moscow. Both were arrested and tried in May 1978 for anti-Soviet activities, but Gamsakhurdia shocked his friends by recanting. Sakharov cancelled plans to travel from Moscow to the trial when he learned that Gamsakhurdia had 'disavowed his human rights activities'. Sakharov recalled, in his memoirs, that 'Gamsakhurdia stated at his trial and again on television, that he regretted his public statements and meetings with foreign diplomats. I don't think it right to condemn anyone for recanting. Human strength has its limitations . . . all the more reason to admire those who stand firm, like Merab Kostava. Left exposed by Gamsakhurdia's capitulation, he refused to yield and continued to conduct himself with courage and dignity in camps and exile.'

Gamsakhurdia's action was a triumph for the Kremlin. Craig Whitney of *The New York Times* and Harold Piper of the *Baltimore Sun* were fined in a Moscow court for reporting that the televised expression of remorse had been fabricated. Gamsakhurdia was still sentenced to three years, but asked for, and got, a pardon in 1979. He had re-emerged as a force in Georgian politics in the independence drive of the previous two years. When he and Kostava were arrested again after the Tbilisi killings, the new prison spell helped remove the stain on Gamsakhurdia's nationalist credentials. Their release after forty days followed intense public pressure. He was forbidden to leave Georgia, but when the president of Czechoslovakia, Vaclav Havel, came to Moscow early in 1990, he pointedly invited Gamsakhurdia to a reception, and the ban was lifted.

Gamsakhurdia's models for the independence struggle he had waged against Moscow were the Irish heroes Roger Casement and Terence MacSwiney, he said. People in Georgia knew that both had died to win freedom for Ireland. Their names appeared in an open letter to Lenin in 1921 written by Gamsakhurdia's father, the famous Georgian novelist and nationalist Konstantine Gamsakhurdia. 'In it he declared that Georgia was not as politically evolved as Ireland, but Georgia would have its own Casements and MacSwineys until it gained full independence', he said. 'They were in my mind when we organised the hunger strikes. That prophesy is being fulfilled today.' One of the high-ceilinged rooms in the mansion had been preserved as a museum to his father, who had managed to work successfully as an author under communist rule.

Gamsakhurdia also vigorously maintained that demands for self-government from the Ossetians played into Moscow's hands. He went further and alleged that they discriminated against Georgians. 'This autonomous region was created by the Bolsheviks', he said in his fluent English. 'Now there is an apartheid there worse than in South Africa. Ninety per cent of government there is Ossetian. Georgian people can't even enter the shops or use transport. When you hear autonomy, you hear apartheid. Moscow created this apartheid. On instructions from Moscow, Ossetians are not punished for their crimes. They fight against us with Soviet flags and pictures of Lenin.' I asked him if he had any contacts with their leadership. 'No, you can't trust any Ossetians', he replied.

Gamsakhurdia's role in the turbulent evolution of Georgian politics helped explain the heavy security. As he accompanied me to the gate, he told me how once when he was leading guests to their car at 3.00 a.m., a hand grenade had been tossed at their feet. It had failed to explode. Violent incidents were becoming commonplace. Georgy Chanturia, head of the National Democratic Party, was shot in the arm in a Tbilisi street. Chanturia had published in his newspaper a story of how a meeting of Soviet dissidents in Prague had passed a resolution criticising Gamsakhurdia's attitude towards minorities. His printing-press had also been attacked.

By the time the first anniversary of the April killing arrived, the hoarding in Rustaveli Avenue had been taken down. A simple monument to the dead had been erected on the steps, which were covered with red carnations and roses. Trestle tables had been placed on the pavements to collect signatures from citizens who wished to renounce Soviet citizenship in favour of Georgian nationality. They were doing brisk business. Local authorities had bowed to the will of the increasingly assertive nationalist movements, and the crimson, black and white flag of independent Georgia flew from public buildings. The army officers' club near the site of the massacre had been ordered to close down, and every lamp post in the city centre was fitted with a set of artificial candles, which flickered on and off like Christmas decorations. Long before 4.03 a.m., the precise moment when the attack by soldiers began a year previously, it was almost impossible to move through the throng in the boulevard. Every balcony on the solid, stone buildings was packed to danger point by people waving flags and holding candles aloft, and the sycamore and plane trees near government buildings were laden down with young spectators. The day coincided with Palm Sunday in the Georgian Catholic church; many carried branches from church services. Thousands of candle-flames lit the roadway with pin-pricks of light throughout the still, warm night. The army assault on Tbilisi, and the Soviet military action in Baku, the capital of Azerbaijan, nine months later had created a momentary solidarity between Christian Georgia and its Moslem neighbour. Among the flags were the blue, red and green of independent Azerbaijan, held aloft by members of its popular front, some of whom had made the 300-mile journey from Baku to Tbilisi on foot to publicise their gesture. The flags of other republics were there too, including Lithuania and Estonia, but conspicuously absent was that of Armenia, where there was resentment towards Georgian nationalists for pursuing neutrality in the Armenian-Azerbaijani conflict. Most Tbilisi Armenians stayed away from the demonstration.

At the climax of the ceremony, the deep tones of fifty Georgian singers, magnified by a stereo system big enough for a rock concert, resonated through the dark boulevards. The ancient battle hymn sung by the mustachioed men of the Georgian ensemble, dressed in black, silver-lined robes with swords and ornate bandoliers, launched a wave of nationalistic emotion through the crowd, who cried and thrust fists in the air. Iraki Tsereteli of the Independence Party proclaimed through the public address system, 'Our duty is to remember the martyrs who died in the struggle for independence. The events of 9 April didn't frighten the people. We are more united now in the struggle with the empire. No tanks will stop us in this struggle.' Georgy Chanturia said, 'A lot of people have come here from other republics. We sometimes learn from others, like the Baltics, but maybe they can now learn something from us in our irreconcilable struggle with the empire.' One of the loudest cheers was for Akaki Asatiani, chairman of the Monarchist Party, which sought to revive the Georgian kingdom abolished by the Russian tsar in 1800 when Georgia was united with Russia.

The anniversary celebrations were preceded by a campaign of destruction of public monuments commemorating seven decades of communist rule. When I arrived the night before, I found masonry and white paint littering the footpath at the opposite end of Rustaveli Avenue. Young men armed with hammers and a pot of white paint and perched on top of a crane had attacked a mural of Stalin on the wall high above the entrance to the Marxist-Leninist Institute – where the monarchist and other new parties had been given premises.

Stalin occupied a peculiar place in Georgian psychology. I found a mighty statue of Stalin, or Joseph Vissarionovich Dzhugashvili, standing in the centre of Gori, an hour's drive from Tbilisi through Tuscan-like valleys of vineyards and orchards where the apple trees were a psychedelic green from insecticide spray. Stalin was born in Gori in 1879. The black, brooding figure in an overcoat of stone was the last public monument to the discredited dictator to remain standing in a public place in the Soviet Union. Gori, overlooked by a crumbling, second-century fortress, had become a place of pilgrimage for those who still revered Stalin, and for the tourists of perestroika, drawn by curiosity to look at the Stalin museum and the little wooden house where the Dzhugashvilis used to live. The two-roomed dwelling was set in public gardens and protected from the elements by a marble arch resembling a miniature metro station, erected by Stalin's secret police chief, Beria, in 1936. Both the museum and the house had been closed for the previous two years as Stalin's crimes were exposed under glasnost, but they could be inspected with a little persuasion. An ancient bemedalled attendant pulled back the hovel door to allow a peep inside at the crude bed where Stalin was born. He wore a Stalin pin in his lapel, 'and Stalin is in my heart, too', he said. It was undoubtedly a favourite line for the tourists, just as the old men sitting nearby, like Vladimir Shevardnadze, took a perverse pride in telling people that they were not ashamed of Stalin, and 'The Soviet Union could do with the type of discipline he imposed.' The younger people in Gori, caught up in the wave of nationalism and anti-communism sweeping through Georgia, had less respect for the dictator, but, as one radical youth said in Stalin Square, 'It's his home town; let him stand there.'

The attitude to Lenin, however, was different. The founder of the communist state was a Russian, and Georgians blamed him for the annexation of Georgia in 1921. In the run-up to the anniversary commemoration, all his statues had been pulled down in Georgian towns and cities, except for the biggest – a huge monument in the main square in Tbilisi which had been put under heavy police guard. In Gori, we were told that the town's big Lenin statue had been pulled down a couple of weeks previously.

A typical old-style party official, well dressed and over-bearing, with a couple of comrades in tow, arrived at the Gori Soviet, an imposing building in Stalin Square, while I was inspecting the Stalin statue in the company of my colleague John Lombard of Australian Broadcasting.

'Is it true', I asked the party official as he stepped out of his black Volga, 'that Lenin's statue was pulled down here in Gori?'

'No, that's not true', he replied, lighting a cigarette.

'But I heard reports that Lenin's statue was toppled.'

'Those reports are wrong.'

'People I talked to say it happened.'

'Nothing like that took place, I can assure you.' The two men accompanying the official looked on, unblinking.

'So where's the town's statue of Lenin?'

'We, er, don't have one', he said.

In that he was correct.

In a rather unkempt public garden beside the Kura, which also flowed through Gori, a five-minute walk from Stalin Square, we found a twelve-foot high stone pedestal. It was empty. The concrete surround was smashed at one side where the massive figure of Lenin had fallen and broken into pieces. A Russian woman, Alla Makharashvili, who lived nearby with her Georgian husband, explained what happened.

'There was a big demonstration here on 6 March', she said. 'They took a vote to get rid of Lenin. Some were against, but most supported the idea. Then a young fellow went and got a crane and they pulled it down with ropes.'

Several other people told the same story. Even the brown-eyed local children who said, 'Stalin – okay', but gave a thumbs-down sign for Lenin and Gorbachev, knew all about the night the statue was destroyed, and that all but one of the Lenin memorials in Georgia had been wrecked. Some had been more difficult to get rid of than others. The statue at Mtskheta, the ancient Georgian capital not far from Tbilisi, was no push-over. The pedestal, on the roadside below the ancient fortress church of the Temple of the Cross, still had a jagged pair of feet stuck to the stone base. Not far away, a hideous modern structure, a giant oval of entwined stainless steel strips erected to typify the friendship of Soviet peoples, stood charred and rusted by the roadside. It wouldn't burn, said the Georgian driver in disgust.

There was no place for Stalin in Tbilisi, however. Two Armenians watching the clearing up after the attack on the Stalin frieze brought me to an alleyway across from the Marxist-Leninist Institute. Lying in the corner among some rubbish was a huge, round copper shell. They turned it over. It was a bust of Stalin, taken the night before from the institute as the choir sang their lament at the commemoration ceremonies. Its face had been smashed in with hammers. 'And they did it themselves; Georgians did it', said the Armenians gleefully.

The nationalist mood swept the communists from power in the autumn 1990 elections. The next time I saw Zviad Gamsakhurdia was in January 1991 on a chilly day when a damp, heavy snow coated Tbilisi. He had just been elected president and now occupied the former party chief's office in the parliament buildings. He had replaced the picture of Lenin behind the desk with a gold-and-blue enamel plate depicting St George armed with a lance, the symbol of independent Georgia during 1918 to 1921. The Lenin statue in the square at the end of Rustaveli Avenue had finally, and officially, been toppled, its admonishing, outstretched hand rocking to and fro as if making one final plea to an unresponsive city before crashing to the ground. Gamsakhurdia's old comrade Merab Kostava had not lived to see Georgia shaking off its ideological chains. He had been killed in a car crash on Friday, 13 October 1989. The tough-looking men who had protected Gamsakhurdia's house had become members of his 12,000-strong national guard. I recognised some of them standing outside the parliament in makeshift uniforms of brown caps and brown leggings tucked into black jackboots. This time they were holding *kalashnikov* automatic rifles.

Gamsakhurdia was still preoccupied with the Ossetians. A nasty little civil war had broken out around the main Ossetian town of Tskhinvali, an hour's drive north of Gori along a road lined with tall poplar trees and infested with magpies. 'They want to throw all Georgians out of Tskhinvali now. Most Georgians fled. Now they are refugees', growled Gamsakhurdia from behind his desk. 'The Soviet government wants to have a pretext for interventions into Georgia. This is also the Baltics' way. They want to make it in the form of calming the situation in south Ossetia. They have no right to have here a state in Georgia. They are here a national minority. Their homeland is north Ossetia, north Caucasus. Here they are newcomers.'

Fearing the loss of their privileged status, the pro-Soviet south Ossetians had ignited Georgian passions by declaring their intention to unite with north Ossetia inside the Russian federation as a new Soviet Republic. Georgian militia and irregulars had invaded the town and then withdrawn to a ring of roadblocks after fierce fighting. Kidnappings and assassinations had become the weapons of the militants of both sides, terrorising the communities who had lived together in Tskhinvali and nearby villages for nearly a century. As I stood at the last Georgian roadblock just outside Tskhinvali, a yellow Zhiguli tried to slip through behind a passing Soviet armoured vehicle, but a dozen Georgian militiamen and vigilantes ran out on to the roadway and forced them to stop. A pot-bellied vigilante with a hunting rifle strapped to his back wrenched open the door of the little car and pulled out the terrified young Ossetian driver by the scarf. 'Where are your documents?' he shouted. 'You stole this car, didn't you? This belongs to a Georgian, doesn't it?' The Zhiguli driver was taken to a building for questioning. Seconds later Georgian militiamen cradling automatics ordered seven Ossetian men from the back of a lorry. The fat man pushed and prodded them, shouting, 'Where have you hidden your guns?' Four of the men were told to run. They did so, as fast as they could.

The red flag flew over Tskhinvali as I walked into the hill town from the roadblock past barricades of shoulder-high concrete sewage pipes blocking a narrow bridge over the Liakhva River. In a general store in the town centre, five strong-boned women sat around a wood stove. The shelves were bare. The windows had been shattered by gunfire. There were bullet holes in the ceiling; one woman produced a frying pan with a neat hole in the centre. They laughed when I said I was from Ireland. The Ossetians call themselves 'Ire' people and joke that 'Ire-land' is their homeland. Their word for water is *don*, and they 'claim' London too. Most moved to Georgia from the Caucasus in the previous one hundred years, seeking better land. They took the Bolshevik side in the revolution and, to the anger of Georgian nationalists, were rewarded with autonomous status in 1922. Now they were under siege. The Soviet army was hesitant to get caught up in the fighting. Electricity supplies had been cut and the only power came from a portable generator which supplied the bakery. There was no heat or water. More than 200 patients shivered in the beds of the local hospital. During the day there was a lull in the constant sniper fire, and children sleighed down the snowy streets or hung on to the bumpers of the few cars that passed by to slide along the roadway. 'We are a cultured people, not wild like Gamsakhurdia says', said Julietta Ostayeva, an elderly, bespectacled teacher with white hair and a tweed suit, who was organising emergency housing for hundreds of distraught people milling round the administrative offices, where Lenin's picture still adorned the walls. The town had a

Stalin Street and a Lenin Street, and in a park an eternal flame burned at a memorial to the Soviet war dead. Six busts of Soviet heroes had been taken from their pedestals at the memorial and thrown in the river by Georgian militiamen, the other two had been defaced with hammers. 'If Georgians want to leave the Soviet Union, we don't', said Yulia Gazaiva, one of the women in the empty store whose husband, like so many Ossetians, was a Soviet army officer.

Despite the Caucasian surroundings, Tskhinvali reminded me vividly of Belfast in 1969. The atmosphere was one of fear; the talk was of pogroms. A street of a dozen houses had been burned down, the homes of Georgians, with only blackened gables left standing like Bombay Street in Belfast after it had been attacked by loyalist extremists. Hundreds of the two-storey stone houses had been damaged in the fighting.

If Casement and MacSwiney were Gamsakhurdia's Irish heroes, there was no doubt who these people were. The Ossetians had become his Ulster unionists.

17

Yalta to Malta

T HERE were few better ways of seeing the world than travelling with Mikhail Gorbachev. In his quest to take the Soviet Union out of its Cold War isolation, the Kremlin leader journeyed to Beijing to make peace with Russia's old enemy, China, to Washington to bury the hatchet with its Cold War foe, the United States, and to the Vatican in order to forge a concordat with the Pope. He became the tourist of his own revolution in world politics. We went with him on the excursions which took the Soviet leader to the gates of the Forbidden City and to the inner sanctums of the Holy City, to the drawing-rooms of London and the dinner-tables of Paris, and, as Gennady Gerasimov of the Soviet Foreign Ministry put it in his inventive way, to Malta from Yalta – two places which had in common a major role in the redrawing of the map of Europe twice in half a century.

Perhaps the most fraught of these historical journeys was the one in which Gorbachev made peace with China in May 1989. The Soviet Foreign Ministry organised a charter flight to bring us to Beijing two days in advance of the visit, the first Sino-Soviet summit in thirty years. On the plane, dubbed Glasnost Three (Glasnost One and Two went to New York and Havana), Gerasimov passed down the aisle, handing out, like holy communion, red souvenir badges displaying a hammer and sickle entwined with a Chinese star, while intoning in English, 'Red is beootiful.'

The first sign we saw at the airport in Beijing, the capital of the world's most populous communist state, read, 'Visa card is everywhere you want to be'. The taxis outside were Volvos, Toyotas and Mercedes. The road into the city centre was smooth. This was a welcome change from Moscow, the other capital of world communism, with its battered old Volgas and its potholes. Almost all Beijing traffic consisted of modern Japanese and European cars. In Moscow the car was king, and pedestrians cringed back at the sound of a horn, but in the Chinese capital the cyclists and pedal rickshaws co-existed easily with the automobile, drifting across main avenues in a never-ending stream and ignoring all traffic signs.

The centre of Beijing had been endowed with a strip of luxury hotels by China's economic reforms of the previous ten years, designed to attract capitalist businessmen and investment. In the Jianguo Hotel I found push-button telephones with direct dialling to every major city in the world – except Moscow. Nor was the Soviet capital included in the international time-clocks above the reception desk, showing the hour in New York, San Francisco, Honolulu, Tokyo, New Delhi, Athens, Rome, Paris, London and Beijing. The hotel had a business room with a fax, and the *Herald Tribune* was delivered daily to the bedrooms. In the lobby, a Filipino ensemble entertained guests sitting around in cane chairs under the latticed glass roof. They crooned, 'You're just too good to be true, can't take my eyes off-ah you'.

Driving around town on Saturday, 13 May, the day after our arrival, our car was delayed at a junction by a line of students with red flags. Soviet officials had confidently forecast that intermittent student protests in Beijing would be suspended during the summit out of respect to the important guests, but when we went to Tiananmen Square, empty that morning, we found a few thousand students with white headbands gathered in front of the monument to the people's heroes. Many spoke English. They told us that 1,000 of their number had started a hunger strike at 2.00 p.m. that afternoon. They said they wanted democracy and openness within the system, and were opposed to autocratic rule and corruption under China's leader, eighty-four-year-old Deng Xiaoping. They wanted glasnost in China and a retraction of Deng's insult that the students were 'a black hand raised against the party and myself'. 'Gorbachev is good, we like him', said a young hunger-striker, giving a thumbs-up sign.

On Sunday morning the Filipino group in the lobby had been replaced by a thirty-member orchestra in evening dress. They played Mozart and Verdi and rounded off with, 'It's now or never'. Several Soviet intellectuals gave a press conference in the international hotel on reforms in the USSR. An actress from Georgia drew pained looks from Russian officials when she said the young students on hunger strike reminded her of recent events in Tbilisi, where twenty demonstrators were killed by troops. After a series of questions in American accents, a Soviet official complained, 'Why do the Americans ask all the questions?' Gerasimov, sitting among the reporters, replied, 'Maybe it is because they don't know the answers.'

The city was full of rumours that Deng has ordered Tiananmen Square to be cleared for Gorbachev's visit. The Soviet leader was to be officially welcomed after his arrival on Monday at the memorial, around which the students had gathered, and official banquets were to take place in the great hall of the people alongside the square. Three times the radio said students should leave the square by 8.00 a.m. on Monday morning. An Australian diplomat in the Jianguo told me 'Five a.m. – that's the time the police will move in.' That evening four white, Italian-made ambulances appeared on the edge of the vast square. A student whose headband read 'Law and Democracy' told the crowd through a loudspeaker, 'In my own opinion we should leave now and be courteous to Gorbachev.' The thousands standing around listened in silence. Another said through a megaphone, 'We will go to the death for freedom.' There was a huge cheer. I decided to stay in the square all night. It was warm, but the steps at the base of the memorial, the only place to sleep, were hard and uncomfortable. Dressed for a summit, not a revolution, my suit was soon creased and dusty. At 3.10 a.m., the chanting and singing of the 'Internationale' died away and people cupped their ears to hear an announcement that negotiations with the communist leaders had broken down. The student strike committee split ten to ten on what to do. They decided to stay because there was no decision to leave. In any event the initiative was beginning to slip to other forces. Hundreds of workers were pouring into the square with banners saying, 'Citizens' Support Brigade'. At 5.00 a.m. nothing happened. A convoy of army trucks drove by on the main avenue and a hunger-striker was carried away, screaming with stomach pains. Eight a.m. came and there was still no move against them. I took a bicycle rickshaw to return the three miles to the Jianguo. Because of the time difference I was able to telephone a new introduction to my story in *The Irish Times*, which included the line, 'as the sun rose this morning over the museum of Chinese history in Tiananmen Square'. They would be reading that in the DART commuter train in Dublin before dawn on the same day, I thought with some satisfaction.

On Monday, Gerasimov told us that Gorbachev's welcoming ceremony had been transferred from the square to the airport. Copies of the Soviet leader's remarks on arrival were distributed, but he did not get a chance to utter them as he was hurried through the terminal. They included, 'We in the Soviet Union follow with great interest the transformations that are unfolding in China.' The students and supporters, by this time numbering 100,000, were jubilant that they still controlled the square. 'It's wonderful, for the first time everyone is talking openly about politics', said a law student. They erected a black flag near the hunger-strikers. Seventy people had been taken to hospital and the number of ambulances had increased to ten. The first in a series of government concessions came in Monday's party-controlled newspapers, which splashed pictures of the demontrations, an unheard of example of Chinese glasnost. Four hundred policemen appeared and made a half-hearted attempt to push the students off the square, but they met a solid wall of people and after a while simply give up. At 4.15 p.m. Gorbachev was expected at the Great Hall for talks with Chinese President Yang. The meeting was put off to 6.00 p.m. We gathered at the north entrance to the Great Hall to see Gorbachev arrive, after first being told he would enter by the east entrance facing the square. This had been changed to the south and then to the north. Four hundred soldiers came jogging by to seal off the side street on the northern side. They carried little wooden stools and were unarmed. At a signal they opened the stools with a loud clicking sound and sat in unison, then rose when a crowd of onlookers gathered to push them back. Gorbachev eventually arrived in his black Zil and headed straight for the back door on the west side, out of sight of the correspondents. 'It's hard to play this game', sighed a Japanese cameraman. The Soviet leader's schedule had included a tour of Beijing, but instead, someone said, 'They took him on a detour of the city.'

The student protest was by then highly organised. Stewards holding hands formed interlocking circles in a honey-comb pattern to protect the hunger-strikers lying on the ground. Ambulances were racing in and out along a special passageway carved through the protestors. By Monday evening 140 students had been taken to hospital, some with internal bleeding. Two hospitals had run out of saline drips. A medical centre had been set up by the monument with students in white coats. Discipline was rigid. A student with a megaphone ordered circles of the honeycomb to stand or sit cross-legged at different times. Long lines of hunger-strikers holding hands were occasionally escorted out of the *cordon sanitaire* to public lavatories across the square. Workers' banners appeared on the edge of the huge crowd and there was a feeling that the protest was becoming a 'now or never' attempt to win real reform.

On Tuesday morning Gorbachev came to the Great Hall once more, again through the back door, for his historic meeting with Deng. A wreath-laying at the monument had been called off as they could not get near it. Throughout the city, excitement was rising as impromptu parades appeared on the main avenues. I came across a massive bicycle jam at a road junction where the air was filled with tinkling bells and cries of 'hoi, hoi, hoi'. Around Tiananmen Square, lines of parked bicycles, all with tiny registration plates, formed an almost impenetrable barrier. White-coated medical students made collections for the protesters, and pedal-carts brought boxes of coca-cola and cartons of cigarettes to the square. Handfuls of cigarettes were thrown among the hunger-strikers. Everywhere people called out, 'hello', and pointed to the students, grinning and shouting, 'good', and giving V for victory signs. On Tuesday afternoon eleven students from the Beijing Drama School started a hunger strike in front of the southern entrance to the Great Hall. They lay side by side on the roadway in blankets, each clutching a red rose. A huge crowd gathered around, blocking the wide avenue, and traffic in the centre began to seize up. Students policed the roadway as a joyous anarchy replaced the city's normal daily life. In the square litter was ankle deep and the still air had become turgid and foul-smelling. The wail of ambulance sirens was now a constant background noise. A broadcasting system set up in the centre of the square had replaced the megaphones and non-stop messages of support were read out. The whole city was behind them, it seemed. Even CBBS, the party-controlled radio station, said there were 'several hundred thousand' people in the square, another victory for openness.

The Soviet camp was by this time in crisis, with Gorbachev's schedule in tatters. Gennady Gerasimov was due to give his press conference at 10.00 p.m. He didn't turn up until midnight and was loudly hissed by the exhausted journalists. He slapped his face in self-deprecation.

On Wednesday morning protestors converged from every direction to the square. The whole city was on the move in peaceful revolt. All the way from the Jianguo Hotel to the square, and as far as I could see in the opposite direction, the eight-lane highway was a mass of cheering, shouting people. There were a million in the square with flags and banners. Volunteer organisers kept parades moving around to avoid a disastrous crush. The Jianguo manager apologised that half his staff hadn't turned up, but the Filipino group was in place, singing a merry 'cha-cha-cha'. An elderly female American tourist asked loudly, 'Where is the shopping centre?' For the first time a taxi did not glide up as soon as she stepped outside. Most of the press corps had by now hired bicycles. In the square, a student gleefully said that workers had joined the protest from the Xiyuan Hotel, which everyone apparently knew was run by the secret police. Bell hops in uniform were parading with flags. The seventeen-storey Beijing Hotel, overlooking the square, seemed a good vantage point to observe the vast multitudes. In the lift a recorded voice said in English, 'First floor, going up'. The elevator carpet was inscribed in English with the word Wednesday. The following day I found it had been changed for one marked Thursday. On the top floor I was shooed away from the windows by hotel officials. Pushing my way back into the square I found some students sitting on petrol cans. They had volunteered to burn themselves alive if the demand for dialogue with the government was not met. A group appeared bearing a banner in English with former president Kennedy's words, 'Let's not negotiate out of fear but do not fear to negotiate.'

Gorbachev addressed the Chinese people on television from the Great Hall, having again entered by the back door. He was then taken out of town to visit the Great Wall, the fate of every important guest. Nixon was reported to have said, 'It's a great wall, isn't it?' Hardly any of the reporters went with him on the one hundred-mile journey. We watched on CNN in our bedrooms as he took the few obligatory steps along the surface, then returned to the streets.

By Wednesday afternoon the centre of the square was like a refugee camp of makeshift tents, with ambulances dashing in and out at breakneck speed. More then 700 hunger-strikers had now been taken to hospital. We gathered again at the north entrance to the great hall, this time for Gorbachev's summit press conference prior to his return to Moscow. Several people broke away from the masses and ran up the steps. Soldiers rushed out from behind the big doors but stewards appeared from nowhere and pushed the crowd back. We were admitted to a huge room with oriental carvings and silk screens. Everyone was in place – some 1,000 journalists, Gerasimov, the official note-takers, the KGB security men, led by the burly figure with a mole on his face – when a Chinese official arrived and screamed hysterically into a microphone that the venue had been changed to the official guest-house where the Gorbachevs were staying. This was some miles away from the city centre. With the roads jammed with people as far as we could see, journalists disappeared in all directions in a futile search for taxis. Accompanied by Bill Keller of *The New York Times*, I found a two-seat bicycle rickshaw. The elderly Chinese driver pedalled us furiously through narrow alleyways to avoid the throng which had paralysed the streets. Even at the government guest-house in the suburbs there were endless parades of people shouting the phrase which echoed through all of Beijing, 'We support the students.'

Gorbachev, who had initially dismissed the students as 'hotheads', clearly thought they were winning and told us of the 'warm, sincere and substantive' support they had given him in a letter he had received. The students had undoubtedly taken their example from Gorbachev's glasnost. What if Soviet students in turn imitated the Chinese? The question was put by Xan Smiley, the Moscow correspondent of the *Daily Telegraph*. 'If a problem of such a nature arose in the Soviet

Union, we would address this problem within the spirit of glasnost and democracy', he replied, indirectly giving a green light for the mass rallies which were to take place in the following months in Moscow.

Despite the wrecked schedule, Gorbachev achieved what he set out to do. The three irritants in Soviet-Chinese relations were resolved – the Soviet occupation of Afghanistan, Russian military build-up on the Soviet-Chinese border, and differences over Cambodia. In a much-photographed handshake with Deng Xiaoping, he had been able to declare Sino-Soviet relations normal for the first time since 1959. The two countries could open their borders again and resume trading, which had been interrupted three decades earlier.

The next day as we prepared to leave on Glasnost Three – Chinese officials had refused to renew our visas to allow us to stay behind – the whole city was in a state of insurrection. Buses had been commandeered and lorries packed with flag-waving people headed for the square. With a loud roar, fifty motorbikes went by the Jianguo, each with a red flag – Beijing's version of the Hell's Angels. The mass movement for democracy and against corruption was turning into an anti-communist revolt. In the afternoon, nature contributed to the drama with a violent thunderstorm. The Australian diplomat told me as we carried our cases out of the hotel, 'There's no going back, nothing will ever be the same again here', words I recalled some days later after the massacre on the square when the democracy rebellion was crushed and the old order was reimposed.

Because of the unrest in Beijing, Gorbachev didn't make it into the forbidden city, the old Chinese capital behind the pagoda on Tiananmen Square. Months later he did, however, penetrate the walls of a city where no Soviet leader had ever set foot before – the Holy City of the Vatican, capital of world Catholicism and avowed enemy of communism.

The meeting was of great significance for the leaders of the communist and Catholic worlds. For Gorbachev it was part of a process of gaining world legitimacy for the Soviet Union in his attempts to integrate its economy with the West, and of winning internal approval from the USSR's Roman Catholics for his reforms. For Pope John Paul it was an opportunity to secure greater freedom of religion inside the Soviet Union, which had broken off diplomatic relations with the Vatican in 1922, and to prepare the way for a papal visit. But some serious questions of protocol had to be decided first. It was one thing to have the Kremlin leader stepping inside the sacred portals of the Vatican, it was quite another to expect the red flag of communism to fly over St Peter's in his honour and to have the brass band of the Holy See play the Soviet national anthem. Such embarrassments were avoided by a diplomatic sleight of hand. President Gorbachev's visit to the Vatican was decreed to be an 'official' rather than a state occasion, thus dispensing with the symbolic trappings. A flashy Italian motorcycle escort conducted the Soviet party in their bullet-proof Zil limousines, which did have little red flags, to the grotto entrance of St Peter's. Here a Vatican Mercedes, with its distinctive SCV number plate, took over to lead the motorcade into a cobbled courtyard in the heart of the tiny ecclesiastical state to which I had been admitted along with a few colleagues to observe the comings and goings.

If Raisa Gorbachev's outfit shocked the waiting Vatican officials as the couple stepped out of their car to be greeted by Pope John Paul in his customary white robes, they didn't show it. Instead of the conventional black outfit and veil which protocol decreed should be worn by the female consort of an official guest, the independent-minded Raisa was wearing a costume coloured, as an Italian commentator described it, 'Bolshevik red', with velvet buttons and collar, and no head covering. While the head of the Roman Catholic church and the leader of world communism – the first, by his own admission, to have been baptised – retired to the pontiff's private study for their talks, Raisa Gorbachev was escorted on a tour of the Vatican museum and galleries. She was overheard telling the museum director how she had come to the Vatican as a tourist in 1971 with her husband and had been disappointed not to have seen the Sistine Chapel as it was under renovation. 'I'm looking forward to seeing it this time', she said. But once more she was thwarted. Time ran out before she could properly study the chapel with its famous Michelangelo frescoes. It was mostly her own fault, however. Raisa Gorbachev, reputed to have once said, 'I'm the atheist in the family', lingered too long in the Stanza Della Segnatura to examine Raphael's paintings depicting the glory and triumph of the church. Raisa ordered that the shutters be closed so that she could better see the ceiling in Raphael's 'Room of the Fire', and disagreed with the museum director over whether Italian and Russian madonnas looked alike. She said they didn't.

When the Pope and Gorbachev emerged to meet with the rest of the Soviet party again, it was immediately obvious that the encounter between two of the most influential world leaders in modern history had gone extremely well. They were smiling and relaxed. Gorbachev had used to the full his extraordinary gift of charm, enabling him to hold the hand of Deng Xiaoping in Beijing one day and to bathe in the warmth of the Pope's hospitality the next. There was no mistaking the rapport established between the Russian party boss and the Polish Pope in their sixty-five-minute private meeting in the pontiff's study. It marked the end of one of the longest Cold Wars of this century – that between the Kremlin and the Vatican. The general secretary of the Soviet Communist Party introduced the Pope to his entourage, which included his foreign minister, Eduard Shevardnadze, whose head nodded vigorously in supplication as he shook the holy father's hand; Alexander Yakovlev, the radical Politburo member whose triumph this visit partly was; Ivan Frolov, editor of *Pravda*; and Lunkov, the Soviet ambassador to Rome, whose wife was properly attired in protocol black. The Pope started his formal speech in Russian and then continued in Italian. The Polish-born pontiff spoke Polish when he met Gorbachev, conversing without interpreters for the first few minutes in his study, according to a priest with whom I had coffee. Any information at all, serious or trivial, was hard to come by in the Holy City. It used to be said that the two most secretive institutions in the world were the Kremlin and the Vatican. The Vatican alone could claim that distinction by the end of the 1980s. Gorbachev, at the conclusion of a short address in which he announced the restoration of diplomatic relations, departed from his script to say that he had invited the Pope to visit the USSR. The Vatican press-corps, watching on a screen in another part of the Holy City, broke into applause. The Pope individually presented all twenty-six members of the Soviet party with papal medals. When Raisa opened the little white box she received, her face registered surprise and delight. She had been given mother-of-pearl rosary beads with a golden cross. As the farewell ceremonies drew to a close, she kept opening the box to peep inside, and called over the heavy-jowled Yakovlev to have a look. The Soviet leader was presented with a reproduction of a mosaic representing Christ on the tomb, and gave the Pope, in return, two facsimile fourteenth-century psalters from Kiev. The Vatican press office provided English language copies of Gorbachev's farewell remarks. Those listening distinctly heard Gorbachev use the word Vatican twice in his speech. Both times it appeared in the translation as the Holy See. We decided that it was probably force of habit (no pun intended) rather than another Vatican sleight of hand.

I left Rome in an Air Malta plane for Valletta and underwent one of the most hair-raising experiences of my reporting career, a cliff-top approach in a force eight gale to the airport in the Maltese capital, on my way to Gorbachev's next encounter with a world leader, President George Bush of the United States. In Malta the angry waters frothed and foamed while wind-whipped waves rose and crashed – and this was only in my hotel swimming-pool. Out on Marsaxlokk Bay, one of the worst gales of Malta's winter kept the US-guided missile cruiser, the Belknap, stormbound. On board was the American president, who had flown from Washington for the summit with Gorbachev. It was to be a meeting which would decide the future of Europe, where democracy movements more potent than those in China were sweeping aside the Soviet-backed governments in all the Warsaw pact countries of Eastern Europe. The elements, however, conspired against it. From the heaving decks of the Belknap, some unkind words may have been hurled into the teeth of the wind about the president's brother, William. It was he, Maltese officials said, who had persuaded George Bush to hold the summit off Malta after visiting the then undoubtedly balmy Mediterranean island in September as a White House representative during Independence Day celebrations. 'He was really impressed with Malta', said a gloomy-faced Arthur Pace, director of the tiny republic's information service, as the gales whipped a long line of US and Soviet flags along the sea front, tearing many of them into shreds. The two-day summit timetable was also in shreds by the time the Soviet leader arrived in Malta's Luga Airport that evening. The Belknap and the Soviet cruiser, the Slava, co-hosts for the meeting, were already pitching and rolling less than a mile offshore.

As it turned out, the Russian obsession with hard currency was to save the day for an exhausted Gorbachev. The luxury Soviet liner, the Maxim Gorky, had been brought to Malta to serve as a rouble-paying hotel for Soviet officials and journalists. Equipped with two stabilisers, the big white pleasure ship nestled solidly against the quay in Marsaxlokk Bay. 'That's where I'll stay', said Gorbachev, abandoning any thought of taking a launch across the choppy waters to the quarters prepared for him on the 600-foot Soviet warship. The summit was rescheduled for the Maxim Gorky – which meant that the US president, who had braved the elements to bed down on the Belknap, had to do all the running – and heaving and bobbing – backwards and forwards across the churning green waters. On Saturday morning he crossed on the admiral's barge to the Soviet liner without too much trouble and bounded up from the fifth to the sixth deck to greet a waiting Gorbachev, saying, 'I'm glad to see you, nice to see you.' As they shook hands, someone asked Gorbachev if he would be reducing Warsaw pact forces. 'The first thing to do', replied the Soviet leader, 'is to eliminate the types of ships which you cannot board in this kind of weather.' The talks were held in a book-lined ship's card-room, across a three-foot wide table used by Scandinavian holidaymakers for games of poker. 'It's so narrow that if we don't have enough arguments we will kick each other', said Gorbachev as they settled down, knees almost touching and their papers overlapping in front of them.

During the morning session and lunch on board the Maxim Gorky, the weather got steadily worse. The launch taking Bush back to the Belknap for a break in the talks had to make several attempts before it docked beside the cruiser, with green-faced secret servicemen frantically trying to ensure that the commander-in-chief of the US armed forces did not end up in the Mediterranean. The Belknap was by this time dragging its anchor, which interrupted ship-to-shore communications, creating further havoc for the presidential party. Maltese pilots on board both cruisers laboured all day to prevent any mishaps. At 6.00 p.m. a pool of reporters allowed on to the Maxim Gorky were told by a tousled-looking White House spokesperson, Margaret Tutwiler, wearing a see-through airforce raincoat, that President Bush was stranded on the Belknap. With him were the US Secretary of State James Baker and other US officials. 'They're all fine', she said, as the admiral's barge alongside the cruiser disappeared in the trough of each passing wave. 'Just fine.' During the afternoon an interpid windsurfer braved the howling gale to sail his board between the Soviet and US warships. He fell off in the mountainous seas but remounted quickly and zipped away, pursued by two patrol boats, one of which eventually caught him up and hauled him on board.

Half an hour's drive away from the bay, in one of the island's old right-hand-drive Ford Cortinas, White House officials were trying to put the best face on the summit farce. 'The president likes this sort of thing – the soup (bad weather)', a spokesman called Sig Rogich told journalists quarantined in the Mediterranean conference hall, once the Holy Infirmary of the Order of St John of Jerusalem. A briefing scheduled for 7.00 p.m. on Saturday by the US and Soviet press secretaries, Marlin Fitzwater and Gennady Gerasimov, was cancelled. We were told that Gerasimov could attend, but he stayed away in solidarity with Fitzwater, who couldn't. Despite Gennady's noble gesture to his stormbound counterpart in not taking advantage of the situation to give the Soviet viewpoint exclusively, the White House decided that scruples were for jettisoning to prevent the US press from dwelling too much on storm damage. Late on Saturday evening a US official called aside a chosen few from the White House press-corps and revealed to them Bush's 'agenda' for the summit and asked them to pass it around. The details were devoured by the news-hungry journalists. This classic piece of damage limitation by the US government dictated the headlines in all America's Sunday newspapers the following day.

If the whole affair was an embarrassment for the Americans, it was a disaster for the Maltese, who had seen the summit as a glorious opportunity to promote tourism on which the island's economy depended. As drenched reporters arrived at the press centre in the conference hall, after negotiating a roadway splashed by giant waves, they were greeted by an electric sign saying, 'Welcome to Malta, island of sun and tranquillity'. Smiling girls behind service desks forlornly offered tourist brochures and the choice of a free holiday in a special draw. The ever-helpful island officials, who said they worked day and night to get everything right, watched unhappily as 2,000 journalists, sent from all over the world to report Malta's moment of glory, spent much of the weekend writing bad-weather stories. 'These are really freakish gales for us', said Mr Pace, who would not have looked out of place as a golf-club secretary in the English southern counties. If anyone in the White House had checked the weather records before deciding on a December sea-borne summit in the Mediterranean, however, they would have found out that the same time the previous year, almost to the day, there had been just such a storm in Malta.

The summits which Gorbachev and the press enjoyed most were those held in the United States. Whatever his battered image at home, the Soviet leader received celebrity status in Washington. Where the Chinese saw a serious Gorbachev well versed in the rhetoric of communist ideology, the Americans perceived a smiling, articulate reformer, committed to reducing nuclear arms and to correcting human-rights abuses, and prepared to take part, as he did with Ronald Reagan during their first Washington summit in December 1987, in a joint sing-along at a White House dinner where the Russian and American presidents crooned verse after verse of the sentimental Russian folk-song, 'Moscow Nights'. At that summit, Gorbachev played Reagan at his own game. Their public debate was conducted in corny one-liners and quotations. Both delved into the works of Waldo Emerson, ignoring the nineteenth-century American philosopher's admonition, 'I hate quotations, tell me what you know.' Reagan selected Emerson's words, 'All history becomes subjective, in other words there is properly no history, only biography.' Gorbachev chose, 'The reward of a thing well done is to have done it.' The Russian leader charmed Nancy Reagan at dinner with his account of the five stage's of a woman's life. First she is a girl, then a young woman, then a young woman, then a young woman, then a dead grandmother. Reagan illustrated how they had become captives to the arms race by recounting the Russian story of a general who was told that one of his soldiers had captured a bear. He asked him to bring it along. The soldier replied, 'I can't, the bear won't let me.' It was an all-American affair with wisecracks and first names. The mood was transmitted to the international press, based in the Marriott Hotel ballroom near the White House. The hundreds of reporters there had everything at hand: telephones on linen-draped tables, fresh coffee from giant urns, iced Coke in silver containers, and a twice-daily floor show from Gennady Gerasimov and Marlin Fitzwater, who turned up to give regular briefings. How were Gorbachev and Reagan making out, they were asked on the first day. 'Well', said Gennady, 'this morning the general secretary smiled at me and the president winked.' 'Hey', said Marlin, 'it was me he winked at.' 'Sorry, I thought it was me', retorted Gerasimov. 'Gennady is always stealing my show wherever he goes', complained Fitzwater. The accumulative effect of this bantering was to convince everyone that the Americans and the Russians were buddies, that the Cold War was over, or, as Gorbachev put it, the winter of their discontent was on the wane.

Gorbachev, however, not only brought to Washington the possibility of reducing world tensions and nuclear arms stocks, he brought his wife Raisa. In contrast to the stereotype of Soviet women as fat and dowdy, Raisa was elegant and slim, a doctor of philosophy – the first self-assured, high-profile Kremlin consort since Nadezhda Krupskaya, wife of Vladimir Lenin. French fashion designer Pierre Cardin called her one of the most elegant women in the world. At home she was the subject of criticism for her high profile, but in Washington she was idolised by society. Inevitably, the American media pitted Raisa against Nancy Reagan and concluded that Nancy was outclassed. The two women patently did not like each other but had to observe the protocol imposed on presidential spouses. This included holding hands when appearing in public. Everyone watched the two hands as they clasped loosely, then parted for a glance at a watch or to point out something of interest, then joined again, casually, as if they belonged to two close friends out for a stroll. Everyone sensed it was a trial for both of them and the hand-holding was ice cold. 'Where does this dame get off', Nancy said once, according to former White House aide Donald Regan.

The force of Gorbachev's personality and tireless energy was central to his achievement in bringing about the major improvement in Soviet-American relations on which the Kremlin's new foreign policy depended, and the subsequent transformation of Europe for which he would eventually be rewarded with the Nobel Peace prize. When he gave a press conference in the Soviet embassy in Washington after his summit with Reagan, his first major encounter with the world's press, the 300 American and foreign journalists paid him a rare tribute. Everyone stood up and several applauded. Gorbachev addressed us for seventy-two minutes, displaying a grasp of detail on every issue, though the lecture irritated many correspondents as it diminished the time for question and answer. One of Gorbachev's great talents, however, was learning as he went along. By the time he returned for the second summit with President Bush in June 1990, he had a greater appreciation of the importance of symbolism and of television 'sound bites' in creating an image in America. His press conference on this occasion was held jointly with the American president, in the White House, with the two presenting themselves as equals. There was no long peroration, and his answers were brief and to the point.

An atmosphere of goodwill was crucial to Gorbachev's campaign to end the arms race, which was draining the Soviet economy, and to win American backing for economic reform. This involved persuading the US administration to drop Cold War barriers, such as the 1972 Jackson-Vanik amendment, which required all countries receiving most-favoured-nation status to allow their citizens to emigrate freely, and an advisory to all American companies and Nato allies not to sell advanced technology to the Soviet Union. Such conditions, which hampered US business dealings with the USSR, reflected the belief expressed only a few years before by Ronald Reagan that the Soviet Union was an 'evil empire'. It was a measure of Gorbachev's persuasive powers that Reagan retracted the charge in June 1988, saying, in the shadow of the Kremlin walls, 'I was talking about another time, another era.' It was also important to Gorbachev to make Russia fashionable, to attract the representatives of big corporations who would set up joint ventures bringing investment and technological know-how to the Soviet Union because it was the new frontier where everybody was heading to invest.

Gorbachev relied most of all on projecting himself. He set out to charm the people and the press. To the horror of US and Soviet agents, he plunged into crowds to shake people by the hand. On his second US summit he made his spokesman redundant by talking to the reporters at every opportunity. He caused consternation in the White House when he emerged from the west wing after a session of talks with George Bush and, spotting a small pool of reporters, headed in their direction to give an American-style briefing on progress to date. White House officials, fearful that Gorbachev would steal the news headlines, frantically propelled Bush in front of the microphones in the rose gardens. He looked slightly needled. Their discussion had ranged over American and Soviet losses in the Second World War. 'I reminded him that I was the only one of the two of us that was old enough to remember it from being there', Bush said with the truculance of someone outsmarted at his own game.

Gorbachev's impromptu meetings with the people meant that we saw more of the Soviet leader in action by accompanying him abroad, than by covering his activities at home in Moscow where walk-abouts were practically abandoned as Gorbachev became a focus for the growing hostility of the people to a system which had brought them close to famine. Gorbachev carefully laid the foundation for the second Washington summit by working the crowds in Ottawa on a stop-over in Canada on his way to the US capital, illustrating that however badly his image was slipping at home, Gorbymania was still a powerful factor in North America. The friendly crowd scenes not only helped create a benign climate for the superpower negotiations, but reminded Soviet television viewers at home of the tremendous assets he brought to the international negotiations as Soviet leader.

They also seemed to give Gorbachev a charge of andrenalin and energy. As he walked through the Sparks Street mall in Ottawa to shouts of 'Gorby, you are wonderful', I could sense from my place in the crowd that he was energised by the waves of goodwill radiating from Canadians. He responded with the charm which had made him the most popular statesman in the West, pressing outstretched hands and smiling and waving. As he approached, I called out 'Mikhail Sergeevich', using the formal method of address common in Russia, where first name and patronymic are used, but not the surname. He came over and grasped my hand. Face to face he looked slightly smaller than I had imagined. Would there be a referendum on a market economy in the Soviet Union, I asked. It was one of the issues of the day. 'Whom do you represent?' he inquired. I told him. He launched into a long explanation of the need for economic change and how the switch to a market economy would cause hardship and would have to be regulated to protect ordinary people. We discussed the technicalities of a referendum and the need for a legal basis. All the time he maintained eye contact and held firmly to my hand. I knew that if I reached for my notebook the conversation would have ended abruptly. He was trying to convince me, not just repeating stock phrases for my newspaper. Raisa reminded him with an apologetic smile that he should be talking to the people and not to the press and he moved on. 'So are you the only Irish correspondent in Moscow?'

he asked over his shoulder. I told him I was. '*Molodyets*', he said, 'good lad'.

Gorbachev came to my own country on his way to Cuba on 2 April 1989, declaring his visit to Ireland was not a stop-over but a milestone, though he stayed at Shannon Airport no longer than it normally took for the refuelling of the aeroflot planes which landed there on their way to Central America. He did not plan a press conference, but I was tipped off by a Soviet official that he would make a brief statement at the end of his short talk in the terminal building with the Taoiseach, Charles Haughey, and would then take one question if put to him in Russian. As the Soviet leader turned to leave after making a few remarks, I called out, once again, 'Mikhail Sergeevich', and true to the unofficial arrangement, he stopped and replied to my question.

A reporter from one of the Irish newspapers came up afterwards and said to me, 'By God, Conor, I didn't know you were on first name terms with the man.'

18

Conclusion: Melting Snow

T HOSE of us who came to live and work in the Soviet capital during the political spring of perestroika soon became preoccupied with another phenomenon of the times, the gradual disappearance of the Russian winter. This was bad news, not good.

The Russian winter begins in November. The Russians have an apt word to describe wet snow – *mokryi* – and mucky it can be, covering the pavements in dirty, ankle-deep slush; after a couple of weeks of this in November, however, in my first year in Moscow, the city was transformed into a winter wonderland. The temperature dropped and the snow turned to fine powder, coating the roofs in crystal white. It eddied down for days, finding its way under doors and into cracks – a pure, light, clean snow that creaked underfoot. The temperature kept falling until it was minus sixteen degrees centigrade. Condensation caught inside the double glazing turned into lace curtains of ice. In the streets the buses and tram windows developed glittering, intricate patterns of frozen breath. The colder it got, the more Moscow seemed to like it. Muscovites are well prepared for winter. All apartments are centrally heated and double-glazed windows are taped up to keep out the icy draughts. At home people leave their boots by the door and live in slippers or stockinged feet. Car owners carry matches to warm car keys so that they unfreeze locks. Despite the cold, ice-cream kiosks continue to do a brisk business. In Gorky Park – better known to Muscovites as Park Kultury – paths are frozen for skaters. On the weekend the metros are full of skiers on their way to the parks and countryside, their skis clipped together and the narrow, curved ends covered by plastic bags. Cross-country skiing is one of the Russians' favourite sports and its devotees quickly learn that there are several different kinds of snow, not all conducive to good skiing. The skis stick in wet snow or if the temperature is near zero. They slither uncontrollably over snow that has thawed and then frozen to the hardness of concrete. On the rare occasions when the temperature drops below minus twenty degrees centigrade, the snow becomes floury and all one can do is plod through it. The more adventurous head out into the forests and fields and spend the day travelling in a

295

long line over fresh snow, taking turns to lead the way and to leave tracks like narrow tram-lines for those behind.

In Moscow the great number of parks make skiing accessible to everyone. Since the Revolution all the big estates have been thrown open, leaving immense areas of forest within the city limits. One of the nearest open spaces to my apartment, Kuskovo Park, had delightful ski runs across a frozen lake in front of a magnificient eighteenth-century palace, which once belonged to the Sheremetyev family. On Saturdays and Sundays on the steep banks of a smaller lake it was hard to find a space as dozens of young people whizzed down the slope and laboured up again with spread-eagled skis, while grandfathers pulled sleighs with tiny children wrapped up like Russian dolls. My favourite place was the countryside around the village of Peredelkino, a thirty-minute drive out of the city, where one could ski for hours through hilly fields and forests and along a curving switchback path beside a stream. The sharp, cold air of winter cheered everyone up. Snow in the West often blocks roads and brings chaos, but winter beautifies and liberates the Russian countryside, freezing the rivers so that they become roads, and coating muddy, rutted paths over which horse-drawn sleighs travel swiftly and smoothly. In Moscow, Russian *troikas*, colourfully painted sleighs pulled by a trotting horse with two trace horses on each side, were a familiar sight at the winter festival in the Park of Economic Achievements every January.

We spent one Christmas skiing on the Volga, about seventy-five miles from Moscow. The ice was covered by snow, except in the centre where it had frozen only a short time before. Under an egg-shell blue sky on Christmas Day, the exposed ice looked like long strips of jade against the white meadows and dark patches of coniferous forest on the banks. The ice was several inches thick, but one needed to develop confidence to ski on the river. At first we kept close to the bank, following the footprints of villagers on the snow, and for a while the track of a bicycle. At least someone had been there before us to test its strength, and if the ice broke perhaps we could struggle ashore. After a while caution was tempered by the sight of fishermen far out on the ice, lone figures hunched here and there on the two-mile wide frozen expanse near the village of Zavidovo, jiggling hand-held fishing lines through holes bored in the ice to catch perch, pike and sturgeon. We stopped to examine old bore-holes near the banks, where the water had frozen with the transparency of thick glass, through which we could see reeds and stones below. Then we came across the wheel marks of a tractor which had driven across the river, and after that we fairly whizzed along, full of confidence, far out from the bank. On Christmas

Day the temperature was several degrees below zero, but we didn't feel the cold in the still air. The snow was perfect, crisp and not too deep, so that the skis found a grip but were not impeded. We were not far from the Moscow-Leningrad highway, but the villages along the bank were primitive hamlets of misshapen wooden houses, unpaved lanes and no shops. We skied up to the lakeside village of Gorodischa. A rectangular hole, ten feet by six, had been cut in the ice for women to rinse their washing. A thin coat of ice formed quickly when it was unattended and it had to be broken afresh each morning.

We stayed in a *dacha* close enough to the river to hear the ice cracking at night as the water level changed slightly. There were a few dozen *dachas* at Zavidovo, cosy, centrally heated wooden bungalows set among birch trees on a bend of the Volga, the glass of the unheated verandas frosted like a scene from a Victorian Christmas card. These could be hired by foreign residents through a government department in Moscow. The little community had a floodlit skating-rink, which was in fact a flooded tennis-court, and a little hotel on the water's edge where the words 'Happy New Year' in German and English decorated the glass door. Tinsel was draped from the moose head above the fireplace in the lobby. The hotel had a billiards table, the Russian version with fifteen big white balls which only just squeezed into the narrow pockets after a perfectly aimed shot. Peter the Great brought the game to Russia, it is said, to teach his officers the value of accuracy. Christmas dinner in the hotel was caviar, *borshch* and pike, which was quite tasty, or beef *shashlik*. The shortages of the outside world intruded on the menu, however. There were no fresh vegetables or fruit. Diners had to bring their own wine.

It was places like Peredelkino and Zavidovo in winter which made life bearable during the chaos and queuing which accompanied the break-down of the economy. However, from 1987 onwards the winters grew steadily warmer. In January 1988 the snow disappeared from Moscow, the coldest capital city in Europe, as a wave of warm air brought record temperatures of five degrees centigrade. In 1989 we had the warmest January since 1882 when Vladimir Ilich Lenin was eleven years old, Alexander III was tsar and a daring new ballet called 'Swan Lake' by Petr Ilich Tchaikovsky was pulling them in at the Imperial Marie Theatre in St Petersburg. That year the average Moscow temperature was 7.2 degrees centigrade above normal. In 1989 it was 7.5 degrees above normal, still fairly cold by West European standards, about three degrees below freezing when night and day temperatures were averaged, but not cold enough to allow people to enjoy the winter. Everyday that January there was a thaw. This wreaked havoc with winter sports, the city streets and the romantic image of the Russian winter. The heaps of once-white snow along the city streets shrank day by day into icy, black slag-heaps, permeated with layers of pollution and hundreds of cigarette ends. Dirty water seeped across pavements and across roads which had no drains. Large icicles from melting snow fell from roofs like daggers, making life hazardous for pedestrians. The skating-rinks and the paths in Park Cultury became sheets of water.

Out in the countryside the snow was too wet for skiing. In the European parts of the Soviet Union, the snow cover disappeared in January altogether. In Minsk, capital of Byelorussia, residents abandoned their skis and took to the sodden forests to pick basketfuls of honey-agaric mushrooms three months earlier that usual. If Napoleon had experienced this weather in 1813 or Hitler in 1942, the history of Russia might have turned out differently. The extremely cold January of 1942 helped stop the ill-equipped Nazi troops in their advance on Moscow. In January 1989, however, the lilacs bloomed in Riga on the Baltic coast. The leaders of the pro-independence movements were quick to equate the mild weather with the thaw in Kremlin policy. 'We can thank the greenhouse effect for our new freedoms', quipped a Lithuanian university professor as we walked through the streets of Vilnius in drizzling rain. (Political thaws might end but the winters stayed warm. When the paratroopers with their light tanks appeared in Vilnius to enforce conscription in January 1991, it was raining.)

Like everywhere else in the world, the weather forecasters in Moscow were the butt of ridicule. A cartoon in *Izvestia*, after a period when the forecast was consistently wrong, showed two clowns preparing a weather summary which said simply the temperature would be somewhere between plus ten and minus ten degrees centigrade. 'Couldn't be more precise', cried one. Newspapers had a contemptuous attitude towards the provision of information about the weather, sometimes not bothering to carry a forecast at all if space squeezed it out. *Pravda* might simply say 'snow' without explaining whether it would snow in the morning, at midday or in the afternoon. Often it didn't snow at all. The problem for the Russian metereological office seemed to be that quite often a blanket of cloud would cover the city for weeks on end, wilfully ignoring the professional predictions and producing rain or snow when it felt like it, or just continuing to impose its depressing presence. I heard a story in Siberia about an inexperienced Buryat medicine man who once predicted a long, hard winter, whereupon his fellow tribesmen began hunting extra seals to bring in surplus stores of fat. Worried that he might have read the signs wrong, the medicine-man put on a suit and went to the meteorological centre in the nearest city to check his prediction. The government weather man there told him that indeed it would be a long, hard winter, he had no doubt about it. Much relieved, he began to leave, then paused at the door to ask the weatherman how he knew. 'Simple', said the metereologist. 'The Buryat tribesmen are hunting extra seals; that's always a sure sign.'

The director of the Moscow weather centre, Alexander Yasilyev, a mild-mannered, English-speaking meteorologist working in his office near the Moscow Zoo with the windows open, threw his hands up in despair and said, 'It's difficult to say what's happening', when I called one February day to ask him about the disappearance of the Russian winter in the wet and miserable January of 1989. Everyday the air masses over Moscow had pushed in from the Atlantic. A couple of days beforehand the same air had been over Ireland, said Alexander Yasilyev. No, he didn't blame the greenhouse effect. Leaping up from his chair he grabbed a piece of chalk to illustrate on a blackboard how the jet stream in the upper atmosphere had created conditions forcing Atlantic depressions over Eastern Europe, but at the same time pushing cold air over India and Bangladesh which were having their chilliest winter in one hundred years. But he acknowledged that the Russian winter was warming up. In the last half-century, there were eight Januaries when the temperature was at least six degrees centigrade above normal. In the previous fifty years there were only two. For three years in a row, 1979, 1980 and 1981, the snow in Moscow thawed on New Year's Eve, a phenomenon which occurred only eight times a century.

I went back to see the director a year later after another mild January and the premature disappearance of winter snows from the streets. For the seventh year in succession, the January temperature had been above normal, he said glumly. In Byelorussia, the Ukraine and the Baltic republics there had been no winter snows and the rivers had remained unfrozen. This time he was more inclined to blame the greenhouse effect. 'This may indicate a real change of climate', he said. 'The principal reason is the change in circulation in the atmosphere. The configuration of the jet stream is different. There may be global reasons for this and one, of course, might be the outflow of greenhouse gases.' He went further. 'I believe after fifty years of studying the weather that the average temperature of the whole atmosphere is getting warmer. It is accelerating now and one could say that in ten or twenty years it will be several degrees warmer here.'

As I watched the miserable faces of Muscovites on the damp week-ends of the winters of perestroika when they should have been skiing or skating, I reflected to myself that for the unfortunate Russians, even the snow had become *deficit*. It was a simile for the times. The lessening of the grip of the harsh Russian winter should have brought less, not more, misery, just as the loosening of the stranglehold of the Communist Party should have improved the life of ordinary people, rather than plunging them into dejection and hardship. But nature, and man, are perverse. It didn't work out that way.

Index